D0934141

Frontier Decision
Support Concepts

Sixth-Generation Computer Technology Series

Branko Souček, Editor

Frontier Decision Support Concepts

Help Desk, Learning, Fuzzy Diagnoses, Quality Evaluation, Prediction, Evolution

Edited by

VITO LEONARDO PLANTAMURA
BRANKO SOUČEK
GIUSEPPE VISAGGIO

A Wiley-Interscience Publication
JOHN WILEY & SONS, INC.
New York-Chichester-Brisbane-Toronto-Sinagpore

This text is printed on acid-free paper.

Copyright © 1994 by John Wiley & Sons, Inc.

All rights reserved. Published simultaneously in Canada.

Reproduction or translation of any part of this work beyond
that permitted by Section 107 or 108 of the 1976 United
States Copyright Act without the permission of the copyright
owner is unlawful. Requests for permission or further
information should be addressed to the Permissions Department,
John Wiley & Sons, Inc., 605 Third Avenue, New York, NY
10158-0012.

Library of Congress Cataloging in Publication Data:

Frontier decision support concepts : learning, fuzzy diagnoses,
   quality evaluation, prediction, evolution / Vito Leonardo
Plantamura, Branko Souček, Giuseppe Visaggio [editors].
      p. cm. — (Sixth-generation computer technology series)
   ISBN 0-471-59256-0
      1. Decision support systems.   I. Plantamura, Vito Leonardo.
II. Souček, Branko.   III. Visaggio, Giuseppe.   IV. Series.
   T58.62.F76   1994   93-45486
   003'.56'028563–dc20   CIP

Printed in the United States of America

10 9 8 7 6 5 4 3 2 1

FLORIDA GULF COAST
UNIVERSITY LIBRARY

CONTRIBUTORS

The IRIS Group presents a forum for international cooperation in research development and applications of intelligent systems. The IRIS International Center is involved in projects, design, measurements, and experiments, as well as in teaching courses and workshops, and consulting. IRIS invites inquires and operates under the auspices of the Star Service S.p.A. The IRIS research coordinator is Professor B. Souček and the Star Service president is V. L. Plantamura. The address is: IRIS, Star Service, Via Amendola 162/1, 70126 Bari, Italy. Telephone ++39 805 484 555. Fax ++39 805 484 556.

WOLFGANG BANZHAF
Department of Computer Science
Institute for Systems Analysis
University of Dortmund
Dortmund, Germany

HYNEK BERAN
H.E.M. Informatics
Prague, Czech

IVAN BRUHA
Department of Computer Science
  and Systems
McMaster University
Hamilton, Ontario, Canada

MARTINA GORGES-
  SCHLEUTER
Kernforschungszentrum Karlsruhe
Institut für Angewandte Informatik
Abteilung Lernende Systeme
Karlsruhe, Germany

JÜRGEN GRAF
SGZ BANK Südwestdeutsche
Genossenschaftszentralbank AG
Karlsruhe, Germany

RAYMOND HO
AND America
Hamilton, Ontario, Canada

GITTE JENSEN
Kjaergaard Industri Automatic
Lesning, Denmark

DUŠKO KATIĆ
Robotics Department
Mihailo Pupin Institute
Belgrade, Yugoslavia

K. KYUMA
Central Research Laboratory
Mitsubishi Electric Corporation
Amagasaki, Japan

E. LANGE
Central Research Laboratory
Mitsubishi Electric Corporation
Amagasaki, Japan

FILIPPO LANUBILE
Department of Information
  Science
University of Bari
Bari, Italy

M. LIQUIÈRE
Faculté de Sciences
Reúnion, France

ROBERT MANGER
Department of Mathematics
University of Zagreb
Zagreb, Croatia

T. NAKAYAMA
Central Research Laboratory
Mitsubishi Electric Corporation
Amagasaki, Japan

GHOLAMREZA NAKHAEIZADEH
Daimler-Benz AG
Forschung und Technik
Ulm, Germany

MIRKO NOVAK
H.E.M. Informatics
Prague, Czech

J. OHTA
Central Research Laboratory
Mitsubishi Electric Corporation
Amagasaki, Japan

M. OITA
Central Research Laboratory
Mitsubishi Electric Corporation
Amagasaki, Japan

EMIL PELIKAN
H.E.M. Informatics
Prague, Czech

**VITO LEONARDO
  PLANTAMURA**
Department of Information
  Science
University of Bari
Bari, Italy

H. RALAMBONDRAINY
Faculté de Sciences
Reúnion, France

BRANKO SOUČEK
IRIS International Center
Star Service S.p.A
Bari, Italy

MARINA SOUČEK
National and University Library
Zagreb, Croatia

JOHN G. SUTHERLAND
AND America
Hamilton, Ontario, Canada

GIUSEPPE VISAGGIO
Department of Information
  Science
University of Bari
Bari, Italy

MIOMIR VUKOBRATOVIĆ
Robotics Department
Mihajlo Pupin Institute
Belgrade, Yugoslavia

CONTENTS

PART II FRONTIER OPTICAL AND PARALLEL SYSTEMS

PREFACE

Customer service and decision support are poised to be the leading areas of revenue growth of companies in the 1990s. Computing is moving into desktop, hand, and pocket calculators. Decision support systems proliferate in cars and houses. A large percentage of them will have to deal with fuzzy and inexact data. Long decision cycles must give way to very quick decisions based on available information. Users will expect systems capable of learning from experience and building personal memory based on association maps. Predictions are that personal assistants and decision support systems for management and manufacturing will dominate the market over the next few years.

This book focuses on frontier decision support concepts merged with concrete applications. It gives detailed explanations for underlying principles and concentrates on concrete examples, real-world problems, and applications. It describes concrete hands-on tools and methods, including details of computer implementation of software packages on PC networks, single-processor machines, and high-speed parallel and optical systems; the amount of processing required; editing and man–machine interfaces; simulation runs; results and performance measurements; block diagrams; ready-to-use recipes and solutions. This is a practical, engineering, and applications-oriented book. Described concepts and applications include:

1. *Help Desk.* Supports people in complex but routine decision making; customer service and support; maintenance and troubleshooting; software development and use; information retrieval executive systems.

2. *Media Decision Support.* Supports information systems and software packages in their work. This includes intelligent data bases, pattern base, de-

ductive hypermedia, association maps, and decision support in EDI and in virtual reality.

3. *Process Decision Support.* Supports business and real-time process control systems. It offers the features of production surveillance, object and pattern recognition, product evaluation, adaptation and learning.

Described concepts are related to the business and to the business process reengineering (BPR) in the following way:

HELP DESK	+	MEDIA DECISION SUPPORT	+	PROCESS DECISION SUPPORT	→	BUSINESS PROCESS REENGINEERING
↓		↓		↓		↓
Manpower	+	Media	+	Process	→	Business, Profit

BPR helps companies ensure competitive advantage in the marketplace. Currently BPR focuses on decision support systems (DSS) and covers a broad range—from simple $1000 Help Desk systems to $1 million executive information systems (EIS) and related business reengineering. The ultimate BPR strategy is *"succeeding through change,"* where only the best intelligent agents survive in a self-modifying system.

Decision support systems have three basic functions: administrative, reference, and intelligence. The administrative and reference functions are determined by conventional technology. Intelligence requires the application of advanced technology. The solution is seen in the technology that integrates reasoning, informing, and serving—IRIS. In other words, IRIS deals with the interaction between reasoning (higher-level cognitive processes and decision making), informing (perception and low-level interpretation of raw data and sensory inputs), and serving (clients, applications, knowledge sites, users).

The application focus is on improving industrial and commercial productivity and quality. The new IRIS concept covers a broad range of applications, from management, banking, financing, and services, through software development and re-use, all the way to material flow, product distribution, production line surveillance, flexible manufacturing, and quality control. In these areas, frontier breakthrough results have been achieved through the IRIS concept. In finance alone, using an IRIS credit-scoring system could result in saving about $100 billion for America, Europe, and Japan.

Recent innovative decision support systems include several award-winning applications built at companies like IBM and AT&T. These applications saved between $1 million and $20 million annually. The programs addressed a range of areas: intelligent CASE tools, customer support, product quality management, troubleshooting, and configuration, and new tools such as Brain Maker, Neuro-Shell, Neuro Forecasting, Top of Mind, Robo Help, and so on.

The IRIS concept integrates four groups of decision support techniques:

- Knowledge-based systems (KBS).
- Case-based reasoning (CBR)
- Associative reasoning and object-oriented pattern base
- Evolution and Optimization

The IRIS decision support pool, described in this book includes KBS, CBR, learning, fuzzy diagnosis, quality evaluation, prediction, evolution and population structure, learning robots for flexible manufacturing, and frontier implementations.

The book is divided into two parts.

PART I FRONTIER TOOLS, FUNCTIONS, AND APPLICATIONS

Knowledge-based systems contain facts, relations between facts, and possible methods for solving problems in the application domain. The inference machine implements algorithms that solve problems and answer user queries by either simply retrieving facts from the knowledge base or by inferring new facts from explicitly stored information in the knowledge base. Inferring new facts involves using general relations or principles that also can be stored in the knowledge base.

Case-based reasoning techniques enable programming by example. Knowledge is stored in the form of experiences or cases that are written in conversational language style. Because it can access, organize, and analyze unstructured information that cannot be captured in data bases (e.g., free-text data), CBR allows the hybrid system to handle people's experiences or cases. It also enables the system to perform broad, shallow reasoning across these cases by matching new cases with existing ones in the case base.

Learning is one of the basic features of intelligence. The concept of learning machines comes from biological models. Learning is effective self-modification of the organism that lives in a complex and changing environment. Learning is any directed change in the knowledge structure that improves performance.

The holographic learning method has been developed recently. Holographic neural technology employs a novel concept in which information is represented by vector orientation on a Riemann plane where very large sets of fuzzy associations are both learned and expressed in one noniterative transformation. Experiments reveal speed-up factors of 10 to 100 times compared with other learning paradigms.

Fuzzy diagnosis is important for decision support in the area of complex, fuzzy, and incomplete data. Three procedures for fuzzy diagnosis are presented and compared: holographic, statistical, and neural.

Quality evaluation is related to the usefulness of the product or of the process. Several quality evaluation systems, based on knowledge, holographic, and neural technologies are described. They include

- Quality control in manufacturing
- Software quality evaluation
- Credit-scoring systems in financing

Prediction or forecasting deals with time series and with nonstationary dynamics. Several models are presented:

- Daily short-term prediction of stock prices
- Long-term prediction of the stock process
- Prediction of global electric power consumption

The aforementioned models compare the predictivity performance of holographic and neural networks, statistical methods, and machine-learning algorithms based on the ID3 procedure.

PART II FRONTIER OPTICAL AND PARALLEL SYSTEMS

Evolution is viewed as a typical optimization problem. The introduction of the concept of population structures, allowing only interactions between geographically nearby individuals, offers a promising extension to the principles of evolution incorporated so far into evolution algorithms. We discuss discrete population structures, known as migration models, and continuous models, known as diffusion, isolation-by-distance, or neighborhood models. Applications include management, manufacturing, robotics, and parallelization. A speed-up factor of 15 times has been achieved, compared with other evolution algorithms.

Learning robots present the base for complex process control. Using decentralized control and computed torque control algorithms, we develop models of neural networks as feedforward robot controllers. The goal is intelligent and flexible manufacturing.

Frontier implementation technology is used to implement a competitive learning system: optoelectronics, including light-emitting diodes, and variable-sensitivity photodiodes. Optical technology is used to implement color pattern recognition systems. The system has been used for Japanese color stamp recognition in the postal service. A recognition rate of 100% has been achieved.

This book presents a unified treatment of previously unpublished methods and results based on research of the IRIS Group. The IRIS group brings together the results from leading American, European, and Japanese laboratories and projects. Each chapter gives a detailed explanation of underlying principles in processes and in systems and presents concrete results, applications, and speedup factors.

This book has been written as a textbook for students as well as a reference for practicing engineers, managers, and information specialists. A minimal undergraduate-level background is assumed, although many fundamentals are reviewed. The treatment is kept as straightforward as possible, emphasizing functions, systems, and applications. The text is rounded out with numerous examples, experimental results, details of working systems, illustrations, flowcharts, program listings, and a bibliography of more than 200 entries. The examples are designed as practical exercises for students and users of intelligent systems. Readers interested in complementary solutions, other related topics, and background on neural, concurrent, and intelligent systems should read this book along with the other Sixth-Generation Computer Technology Series books listed on the page opposite the title page. These books are independent, mutually supporting volumes.

ACKNOWLEDGMENTS

We acknowledge the encouragement, discussions, and support received from our teachers, collaborators, friends, and colleagues. We are grateful for the grants supporting our research. We thank the institutions where we performed the experiments and research with intelligent systems. The institutions are listed next to the contributors' names. Special thanks to Miss Luciana Palmisano, Mrs. Vladimira Zlatić, Mrs. Lisa Van Horn, and John Wiley's editors and reviewers, for an outstanding job in preparation, supervising, and copyediting the manuscript.

VITO LEONARDO PLANTAMURA
BRANKO SOUČEK
GIUSEPPE VISAGGIO

Bari, Italy

PART I

Frontier Tools, Functions, and Applications

Decision Support for Business Process Reengineering

Help Desk Projects, Software and EDI

The Holographic Learning Cell—A Quantum Perspective

Stimulus Preprocessing for Holographic Neural Networks

Classification with Holographic Neural Networks

Quality Control in Manufacturing Based on Fuzzy Classification

Quality Evaluation in Software Reengineering Based on Fuzzy Classification

Software Quality Metrics as an Input to Fuzzy Classifiers

Neurological Fuzzy Diagnoses: Holographic versus Statistical versus Neural Methods

Holographic Decision Support System: Credit Scoring Based on Quality Metrics

Credit Scoring Based on Neural and Machine Learning

Symbolic-Numeric Learning and Classification

Time Series Prediction by Artificial Neural Networks: Electric Power Consumption

Application of Learning Algorithms to Predicting Stock Prices

CHAPTER 1

Decision Support for Business Process Reengineering

VITO LEONARDO PLANTAMURA
BRANKO SOUČEK
GIUSEPPE VISAGGIO

1.1 INTRODUCTION

Decision support systems help to resolve complex problems in management and in manufacturing. They could be divided into three classes:

1. *Help Desk.* Supports the person in complex but routine decision making, customer service and support, maintenance and troubleshooting, software development and use, information retrieval, product support.
2. *Media Decision Support.* Supports the information systems and software packages in their work. This includes intelligent data bases, pattern base, deductive hypermedia, association maps, decision support in EDI.
3. *Process Decision Support.* Supports real-time business and process control systems. It offers the features of production surveillance, object recognition, product evaluation, adaptation and learning, robot support.

The basic task in a decision support system is either diagnosis and recovery or problem classification and referral. In most domains, quick response time is critical. Typically, the problem definition comes in as free-form text or signal patterns with vague or poor symptom descriptions. Somehow this vague, unstructured information must be used to focus the system on a small set of possible diagnoses to explore with further questions. Determining and asking the customer the fewest questions required to resolve the problem in the ques-

Frontier Decision Support Concepts, Edited by V. L. Plantamura, B. Souček, and G. Visaggio.
ISBN 0-471-59256-0   © 1994 John Wiley & Sons, Inc.

tion-and-answer phase of problem resolution can be very tricky. The process of elimination-type questioning needs to be as focused as possible so as not to waste too much time eliminating unlikely possibilities. The same is true in systems based on machine learning, where questions and answers are replaced by training and testing sets [1–8]. These issues all need to be taken into account in building an effective decision support system. In general, Help Desk is a software solution that enables a customer service organization to expand its problem resolution capabilities without additional personnel or training. It is an integrated approach to customer support, encompassing a diagnostic system, a hypertext reference facility, and a problem-related data base system. Similar functions are also present in Media Decision Support and in Process Decision Support.

Work in this domain aims to expand the application potential of high-performance decision support systems, to demonstrate the cost-effective merge of applications currently running on conventional systems with decision support environments, to act on new applications that will foster the mastery of new functionalities and levels of performance, and to develop next-generation decision support technology and systems, especially those that improve application transfer or development and that are easy to use. The application focus is on improving industrial and commercial productivity. The high-performance systems addressed concern PCs, parallel processing systems, shared-memory and distributed-memory multiprocessors, clusters of workstations for high-performance applications, and the integration of high-performance subsystems into distributed client/server relationships.

Decision concepts support two areas:

1. *Applications Involving Complex Decision Support.* Applications in areas such as banking, financing, management, command and control, and real-time engineering processes place a major premium on the need for rapid but well-founded management decisions, often in the context of variability in the quality and quantity of available input data. Developments are described that provide significant increases in the level of intelligent support offered and that improve the effectiveness of the information presentation. These developments result in identifiable and measurable improvements in decision making. The goals are to

- Maintain current knowledge of the domain and update continually
- Reduce handling time and eliminate errors
- Spot difficult problems for special handling
- Make on-the-job training possible to reduce training costs
- Capture expertise and make it available to all customers
- Improve the business processes, products, and customer service
- Do it as cheaply as possible

Applications include knowledge-based troubleshooting systems, intelligent information management systems (including text retrieval systems, call classification systems, case retrieval systems, interactive electronic technical manuals), force planning and dispatch systems, maintenance planning applications, and analysis and use of field feedback data.

2. *Improvements in Quality of Use.* Activities to measure the effectiveness in the use of software-intensive applications at the organization, economic sector, or cross-sectional level include production surveillance and quality control systems. These are crucial for successful manufacturing. These systems are capable of learning which produced object belongs to which class. The applications are numerous: sorting bottles by color, sorting waste bags, checking colors in a print process, classifying seeds, checking for a missing object in a crate, quality control inspection of welds produced by roll machines. Of course, for each application it is necessary to have the proper sensory device. An important new application area is decision support systems for software quality evaluation and development.

In the study of these problems, it was discovered that they all carried out three basic functions: administrative, reference, and intelligence. Two of the functions (administrative and reference) were determined to be functions of conventional technology; the third, intelligence, requires the application of advanced technology.

Neural nets, case-based reasoning, electronic manuals, and semantic network techniques are all approaches to the central problem of customer support—diagnosis. Each approach is an appropriate technology for a given environment as characterized by problem size, problem complexity, and availability of expertise. Other technologies such as voice-response systems, knowledge-acquisition aids, and systems to analyze field feedback reports are all useful but secondary to the primary goal of finding out what the customer's problem is and then fixing that problem. The work over the last half-dozen years has been oriented toward finding better ways to solve large and complex diagnostic problems where expertise is available from service practitioners. The solution is seen in the technology that *Integrates Reasons, Informs,* and *Serves* (IRIS). The concept of IRIS, as defined by Souček [1–6], is outlined in Figure 1.1. The concept integrates four groups of decision support techniques:

1. Knowledge-Based Systems (KBS)
2. Case-Based Reasoning (CBR)
3. Associative reasoning and object-oriented pattern base
4. Evolution and optimization

1.2 KNOWLEDGE-BASED SYSTEMS

A set of programmed rules that could perform at, or near, the level of a human expert in a specific domain is called an expert system. Expert systems are being developed to diagnose diseases, locate mineral deposits, configure complex computer hardware, assist managers with complex planning and scheduling

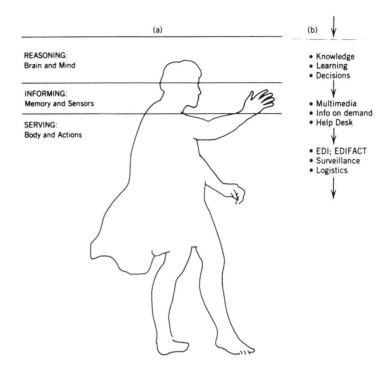

Figure 1.1 *Integration of Reasoning, Informing, and Serving (IRIS): (a) IRIS in living organism. (b) IRIS in man-made systems. Silhouette adapted from P. P. Rubens.*

tasks, and aid mechanics in troubleshooting. Only recently have expert systems and related hardware become fast enough for applications in real-time business processing, process control, and robotics.

With few exceptions, most projects to date on the construction of expert systems for problems with decision support have relied on rule-based reasoning methods. These systems are referred to as rule-based because inference is performed through the logical chaining of If-Then rules, acquired from an expert. The logic on which these systems are based assumes certainty in the relationships among observations and disorders.

Expert systems can usually be viewed as composed of two modules: a knowledge base and an inference machine. This structure nicely reflects the two main tasks of knowledge engineering: representing and storing large amounts of problem-domain knowledge in the computer, and actively using this knowledge for solving problems and answering user queries.

The knowledge base contains facts, relations between facts, and possible methods for solving problems in the domain of application. The inference machine implements algorithms that solve problems and answer user queries by either simply retrieving facts from the knowledge base or by inferring new facts from facts explicitly stored in the knowledge base. Inferring new facts involves the use of general relations or principles, which can also be stored in the knowledge base.

A production system is defined by a set of rules, or productions, which form the production memory (PM), together with a data base of assertions called the working memory (WM). Each production consists of a conjunction of pattern elements, called the left-hand side (LHS) of the rule, along with a set of actions called the right-hand side (RHS). The RHS specifies information to be added to (asserted) or removed from WM when the LHS successfully matches against the contents of WM. In operation, the production system repeatedly executes the following cycle of operations:

1. *Match.* For each rule, it determines whether the LHS matches the current environment of WM. All matching instances of the rules are collected in the conflict set of rules.
2. *Select.* It chooses exactly one of the matching rules according to some predefined criterion.
3. *Act.* It adds to or deletes from WM all assertions specified in the RHS of the selected rule, or it performs some operation.

During the selection phase of production system execution, a typical interpreter provides conflict-resolution strategies based on how recent the matched data in WM are and on syntactic discrimination. Rules matching data elements that were more recently inserted in WM are preferred, with ties decided in favor of rules that are more specific (i.e., have more constants) than others.

In general, rules are of the If-Then form, but they can have different interpretations. Some examples follow:

If precondition P, then conclusion C.

If situation S, then action A.

If conditions $C1$ and $C2$ hold, then condition C does not hold.

A more concise notation is often used: $C \rightarrow A$. The meaning of this depends on interpretation; that is, "if condition C, then action A."

Basically an expert system could operate in two ways:

1. *Data-Driven Forward-Chaining Mode.* At every computational cycle, the LHS of the set of rules are examined to determine which rules are satisfied by the data pattern in the storage.
2. *Goal-Driven Back-Chaining Mode.* At every computational cycle, the RHS of the set of rules are examined to see if a desired goal be can be found.

Programming of an expert system can be done in a high-level language. Artificial intelligence (AI) programmers commonly use LISP or PROLOG.

LISP consists of operators that facilitate the creating of programs that manipulate lists. Commercial LISP machines have been developed, such as the Symbolic 3600 series. Lists are the fundamental data structures in LISP, and their implementation must allow for rapid access and compact storage. They are achieved through a stack-oriented architecture. Most LISP instructions are executed in one machine cycle. The architecture also provides for incremental compilation so that each new function can be compiled independently of the rest of the program of which it is a part.

PROLOG contains constructs that make it easy to write programs that manipulate logical expressions. The execution of a PROLOG-based program can be speeded up by exploiting various kinds of parallelism. AND parallelism refers to the simultaneous execution of logically ANDed clauses. OR parallelism refers to the concurrent search for alternative solution paths. The best-known PROLOG machine is a parallel inference machine (PIM) multicomputer under development at ICOT in Japan, as a part of the Japanese fifth-generation computing project.

We use the simple "animal game" to explain the operation of the expert system. Figure 1.2 illustrates a semantic net of the animal hierarchy. The top level represents specific animals (species). The middle level defines broad classes such as mammals, birds, and fish. The bottom level lists the characteristic features: gives milk, eats meat, and so on. The expert system generates the results by using production rules. Some of the rules used for the animal game are listed in Figure 1.3.

Figure 1.4 shows the trace of the goal-driven backward-chaining operation, identifying a tiger.

In complex real-life systems, assumption of determinism between observation and causes is typically invalid. In such cases we can no longer state that rules and facts are certainly true or certainly false. Instead a multivalued form of logic is used and the resulting form of inference is called inexact. Most diagnostic expert systems to date attempt to deal with uncertainty by extending rule-based systems to allow experts to express uncertain relationships.

The common approaches to inexact reasoning in expert systems can be categorized as

1. Bayesian approach
2. Certainty factors approach
3. Theory of evidence approach
4. Fuzzy logic approach

In the Bayesian approach, uncertainty is viewed as probability; in the certainty factor approach, uncertainty is viewed as a degree of confirmation; in the theory of evidence approach, uncertainty is viewed as a degree of belief; in the fuzzy logic approach, uncertainty is viewed as a degree of set membership. Since each approach has a different perspective on uncertainty and each of them

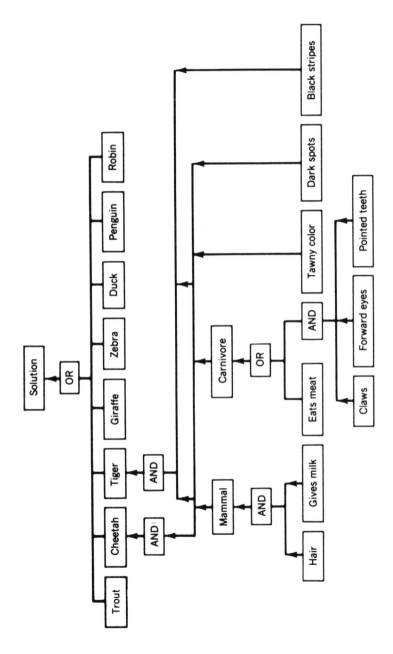

Figure 1.2 *Semantic net of the animal hierarchy. (Adapted from Lewis and Lynch [9]).*

1. IF has-hair AND gives-milk THEN is mammal
2. IF eats-meat THEN is-carnivore
3. IF has-pointed-teeth AND has-claws AND has-forward-eyes THEN is-carnivore
4. IF is-mammal AND is-carnivore AND has-tawny-color AND has-dark-spots THEN is-cheetah
5. IF is-mammal AND is-carnivore AND has-tawny-color AND has-black-stripes THEN is-tiger

Figure 1.3 *Some of the "animal-game" rules. (Adapted from Lewis and Lynch [9]).*

manipulates uncertainty information in a different way, there does not seem to be one approach that is "best" for all situations.

The certainty factor (CF) model has been widely adopted by expert system developers for medicine, customer service, and other application areas. The term *certainty* or *confidence factor* is used to refer to truth values. The truth value for "John is male" is 100, while the truth value for "John likes wine" may be 70.

Let *A* and *B* be clauses. According to Parsaye and Chignell [10], to perform inexact reasoning using backward-chaining inference, we need to define four basic formulas for

CF(not *A*)
CF(*A* and *B*)
CF(*A* or *B*)
Combine(*A*,*B*)

Attempting to deduce "is-mammal"
  Using Rule 1
  Is this true: animal "has-hair"? YES
  Is this true: animal "gives-milk"? YES
  Rule 1 deduces animal "is-mammal"
Attempting to deduce "is-carnivore"
  Using Rule 2
  Is this true: animal "eats-meat"? YES
  Rule 2 deduces animal "is-carnivore"
Attempting to deduce "is-cheetah"
  Using Rule 4
  Is this true: animal has "tawny-color"? YES
  Is this true: animal has "dark-spots"? NO
  Rule 4 failed to deduce "is-cheetah"
Attempting to deduce "is-tiger"
  Using Rule 5
  Is this true: animal has "black-stripes"? YES
  Rule 5 deduces "is-tiger"

Figure 1.4 *The trace of the process; identify a tiger. (Adapted from Lewis and Lynch [9]).*

The formula for Combine is needed to calculate the combined certainty when two or more rules support a hypothesis. Different methods have been suggested for defining these formulas; for instance, the following definitions are based on fuzzy logic and certainty theory:

$$CF(\text{not } A) = 100 - CF(A)$$

$$CF(A \text{ not } B) = \text{minimum}[CF(A), CF(B)]$$

$$CF(A \text{ or } B) = \text{maximum}[CF(A), CF(B)]$$

$$\text{Combine}(A,B) = CF(A) + CF(B) - [CF(A) * CF(B)/100]$$

Alternative and complementary methods include associative reasoning, object-oriented pattern base and case-based reasoning.

1.3 CASE-BASED REASONING*

1.3.1 Similarity

Case-based reasoning (CBR) is an alternative to current expert systems techniques for the development of applications. Case-based reasoning involves applying experience as represented in past similar cases to analyze and solve current problems. CBR systems have been designed to handle such diverse tasks as planning, design, diagnosis, argumentation, and negotiation. CBR is a new AI methodology and has recently received much attention from the AI community. CBR has rapidly matured into a technology. Various industrial research AI laboratories around the world are now supporting projects that utilize CBR and a number of software companies are already marketing CBR shells.

It is claimed that case-based reasoning is the essence of how human reasoning works, or in other words, case-based inference is believed to be the most basic element of reasoning [11]. Rules (i.e., abstract knowledge) are the most important cognitive mechanisms, although no doubt there are other kinds of knowledge. Only when there is no rule directly applicable, will cases (or analogous knowledge in general) be used.

Case-based reasoning is performing the following steps:

- INPUT—receive data
- INDEX—find relevant pointers;
- RETRIEVE—find relevant cases based on indices;
- ADAPT—modify the retrieved cases for the current situation;

---

*Section 1.3 is based on Barletta and Mott [12]. Courtesy and copyright © 1992 by Barletta and Mott.

- TEST, REPAIR and STORE—try out the solution and store it into the case base after it is turned into a correct form.

This entire process is construed to be sequential and iterative.

According to Barletta and Mott [12], regardless of which sources of knowledge are used to help the customer or which set of questions had to be asked to arrive at a successful resolution of the customer's problem, the relevant pieces of information can be summarized into a reusable "case." If we see a similar case in the future, we should be able to use our past cases as a guide to solving the current problem in a consistent and efficient way. A case embodies all of the implicit or explicit knowledge that was used by the customer service representatives (CSR) to help arrive at a solution. These may include conclusions that they drew from the customer's description of the problem, follow-up questions they asked the customer, discussions with a supervisor or co-worker, sections in a manual, or intuitions about the likely cause of the problem that just happened to be correct. The representation for a case is a set of features (the simpler the better) describing the problem situation and what was done about it (i.e., the solution or outcome). One key issue in building a case-based system for Help Desk problems is to capture this case knowledge in a consistent and simplified form that can be used by case indexing and retrieval algorithms. The other key issue is choosing the correct indexing and retrieval technique to match the needs of the particular Help Desk being built.

Following an initial problem description, the help user could employ one of four types of case indexing/matching approaches to help resolve a given case: (1) template matching, (2) nearest-neighbor matching, (3) inductive indexing, and (4) prototype indexing. The first two approaches, template matching and nearest-neighbor matching, provide the user with more dynamic case retrieval capabilities, requiring little or no preindexing of cases at the expense of retrieval accuracy and speed. The second two approaches, inductive indexing and prototype indexing, allow the user to build more accurate and efficient retrieval structures at the expense of dynamic adjustment. Finally, these techniques can be combined to take advantage of the inherent strengths of each. Barletta and Mott [12] define the four indexing/matching approaches in the following way.

Template Matching. Template matching is similar to making a data base query. It allows an experienced CSR to retrieve cases with a specific set of features and values, presumably those that best describe the current problem. The CSR can then browse through the retrieved cases, asking more questions of the customer or making additional, more specific queries based on the insights gained while browsing or asking questions. Each template match reduces the relevant case set by the criteria specified by the CSR. Case data can be entered and updated anytime during this process, so it is inherently interactive. This is not a technique for the novice CSR, but it allows the expert to use his expertise to avoid unnecesary overhead in using techniques.

Nearest-Neighbor Matching. Nearest-neighbor matching is the type of re-trieval most people associate with case-based reasoning. The goal is to find the best case by applying a similarity function to the input case. The *similarity* function does a pairwise comparison of each of the features of the input case and existing cases in the library to come up with an overall similarity score for each case in the library. Most nearest-neighbor matching schemes allow the user to apply a set of weights to the features (a weight vector), allowing certain features to affect the similarity score of cases more than other features. Because most nearest-neighbor matching techniques do a linear of near-linear scan of the case library, retrieval time is affected as the case library grows. Nearest-neighbor matching is a good technique to use if there are few cases in the case library and the number of possible diagnostic categories is large.

In a CBR system the question answering and retrieval would be performed until the CSR was satisfied that the input case matched closely enough with a retrieved case or that the scores were starting to degrade, indicating an exception case. The solution for the best matching case would then be suggested to the CSR as the best solution of the current input case:

$$\text{Total score} = \frac{\Sigma\,(\text{Similarity}[(\text{In}\,[i],\,\text{Ret}\,[i])*\text{Weight}\,[i])}{\text{Sum of weights}}$$

where
i = each feature used for matching
In $[i]$ = input case value for i
Ret $[i]$ = retrieved case value for i
Similarity ( ) depends on the field types being compared
Similarity scores range from 0 to 100 (100 = a perfect match)

Inductive Indexing. One problem with using nearest-neighbor techniques ex-clusively is that, as the size of the case library grows, the technique becomes harder to use because it takes too long to retrieve cases. A bigger problem with just using nearest-neighbor matching is that it has no way of handling subtle differences in cases that can have a major impact on determining the correct outcome. Even weighted nearest-neighbor matching cannot overcome this prob-lem beacuse, even though one feature may be more important than another, in general there may be specific times when the other feature will be much more important than another; in general, there may be specific times when the other feature will be much more important. The problem is that nearest-neighbor matching has no way of addressing the contextual importance of features in different circumstances.

Fortunately, inductive machine-learning techniques can be used to help in-dex cases so that they cannot only be retrieved more efficiently but also more accurately, taking into account the contextual importance of features (especially ones that are parsed from text descriptions of the problem). Inductive techniques like CART and ID3 can enable us automatically to derive the contextually relevant indices for accurately retrieving cases and fashion those indices into an efficient decision tree for retrieval purposes,

Prototype Indexing. The reason that rule-based expert systems seem like a viable approach to building Help Desk applications is that there are usually some easily definable rules specifying or clarifying many of the problems that come in to a Help Desk. The problem in using a purely rule-based approach comes from the difficulties in building and maintaining the rules that go beyond those easy-to-define rules for getting a rough idea of the problem. It is not that rules are not valuable or relevant, but that it is often hard to build a system only with rules. We can take advantage of those easy-to-define rules in a case-based system by building a network or "prototypes," while avoiding the difficult task of writing the more difficult rules by using induction and case retrieval. In essence, we can take advantage of knowledge that is easily described to assist in the indexing process and derive the knowledge that is hard to describe using inductive techniques. An additional advantage of using a prototype structure is that it enables multiple paths to be retrieved from a single input case, allowing multiple hypotheses to be explored simultaneously. Prototype structures can also be used in conjunction with nearest-neighbor techniques when induction is not viable.

It is important to note that CBR systems are not designed to operate as a problem solver independently of a human operator. The CBR system si designed to be an intelligent assistant, providing information and recommendations to the best of its knowledge but leaving the final decision and actions to the user. Also it is expected and desired that users enter new cases into the case base with little expert intervention.

Alternative and complementary methods include associative maps, object-oriented pattern bases, and pattern addressable memories.

1.3.2 Barletta–Mott Representation of a Help Desk Case

The main issue we will explore in this section is what kinds of information we can effectively represent and use as cases for our help desk. As was previously stated, a case should contain the description of relevant information needed to resolve the problem, and how the problem was resolved or categorized for passing up to a higher level help desk. We will break useful case information into two groups. The first group is the information that is directly usable by the case-based system to index and retrieve help desk cases. The second group is information that is valuable to the end user (i.e., CSR) but not directly usable by the case indexing and retrieval mechanism because adequate indexing and retrieval mechanisms don't exist yet.

Information that could be used by a CBR indexing system are:

- Short texts describing the problem situation—for example: My computer crashes when I try to print a file from Word®.

- Numbers, dates
- True/false queries—for example: Is the printer on?
- Symbols (i.e., nonnumeric, enumerable types)—For example: colors, Model types, subjective ratings (e.g., high, medium, low), etc.
- Lists of the above-mentioned types—for example, the names of all the applications running on the system, or the last five temperature readings from some gauge.

Information that would be useful for the CSR to have but can't be used by a CBR indexing system are:

- Freedom text from manuals or other large documents
- Pictures, diagrams, and drawings
- Sounds

This type of nonindexing information could be incorporated into the case either directly or via a reference to the appropriate document or drawing. The focus of the remainder of this section will be on features that can be used by indexing and retrieval mechanisms of current CBR systems.

If we view a Help Desk case as an initial description of a problem, a set of questions that are subsequently asked by the CSR to further clarify the problem, and an outcome or resolution to the problem, one possible representation for a computer Help Desk case might look like the one shown in Figure 1.5.

The underlying case record contains the union of all the potentially relevant case features (i.e., symptoms, questions, answers, and solutions) used to solve all known problems in the domain. That is, all the data describing the initial symptoms and all possible questions and answers related to resolving problems from the initial symptoms would be represented in the case record. Any single case will have only a small subset of the record actually filled in, since it would represent a tiny part of the problem domain. Although Figure 1.5 shows all the possible questions in a single form where most of the values are N/A, it would be just as easy to display cases so that only the fields that had values showed. What the CSR sees is totally up to the developer of the Help Desk interface. Under the interface, however, all the unique features (i.e., questions) of all the cases in the library will be present and available if needed.

Using Text As An Indexing Feature. The basic goal in case retrieval is to compare cases on a feature by feature basis and choose the case that matches best relative to the indexing strategy used. This type of technique is fairly easy to understand when thinking in terms of numbers, dates, true/false, and even symbols: four is closer to three than five is so the case with three is a better match, or, a 386 chip is closer to a 486 chip than it is to a 68040 chip so the 486 chip case is a better match, or, the list (a b) is closer to the list (b c) than it is to the list (c d) etc. But, how does this work on freeform text? The short

The Case Record

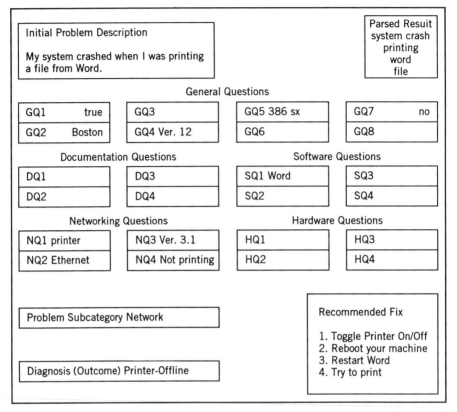

Figure 1.5 *A representation of a Help Desk case. From Barletta and Mott [12].*

answer is, it doesn't. However, if we can turn the freeform text into one of the other field types, it becomes possible.

Even though we can't reliably perform a semantic parse of the freeform text (not because it isn't possible but because it would take much too long to build and maintain such a parser) we can fairly easily extract key words out of the text. For example, we could take an initial problem description such as "My system crashed when I was printing a file from Word®" and turn it into a list of symbols—system, crashed, printing, file, Word®. A simple lexical parser could look for words we thought were relevant, get rid of words we didn't want such as my, when, I, was, etc., and keep track of any new words that we hadn't seen before. Words that we wanted to look for could be organized into hierarchies of values that could be used by the indexing system to match words that were essentially synonyms. A CBR shell like ReMind would use its Symbol Editor in conjunction with its Formula Editor to allow the developer to build and maintain lexicons, and transform texts into lists of symbols for indexing and retrieval. The problem with using freeform text in this way is that the case matching process is at the mercy of the people entering in the text. Too much description and a case might be missed. Too little description and too many cases are retrieved. Different terminology, even with synonyms maintained, make things tenuous at best. We believe that freeform text should be avoided if at all possible for use in the indexing process because it will lead to unpredictable and unreliable results over the long run. However, if used only where absolutely necessary and in conjunction with more structured feature types, it can be used reasonably effectively.

Since the case representation contains all the potentially relevant features of all the cases in the library, and a small percentage of features are actually filled out in each case, the key issue in using this type of representation for help desk problems is determining which features (i.e., questions) to use in a new situation. This is the problem that the indexing and retrieval mechanism must address.

When choosing the appropriate case-based indexing and retrieval strategy for a given help desk application there are several questions to keep in mind.

- *What is the ratio of cases to problem outcomes?* If the ratio of cases to problem outcomes is high then inductive techniques are the best bet. If the ratio is low, nearest-neighbor techniques are an alternative.

- *How many cases do I have?* The number of cases often dictates the type of technique that should be used. If there are going to be a large number of cases but inductive techniques can't be used then try combining nearest neighbor with prototype indexing.

- *Are there easily describable criteria for quickly getting to an appropriate subset of cases?* If there are easily defined rules for quickly getting to a ballpark answer then prototype indexing makes sense regardless of which if any secondary retrieval technique is used.

- *How often do I encounter completely "new" problems?* If brand new problems are the norm rather than the exception, static indexing structures such as inductive or prototype indexing may not be appropriate. If features or outcomes are constantly changing, templates or nearest-neighbor matching may be the only alternative.

- *How much do my CSRs know about the problems they must resolve?* If CSRs are experts, then more dynamic retrieval techniques like templates and nearest-neighbor matching may provide the flexibility an expert will demand. The only problem comes with using these techniques on large libraries. Think about splitting the case libraries into separate problem specific libraries. If CSRs are novices they will need all the help they can get. Take advantage of induction and prototype indexing as much as possible to minimize confusion and errors, while speeding retrieval.

- *Do I want my system to handle exception situations, or common situations?* If you use some other system to handle the most common situations and want to use CBR to handle the tough cases, nearest-neighbor matching or inductive techniques can provide benefits. NN matching gives flexibility in dynamically searching for relevant cases, but inductive indexing can provide insights into the features that tend to lead to certain types of exceptions, so they can be moved into the common situation system. If the CBR system is to be used to handle just common situations, inductive indexing is almost always the best choice unless the number of available cases is small (which is not likely since these are supposed to be common situations).

1.4   ASSOCIATIVE REASONING AND OBJECT-ORIENTED PATTERN BASE

Associations are the bases for intelligent behavior of living organisms. Received sound invokes the shape of an animal in the night; smell invokes the kind of food; a broken branch signifies that a dangerous predator may have passed through.

Human memory is organized in an associative manner. Unlike inputs to digital computer memory, inputs to human memory are not addressed sensory patterns or parts of patterns. Given an input, the memory has the ability to recognize this input as being similar to some stored pattern. A striking example of this associative recall is the ability to recollect the words of a song after hearing a snatch of the tune. The visual system, too, is capable of recognizing an object in the presence of distractors or even when part of the object happens to be occluded. Efforts to incorporate these properties in artificial systems have been quite successful, and a number of associative memory models have been suggested. Artificial associative memories have the desirable properties of generalizing over Hamming distance and pattern completion. The human visual system, however, has abilities that far exceed these simple associative memories. Shown a scene, a human is able to recognize most of the objects in the scene independently of where they may be in the visual field. Recognition of objects by the human visual system is invariant to a set of transformations of the input image. The object can be translated anywhere within the visual field, rotated or distorted to a certain degree, or scaled up or down without degrading accuracy of recognition. Most artificial associative memories do not provide these properties of invariance, and it is desirable to incorporate these properties in artificial systems. Research in this direction is based on learning.

A large number of man-made learning systems has been developed so far. They follow three basic paradigms: artificial neural networks (ANN), rule sets, and hybrids.

Various ANN models have been proposed in the literature [1–8]. These models can be differentiated on the basis of whether the network is single or multilayer and whether it is feedforward or has feedback.

The computation involved in most ANN modes, however, conforms to a common form. The neural networks (connectionism) adhere to the following general model. A neural network consists of interconnected simple neurons. The input signals received by a neuron are multiplied by appropriate weights and summed to yield the overall input to the neuron. The output of the neuron is produced by applying a function f_i, called the activation function, to the weighted sum.

The update step can be formally described as

$$a_i^{k+1} = f_i\left(\sum_{j=1}^{n} w_{ij} a_j^k \right)$$

Learning is defined as a modification of synaptic weights that encodes patterns into the ANN. Learning can be supervised or unsupervised. In unsupervised learning (e.g., Hebbian learning), the weight of a link is updated based on local information available to the neurons by the link. Supervised learning, on the other hand, requires the presence of an external "teacher." The teacher modifies the weights based on the error between a desired response and the actual response to an input. One of the most popular learning schemes for multilayer neural networks is the back-propagation algorithm. Back propagation is a supervised learning mechanism that minimizes the mean-squared error between the desired and actual output values. One of the reasons that it is used to solve real-life problems is that it is computationally cost effective. There are two phases to the back-propagation algorithm. In the forward phase, the training pattern is input to the network and activations of the neurons are updated until the output emerges at the output layer. This output is compared with the desired output for that pattern, the error signals are propagated back through the network, and the weights are updated. The computational complexity of the backward phase is the same as that of the forward phase. To fully capture the potential of learning paradigms, ANN models have to be implemented in hardware.

Both symbolic and neural computing have difficulty in expressing associations. The holographic neural technology presents a major breakthrough in fuzzy associations. A holographic network superimposes a very large set of analog stimulus-response associations within the individual neuron cell. The holographic process involves representation of information within the stimulus and response field by vector orientation in a generalized complex domain. The holographic process utilizes the inherent properties of vector transforms to enfold very large numbers of stimulus-response associations onto an identical set of complex vectors. Digitization of the information-enfolding process facilitates a neural system whereby a thousand analog stimulus-response associations may be easily enfolded onto a single neuron of relatively small size. Simulation results for holographic systems indicate data storage capacities and effective rates of processing at a level that is orders of magnitude beyond current neural network theory and practice.

According to Sutherland [13, 14], this feature is characteristic of the holographic process due to the manner in which highly accurate responses are

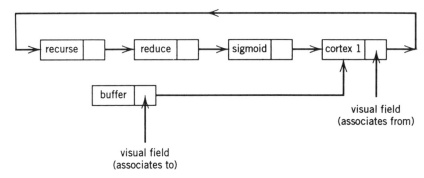

Figure 1.6 *Configuration for the recurrent associator demonstration [14].*

generated on a single-pass decoding transformation. An illustration has been constructed to emulate this characteristic of linear association. The example constructed consists of a cortex cell arranged within a recurrent structure as illustrated in Fig. 1.6. The response field from this set of neural cells is averaged down to an 8 × 8 array and fed back into the stimulus input field for the cortex cell. During encoding, 20 related visual images are exposed in sequence to the network as stimulus pairs. These association pairs are encoded in such a manner that supplying the stimulus field with one pattern will evoke as a response the generation of the previously associated output image (Fig. 1.7).

During the decoding (or expression) portion of these applications, one of the visual images selected by the user is provided as the initial stimulus to the array of neuron cells. The user also has the option of applying a variable degree

Figure 1.7 *Display illustrating the recurrent associator concept [14].*

of random distortion to this initial input pattern. On each subsequent execution cycle, the cortex cells express an association along a linear sequence. The associations enfolded within the cell are thereby regenerated as a sequence of visual patterns, expressed in their temporally connected order. The example enfolds two disconnected trains of visual associations within the neural cell, each of 10 images. Depending on which initial pattern one presents to the neural engine, the system will course through one of the two sequences of visual associations. Applying the above concepts within an expert system application, one may view the input field not as visual images but as input-state conditions. For instance, an input field consisting of, say, 1000 values may store the input-state conditions to a diagnostic system. The holographic system may enfold a vast number of scenarios for those state conditions and associated diagnostic responses onto the neural system. In this manner, the expert system need not parse through a logical or heuristic tree structure. The holographic process permits all input/output scenarios to be enfolded onto the same correlation elements, and one stimulus pass through the neural system will generate the closest associated response.

One fundamental feature of the holographic pattern base is that the user is provided with a model that closely resembles the object in the real world. The object class persists after program activation and termination, and it remains accessible in subsequent programs. In this respect, the holographic pattern base is a fuzzy complement to classical object-oriented data bases, IMS, CODA-SYL, and SQL.

Direct representation and manipulation of certain types of objects is available, including the three most fundamental aspects of the object paradigms: encapsulation, inheritance, and object identity. This is of special importance when dealing with multimedia (codes, images, speech).

Object-oriented holographic models provide a natural representation for multimedia, as well as for fuzzy processing. High-level processing is based on three categories of cells: input, operator, and neural. The object is accessed and modified only through these interface cells. The internal implementation details, data structure, and storage elements used to implement the objects and operations are not visible to the user accessing and manipulating the object. The holographic model is viewed as a collection of independent objects that communicate with each other through high-level cells or procedures.

Figure 1.6 is an example of a high-level structure. It uses standard processing cells, available in a holographic system. Cells used in the example include the

Buffer, which receives the digital image (the stimulus, or the response)

Recourse, which establishes the recurrent configuration

Reduction, which averages adjacent elements in the input data field

Sigmoid, which is symmetric redistribution of phase orientation

Cortex, which executes the fundamental encode/decode/commutative holographic processes

The holographic pattern base presents a fundamental diversion from the standard neural systems:

- Stimulus-response associations are both learned and expressed in one non-iterative transformation. In some applications holographic learning is 100 times faster than neural learning.
- A single holographic cell can replace a large connectionist network.
- The holographic pattern base provides a natural representation for multimedia. It presents a complement to the object-oriented data base.
- The user's attention is shifted to pre- and postprocessing.
- In many application areas holographic networks are strong competition to neural networks and rule-based expert systems.

Expert systems have proven to be effective tools for mimicking an expert's problem-solving techniques when the expert can explicitly state the necessary rules, but they have failed to capture the "soft" knowledge that experts cannot put into words. Fuzzy associators, however, are fully capable of discovering this hidden information by observing samples of an expert's behavior during a problem-solving task. As independent systems, or working together with conventional expert systems, fuzzy associators can reduce development and maintenance costs and provide customer service by automatically learning rules.

The described technique leads in the direction of reasoning systems whose behavior resembles that of a human mind. The systems should be able to describe, evaluate, and approximate information with some degree of fuzziness, uncertainty, or incompleteness. The ultimate goal is the intuitive information processing that humans display: unconscious, integrated, analog, parallel, and distributed reasoning, pattern recognition, probabilistic reasoning, and inductive reasoning in situations of incomplete or fuzzy information. See Chapters 3 to 10.

1.5 EVOLUTION AND OPTIMIZATION

Evolution and optimization are very frequent decision support functions. The genetic algorithm is a form of artificial evolution. The genetic algorithm implies the existence of a set of different network configurations (population), a method of configuration quality estimation (fitness), a way of concise configuration representation (genotype), and the operator for genotype modification (such as crossover and mutation).

The basic idea of the genetic algorithm is as follows:

Create initial population of genotypes and structures to be optimized;
Evaluate structures in the population;
REPEAT

Select genotypes, forming the new population;

Form new genotypes, recombining the old ones;

Evaluate structures created according to new genotypes;

UNTIL terminating condition is satisfied.

The key steps are the parent selection and the formation of new genotypes. Parents are selected based on their fitness. The better ones have a greater chance of being selected. New genotypes are found by genetic operators, the most important of which are crossover and mutation. The crossover operator builds a new genotype of bits from each parent. In this way an offspring is formed that has characteristics of both, already well-adapted, parents. The mutation operator changes genotype bits in a random manner with a low probability, sustaining in this way population diversity.

A few examples where the genetic algorithm and related selection processes could be an alternative to other decision support functions are the following:

1. *Recognition.* To recognize a word, we almost need to know which word we are looking for. Elements of recognition ignite the process of domination. This process, after a while, will feed back to the elements that caused it to happen in the first place.

2. *Context.* Context is needed to understand the text, but the text provides information on what the context is. Hence, we start with an initial population of many possible contexts. Specific words in the text enforce the domination of a particular context, and, conversely, the context enforces the words in the text.

3. *Goal Selection.* All potentially executable goals form the initial population. Initial success in execution of the goal will further enforce the goal; the more resources and supports from the environment will go toward it.

4. *Rule Learning.* The process starts with a diverse set of rules. When rules are successful, they gain in strength; otherwise they become weaker.

1.6 THE IRIS ENGINEERING

To develop a high-quality decision support it is necessary to integrate several processes and paradigms. IRIS is a bridge or a chain of links that orthogonally connects processes offering an integrated solution (Fig. 1.1):

- Integrated reasoning information systems
- Integration rules, interactions, and standards
- Integration of resources, infrastructure, and service
- Integration and reuse of information and of software

The technological backbone of the IRIS decision support concept is to integrate features of fuzzy, crisp, parallel, neural, and knowledge-based processing with holographic networks composed of complex numbers or vectors. The holographic method presents a fundamental diversion from both connectionist neural computing and from rule-based reasoning. First experiments in the field of financial application indicate that training the holographic network could be 100 times faster than training a neural network. A modified holographic-symbolic network provides a natural medium to integrate learning, knowledge, fuzzy, and parallel processing.

In the IRIS concept an integrated reasoning and informing service consists of a number of pools of holographic network crisp-fuzzy reasoning functions and of a pool of functions enabling access to heterogeneous and autonomous multidata/multimedia information sources. The learning capability of the system—the training sets will come from the data bases keeping the past experiences and behaviors, as well as from the human operators and inputs—will enable an enterprise to exploit incomplete and complex data in distributed and heterogeneous data bases in order to enable rapid but well-founded management decisions in context of complex, incomplete, dynamic, and fuzzy problems that typically occur in financing, software production, aircraft control, energy, ecology, climate, chemical engineering, and other areas.

Based on the first experiments, major breakthroughs are possible with substantial saving for users. Only in credit scoring is it possible to save up to DM 15 billion for a country like Germany. Also fuzzy-crisp-multimedia decision support systems are a billion-dollar market.

IRIS established a new level of cooperation between component technologies: knowledge, case base, learning, adaptation, evolution, optimization, and so on, jointly work on the common goal, decision support. Figure 1.8 outlines the relation between components technologies and IRIS engineering that integrates them. The background on both can be found in the sixth-generation series of books [1–8].

No single component technology can yield the optimal way of creating a powerful decision support system (DSS). The solution is a hybrid, integrated system. Its structure depends on the application. IRIS engineering offers six models of integrated hybrids.

The *loose-coupling* model uses separate and independent components (KBS, CBR, neural networks etc.) as stand-alone modules that communicate via data files. The *tight-coupling* model uses separate and independent component modules that communicate via parameter or data passing. The *fully integrated* model is so unified that the distinction between the component moduls is blurred. The model uses shared data structures and knowledge representation. An example is a neural network node that represents part of a rule. The *EDIFACT model* offers the standardized messages to communicate between component modules. The UN EDIFACT standard covers data elements, codes, segments, and syntax rules. See Chapter 2. The *core-pool system* is composed of a core DSS and a pool of components. A core DSS utilizes models and/or analytical techniques

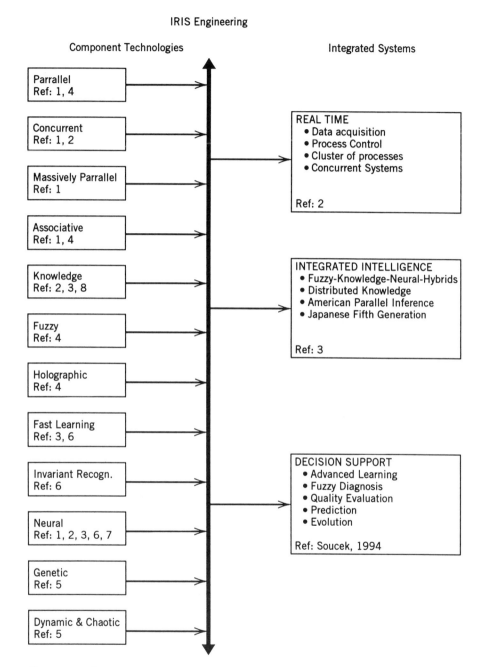

Figure 1.8   *Component technologies vs. IRIS engineering vs. integrated solutions. Relations to the sixth-generation series of books [1–8].*

and deals with internal and external data bases and with user interfaces. A pool of components (KBS, CBR etc.) supports knowledge and learning functions related to narrow problem domains. The *distributed model* covers message-passing, marker-passing, and value-passing, using networked, concurrent, parallel, and optical platforms. For examples, see Chapters 15 to 18.

IRIS hybrid systems combine KBSs with other technologies, such as neural networks, CBR (case-based reasoning), genetic algorithms, virtual reality, and multimedia.

CBR and rule-based reasoning complement one another.

Rules handle big chunks of problem domains well, but they are less useful or cost effective in the boundary areas where subtle contexts tend to exist. Cases, on the other hand, can model entire domains if you assemble enough cases to cover every problem area in the domain.

A neural network adds accuracy and fault tolerance to a KBS, and a KBS can explain why a neural network behaves as it does. KBSs gain better search-and-development capabilities when merged with genetic algorithms. In other words, logical and crisp nature of a KBS complements the numeric, associative, self-learning and fuzzy nature of neural and holographic networks and evolution algorithms.

This book deals with a new area, decision support. It covers advanced learning principles and their implementations, fuzzy diagnosis, quality evaluation, prediction, and evolution. The above is a new set of features for Help Desk, for Media Decision Support, and for Process Decision Support.

In decision support, IRIS integrates the feature of fuzzy, crisp, parallel, neural, and knowledge-based processing with a holographic network composed of a complex number of vectors. A pattern (content) addressable memory could be developed with holographic symbolic networks, capable of enfolding association in the sense that one input pattern will induce the issuance of the second, thus subsequently inducing the issuance of a third, and so on. Such a sequence may be configured to form an engine for applications within a fuzzy expert or diagnostic system. An intelligent data base would be used for crisp processing. The information in the IRIS system is represented as digital codes (data files, text, links) and patterns (information sets, pictorial symbols, labels, image, sound). Processing and reasoning are going through the fuzzy-crisp steps. In this way an intelligent I/O-parallel-data base system is formed that could access information in a flexible manner in a way that resembles the operation of human reasoning.

The IRIS pool performs

- Processing and reasoning by association and by analogy
- Fuzzy-holographic-distributed processing
- Crisp-fuzzy associations across data, documents, and multimedia

Multiple crisp-fuzzy-holographic associators integrate these operations within the same correlation media. Integration platforms are PCs, C language, and workstations. A graphic user interface will integrate multimedia and knowledge.

The features of the IRIS pool include

- Intelligent I/O–parallel processing–data base–fuzzy associations
- Detection of usual and unusual patterns in information sets and in data bases; recognition of image and of voice
- Dealing with partial and inexact information, and making educated guesses based on what has been before and what is stored in a fuzzy associative memory
- Combining the information in text, image, and sound form
- Reasoning based on data patterns as well as on data pattern structures, including categories of hierarchies among objects
- Vertical associations as well as lateral reasoning based on side links and branches

The IRIS pool could be used in three ways:

1. As stand-alone fuzzy-crisp associators
2. In a system with other modules as a decision support
3. In a network of distributed federated systems, as fuzzy-crisp nodes, and decision support subsystems

The user is free to select the right functions from the IRIS pool and to connect them in a topology as required by application. Many function/application examples are described in Chapters 3 to 18.

1.7 TOOLS, METHODS, AND APPLICATIONS DEVELOPED BY THE IRIS GROUP

The IRIS group is composed of leading American, European, and Japanese laboratories. They offer concrete IRIS tools and solutions. Each solution presents the frontier in its field, and some solutions are quite complex. Yet, if there is no pain, there is no gain say the financial gurus and analysts of the leading think tanks. The IRIS group provides the necessary knowledge, experience, tools, and methods. It offers

Concrete real-life, ready to use, off-the-shelf solutions
Custom solutions, service, and products
Flexible training, learning, and expert knowledge
New concepts

The tools and methods include

Learning for decision making
Fuzzy diagnosis
Quality evaluation
Prediction
Evolution and population structure
Learning robots and flexible manufacturing
Frontier implementation

1.7.1 Learning for Decision Making

Learning is one of the basic features of intelligence. The concept of learning machines comes from biological models. Learning is effective self-modification of the organism that lives in a complex and changing enironment. Learning is any directed change in the knowledge structure that improves the performance.

The holographic learning method has been developed recently. Holographic neural technology employs a novel concept in which information is represented by vector orientation on a Riemann plane where very large sets of fuzzy associations are both learned and expressed in one noniterative transformation. The holographic neural process ideally embodies the concept of content addressable memory. Multiple pattern associations, at nearly arbitrary levels of complexity, may be enfolded onto a neural cell. Encoded responses or "outputs" may subsequently be generated or accessed from the cell via content of input. Input fields may be representative of addressing schemes or "syntax," and are transformed in an inherently parallel manner through all of the content "addresses" enfolded within the cell. In response to an address or stimulus signal, the cell regenerates the associated output data field, indicating also the degree of confidence in that output association. The holographic process can be structured to operate directly within the context of content addressable memory, whereby input–output associations enfolded within a given memory "cell" are expressed directly through content of input.

Holographic-fuzzy classifiers operating in PC, C, Windows, environment are described. They include the symmetrical transformation/nonlinear expansion preprocessing routines and the holographic discovery/development packages. The classifiers deal with financial, biomedical, power, and geophysical problems. Experiments reveal speedup factors of 10 to 100 times compared with other learning paradigms.

1.7.2 Fuzzy Diagnoses

Most diagnostic expert systems to date attempt to deal with uncertainty by extending rule-based system to allow experts to express uncertain relationships. One such extension is the certainty factor model. The CF model has been widely adopted by expert system developers for medicine, customer service, and other application areas.

The most traditional is the application of statistical techniques, and several models have been advanced. Perhaps most notable among them is the Bayesian approach using Bayes' theorem to update probability estimates based on observed data. The second technique is to apply developed and evolving techniques such as fuzzy logic in both its deterministic and stochastic forms.

Three procedures for fuzzy diagnoses are presented and compared: holographic, statistical, and neural. All three have been used for the same task, namely neurophysiological diagnosis. The diagnosis is based on the brain stem auditory evoked potentials (BSAEP) classification. The BSAEP are generated in response to brief auditory stimuli involving characteristic spike potentials. Diagnostic accuracies of 96% (holographic), 88% (neural), and 84% (statistical) have been achieved.

1.7.3 Quality Evaluation

Quality is related to the usefulness of the product. It describes the differences between ideal features that the user would like to have and the real features of the product, process, or service.

Several levels of quality have been defined. Quality control (QC), the first level, is based on the identification and separation of good and bad in all phases of the control of production. Quality assurance (QA), the next level, is based on the requirements and recommendations in ISO 9000 of the International Standardization Organization (ISO). Computer-aided quality assurance (CAQ) is the next level, and is based on the use of computers in all phases relevant for quality. Total quality management (TQM) is the next goal. It integrates all the functions, the motivation of workers, and the management and manufacturing processes. In other words, TQM is related to IRIS.

Quality control in manufacturing is crucial for succesful production. The quality evaluation systems are capable of learning which produced object belong to which class.

Software quality evaluation, based on learning of quality metrics, is described. A software metric is obtained from observations made on the products or processes. Some examples of software metrics are the number of instructions in a module, the number of variables in a program, the development cost of an application, and the number of errors occurring during testing. Evaluation of software products and processes, using knowledge-learning-holographic methods, is described.

Quality evaluation is crucial for decision making in financing and banking. Loan and credit scoring based on learning is described in detail. Credit demand has increased rapidly in recent years. Private households in Germany have applied, on average, for DM 28.4 billion new credit in 1990–1991. Also, private companies have increased credit demand. Recently, one finds some knowledge-based credit-scoring systems developed with expert system technology. In practice, many of the attributes used to characterize credit applicants are qualitative, and, as is well known, discriminance analysis is not an appropriate tool in such circumstances. On the other hand, in development of knowledge-based credit-scoring system, normally, one is encountered with the typical knowledge-acquisition bottleneck problem. Also as an alternative to such approaches, one can consider the application of neural nets and machine-learning algorithms.

In this book we discuss the performance of different approaches that can contribute to automating the credit-granting procedures. We concentrate, in particular, on the application of machine learning and neural network approaches in solving the credit-scoring problem. To evaluate the different approaches, we use several real-world data sets. The empirical results of the evaluation procedures are reported and discussed. The results show that machine-learning-based classification approaches can be regarded as a very efficient alternative to implementing the credit-scoring systems.

Holographic classification in terms of good versus bad clients has been performed. It leads to the elimination of 88% of financial losses while reducing the good client prospective by only 13%. Training and testing sets contain 650 client vectors each. The entire training/recall process required approximately 5 min (versus 8 h for the connectionist package).

It is estimated that about DM 15 billion of the granted credit to the private companies in Germany will never be paid back. Hence, holographic credit scoring can offer substantial savings to financial institutions. This system combines a new method for symmetrical preprocessing with the two levels of holographic learning. It outperforms other paradigms in speed as well as classification accuracy.

1.7.4 The Prediction

Time-series prediction or forecasting is a very important component of management decision models. Besides the application of the traditional methods like technical and fundamental analysis or quantitative classical statistical methods, attention has recently focused on the application of neural networks. Different methods and algorithms are discussed.

In particular, the most difficult systems to predict are those with nonstationary dynamics, where the underlying behavior varies with time, such as short- and long-term financial time series, electric power network consumption over several days, weeks, or months, daily temperatures, and water level.

Several models are presented. (1) Daily short-term prediction of stock prices on the German market DAX (Deutcher Aktienindex). In this model different information like the change of Dow Jones and Nikkei indices, U.S. bonds, German Bund-Future, exchange rate DM/USD, and a technical indicator act as exogenous variables. (2) Long-term prediction of DAX development. In this model, fundamental descriptions like profit expectations, U.S. and German interest rates, and business climate index are considered exogenous variables to estimate the "fair value" of DAX and to forecast development one year ahead. (3) Prediction of global electric power consumption. The data in the West-Bohemian region were available for the last two years, having been monitored every hour. The method of prediction uses the special multilayer neural network.

The aforementioned models compare the predictivity performance of neural networks, statistical methods, and machine-learning algorithims based on the ID3 procedure.

1.7.5 Evolution and Population Structures

Evolution is viewed as a typical optimization problem. Nature is the result of a large-scale evolution experimentation on earth. Not only nature, but the evolution process itself evolved. We might expect that during the more than a thousand million years of action of biological evolution an optimization strategy has evolved that is very efficient and complex in the mode of operation.

Evolution algorithms are inspired from analogy with biological evolution. Adopting the complex mechanism of nature to offer the possibility of a general-purpose adaptive search algorithm assumes the identification of the main operators. The models of simulating evolution are based on a reproduction and selection model. The optimization model operates on a finite, and usually small, ensemble of individuals called the population, via the operator's selection, mutation, and crossover.

The adaptive search process of the traditional evolution algorithms, as genetic algorithms and evolution strategies, is sequential and guided by global information and global rules. The introduction of the concept of population structures, allowing only interactions between geographically nearby individuals, offers a promising extension to the principles of evolution incorporated so far into evolution algorithms. We discuss discrete population structures known as migration models and continuous models known as diffusion, isolation by distance, or neighborhood models.

The advantages of introducing a population structure are threefold. First, the algorithm becomes explicitly parallel and may be run, for example, on a network of machines giving an expected linear speedup. Second, the introduction of a population structure also improves search behavior in terms of the time/quality trade-off, final quality, and robustness; that is, compared with the same algorithm without population structure, the algorithm is faster and generates better solutions with greater probability. Third, the algorithm may focus its search on several optimal solutions in a single run, an important aspect for at least some applications.

The traveling salesman problem is used to present an application case study. It is a combinatorial optimization problem that is easy to state and yet very difficult to solve optimally. An evolution algorithm with a continuous population structure is described in detail, and simulation results illustrating the advantages of the enhanced algorithm are presented. Applications include management, manufacturing, robotics, and prosthetics. A speedup factor of 15 times has been achieved, compared with other evolution algorithms.

1.7.6. Learning Robots and Flexible Manufacturing

Learning the motion presents the base for complex process control and robotics. Since the exact dynamics of the controlled object are generally unknown, it is possible to use a neural network model and appropriate learning rules by which an internal model of inverse robot dynamics is acquired during execution of movement. Also, neural networks have great potential for application in intelligent systems, where controller or robot would be able to learn from its experience to recognize changes in environmental conditions, reach them, or make decisions based on changing manufacturing events. Using decentralized control and computed torque control algorithms, we can develop models of neural networks as feedforward robot controllers.

Based on repetitive trials (i.e., repetitive execution of the working task and position and velocity errors during execution), a training network controller can be realized. In this way, the control algorithm is redistributed between feedforward and feedback loops, resulting in fast response and improved system performance. The goal is intelligent and flexible manufacturing.

1.7.7 Frontier Implementation

The new level of quality could be achieved by using new concepts or new implementation technology, or, even better, combining the two. Very new technology is optoelectronics, including light-emitting diodes and variable-sensitivity photodiodes. Optical technology is used here to implement a color pattern recognition system, based on the learning concept of mode competition.

The concept of mode competition is based on experience in nonlinear dynamics: Systems composed of many subsystems often show global behavior determined by just a few ''modes'' binding together the underlying subsystems. By analyzing the time development of the strength or amplitude of these modes, we can formulate general equations governing many different systems. It turns out that, usually, subsystems cooperate to form global modes that compete for domination of system conditions such as energetic input, boundary constraints, interconnection between subsystems or fluctuations that favor them over others. The whole concept could therefore also be seen as an extension and generalization of Darwin's concepts for adaptation to the inorganic world.

The system has been used for Japanese color stamps recognition in the postal service. A recognition rate of 100% has been achieved.

1.8 EXAMPLES OF BUSINESS PROCESS REENGINEERING

The IRIS concept covers a broad range of applications, from banking, financing, and services, through software production and reuse, all the way to production line surveillance, flexible manufacturing, and quality control. In these areas, frontier breakthrough results have been achieved through the IRIS concept. These are described in Chapters 3 to 18. Three demonstrators in important application areas are outlined here: banking and financing, software engineering and manufacturing, and quality control.

1.8.1 Banking and Financing

The bank should be able to use past cases as a guide to solving current problems consistently and efficiently. A case embodies all of the implicit or explicit knowledge that was used to help arrive at a solution. These may include conclusions based on the customer's description of the problem, follow-up questions to the customer, discussions with a supervisor or co-worker, sections in a manual, or intuitions about the likely cause of the problem that just happened to be correct. The representation for a case is a set of features (the simpler the better) describing the problem situation and what was done about it (i.e., the solution of outcome). One key issue in building a case-based system is to capture this case knowledge in a consistent and simplified form.

The resulting financial service and support systems and IRIS Help Desk are based on new knowledge, learning and multimedia technologies. The service is intended for management, offices, and customers, and is based on intelligent data bases and on fuzzy reasoning and forecasting. The desired financial services are listed here.

1. *Credit Risk Analysis.* Credit risk analysis of prospective borrowers and insurance policyholders is undertaken. The service can be of enormous benefit to lending institutions in minimizing losses incurred through client loan default. It is possible to achieve 90% accuracy in client classification on what had previously been considered unanalyzable data.

2. *Fuzzy Reasoning and Trend Detection in Time Series.* Fuzzy holographic matrices will be used to produce an approximate answer. Such a system can forecast the effects of price rises, new government proposals, decrease/increase in exports, inflation rates, exchange rates, and seasonal trends.

3. *Credit Card Fraud.* This application requires sufficient accuracy in prediction to make verification feasible considering the attendant risk and resource expended on ''false positive''; the number of actual frauds is a small fraction of the total transaction, and excessive false positives incur a liability in terms of client confidence by requiring manual verification of the transaction. The holographic network may have sufficient reliability to make fraud detection a practicable application.

4. *Money Market Analysis.* This is a daily recommendation based on fuzzy forecasting for market and currency exchange rates for the next week. It is necessary to compile a stock and commodities trading system using both technical (i.e., price/volume) and fundamental data for companies listed on exchanges. This application appears to provide the most significant opportunity within the financial sector, because very large investments are in question.

5. *Direct Marketing.* Many companies are substantially reliant on direct marketing techniques for sales of service or products. This, naturally, includes banks in their promotion of credit and banking services. Some of the more progressive direct marketing agencies have resorted to neural network techniques to optimize their "hit" ratios. Such analysis with holographic networks can display results that substantially exceed other methods.

6. *Stock Purchasing Decision* The investor will use the system to browse through information on different companies, focusing on those aspects of a company's financial performance that are most relevant to the stock investment decision: the number of investors, the price-to-earning ratio, the price of the stock, annual sales, and current liabilities of the company. Financial status is important. Is the company a Fortune 1000 company, or one of the leading companies in the region, country, or world.

Techniques, concrete applications, and results related to banking and financing are presented in Chapters 3 to 6, 10 to 13.

1.8.2   Software Engineering and Reengineering

Software production and reuse directly depends on the

- Software quality metrics
- Software quality evaluation
- Quality of software house management
- Quality of the software production line

The *IEEE Standard Glossary of Software Engineering Terminology* reports the following definitions for software quality.

1. The totality of features and characteristics of a software product that bear on its ability to satisfy given needs; for example, conform to specification
2. The degree to which software possesses a desired combination of attributes
3. The degree to which a customer or user perceives that software meets his or her composite expectations
4. The composite characteristics of software that determine the degree to which the software in use will meet the expectations of the customer

Therefore, several software quality factors are identified: correctness, reliability, efficiency, integrity, usability, maintainability, testability, flexibility, portability, reusability, and interoperability.

In software engineering and maintenance, as well as in reuse and reengineering, it is necessary to evaluate the software components. The evaluation is based on software metrics, which cover both products and processes. The desired steps include the following:

a. The compiler or the user performs the compilation in reverse and decomposes the code into independent segments or modules. The result is the library of available modules.
b. Each candidate module is described in terms of a collection of metrics. The metrics could be binary, discrete, or continuous.
c. The modules are classified into well-structured and poorly structured code groups. The classification system is based on learning, using the training set with the known examples of both kinds of modules.

The solution is seen in developing two groups of software packages: ADAM (acquisition of data and metrics) should resolve steps a and b, and EVA (evaluation of software modules, using knowledge-learning-holographic methods) should resolve step c.

With a training set of well-structured and poorly structured modules, each described in terms of the appointed software metrics, fuzzy-holographic association maps will be produced. The maps will be used to recognize other well-structured modules in terms of their fuzzy metric properties. In the maps, analog information content is assigned to the phase orientation of the vector. The associated vector magnitude indicates the confidence, bounded within a probabilistic range (0 to 1).

The user can establish a threshold level about a given confidence value to define the categories of modules. EVA should be composed of three modules: analysis/classification, simulation testing, user-friendly interface. The package can be used for evaluation of software modules produced by a controlled group of students, obtained from a software house, or derived from a large data base. Special attention should be focused on the software-multimedia domain.

Techniques and applications related to software engineering are presented in Chapters 1, 2, 3, 4, 5, 7, and 8.

1.8.3 Manufacturing and Quality Control

Improvement of quality, performance, reliability, maintainability, and accessibility of the products and processes is one of the major goals of the industry in order to improve the competitiveness. Recent investigations show that, especially in uncertain and unpredictable situations, management and operators have to be provided with the best possible awareness of the situation. This knowledge has to be derived from partial, incomplete, and inconsistent data based on internal as well as external status of the production environment.

On-line support systems for the operators of a modern production line need to provide comprehensive situation awareness and tactical recommendations for decision making in order to prevent human beings from becoming the limiting factor for system performance, but put man into action where he is unique as system manager and final decision executor. The extraordinary situation in this area is characterized by extreme demand on very fast response time. In case of emergency the operator has to make decisions in milliseconds.

The coordinator of a growing number of demanding subsystems during the decision-making process imposes additional workload and, in consequence, operational problems to the operators of such integrated systems.

Production surveillance and quality control systems are crucial for successful manufacturing. These systems are capable of learning which produced object belongs to which class. Some examples follow.

To train the system, one presses the class 1 button, and some class 1 objects are sent down the conveyor. The same procedure is followed for class 2 objects. Then the production button is pressed and the system is fully operational, classifying by experience it has gained about what the difference is between the two classes. Applications are numerous: sorting bottles by color, sorting waste bags, checking colors in a print process, classifying seeds, checking for missing object in a crate, quality control inspection of the welds produced by roll machines. Of course, for each application it is necessary to have the proper sensory device.

In the analysis of NIR (near-infrared reflection) data, a sample is exposed by infrared light, and the reflection of the infrared light is measured as a percentage of light exposed. The amount of data measured depends on the sample to be analyzed. These data are used to predict the proportion of protein, water, and other materials in the sample. This method is faster and cheaper, but not as accurate, than a laboratory chemical test.

Current R&D activities indicate that the technology of early knowledge-based systems as well as neural network technology may not be adequate to satisfy hard real-time constraints in the aforementioned environments. The IRIS concept offers high-speed, high-quality hybrid solutions.

Techniques and applications related to production surveillance and manufacturing are presented in Chapters 3 to 6, 12, 15 to 18.

1.8.4 Generalized Description

The three application fields are summarized in Table 1.1. In the discussion, ( ) refers to the row of Table 1.1. In all three cases the human decision maker (4) is confronted continuously during the work with the need of making quick decisions in the presence of uncertainty. Increasing system and scenario complexity means that users have to cope with larger amounts of data in a shorter time by correlating this information flow mentally under stress conditions. For a single event they might be able to manage the situation, but for several simultaneously appearing problems it is impossible for human beings to solve the problems, taking into account all effecting constraints. Therefore it becomes more and more important to provide suitable workplace (3) decision support systems.

TABLE 1.1 Summary of Three Field Applications

1	Application field	Banking and financing	Software engineering	Manufacturing and quality control
2	Environment	Executive level	Executive level	Factory
3	Workplace	Office	Office	Production line
4	User, decision maker	Manager	Manager	Operators
5	Information source on internal situation	Management information system	Management information system	System status Monitoring system
6	Information source on external situation	External data sources	External data sources	External data sources
7	Critical scenarios	Accept, modify, reject	Accept, modify, reject	Preparation, stop, continue
8	Needs	Comprehensive situations awareness, strategic and tactical recommendation for decision making	Comprehensive situations awareness, strategic and tactical recommendation for decision making	Comprehensive situations awareness, strategic and tactical recommendation for decision making
9	Information sources	Data bases, external	Data bases, external	Sensor, remote sources
10	Procedures	Financial decision, credit and customers scoring, forecasting and prediction	Forward engineering, reengineering, reuse, quality assessment, maintenance	On-line classification of products, on-line learning and adaptation
11	Response time	Minutes	Minutes	Milliseconds

A basis for making high-level decisions in the workplace requires a continuous flow of precise and consistent information of internal (5) and external (6) situation. The information source on the internal situation is system status monitoring or management information systems.

The growing number of information sources (9) requires means for merging this partial, incomplete, and inconsistent information about the same object from different sources to one consistent information source for the user.

Common to all three applications is the need to make fast and accurate decisions in complex, fuzzy, and partially undefined environments.

Computing architectures take many forms, but the most common form is the client/server configuration, shown in Figure 1.9. Resolve, shown in Figure 1.10, aids support personnel in answering customers' questions. Because it is a client/server system, Resolve resides on both the desktop component and the knowledge server. A support person enters problem information and Resolve generates queries on the information and submits them to the knowledge server. If the answer isn't there, Resolve sends the queries to the information servers, which could be data bases in other parts of the company. Resolve filters and returns the results of the queries to the support person. The common goal is integration of reasoning, informing, and serving.

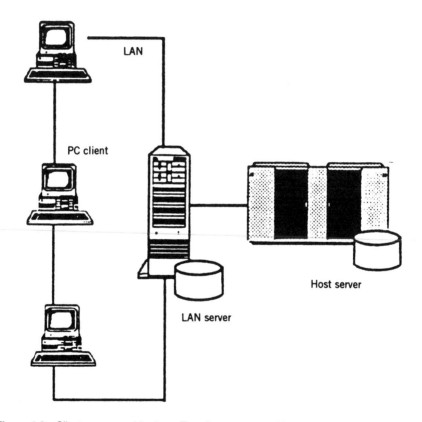

Figure 1.9 *Client–server architecture. The client–server architecture consists of one or more client computers (generally LAN-based PCs), associated data-base servers, communication gateways, and optional host computers. The GUI and end-user applications reside on the PC; data required for end-user interaction is stored on the server, and corporate data remains on the host computer. In a client–server application, the user interface and business-specific functions run on the client, which is typically a PC or workstation in a windowed environment. Client applications provide an intuitive GUI, customized procedural logic, and the ability to access data on local or remote data base servers and host computers.*

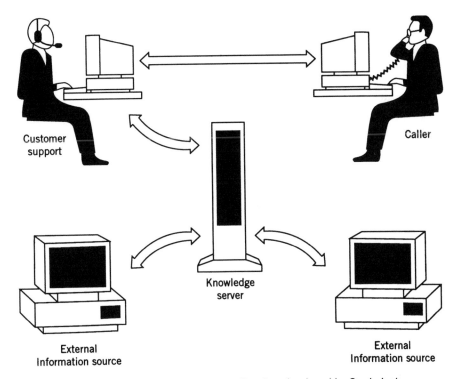

Figure 1.10 *The advanced system, Resolve, developed by Symbologic.*

REFERENCES

1. B. Souček and M. Souček, *Neural and Massively Parallel Computers*, Wiley, New York, 1988, p. 460.
2. B. Souček, *Neural and Concurrent Real-Time Systems, The Sixth Generation*, Wiley, New York, 1989, p. 387.
3. B. Souček and IRIS Group, *Neural and Intelligent Systems Integration*, Wiley, New York, 1991, p. 664.
4. B. Souček and IRIS Group, *Fuzzy, Holographic, and Parallel Intelligence*, Wiley, New York, 1992, p. 330.
5. B. Souček and IRIS Group, *Dynamic, Genetic and Chaotic Programming*, Wiley, New York, 1992, p. 650.
6. B. Souček and IRIS Group, *Fast Learning and Invariant Object Recognition*, Wiley, New York, 1992, p. 279.
7. T. Hrycej, *Modular Learning in Neural Networks*, Wiley, New York, 1992.
8. R. Sun, *Integrating Rules and Connectionism for Robust Commonsense Reasoning*, Wiley, New York, 1994, p. 273.

9. J. W. Lewis and F. S. Lynch, GETREE: A knowledge management tool, *Proc. Trends and Applications. Automatic Intelligent Behavior, Applications and Frontiers*, IEEE, New York, 1983.

10. K. Parsaye and M. Chignell, *Expert Systems for Experts*, Wiley, New York, 1988.

11. *Proc. Workshop on Artif. Intelligence for Customer Service and Support*, Monterey, Calif., March 3, 1992.

12. R. Barletta and S. Mott, Techniques for employing case-based reasoning in automated customer service help desk, in *Proc. Workshop on Artificial Intelligence for Customer Service and Support*, Monterey, Calif., March 3, 1992.

13. J. Sutherland, A holographic model of memory, learning and expression, *Int. J. Neural Syst.* 1(3) 259–267 (1990).

14. J. Sutherland, "The Holographic Neural Method," in B. Souček and IRIS Group, *Fuzzy Holographic, and Parallel Intelligence*, Wiley, New York, 1992.

CHAPTER 2 ─────────────

Help Desk Projects, Software, and EDI

MARINA SOUČEK
GIUSEPPE VISAGGIO

2.1 INTRODUCTION

Decision support software projects lead to a strong partnership between developer and user. In this area a strong partnership is crucial; the user holds the balance of power. The software package structure is formalized by application experts and design experts, typically in the form of deduction flows.

This chapter discusses advanced implementation technologies, including rules in relational database, parallel structures, associative processors, fuzzy association maps, task-process hierarchy, model-based reasoning, knowledge as a data concept, intelligent computer-aided instructional system, client–server concept, graphical user interface, and others. Software development tools for decision support systems follow two lines: Help Compiler or Hypertext.

Decision support software represents a large share of the software market. As the information society becomes more sophisticated, the software required grows larger and more sophisticated. There is an accumulation of software that requires maintenance, and the knowledge that a software engineer must have increases, according to a Japanese study. In the year 2000, the software market will grow to 35,600 billion yen or $300 billion, and 2 million software engineers will be needed. The supply of software engineers based on present measures for fostering engineers and availability is estimated at 1 million in that year. A gap between supply and demand of 1 million engineers will exist. Systems engineers will be in short supply, and the shortage of high-quality engineers needed for a high-information society will become more decisive.

Frontier Decision Support Concepts, Edited by V. L. Plantamura, B. Souček, and G. Visaggio. ISBN 0-471-59256-0   © 1994 John Wiley & Sons, Inc.

To resolve the problem, an enhancement of the education and training for systems engineers combined with new technological concepts is needed.

We advocate two new concepts:

1. Mixing programmed modules based on predefined operations inherited from the designer, with adaptive modules that are able to learn and in this way handle new and unusual situations.
2. Development of standard messages for communication between decision support systems: message standards, similar to EDI/EDIFACT would enable the integration of software packages, knowledge, and intelligence that come from many sources.

The chapter ends with a review of decision support software projects. These are large-scale knowledge/reasoning Help Desk systems operating in real time. Typically, three to six persons are needed, and the development period is one to two years. The resulting intelligent systems represent parts of the global neural systems (GNS). Intelligent GNS used by industry and commerce remove the remaining technical barriers to a global electronic village.

The reviewed projects include:

American customer service and support projects

European strategic program for research and development in information technology (ESPRIT)

Japanese national priority projects

International SWIFT-EDI financial network projects

2.2 DEFINING THE SYSTEM

Decision support system applications in on-line or real-time environments, such as troubleshooting, customer service, banking, automated factories, and continuous and batch process plants, typically involve reasoning on large complex systems. A two-stage development approach, which includes an on-line phase, is recommended. First create and test an off-line prototype of the system being modeled and analyzed, and then integrate and scale up the prototype into the on-line environment. If the eventual goal is to build a closed-loop system, such as an automated machine controller, it is recommended that the second stage include the development of an intermediate open-loop system, with the knowledge systems acting in the capacity of an operator's assistant.

Not surprisingly at each stage different issues arise that are addressed by different aspects of decision support technology. In the first stage the knowledge system developer's efforts focus on understanding how best to represent the system of interest in order to build a computational model that can be reasoned over and analyzed by other components of the application. At this point the developer is concerned principally with how easily and rapidly scale models of the system being analyzed can be prototyped; the issues of real-time performance and on-line integration are secondary.

While the model developed in the first stage serves as the basis for the on-line real-time application, new issues emerge as the application is moved from the off-line to the on-line environment. The developer must now deal with the following issues of real-time performance and on-line integration:

1. Human-machine interfaces
2. Machine-machine interfaces and configuration
3. Data transfer rates
4. Impact on real-time performance
5. Hardware configurations for industrial or office environments
6. Reasoning speed
7. Concurrence of data with the reasoning process

The reasoning steps are formalized by application experts and design experts in the form of deduction flows. These are similar to traditional data flow diagrams and represent incoming events, time-outs, objects, and reasoning steps.

2.3 SOFTWARE DEVELOPMENT MODELS

According to Yeh [1], in typical, large software systems, requirements cannot be completely defined until the bulk of the system is built and used. But the system cannot be built without specifying what is to be built. Thus, the activities of requirements, design, build, evaluate, and use need to occur in a more ongoing, intertwined, and mutually supporting way rather than proceeding along the lines of previous definitions, as is usually the case.

In order to manage the increasing breadth and complexity of software systems, several development models have been used during the past 35 years. The "code and fix" model used in the 1950s and early 1960s provided too much flexibility. The resulting systems were difficult to test and maintain. The waterfall model (Boehm [2]) provided more structure. This model stressed extensive documentation and testing, frequent customer involvement, and "building systems twice" because requirements and design are too difficult to get the first time. Unfortunately, this model was adopted in practice with more rigidity and structure than suggested, and "building it twice" turned into "build it once, then fix it." As such, waterfall development as practiced now has a single-version product focus.

The evolutionary model (McCracken and Jackson [3]) provided a multiple-version product focus by suggesting expanding operational product growth incrementally as a means of expanding the product as requirements evolve. This model explicitly acknowledged the fact that it is not generally possible to completely define the requirements of complex systems up front. The importance of a process focus in software development is clearly explained by Humphrey's maturity level study [4]. The spiral model [2] was the first to explicitly introduce multiple cycles of planning, prototyping, and so on, for risk management and dynamic process organization.

According to Yeh [1], it seems that these process models and practices are all aimed at achieving efficiency by wrestling with three fundamental points of conflicting needs:

1. Stability versus flexibility
2. Modularity versus essential interconnectivity
3. Broad, long-term scope versus narrow, immediate focus

These are indeed difficult balancing acts. Therefore, despite the evolution of models, many experts suggest that dramatically new concepts and methods are needed to tackle the software problem.

The IRIS concepts for the development of decision support software include the following steps:

1. Rule-based representation of knowledge is used first including, forward and backward chaining of knowledge, knowledge frames, knowledge world, truth maintenance systems, schemas, fuzzy cognitive maps, expert systems, and model-based reasoning.
2. Creating specialized case-based reasoning modules for specific types of tasks, with limited adaptation.
3. Mixing specialized modules with more general adaptive networks to handle new and unusual situations.
4. Mixing adaptive and programmed modules.

In general, the best way to simplify the design is to introduce modular, hierarchical structures, in which different modules are only loosely coupled. This corresponds to the feature extraction theory and group selection theory of the brain, described by Edelman and Mountcastle [5]. There should be a variety of modules, capable of certain predefined operations inherited from the designer (natural, born with) and able to learn a slightly more difficult set of tasks (nurtured).

2.4 IMPLEMENTATION STRATEGIES

Several implementation strategies are possible, depending on the application area. The expert-system-based *Help Desk* generates results by using production rules. The number of rules could run into thousands. In a standard computing environment it would take a long time to execute a single cycle of the production system.

For inference, the entire rule base had to be loaded in the main memory. For a large rule base that grows at a steady rate, system performance is limited by the available memory. Also, simultaneous use of the knowledge base by multiple users degrades performance.

Representing the rules in a relational data base model allows them to reside on disk and matching can be done much more efficiently [6, 7, 8]. The increase in the size of the knowledge base, as well as the simultaneous use by multiple users, does not linearly degrade performance (Perikh and Chisholm [6]).

The "If" part of the rules is represented in a relation that contains the rule identifier and symptoms as attributes. The attributes contain the value of the corresponding symptom. In most cases only a subset of the symptoms has values. The others are stored with null (for string) or zero (for numerical) values. The text for each field of the "Then" part of the rules is stored in a relation with the corresponding rule identifier. The footprint of the given case is matched with each rule, where each symptom with either a nonnull or a nonzero value in the rule is matched with the value of the corresponding symptom in the footprint. In a successful match, the description and solution are retrieved from the corresponding relation with the same rule identifier as the matched one. If there are multiple matches, the tests suggested for the "technique for confirmation" help in identifying the appropriate rule for the analysis.

The parallel structure of an associative processor or fuzzy association map is well suited for a high-speed, *Media Decision Support* and real-time expert system. The number of rules can be easily ANDed or ORed and executed in one cycle. Typically, a disjunctive normal theorem is used to compress or distribute Boolean expressions used in production rules. The execution time required for the parallel search in an associative processor is independent for the number of rules. Hence, thousands of rules could be processed at high speed. In this way a microsecond response time is possible. This fact opens the door for high-speed real-time decision support systems.

During the execution of deduction flow, the system may start specific tests or branch to a subflow. According to Phelps et al. [7], using rules for coding these kinds of flows is not always suitable. Most of the actions started in a flow, as well as the control of the flow itself, are of a procedural nature. When we receive a new message that indicates that a previous deduction flow is invalid, this flow must be interrupted, test procedures must be stopped, and so on.

To organize a large knowledge base, with hundreds of deduction flows and their procedures, the concept of a *task-process hierarchy* has been introduced [7]. A task can be a deduction flow or a complicated test or other complex system function of application itself. To each task corresponds a control flow and a data flow. A task procedure is responsible for supervising the control flow of the task, which is designed as a kind of a state machine.

A task may start one or more processes to execute single steps of the task. Examples are sending a command and waiting for a response, interacting with the user interface, and so on.

Tasks and processes are represented by objects with their associated procedures. The objects carry control information and are used to create relations between several tasks and between tasks and the associated objects of the application model. Using these relations we can easily associate several applications components to one task, or one application component can be related to several parallel ongoing deductions.

Process decision support systems are automatic fault diagnosis, factory cell simulation, and knowledge-based business and process control. These decision support systems follow the concept of model-based reasoning. The model contains an explicit description of a domain, objects, relationships between objects, and a taxonomy of the object classes.

The processing strategy at each rule level is a standard backward-chaining process; hypotheses are tested in sequence. A unique characteristic of the expert's strategy is subdivision of the problem into two levels. The expert first determines the subsystem in which the fault occurred. He or she then identifies the faulty component within that subsystem. The diagnostic expert system decomposes the problem according to this strategy. One set of rules determines which subsystem is faulty according to heuristics that examine the pattern of input data. The second set of rules, within the context of the subsystem, determines which component is faulty by examining measurements in the subsystem. These two sets of rules are invoked separately—the first set by a top-level command to start the diagnosis, the second set by the first set's successful conclusion.

Distributed problem solving (DPS) refers to the cooperative solution of problems by a group of decentralized and loosely coupled problem solvers (or agents, knowledge sources, actors). Two closely related issues attract a lot of attention in DPS research, namely, how to deal with uncertainty and how to solve complicated problems efficiently by cooperation and interaction among distributed problem-solving agents.

According to Deng and Chang [9], DPS consists of three phases: problem decomposition, subproblem solution, and answer synthesis. The second and third phases are often combined. There are two major forms of interaction among distributed agents: task sharing and result sharing. Task sharing refers to the form of cooperation in which agents share the computation load for the execution of subtasks of the overall problem. A typical example is the contract net framework. Result sharing refers to the form of cooperation in which computation agents assist each other by sharing partial results, based on somewhat different perspectives on the overall problem. A typical example of this type of cooperation can be found in blackboard-based systems.

Schmitz [10] supports the approach called *knowledge as data*. It has been noticed that various talented knowledge engineers and programmers spend months coding all the knowledge related to a particular domain into a network of backward- and forward-chaining rules, agenda conditions, probability factors, and so forth, only to find that by the next version/release/patch update of this domain some or most of the knowledge had become obsolete.

Support systems for software products are very different from other diagnostic systems like, say, hardware support, MYCIN-like systems, and others. Instead of being able to build up to a "perfect" and fairly stable set of expert knowledge, customer support information for software products is typically very dynamic and can change daily and weekly, depending on patches, releases, versions, latest fixes, workaround, and other factors. As such, it does not make sense to try to capture all the expert knowledge inside an inference engine, even if this results in a theoretically elegant system with AI techniques galore. The goal should be to develop a system in which anybody would be able to delete or edit a particular resolution path. All the knowledge related to a particular problem X, or containing question X somewhere down the tree, or containing answer X somewhere down the tree, and so on, needs to be accessible on a data level. Otherwise, the gap between knowledge acquisition and on-line availability is just too big.

For some decision support project it is good to incorporate an *intelligent computer-aided instructional (ICAI) system* that will enable users to be trained in system diagnostics on interactive video machines. ICAI will teach system diagnostics through the use of graphic symbols and interactive video technology, and it should be designed to augment advanced individual training (AIT) platform instructional techniques. The hardware configuration typically consists of an interactive video-disk system with full keyboard and direct manipulation data input (light pen/touch screen) capability.

Client–server computing plays an improtant role in decision support projects. Intel 486 microprocessors currently provide 20 to 30 million instructions per second (MIPS) processing power at a cost of $75 per MIPS and up to 500 MB of RAM. The Intel pentium chip increases processing power to 100 MIPS per processor and reduces the cost per MIPS to only $37. At this price, MIPS are essentially free.

Most client–server applications are relatively simple decision support systems that access distributed data, integrate data from multiple applications, and present information to the end user under the control of a *graphical user interface (GUI)*. The user is trained in color, animation, and the use of various interface tools (mice, goggles, virtual reality gloves).

The GUI provides a consistent "look and feel" for user interaction with applications that are compliant with the standard. Although there is no formal industry-standard GUI, the widely used Microsoft Windows GUI acts as a de facto standard. While Windows is by far the most popular client GUI, there is interest in additional GUIs, including the Macintosh, Unix under Motif, and even OS/2 Presentation Manager. Most client–server tools will eventually support multiple GUIs from the same specification.

2.5 DEVELOPMENT TOOLS

Computer-aided software engineering (CASE) tools assist users with the various software development activities of the software development life cycle. CASE tools support all the aspects of system design and construction. Depending on their functionality, CASE tools may be classified as upper and lower. According to Papazoglou et al. [11], upper CASE tools include tools that support techniques such as structured analysis, conceptual data modeling, and techniques such as pseudocode specification, action diagrams, or mini-specs. Lower CASE tools constitute traditional fourth-generation systems (i.e., application generators with tools for dialogue design, screen painting, automatic generation of data base schemas, code generation, etc.). Both upper and lower CASE tools must have connections to implementation tools that facilitate code production—for example, program development tools, such as editors and command interpreters—and manipulation activities, for example, language-specific tools such as compilers, linkers and loaders, symbolic debuggers, and test tools. A tool can be viewed as comprising a set of functions that accept as operands (and manipulate) the various objects created by other tools or users. Commands (i.e., invocable tools services) are essentially interpreted as the application of tools on objects and the production of new objects as a result of applying tools operators on input objects.

In general there are two ways to create a help system in a PC/workstation environment: use of a Help Compiler or use a proper Hypertext system.

2.5.1 Help Compiler

The main advantage of the use of a Help Compiler is that you can use a common text editor and a common graphic tool. These tools have to be able to create text and graphic formats that can be read by the Help Compiler. Usually good text editors like WINWORD or WordPerfect can create the necessary formats. The disadvantage is that you need a COMPILE to get the Help System, so you cannot see the result while you create the system.

Examples of tools are

- MS Help Compiler for Windows; the documentation is included in the SDK (software development kit) for Windows 3.1. The HELP function of Windows were programmed using this compiler.
- OS/2 Help Compiler for OS/2 2.0; the documentation *Information Presentation Facility Guide and Reference*, the software is included in the developer's toolkit for OS/2 2.0
- Similar tools exist for UNIX.

2.5.2 Hypertext Systems

The main advantage of Hypertext systems is the interactive development of the Help system. Disadvantages are that people usually design the Help system improperly, and there are some restrictions on importing other documents.

Examples of tools are

- Hypercard for Apple Macintosh (its part of the system)
- Supercard for Apple Macintosh (a separate tool)
- Toolbook for Windows (a separate tool)

For details see the manuals of commercial tools.

Decision support applications require implementation of several client–server software layers. Support for these software layers is provided by widely used client–server development tools, such as Power-Builder from Powersoft Corp., Easel Workbench from Easel Corp., SQL Windows from Gupta Technologies, and Mozart from Mozart Systems Corp. These development tools generate complete client–server applications that run in multiple-operating-system environments and network environments and provide transparent access to a variety of relational data base management systems and intelligent gateways.

Many different topologies and deduction flows could be created, using commercially available shells, development tools, and platforms. Typical features provided by such tools are presented in examples of NEXTRA system (Fig. 2.1), ReMind system (Fig. 2.2), KAPPA-PC (Fig. 2.3), Open Interface (Fig. 2.4) and Knowledge Pro (Fig. 2.5).

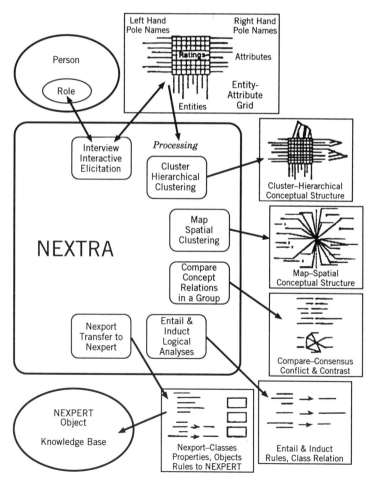

Figure 2.1 *NEXTRA functionality.*

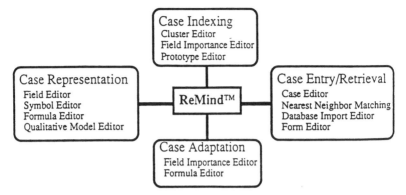

Figure 2.2 *ReMind functionality.*

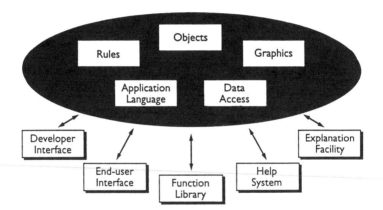

Figure 2.3 *KAPPA-PC.*

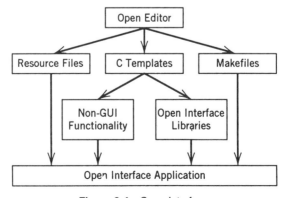

Figure 2.4 *Open Interface.*

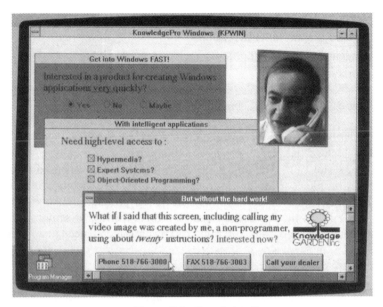

Figure 2.5   *Knowledge Pro.*

2.5.3   ReMind (Cognitive Systems)

ReMind is designed to provide case library developers with a variety of tools for representing, indexing, and retrieving cases in a variety of domains, including Help Desks. The system provides graphical editors for attacking all of the relevant aspects of building a case-based Help Desk. Once the case library is built, C function libraries are available to allow the case library to be accessed and updated from any other program that can make calls to C. This allows for maximum flexibility in delivering case-based applications in a variety of environments and interfaces.

2.5.4   KAPPA-PC (Intellicorp)

The Kappa-PC application development system is the hybrid PC tool that combines critical technologies essential to the rapid development of low-cost, high-impact business applications. Solutions created in the KAPPA-PC environment have shown a high return on investment in a wide range of desktop and laptop PC applications, including Help Desks, order processing, sales support, inventory control, and manufacturing. KAPPA-PC allows you to develop and deliver powerful applications that become timely, cost-efficient solutions to critical business problems.

Major Elements

1. True object-oriented development
2. Interactive, graphical development environment

3. Powerful, high-level application development language
4. Integrated graphic interface libraries
5. Intelligent links to popular software
6. Expert system tools

Applications of KAPPA-PC include:

Product Selection. Customer service officers use the KAPPA-PC application to suggest which of the bank's products and services would be best, based on the customer's situation. The object system in KAPPA-PC was used to model the customer profile, containing information such as age, income, and investment objectives. Objects were also used to model product and service information. Using rules, the application captured the expertise of senior customer service officers to match bank offerings to the customer's needs and requirements.

Foreign Currency Exchange. With the success of the product selection application, the bank decided to tackle the ever-changing foreign currency exchange market. The bank provides information on foreign banks and currencies to customers who want to send money to another country.

Product Configuration. A producer of printer, copier, and camera equipment has purchased KAPPA-PC and is evaluating the possibility of using it to configure printers. This company markets a line of very powerful and sophisticated printers consisting of many different components. Thus, each printer can be designed for a customer's environment.

Quality Assurance. A major computer manufacturer is investigating the possibility of using KAPPA-PC to help in expediting CPUs through testing queues. This company has a number of different rack testers in which they place CPUs for undergoing a battery of tests. The facility is completely automated with CPUs being sent to queues and pulled off of queues based on a number of selection criteria.

Network Diagnostic Aid. A large Asian telecommunications corporation is working with an IntelliCorp distributor on a prototype for a network diagnostic aid. Information required by the service organization for diagnosing customer problems was encapsulated in the form of objects and slots. An easy-to-use graphic interface for entering this information was built using the graphics tools in KAPPA-PC.

Organization Chart. A management consultancy does work for a number of companies to help determine the implication of changing corporate structure on employee organization. As a result of a merger or leveraged buyout, the system helps the user build the new employee organization chart.

2.5.5 Open Interface (Neuron Data)

Open Interface Elements is one of the most powerful and flexible GUI application development tools available today. With Open Interface, developers can design any type of graphical interface for their application, for virtually any environment, while they reduce development effort by as much as 50%. The most advanced version of Open Interface yet, Open Interface 3.0, gives developers even more flexibility, power, and extensibility with new widgets, a new script language, and new C++ support. Open Interface is the key to developer productivity.

Open Interface consists of Open Editor, a WYSIWYG interface development environment, and the platform-specific Open Interface run-time libraries.

Open Editor is used to lay out the components of an application's GUI. Simple point-and-click operations are used to design and edit windows, menus, list boxes, buttons, and so on. Open Editor then generates three files: resource files, C templates, and makefiles. Once these files have been generated, the developer must customize the C templates to add the interface logic and back-end functionality. Finally, to complete the application the makefile is used to compile the code and to link it to the non-GUI functionality and to the Open Interface libraries.

To port an application to another platform, the resource files and C source code files are transferred to the target environment using a network or some magnetic media, and then recompiled and relinked with the Open Interface libraries for that platform.

The Neuron Data Elements architecture incorporates tools and integration layers:

Elements. Elements are portable software modules that provide complete tool functionality for specific application development tasks. The first four elements in the architecture are GUI, data access, rules, and objects. Each element includes a set of portable application services, such as portable memory and print management, file I/O, and event management. The GUI element is derived from Neuron Data's market-leading Open Interface GUI development tool, and the rules and objects elements are derived from the company's NEXTPERT OBJECT knowledge-base application development tool. The data access element is a new module that provides developers with high-level, transparent access to multiple flat-file, object-oriented, and relational data base management systems and other data sources.

Integration and Development Layers. Integration and development consist of visual editors, an extensible, message-based script language, and 3GL facilities, all of which developers can access from any of the elements. Although developers may use any of these layers to integrate the elements, the script language provides the most complete and functional integration capabilities. This language incorporates the power and performance of a 3GL in a functionality-specific, feature-rich scripting facility that delivers rapid application development. The Neuron Data script can accommodate any industry-standard application programming interfaces (APIs), C and C++ libraries, and subroutines. Developers can tailor the language by simply registering application logic as events and verbs in the script's library.

2.5.6 Knowledge Pro (Knowledge Garden)

Knowledge Pro Windows is a tool for developing fast, runtime free, Windows applications in record time. Interactive design tools and easy-to-learn commands help the novice programmer become productive after just a few hours. A rich, object-oriented language and advanced features for adding intelligence and depth give experienced Windows developers the sophisticated tools essential to modern program design. Applications written in *Knowledge Pro* range from intelligent forms for the National Institute of Health to a totally integrated point of sales environment for Avis Leasing field operators.

2.6 DECISION SUPPORT AND ELECTRONIC DATA INTERCHANGE (EDI)

A group of decision support systems are related to electronic data interchange (EDI). *EDI is the computer-to-computer transfer of routine business transactions using approved standards for form and content*, Fig. 2.6. The same philosophy could be followed in decision support systems.

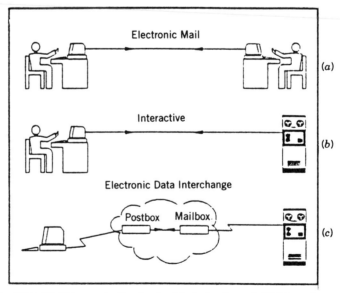

Figure 2.6 *Integration/communication levels: (a) electronic mail; (b) interactive communication; (c) electronic data interchange (EDI).*

In the classic EDI example, a customer generates electronic purchase orders from an application, converts them into a nationally approved standard form, and transmits them to a vendor. The vendor receives the data and translates it into a format that can be passed to the order entry system. To the parties involved, EDI means no paper, no mail delays, no keying, and no keying errors. The whole process takes a minimum of labor and elapsed time. Vendor and customer work together to cut their administrative costs and overhead, improve delivery and service levels, speed orders, and reduce inventory. They become electronic trading partners.

In operation, EDI is the interchange of agreed messages between trading partners. These messages cover applications in trading, transport, customs, insurance, manufacturing, banking, and financing. The interchange itself takes places across telecommunication networks provided by public or private tele-communication or value-added network services.

With information becoming increasingly widespread thanks to EDI, and with all the facilities that are available, businesses are in danger of being swamped with information. The problem is to check the validity of the information and separate the wheat from the chaff. New reasoning techniques could make it possible to carry out validity checks and obtain a clearer idea of where the relevant information is to be found. Reasoning involves a whole series of processing operations that could be included in the Help Desk, to assist the network operators as well as the customers. The main thing is to know at what point in the chain businesses should intervene to obtain the information they require.

2.7 EDIFACT STANDARD MESSAGES FOR DECISION SUPPORT

EDI and standards are synonymous. EDI standards, similar to a language, consist of a grammar (syntax, rules for structuring data elements in segments and segments within a message), and a vocabulary of words (data element directory, segment directory, and message directory).

Communication would break down if interchanging partners did not follow agreed standards, leading them from an intolerable mountain of paper documents to an electronic "tower of Babel," especially in international EDI.

The development of industrywide, national and international message standards has made the widespread use of EDI feasible. Message standards are needed to avoid a proliferation of closed EDI systems and the widespread incompatibility that this entails. They are independent of the hardware used, the type of application, the communications protocol, and the data communication media.

There are four basic aspects to message standards: data elements, codes, message segments, and syntax rules.

1. *Data elements* are the lowest level of data, such as the day of the month or an order date.

2. *Codes* are used to represent data elements. One simple exchange is using a two-digit country code instead of the full name. The use of codes helps to overcome language differences.
3. *Segments* are groups of data elements, such as the recipient's name and address.
4. *Syntax rules* provide the grammar for the construction of messages; they determine the position of data elements and segments within a message.

The international standards in question and supporting directories are

UN-EDIFACT syntax rules (ISO 9735) for structuring data into messages. This standard has also been adopted by CEN (the European Committee for Standardization) as EN 29735.

UN-Trade data element directory (ISO 7372), the building blocks used for the defintion of standard EDI messages.

UN-EDIFACT segment directory standard segments such as name and address, interchange header or tailer segments.

UN-EDIFACT standard message directory. Standard messages fulfilling specific trading functions, such as invoicing, ordering, customer clearance, bills of lading.

UN-EDIFACT code sets internationally agreed codes for countries, currencies, terms of deliveries, terms of payments, modes of transport, type of packages.

The next logical step is to define and develop EDIFACT standard messages for communication between decision support systems.

The EDIFACT standard messages for decision support will enable existing sources of information to be used to better effect without necessarily forcing businesses to restructure their information sources to suit the need of users. The manager will be able to describe his activities in nonstructure terms, in everyday language: The new systems will be capable of receiving this type of message and transforming it into the kind of structure information the user requires.

Reasoning and statistical survey can also be accompanied by a whole range of services that did not exist before, with a user friendliness and efficiency that will greatly simplify life for businesses. The aim is to integrate more completely into systems procedures for linking microeconomic data to macroeconomic data, models, inference, forecasting, and so forth, and to incorporate techniques that can be used with great efficiency without danger of disclosing information.

In exchange for the information they supply, businesses want access to information on other sectors. This ''return information'' could become much more personalized, faster, more efficient, and more systematic. Current efforts to develop the concept of metadata will make it possible to invest numerical data with a whole series of comments and information that will help businesses to interpret the statistics and ensure that they were well employed.

The development of standard messages and decision support systems, which enable the user to carry out increasingly complex and detailed analyses, hitherto the preserve of large businesses, will enable their smaller counterparts to use the information too and will permit all partners to compete on more equal terms.

At the moment, most EDI is processed in batches; that is, EDI messages are prepared and batched together to be sent or retrieved when the sender and receiver require. In the future, some EDI transactions may be handled by real-time dialogue between trading partners. The Open Systems Interconnections (OSI) transaction processing (TP) standard defines protocols to coordinate processing of an on-line transaction on two or more systems. This standard is currently under development and is foreseen as forming the basis for real-time (interactive) EDI in the future.

In this role, skills and expertise are shared among the members of a business network. Very close, and specialized, commercial relationships will be required and the opportunity exists for cooperating organizations to establish sustainable competitive advantage. A U.K. example would be the relationship between Courtlands and Marks and Spencer for clothing design. Using AI, CAD/CAM, and EDI technology, retailing, design, and manufacturing expertise are effectively being shared electronically in a unique relationship. An example is the INS-EDISWITCH System.

2.7.1 INS-EDISWITCH Intelligent Action and Decision Making

The INS-EDISWITCH can act as an intelligent information manager making decisions based on "rules" and directing EDI information as a result (Figs. 2.6 and 2.7). Consider an example where an organization purchases the same product from several suppliers. The organization's purchasing system generates orders for all product lines, and these orders are presented to the INS-EDISWITCH for delivery using electronic data interchange. The purchasing division of the organization has negotiated different commercial terms with various suppliers of the product. The terms vary, depending on price, quantity, delivery time and so on. These terms of trade are held in a purchasing guidelines data base, owned and controlled by the organization.

As the INS-EDISWITCH receives the orders from the purchasing system, it is not yet clear which is the best supplier to purchase from. So the INS-EDISWITCH inquires from the purchasing guidelines data base and directs the orders accordingly. This intelligent action ensures that the best suppliers are selected according to criteria held within the orders.

Having placed the orders, the INS-EDISWITCH generates a management information report and sends it via the organization's electronic mail service to the relevant individuals. This reporting function is performed in real time rather than as a result of an end-of-month consolidation. With this real-time information, the individuals responsible for purchasing can be kept up to date regarding the amount of business being placed with each supplier, thus enabling them to renegotiate better and better commercial terms.

Intelligent Action & Information Manager

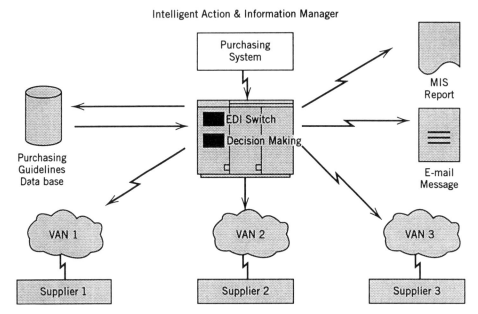

Figure 2.7 *INS-EDISWITCH intelligent action and decision making.*

Hence, the INS-EDISWITCH brings together the organization's automated purchasing processes and the people who make the decisions, adding value to the business and providing the right information to the right people at the right time.

2.8 PRESENT AND FUTURE LEVELS OF INTEGRATION: 6C

According to Winograd [12], the 1990s will see an acceleration of the progress from connectivity to compatibility to coordination. With widespread networking and universal low-level protocols, soon the basic *connectivity* of computers will be taken for granted in the same way, as the connectivity of roads and of telephones. Next comes *compatibility*: the task developed on one computer can work with the task developed on another computer. This becomes possible through the creation of comprehension standards for languages, data bases, communication protocols, and interaction architectures.

According to Winograd [12], the third level, *coordination* is a central issue. For users the purpose of integration is not to share data or to connect processors but to integrate the work: customers, orders, products, designs, and the myriad of specialized things that appear in a different endeavor. Over the next few years, the development of conversation and action systems will create people-centered systems that bring new clarity to the coordination of human action.

In the field of intelligent systems Souček [13] has defined three more levels of integration, aiming at cognition, conception, and conscience.

Cognition means integration of knowledge and intelligence that come from many sources, using a new set of EDIFACT messages. The result is a system with a higher intelligence quotient (IQ). Cognitive integrated systems should have increased ability to categorize objects into classes of equivalence, to recognize association, to learn new concepts, and to generalize and reason.

Conception means integration that automatically and adaptively creates new observables and new devices: Artificial life (AL) is a new scientific and engineering discipline. The AL device must be able to search for a possible solution outside of the reality of what we already know and can specify.

Conscience is the ultimate integration level. Intelligent systems should be created, having in mind noble applications. The systems should be able to distinguish good and evil. Its most important feature should be *global thinking*.

Many decision support projects are in progress. Small subsets of American [8], European [14], Japanese [13, 15], and international EDI-SWIFT [7] projects are outlined in Sections 2.9 to 2.12.

2.9 AMERICAN CUSTOMER SERVICE AND SUPPORT PROJECTS

APEX deals with the task of applying advanced automation techniques to the development of acquisition plans.

ATC helps Apple technical coordinators install, maintain, update, and troubleshoot systems and networks.

BCS (Boeing Computer Services) aids in the diagnosis of problems related to the local computer communications network and to assist Help Desk personnel in the handling of equipment trouble calls.

CANASTRA (Crash ANAlysis Troubleshooting Assistant) is a knowledge-based system developed at Digital Equipment Corporation to assist customer support engineers in analyzing operating system crashes.

CASE-ACE has to solve a variety of problems, related to hardware/software installations as well as printing, local area network (LAN) technologies, information engineering methodologies, Cobol code generation, operating systems, analog-to-digital (AD) cycle concepts, AI concepts, and other functions.

CONMAN is a research prototype decision support system for planning software upgrades or installations. Determining the impact of a proposed system revision is a complicated and time-consuming task. Incorrect installations or system incompatibilities can potentially create nonusable systems or customer support Help Desk phone calls.

DIAGNOSTIC ADVISOR addresses the issue of scarce, distributed, or vanishing expertise within a Help Desk organization. It also addresses the problem of ever-increasing levels of complexity of products and services to be supported.

DBB (Distributed Big Brother) is a distributed network management system consisting of cooperating autonomous computing agents.

DITS is an ICAI system that enables students to be trained in system diagnostics on interactive video machines.

DSC service support package integrates a knowledge-based troubleshooting system, interactive electronic technical manuals, and data bases with the existing DSC programming tools.

DSS is an expert system development environment used by expert trouble-shooters of complex electrical, electronic, and/or mechanical equipment to build knowledge bases for field and Help Desk assistance.

LIBRA provides both an end-user interface for knowledge capture and an "advice server" for transaction-based intelligent response.

REMIND offers a variety of indexing and retrieval approaches to Help Desks, each requiring potentially different indexing and retrieval strategies.

STARREP is a rule-based user system that provides an integrated interface to multiple operations systems (OSs).

2.10 EUROPEAN STRATEGIC PROGRAM FOR RESEARCH AND DEVELOPMENT IN INFORMATION TECHNOLOGY

AZZURRO aims to develop advanced data fusion techniques to handle numerical and symbolic data. The results might be relevant to control applications.

CHARADE aims to develop a platform for integrating advanced techniques for situation assessment and for intervention planning in emergencies. It will also allow differences in reasoning approaches at both technical and application levels. One application considered is planning and resource allocation in command and control systems. Also, its emphasis on aspects of human/computer interface will be worth noticing.

EDS application of parallel processing to large-scale commercial decision support applications will indicate problems and limitations that the IRIS concept might have to consider.

EMS aims to develop a general framework for data fusion in an environmental monitoring system. The works in this project regarding a fusion technique for sensor data and monitoring techniques for situation assessment, interpretation, and prediction might be relevant to the control application of the IRIS concept.

F3 aims to develop a methodology to be used in requirements engineering to transform requirements that are usually incomplete and expressed in informal terms into complete, precise, and consistent specifications in formal notation.

HANSA aims to develop an architectural framework and a software toolkit for business decision support applications, such as banking asset forecasting. Its relevance to IRIS is stressed by its aim to establish an open-ended environment for application building tools integrating standard commercial software with shells for knowledge-based systems (KBS), neural networks, and genetic algorithms.

HINT aims to develop a heterogeneous development environment using neural networks, fuzzy logic, model-based reasoning, and expert systems. Since the architecture will be kept open for integration of further modules, some kind of symbiosis of the HINT and IRIS tools may become feasible.

HUMANOID aims to take advantage of advanced hardware graphic work-stations and computers, to design a real-time parallel system for simulating "virtual humans" in all situations involving human beings, such as aircraft cockpits.

PAPAGENA aims to develop a programming environment for parallel ge-netic algorithms to be applied for implementing a credit marketing and risk assessment decision support tool.

TRACS. Although the application domain of this project—vessel traffic con-trol applications—is not related to IRIS application targets, its concept of using a real-time user console that supports sophisticated prediciton models for han-dling critical situations and a parallel processing system for handling a large amount of critical data coming from sensors in real time could be relevant.

UNITE aims to product techniques for integration of knowledge model par-adigms including fuzziness and for cooperation between KBSs in industrial environments, such as hospitals and space control centers. The results of this project, which is based on methods such as KADS, will be very useful as a baseline for comparison with output of IRIS systems, based on the new fuzzy-crisp associations and holographic networks, especially in terms of performance and speed of knowledge acquisition.

2.11 JAPANESE NATIONAL PRIORITY PROJECTS

In Japan three programs of high national priority are supporting very large and expensive projects based on the development of semiconductor parallel and fuzzy devices and on rule-based logic programming. These programs are fifth-generation computer systems (FGCS), laboratory for international fuzzy engi-neering (LIFE), and new information processing technology (NIPT), and real world computing (RWC).

Real world computing program is the successor of the fifth-generation com-puters systems program and seeks to research the computer technology of the future, such as massively parallel systems, neural networks and optical com-puters.

It is assumed in the RWC program that the solution to the grand challenges must start at foundation principles (i.e., the solution's algorithms). We need to attain a method of operating computers, where the problem to be solved no longer has to be algorithmically described clearly and fully with all parameter values. Instead, solution methods must be developed which still function if no full algorithmic description of the problem exists, or if not all parameter values are known. The system should be able to calculate the most probable solution, on the basis of statistical models. In total, the RWC program should run for 10 years with a total budget of 60 billion yen ($500 million).

2.12 INTERNATIONAL SWIFT-EDI FINANCIAL NETWORK PROJECTS*

The Society for Worldwide Interbank Financial Telecommunication (SWIFT) has developed several decision support systems.

2.12.1 INCA

This project used expert system technology to assist the network operators to control the SWIFT I network. INCA (intelligent network control assistant) is an expert system designed and implemented on a UNIX workstation. The system automates receipt of alarms from the network and filters and correlates them. When it identifies the cause of a problem, it takes actions to alleviate the problem by sending corrective commands to the network. All this functions in real time. Most of the received alarms can be dealt with automatically, without the need for operator intervention. Thus, the size of the operator force needed to control the network was drastically reduced while control quality improved.

2.12.2 ANDES

ANDES has been designed in three hierarchical layers:

1. A monitoring system providing connections to the SWIFT II network receiving and parsing alarms and displaying a real-time view of the network status to the operators. The interface is graphical in nature and has been designed to provide a high overview of the network on one screen. Special attention has been given to the design of mechanisms to focus the operator's attention on problem areas.
2. The diagnostic layer of the ANDES system reasons on the incoming events in order to concentrate the operator's attention on underlying problems and advise on their nature. Some network messages inform about status changes of network components. Others give information that indicate symptoms of problems, but are not directly linked to a state of a component or a set of components.
3. A problem correction layer sends commands to the network to alleviate problems. These commands are selected by the reasoning mechanisms used in the diagnostic layer. The system will show to the operator in all situations what it is doing automatically, and for some problems it will suggest actions that the operator can confirm or cancel. When the operator confirms an action, it is executed by the system, and the system will ensure a follow-up of the progress and results of the action. It will warn

*Section 2.12 is based on Phelps, Ristori, Aerts, Mukherjee, and Thomae [7].

the operator about the results or about eventual problems with the action that was started.

2.12.3 SIRIUS

SIRIUS, SWIFT's Intelligent Resource for International User Support, is an intelligent integrated Help Desk system for SWIFT user support groups, the SWIFT interface to users in the worldwide banking community. It is implemented on UNIX workstations using the RT Works expert system shell.

SIRIUS is an intelligent productivity enhancement tool for SWIFT user support. SIRIUS comprises Hypertext manuals, real-time deductions, processing of events, an event manager, electronic messaging calendars, and a front-end interface to SWIFT's internal E-mail and problem management systems. One goal of SIRIUS is to allow SWIFT to become more active in dealing with user problems. If there is a problem that is impacting users, ideally user support should know about the problem prior to the user calling in.

2.13 SOFTWARE INTEGRATION

Program development, modification, and start-up are considerably simplified by breaking programs into small, clearly defined blocks. Program development costs can be reduced by using standard function blocks for recurrent complex functions. Standard function blocks are off-the-shelf software modules that can be merged into programs written by the user. They can be called many times during program execution and supplied with the required parameters. Good examples are the standard function block libraries for programmable controllers, including the Allen-Bradley Pyramid Integrator™ family and the Siemens Simatic S5™ family, among others. Siemens claims over 100,000 Simatic installations worldwide, running the same software modules.

The ultimate modules are software components delivered as absolute, binary code on electrically programmable read-only memories (EPROMs), disks, or tapes. This eliminates source code manipulations, recompilations, system generation (SYSGEN), and other hazards and labor required to integrate with more traditional, off-the shelf software. Each absolute software component has a private configuration table, supplied by the user and containing application- and hardware-related parameters relevant to its operation table somewhere in RAM or ROM and plugging the address of its configuration table into the software component interconnect bus. This kind of approach is supported, for example, by the Software Components Group Inc.

Powerful software environment increases productivity by allowing the developer to focus on the conceptual level of the problem, without being preoccupied with lower-level details. The software environment should include sophisticated networking and communications capabilities, permitting easy integration of knowledge-based applications with other systems and applications. Software vendors are currently proposing a variety of integration tools: Prodea Synergy (Windows) with Visual Basic or Toolbook; General Magic's Telescript (Communication), Magic Cap (PDA), and others.

REFERENCES

[1] R. T. Yeh, System development as a wicked problem, *Internat. J. Software Eng. Knowledge Eng.*, 1(2), 117 (1991).

[2] B. Boehm, A spiral model of software development and enhancement, *Comput.* 21, 5 (1988).

[3] D. D. McCraken and M. A. Jackson, "Life Cycle Concept Considered Harmful," Software Eng. Notes, ACM, April 1982.

[4] W. S. Humphrey, *Managing the Software Process*, Addison-Wesley, Reading, Mass., 1989.

[5] G. M. Edelman and V. B. Mountcastle, *The Mindful Brain*, MIT Press, Cambridge, Mass., 1978.

[6] M. Perikh and M. Chisholm, CANASTRA, from prototype to product, in *Proc. Workshop on Artificial Intelligence for Customer Service and Support*, Monterey, Calif., March 3, 1992.

[7] R. Phelps, F. Ristori, W. Aerts, D. Mukherjee, and L. Thomae, "The Use of Expert Systems in Improving Service Quality at S.W.I.F.T," The S.W.I.F.T. Report 1992.

[8] *Proc. Workshop on Artificial Intelligence for Customer Service and Support*, Monterey, Calif., March 3, 1992.

[9] Y. Deng and S. K. Chang, "A framework for the modeling and prototyping of distributed information systems," *Internat. J. Software Eng. Knowledge Eng.*, 1(3), 203 (1991).

[10] N. Schmitz, CASE-ACE, knowledge ware's internal AI tool, in *Proc. Workshop on Artificial Intelligence for Customer Service and Support*, Monterey, Calif., March 3, 1992.

[11] M. P. Papazoglou, L. Marinos, and N. G. Bourbakis, The organizational impact of integrating multiple tools, *Internat. J. Software Eng. Knowledge Eng.*, 1(2), 165 (1991).

[12] T. Winograd, "What lies ahead?" *Byte*, 350, (January 1989).

[13] B. Souček and IRIS Group, *Neural and Intelligent Systems Integration*. Wiley, New York, 1991, p. 664.

[14] *ESPRIT Synopses Information Processing Systems and Software*, 1991 and 1992 Commission of the European Communities, Brussels.

[15] T. Ichiko and T. Kurozumi, "Current Results in Japanese Fifth Generation Computer Systems," in B. Souček and IRIS Group, *Neural and Intelligent Systems Integration*, Wiley, New York, 1991.

CHAPTER 3 ────────────────────

The Holographic Cell:
A Quantum Perspective

JOHN G. SUTHERLAND

3.1 INTRODUCTION

The connectionist belief within Artificial Intelligence (AI) maintains that associative processing may be accomplished in the construction of multicellular structures, which, in some manner mimic the interconnectivity of biological neuron cells. The holographic model of neurological function takes a different viewpoint; maintaining that more powerful cognitive properties may be observed within simpler structures displaying the morphology of individual cells, in particular these falling within the stellate and pyramidal class (Fig. 3.1). Furthermore, supporters of the holographic paradigm maintain that a large capacity for learning, dynamic features of memory and attention may be observed from relatively general transforms; these transforms realizing properties implicit within manifolds constructed from a more universal scalar (i.e., the complex number). Students of the complex variable understand that such quantities form a superset of those scalars defined within real valued systems. Of particular interest is the complex product operation whereby a coincident phase rotation occurs for any set of complex scalars defining a path from the origin to a point in the Argand plane. This commutative aspect is used within the holographic neural model to facilitate an *enfolding* of information. Enfolding is a term used here to represent the superposition of stimulus–response associations or mappings onto the same set of complex scalars. Information as represented within the holographic neural process may be further broken down

Frontier Decision Support Concepts, Edited by V. L. Plantamura, B. Souček, and G. Visaggio.
ISBN 0-471-59256-0   © 1994 John Wiley & Sons, Inc.

Figure 3.1 *Morphology of the pyramidal and stellate cell.*

into basic units, referred to in this discussion as *association quanta*. From this perspective, one quanta provides a quantitative representation of the elementary unit used within the holographic process to establish a mapping or association between stimuli and associated responses.

Further to this discussion, results from empirical studies are shown illustrating the characteristics exhibited by the cell's memory storage components (i.e. complex correlation set) following a protracted learning. This covers the situation in which the number of stimulus–response patterns learned by the cell exceeds the number of synapses. Empirical studies based on random statistical tests (Monte Carlo techniques) indicate that growth of complex scalar magnitudes within an unattenuated memory exhibit an asymptotic behavior. Within this chapter, an outline of the underlying theory behind holographic neural technology is presented from the perspective of a quantized system. Also presented is a discussion of the asymptotic behavior on correlation magnitude, and attendant implications of memory and memory decay.

Current theories in computational intelligence flow to some extent from a concept initially proposed in [1], known as the Hebb hypothesis. That is to say, learning mechanisms are located near the synapse and are activated in some manner through coincident stimulation at both the pre- and post-synaptic clefts. Recent neural theory has elaborated on this considerably, leading to a profusion of gradient-descent-type models, whose core aspects are built upon the real-valued inner product. The holographic model described in this chapter presents a somewhat different viewpoint and suggests the possibility of a complex representation for information (Fig. 3.2). Within this format, information is represented by phase orientation (θ) and a confidence level assigned as magnitude (λ) of the complex scalar.

Some general characteristics in the intracellular transmission, particularly regarding the periodicity of synaptic activation may support the hypothesis of a complex representation for information. For instance, consider the functional block representation of a cell presented in Figure 3.3. Multiple input lines receive pulse-modulated signals from an effector pathway, in response to which

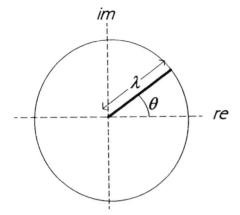

Figure 3.2 *Complex representation for information.*

similarly modulated signals are delivered via the cell's axonal process. One may interpret these signals in a variety of ways, again the predominant viewpoint maintaining a belief that pulsed frequencies are translated into real-valued scalar quantities. If one considers a more generalized mathematical domain, the signal transmission format illustrated in Figure 3.2 suggests an equally feasible mode of intercellular communication. The holographic model proposes the use of modulated waveforms to facilitate analog transmission of complex scalars along dendrites, axons, and their collaterals. From an engineering perspective, one practical means for the analog transmission of complex scalars along a single transmission line is through a waveform employing both frequency and amplitude modulation. Frequency and amplitude within such a signal transmission format may be used to communicate a proportional phase and magnitude in the complex scalar. Such a transmission format concurs with the format of electrochemical impulses observed in biological neuron cells. Far more important, however, are the operational features that may be observed within single cell structures when the complex representation is used. These features are described in [2, 3] and briefly in the following discussion.

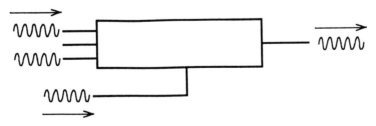

Figure 3.3 *Block diagram of a cortical cell.*

3.2 KNOWLEDGE REPRESENTATION

For the holographic system, the basic unit of measurement or scalar is again a complex value, ideally lying within a distribution displaying a circular or cardiod geometry when observed on the Argand plane. Qualitatively, such measurements may be represented simply as:

$$\lambda e^{i\theta} \tag{3.1}$$

Within the holographic neural model complex scalars may be viewed to contain an information or semantic component as represented by the phase orientation (θ), and a level of confidence in that information represented by the magnitude (λ). An ideal representation for magnitude or confidence is found when the complex scalar is reasonably bounded within a unit circle about the complex origin. Defining a probabilistic bound for confidence enforces numerical stability and permits a logical congruency in the mediation of confidence for response recall, as well as permitting a weighting to be assigned for the influence of individual input stimuli. Associations are represented and stored as *phase angle differences* between connected stimuli and responses. For instance, one element of a stimuli may be represented by phase orientation θ_1 and an associated response by θ_2. A measure of association representing the stimulus to response mapping is simply the phase angle difference:

$$\theta_{diff} = \theta_1 - \theta_2 \tag{3.2}$$

One could state that the complex quantity (θ_{diff}) represents one quanta of association within the holographic model. The range of features governing intelligence naturally proceeds far beyond simple association, however on further investigation of secondary effects, some of which are discussed in this overview, the above postulate becomes somewhat more palatable. Again within the halographic representation, a quanta of intelligent association is defined explicitly as *the phase angle difference between an associated stimuli and response*. The mathematical properties outlined here illustrate a basis for the superposition of a vast number of such association quanta defining stimulus–response association onto a single set of complex scalar quantities, subsequently displaying the ability to recall such associations. By using a fixed size of correlation vector (number of synapses) and a fixed number of computations, the holographic cell is capable of re-expressing prior learned stimulus–response associations at a high level of accuracy. Determinism in the operation of the cell relates not only to the generation of a semantically oriented response as expressed through phase orientation, but a magnitude which displays a congruency in the level of confidence or recognition of the stimuli. The holographic cell displays a further aspect in the ability to respond appropriately to the space of unknown or unlearned stimuli through generation of a low confidence in the response recall. The information storage capacity for holographic cells is considerably greater than conventional ANS systems, in that; one cell is capable of learning and recalling extremely large numbers of stimulus–response associations. A high-level of recall accuracy (i.e., < 1% relative error) is typically attained following less than 4 training epochs. This pattern storage capability has been verified for single holographic cells possessing up to 64K synapses and having learned up to 64K randomly generated stimulus–response patterns. This quantity of stimulus pattern prototypes normally would require in excess of 4 billion bytes of conventional memory.

The concept of an enfolding of information, and corresponding increase in information density, are supported by particular commutative properties found within the complex number system. To illustrate, one such complex quantity may be described by the following relation, describing a path from the complex origin to a point (A) in the Argand plane (Fig. 3.4) where:

$$A = \lambda e^{i\theta} = \sum_{j=1}^{N} \alpha_j e^{i\vartheta_j} \tag{3.3}$$

The distance A may be defined as a summation of complex scalars forming a path from the origin to the point located at phase angle θ and magnitude λ. In other words, the complex scalar may be defined by any subset within the potentially infinite set of all possible paths leading from the origin to point A. When viewed as associative storage elements (i.e., synapses) each of the component scalars defines one quanta in respect of the learned stimulus to response associations.

Recall of such associative information is possible due to the commutative properties of rotational translation (i.e., complex multiply) imposed upon those component scalars and from which the aggregate scalar (A) is derived. Within real number systems and considering the effect of a simple multiply operation, the set of component vectors is increased or reduced proportionally in magnitude. A similar effect occurs within the complex realm, however, along two

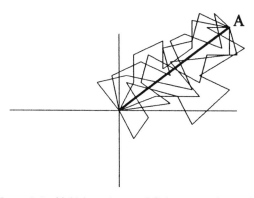

Figure 3.4 *Multiple pathways defining a complex scalar.*

complete degrees of freedom—that is the magnitude and phase orientation. Reiterating, the complex multiply operations possess an interesting property whereby any phase rotational operation (multiplication) imposed on the aggregate scalar produces an equivalent rotation on each element in the set of component scalars from which it is comprised. This is illustrated numerically by performing a product operation on the complex summation in Eq. (3.3) considering:

$$\lambda e^{i\theta} \cdot e^{i\delta} \tag{3.4}$$

By solution of the following simple equality

$$\lambda e^{i\theta} \cdot e^{i\delta} = \alpha_1 e^{i(\vartheta_1 + \delta)} + \alpha_2 e^{i(\vartheta_2 + \delta)} + \alpha_3 e^{i(\vartheta_3 + \delta)} + \alpha_4 e^{i(\vartheta_4 + \delta)} \tag{3.5}$$

or diagramatically as in Figure 3.5.

Once one acknowledges and gains a reasonable understanding of this rotational aspect of complex operators, there comes the realization that important aspects of information may be preserved within an aggregate set of complex scalars as *enfolded* within the complex summation. This aspect becomes very apparent when dealing with sets of aggregate scalars forming complex manifolds. Such enfolded association quanta, despite an apparent inaccessibility, can be modified in both their magnitude and phase allowing the embedded information [i.e., phase differences as per Eq. (3.5)] to be manipulated in an organized manner. Eq. (3.6) illustrates an enfolding of four-analog input to output (or stimulus–response) mappings onto a correlation set comprised of four complex scalars. Four stimulus patterns are presented by the following matrix:

$$[S] = \begin{vmatrix} \lambda_{1,t_1} e^{i\theta_{1,t_1}} & \lambda_{2,t_1} e^{i\theta_{2,t_1}} & \lambda_{3,t_1} e^{i\theta_{3,t_1}} & \cdot \\ \lambda_{1,t_2} e^{i\theta_{1,t_2}} & \lambda_{2,t_2} e^{i\theta_{2,t_2}} & \lambda_{3,t_2} e^{i\theta_{3,t_2}} & \cdot \\ \lambda_{1,t_3} e^{i\theta_{1,t_3}} & \lambda_{2,t_3} e^{i\theta_{2,t_3}} & \lambda_{3,t_3} e^{i\theta_{3,t_3}} & \cdot \\ \cdot & \cdot & \cdot & \cdot \end{vmatrix} \tag{3.6}$$

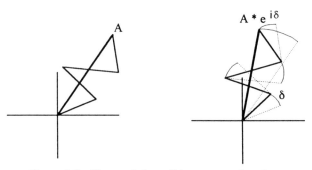

Figure 3.5   *Phase rotation within component vectors.*

Similarly for the associated responses:

$$[R] = \begin{vmatrix} \gamma_{t_1}e^{i\phi_{t_1}} \\ \gamma_{t_2}e^{i\phi_{t_2}} \\ \gamma_{t_3}e^{i\phi_{t_3}} \\ \gamma_{t_4}e^{i\phi_{t_4}} \end{vmatrix} \tag{3.7}$$

A basic learning is performed by evaluating the complex inner product:

$$[X] = [\overline{S}]^T \cdot [R] \tag{3.8}$$

Solution of Eq. (3.6) to (3.8) leads to the type of rotational translations illustrated in Figure 3.5 and described in the following for each correlation value x_j of $[X]$:

$$x_j = \lambda_{t_1,j}\gamma_{t_1}e^{i(\phi_{t_1}-\theta_{t_1,j})} + \lambda_{t_2,j}\gamma_{t_2}e^{i(\phi_{t_2}-\theta_{t_2,j})} + \lambda_{t_3,j}\gamma_{t_3}e^{i(\phi_{t_3}-\theta_{t_3,j})} + \lambda_{t_4,j}\gamma_{t_4}e^{i(\phi_{t_4}-\theta_{t_4,j})}$$

$$\tag{3.9}$$

The complex scalar x_j again has been generated from a set of stimulus–response associations represented in terms of phase angle differences (i.e., $\phi_t - \theta_{t,j}$). Through the equality expressed in Eq. (3.5), any subsequent multiplication by the complex conjugate of a prior learned stimulus induces a reverse rotation on the set of association quanta embedded within each complex correlation value. For any prior learned stimulus, a subset of these association quanta is rotated back to the original phase orientation of the associated response; this operation performed through the complex inner product in the decode transform:

$$R' = \frac{1}{c}[S]' \cdot [X] \tag{3.10}$$

A residual term is concurrently generated by a mapping of the stimulus through the set of noncongruent, prior encoded stimulus–response associations. In effect, the set of all association quanta undergoes an equivalent rotational translation in proportion to the respective s_j terms (as illustrated in Fig. 3.5). Considering the decode transform for only the association quanta known to be within this set, one may expand Eq. (3.10) to obtain a decomposition of the response recall. Using a stimulus pattern $[S]'$ for response recall and having elements described by:

$$s_j' = \beta_j e^{i\varsigma_j} \tag{3.11}$$

Equation (3.10) may be re-expressed in an expanded notation:

$$
R' = \frac{1}{c} \{ \beta_1 e^{i\zeta_1} \{ \lambda_{t_1,1} \gamma_{t_1} e^{i(\phi_{t_1} - \theta_{t_1,1})} + \lambda_{t_2,1} \gamma_{t_2} e^{i(\phi_{t_2} - \theta_{t_2,1})}
$$

$$
+ \lambda_{t_3,1} \gamma_{t_3} e^{i(\phi_{t_3} - \theta_{t_3,1})} + \lambda_{t_4,1} \gamma_{t_4} e^{i(\phi_{t_4} - \theta_{t_4,1})} \}
$$

$$
+ \beta_2 e^{i\zeta_2} \{ \lambda_{t_1,2} \gamma_{t_1} e^{i(\phi_{t_1} - \theta_{t_1,2})} + \lambda_{t_2,2} \gamma_{t_2} e^{i(\phi_{t_2} - \theta_{t_2,2})} + \lambda_{t_3,2} \gamma_{t_3} e^{i(\phi_{t_3} - \theta_{t_3,2})}
$$

$$
+ \lambda_{t_4,2} \gamma_{t_4} e^{i(\phi_{t_4} - \theta_{t_4,2})} \} + \beta_3 e^{i\zeta_3} \{ \cdots \} + \beta_4 e^{i\zeta_4} \{ \cdots \} \} \tag{3.12}
$$

Regrouping only those terms corresponding to a prior encoded mapping (i.e., the stimulus–response association corresponding to stimulus set at t_2), one obtains the following solution:

$$
R' = \{ \beta_1 \lambda_{t_2,1} \gamma_{t_2} e^{i(\phi_{t_2} - \theta_{t_2,1} + \zeta_1)} + \beta_2 \lambda_{t_2,2} \gamma_{t_2} e^{i(\phi_{t_2} - \theta_{t_2,2} + \zeta_2)} + \beta_3 \lambda_{t_2,3} \gamma_{t_2} e^{i(\phi_{t_2} - \theta_{t_2,3} + \zeta_3)}
$$

$$
+ \beta_4 \lambda_{t_2,4} \gamma_{t_2} e^{i(\phi_{t_2} - \theta_{t_2,4} + \zeta_4)} + R_{res} \tag{3.13}
$$

In Eq. (3.13), we impose a condition whereby the new stimulus pattern used in the decode $[S]'$ approaches the prior encoded stimulus pattern for t_2,

$$
\zeta_j \rightarrow \theta_{t_2,j} \tag{3.14}
$$

Equation (3.12) simplifies to a solution for phase orientation which is in fact the associated response vector (R at t_2) plus a residual term

$$
R' = e^{i\phi_{t_2}} \cdot \frac{1}{c} \sum_{j=1,4}^{4} \beta_j \lambda_{t_2,j} \gamma_{t_2} + R_{res} \tag{3.15}
$$

This summation also provides a combinational effect on the confidence values that have been assigned to each of the stimulus and response elements over both the learning and recall transforms. This aspect of operation mediates confidence levels within the generated mappings during learning as well as response recall. In the simplest case, unity confidences may be assigned to all stimulus–response values. The normalization term (c) is set to the dimensionality of the stimulus set (i.e., 4 in this example). Relation Eq. (3.15) then reduces to the following:

$$
R' = e^{i\phi_{t_2}} + R_{res} \tag{3.16}
$$

The component $e^{i\phi_{t_2}}$ defines the contribution produced by one association enfolded within the complex correlation, these terms lining up along the initial response phase orientation and exhibiting unity in the magnitude. The residual (R_{res}) depends not upon any individual association but upon the relationship between the new stimulus $[S]'$ and the set of noncongruent association map-

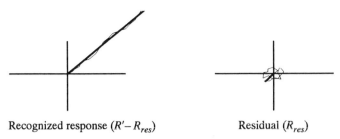

Recognized response $(R' - R_{res})$ Residual (R_{res})

Figure 3.6   *Illustration of response real and residual.*

pings in $[X]$. This residual term may be expanded as follows:

$$R_{res} = \beta_1 e^{i\zeta_1} \cdot \sum_{\substack{T=t_1,t_4 \\ T \neq t_2}} \lambda_{T,1} \gamma_T e^{i(\phi_T - \theta_{T,1})} + \sum_{\substack{T=t_1,t_4 \\ T \neq t_2}} \lambda_{T,2} \gamma_T e^{i(\phi_T - \theta_{T,2})} + \cdots$$

(3.17)

This residual is attenuated by a characteristic displayed in the physical world known as Brownian movement; when the cell is presented with certain nonrestrictive conditions concerning the distribution of data. The active ingredient here relies upon the statistical feature that a summation of approximately random steps within an orthogonal N dimensional coordinate system approaches an asymptote over large samples at the square root of the number of steps. The manner in which the noncongruent mappings are attenuated in the response recall requires that the phase orientations over the set of association quanta assume an approximately uniform distribution over the $0-2\pi$ phase range. In an attempt to visualize the aforementioned process, the following illustrates the generated response component for the recognized stimulus pattern and residual for all other nonassociated mappings arising from a response recall: (Fig. 3.6.)

3.3 PREPROCESSING AND SYMMETRY CONSTRAINTS

One finds that the preceding condition of symmetry can be satisfied in a large number of cases by implementing a sigmoidal conversion of real valued data to appropriate phase angle representations. Other conversion formats may potentially comprise any single valued and continuous function bounded within 0 to 2π (Fig. 3.7). A limited example of sigmoidal type functions is shown in Eq. (3.18), and these despite their simplicity exhibit a high level of generality in terms of the types of distributions they are capable of mapping to a reasonable state of symmetry. Illustrated are the standard sigmoid and the arctan functions:

$$\theta_{\text{sigmoid}} = 2\pi (1 + e^{\kappa(\mu - x)/\sigma})^{-1}$$

$$\theta_{\text{arctan}} = 2 \arctan \left(\kappa \frac{(\mu - x)}{\sigma} \right)$$

(3.18)

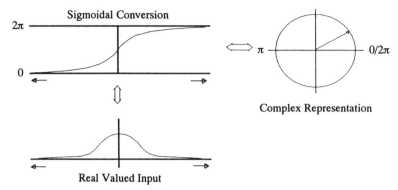

Figure 3.7   *The sigmoidal transformation.*

where κ = proportionality constant
μ = mean of the input distribution
σ = standard deviation of the input distribution

The placement of sigmoidal type transforms as a preprocessing function illustrates a further divergence from conventional backpropagation techniques which generally apply the preceding types of transforms as a post-processing feature primarily to enforce numerical stability. The position and form of this preprocessing transform are more consistent with some aspects of biological receptor neurons (i.e., retinal cells) which convert a measure of intensity in the given sensory modality using an approximate sigmoidal function. Other features are exhibited by these input transformations in their characteristics of mapping normal or Gaussian distributions to the ideal symmetric state. This feature and other aspects of input preprocessing are discussed further in [3].

3.4   HIGHER-ORDER SYSTEMS

An important aspect in the representation of semantic information through phase orientation and rotation is the ability to construct higher-order relationships in a manner that maintains numerical stability as well as consistency with respect to the measure of confidence. For instance, assuming all stimulus inputs have been assigned a unity level of confidence, any higher-order terms constructed from the stimulus basis set will correspondingly display a confidence of 1.0. This aspect has a number of important implications regarding the numerical stability of the system, and obviates the need to enforce stability through post-processing features, such as thresholding. Such higher-order relationships comprise the set of all possible unique combinatorial groups derived from the input basis set [5] and their conjugates. In general, these higher order terms may be represented by:

$$s_k = \prod_{m=1,4} \lambda_{r(k,m)} e^{i\theta_{r(k,m)}} \tag{3.19}$$

The $r(k, m)$ term defines any arbitrary relation which selects terms from the basis stimulus set, using a function whose independent variables are the expanded correlation set index k and product set index m. From the perspective of recall accuracy and generalization, it is more efficient to select only unique combinatorial products from the stimulus basis set, again this basis set defining only first-order inputs as well as the complex conjugates. Certain features of probabilistic consistency are also observed in that the confidence associated with any combination of higher-order relationships mains the net probabilistic combination of all the component terms. For instance, assuming a probabilistically bounded confidence assigned to each of four terms and from which we generate a fourth-order statistic, the net confidence of that fourth-order term is:

$$|s_k| = \lambda_1 \cdot \lambda_2 \cdot \lambda_3 \cdot \lambda_4 \tag{3.20}$$

Practically speaking, this capacity for the stable inclusion of higher-order relationships permits individual cells to map large numbers of stimulus–response associations using a fixed bound in the dynamic resolution of the complex connection "weights" and avoids problems associated with numerical stability. The order of these terms also provides a high level of control in the generalization characteristics displayed by the cell. The general characteristics observed as one increases the order and number of terms fed directly into a cell are:

1. The number of distinct or uncorrelated stimulus–response associations that may be encoded into a cell increase linearly with the number of product terms generated,
2. The regions of generalization become more narrowly defined as one process towards higher-order product terms from the stimulus basis vector.

3.5 ATTENTION AND MEMORY PROFILE

This basic encoding scheme permits learning to proceed independently for those mapping which have previously been learned within the cell. The accuracy of recall over multiple associations and stability of operation may be further enhanced by allowing a recursive facility in which learning is mediated by what has been learned in the past. This aspect should ideally control the rate of learning or attention in inverse proportion to the novelty of the stimulus–response association. Such an enhancement to encoding may be accomplished needing only an intracellular feedback mechanism, thus avoiding the need for multiple layers or cells within such associative systems. The operations involved in this feedback are straightforward and involve the following steps:

1. The cell generates a response from new stimuli being mapped through the memory previously enfolded within the cell.

2. Internally, the cell evaluates the difference between the generated response and the desired response for that stimulus association.

3. The above vector difference in the response is encoded in association to the new stimulus.

The above process allows the cell to generate an exact mapping of new stimulus to desired response within one transform, and enhances stability of the system by allowing the cell to learn differentially over novel versus prior learned associations. The enhanced encoding process considering only one value in the response is given by:

$$[X]+ = \overline{[S]}^{T} \cdot \left(R_{des} - \frac{1}{c} [S] \cdot [X] \right) \qquad (3.21)$$

where R_{des} = desired response and
$[X]; [S]$ = linear matrices containing only a single pattern

One final aspect of this discussion is in respect to the effects observed on training the cell to a point of saturation. This state may be reached by encoding a cell with randomly generated stimulus–response mappings whose range of values assumes a reasonably uniform distribution over the 0–2π phase range. A similar characteristic is observed in the encoding of Gaussian distributed data transformed through the sigmoidal preprocess operation. Two interesting features occur at the limit of saturation encoding:

1. The magnitude or confidence in the generated response approaches a mean of unity producing a recognition response over the entire state space for the stimulus.

2. The mean magnitude of the complex correlation values asymptotically approaches a deterministic limit. The limits of this magnitude, illustrated in Figure 3.8, are given random associations encoded over a range of cell sizes.

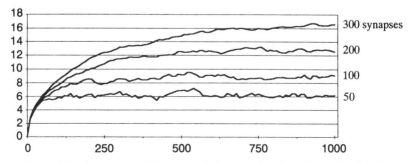

Figure 3.8 *Average correlation magnitudes as a function of encoding density.*

From the perspective of the conceptual development of the complex number based holographic neural model, this asymptotic limit shows that the cell may continue to proceed in encoding without imposing a requirement for the decay of associative mappings previously learned. This has several important implications, one of which relates to memory decay. The applications tool HNeT has a facility to control memory decay within the encoding (cortical) cells and performs this in a rather straightforward manner, through a thresholding of the average magnitude within the correlation set (synapses). This system attenuates correlation magnitude by a variable factor to bring average magnitude down to the imposed threshold. In effect all mappings that had been previously learned within the cell are attenuated by a proportionate factor. Long-term or permanent memory is implemented by setting a threshold at or above the asymptotic point, and shorter term memory by setting the threshold below the asymptote. Experimental results using Monte Carlo generated stimulus–response associations illustrate this asymptotic approach to a state of saturation encoding for a range of cell sizes. Given any number N of synaptic connections into a cortical cell, this asymptote in the correlation magnitudes may be approximated by:

$$\sqrt{N}$$

The affects resulting from memory decay can be discussed in the following general terms. Shorter term memories exhibit a lower level of confidence (magnitude in the response) over a greater proportion of the input space. Concurrently, however, those associations that have been learned more recently in the past are re-expressed at a higher level of accuracy (reduced fuzziness). For long-term memory, the holographic cell has a tendency to assume a unity mean in the recognition response over the extent of the input space allowing little discrimination between recognized and nonrecognized stimuli. In other words, the entire state space is recognized to some degree and influences may result from a large number of overlapping association quanta. The accuracy of recall (or fuzziness) is somewhat greater for recent knowledge acquisitions in the long-term or permanent memory profile.

3.6 CONCLUSION

As discussed earlier, these operational features have been developed from the conceptual perspective of a deterministic manipulation of intelligent associations, each enfolded within sets of complex scalars through summation of phase differences. The preceding asymptotic limit presents an interesting possibility, whereby, given the requirement for a finite dynamic range and resolution in the correlation values, an unrestricted number of *association quanta* may be encoded within the holographic cell without need for attenuation. As in the initial representation, any phase rotation on the aggregate vector imposes a coincident rotation on the set of component vectors, and these association quanta aside from being deterministically fixed through encoding, are quantitatively unbounded within a finite resolution complex manifold. The asymptotic effect in the correlation magnitudes has important implications with respect to memory decay and as well as hardware requirements the data storage of synaptic ''weights.'' The arguments presented here for association quanta present an alternate and hopefully clarifying perspective in holographic-based learning and recall.

REFERENCES

[1] D. Hebb, ''The First Stage of Perception: Growth of the Assembly,'' in *The Organization of Behavior*, Wiley, 1949, pp. 60–78.

[2] J. Sutherland, Holographic model of memory, learning, and expression, *Internat. J. Neur. Syst.*, 1 (3), (1990) pp. 256–267.

[3] J. Sutherland, ''The Holographic Neural Method,'' in B. Souček, ed., *Fuzzy, Holographic, and Parallel Intelligence*, Wiley 1992, pp. 7–92.

BIBLIOGRAPHY

D. Gabour, Associative holographic memories, *IBM J. Res. Develop.*, 13, 156–159 (1969)

D. J. Wilshaw, O. P. Buneman, and H. C. Longuet-Higgens Non-holographic associative memory, *Nature*, 222, 960–962, (1969).

Pribram, K. H., *Scientific American*, 220, 73 (1969).

Teuvo Kohonen, Correlation matrix memories, *IEEE Trans. Comp.*, C-21, 353–359 (1972).

CHAPTER 4 ————————————

Stimulus Preprocessing for Holographic Neural Networks

ROBERT MANGER
VITO LEONARDO PLANTAMURA
BRANKO SOUČEK

4.1 INTRODUCTION

Artificial neural networks are a powerful problem-solving paradigm, which can be used for various purposes, including pattern recognition, classification, prediction, simulation, and associative reasoning. The paradigm is based on mimicking the behavior of neural tissues found in living beings. Thus the solution to a problem is constructed by forming a set of suitably interconnected basic processing elements (so called artificial *neurons*). For an input (i.e., *stimulus*), this network automatically produces an output (*response*). At the same time, the network has the ability to "learn" a given collection of stimulus-response associations, and afterward it becomes able to reproduce and generalize those associations.

There are many variants of the neural networks paradigm presently in use, which differ in neuron properties, network topology, and learning algorithms. The most popular type are *backpropagation layered* networks [1, 2]. A new, and to our opinion very promising type are *holographic* networks, which have recently been proposed by Sutherland [3, 4].

The main properties of holographic neural technology are presented in Chapter 3. So the reader is advised to review that chapter if necessary. Here, we repeat only a few most important points.

First, a holographic neuron is much more powerful than a conventional one, so that it is functionally equivalent to a whole conventional network. Next,

Frontier Decision Support Concepts, Edited by V. L. Plantamura, B. Souček, and G. Visaggio.
ISBN 0-471-59256-0 © 1994 John Wiley & Sons, Inc.

information is internally represented by complex numbers operating within two degrees of freedom (phase and magnitude). Both input to a neuron (now called a stimulus) and output from a neuron (called a response) are vectors composed of complex numbers. A neuron internally holds a complex matrix that enables monitoring stimulus-response associations. Many associations can be enfolded onto the same matrix. Both learning and producing a response are realized through simple matrix operations. Finally, holographic networks are available on PCs through an emulator called HNeT (holographic neural technology) [5].

There is no need to build massive networks of holographic neurons; for most applications one or few neurons are sufficient. In the process of network design, the emphasis is shifted from the choice of topology to the choice of adequate data pre- or postprocessing.

Two kinds of preprocessing are of fundamental importance within the holographic neural process. *Stimulus symmetrization* ensures reasonable accuracy in reproducing learned stimulus-response associations. *Stimulus expansion* increases the number of stimulus-response associations that can accurately be encoded into a neuron. For both kinds of preprocessing, standard methods are provided in HNeT.

Holographic networks seem to be very suitable for analog problems, where stimuli are given as analog signals, which are in turn represented by very long arrays of numbers. However, we have tried to apply holographic technology to semidiscrete problems where a stimulus consists of only few values taken from (possibly different) analog or discrete domains. We have been motivated by banking applications such as financial ratio analysis, stock forecasting, and so on [6]. According to our experiments, holographic networks are also appropriate for semidiscrete problems, provided that some additional (nonstandard) preprocessing methods are available.

In this chapter we review the standard preprocessing methods implemented in HNeT, and propose two new methods, one for each of the two types of preprocessing. We also describe the situations where these new methods are useful. We believe that our proposals greatly enhance the applicability of holographic networks. The chapter is organized as follows. Section 4.2 is concerned with stimulus symmetrization, while Section 4.3 deals with stimulus expansion. Section 4.4 describes our implementation of the proposed methods. Section 4.5 lists some experimental results. Section 4.6 gives concluding remarks.

4.2 STIMULUS SYMMETRIZATION

The holographic process requires phase elements within the stimulus vector to display a highly symmetrical (i.e., uniform) distribution in orientation about the origin of the complex plane. The ability to enfold multiple stimulus-response associations onto the same matrix is derived from the manner in which complex numbers are summed within a symmetric system. Assuming a uniform distribution of orientations, the error terms, whenever present in a response, tend to neutralize in a manner analogous to random walk [3, 4, 5].

If original stimulus data are not symmetric, some form of preprocessing is needed to assure the confidence of response. Such preprocessing, called *stimulus symmetrization*, should redistribute complex elements within the stimulus vector to achieve a uniform phase distribution.

The original HNeT system provides a standard method for stimulus symmetrization based on the *sigmoid* function [3, 4, 5]. According to that method, an element of the stimulus vector, say $\lambda e^{i\theta}$, is transformed into $\lambda e^{i\psi}$, where

$$\psi = \frac{2\pi}{1 + \exp\left[(\mu - \theta)/\sigma\right]}$$

Note that only phase elements are transformed, while magnitudes remain unchanged. In the above expression, μ is the mean of the distribution for phase elements θ, and σ is the variance of the same distribution. According to [5], the sigmoid method performs a mapping of distributions displaying approximate Gaussian form to a fairly uniform state.

Although satisfactory in many cases, the standard sigmoid transform is not appropriate if the original data distribution differs from Gaussian. The latter can happen quite easily, especially if the stimulus consists of only few elements originating from different domains. Therefore we propose an alternative method for stimulus symmetrization, which takes into account the actual distributions of phase elements within the stimulus vector. The method is derived from the following observations.

Suppose that the starting domain is composed of numbers θ in the range $[0, 2\pi)$ with an arbitrary distribution $f_1(\theta)$. This domain should be converted into another representation, with elements ψ also in the range $[0, 2\pi)$, but with a uniform distribution $f_2(\psi)$. It is necessary to find the proper conversion curve $\psi = g(\theta)$.

Since the starting value θ is a random variable, ψ will also be a random variable. If θ has a distribution function $f_1(\theta)$, then ψ has a distribution function $f_2(\psi)$, which depends on $f_1(\theta)$ and on $g(\theta)$. The easiest way to determine the resulting distribution function $f_2(\psi)$ is as follows: If there is a continuous one-to-one correspondence between θ and ψ, then the probability that the original variable is in the range $(\theta, \theta + d\theta)$ must be equal to the probability that the resulting value is in the range $(\psi, \psi + d\psi)$. Hence,

$$f_1(\theta)\, d\theta = f_2(\psi)\, d\psi$$

$$f_2(\psi) = f_1(\theta) \cdot \frac{1}{d\psi/d\theta} = f_1(\theta) \cdot \frac{1}{|g'(\theta)|}$$

The resulting distribution $f_2(\psi)$ is a function of $f_1(\theta)$ and of the derivative of the transfer function, $g(\theta)$. The absolute value of the derivative is taken because a distribution function cannot have negative values. From this expression, one can find the transfer function $g(\theta)$, which will transform an original distribution $f_1(\theta)$ into a new desired distribution $f_2(\psi)$.

$$g'(\theta) = \frac{f_1(\theta)}{f_2(\psi)}$$

$$g(\theta) = \int_0^\theta \frac{f_1(\bar{\theta})}{f_2(\psi)}\, d\bar{\theta} + C$$

Since we are interested in producing a uniform distribution $f_2(\psi)$, we can write

$$f_2(\psi) = K = \text{const}$$

and consequently

$$g(\theta) = \frac{1}{K}\int_0^\theta f_1(\bar{\theta})\, d\bar{\theta} + C = \frac{1}{K} F_1(\theta) + C$$

Here, $F_1(\theta)$ is the cumulative or integral distribution function of the variable θ. Since the uniform distribution is defined in the interval between 0 and 2π, it follows that $K = 1/2\pi$. The constant C can be obtained from the boundary condition for $g(\theta)$:

$$g(2\pi) = 2\pi = 2\pi \cdot 1 + C \Rightarrow C = 0$$

So the required transfer function is

$$\psi = g(\theta) = 2\pi \cdot F_1(\theta)$$

Our optimal stimulus symmetrization method for holographic networks consists of the following:

- Estimate the distribution function $f_1(\theta)$ for a chosen phase element θ within the given stimulus vector.
- Compute the corresponding cumulative function $F_1(\theta)$.
- Transform the phase element θ into ψ using the foregoing relationship.

Since various phase elements within the same stimulus vector can be drawn from different domains, each element can have its own distribution function. Therefore, the process must be repeated for each domain.

4.3 STIMULUS EXPANSION

As any neural system, a holographic neuron produces only approximate responses to learned stimuli. Even if an ideal symmetry of stimulus data distribution is achieved, the phase recall error is still expected to be [4]

$$\phi_{error} \approx \frac{1}{\pi \sqrt{8}} \tan^{-1} \left(\sqrt{\frac{p}{n}} \right)$$

Here n is the length of the stimulus vector (i.e., the number of vector elements), and p is the number of stimulus-response associations learned. Increasing the number of learned associations also increases the noise until it becomes intolerably high. So the learning capacity is limited, and it depends on the length of the stimulus vector.

For the problems where the stimulus vector length is small, the number of associations that can be accurately encoded is also small. The only way to increase the learning capacity is to artificially increase the stimulus vector length and to hope that the relation above will still remain valid. Such a preprocessing operation is called *stimulus expansion*.

The original HNeT system provides a standard method for stimulus expansion. It is based on switching to higher-order product terms, generated from elements stored within the original stimulus vector. These terms or "statistics" form a set of unique combinatorial product groups of the specified order. For instance, let the original stimulus vector be

$$S = [\lambda_1 e^{i\theta_1}, \lambda_2 e^{i\theta_2}, \lambda_3 e^{i\theta_3}, \lambda_4 e^{i\theta_4}]$$

By using the standard expansion method with the order of statistic 2, this vector could be transformed into

$$\bar{S} = [\lambda_1 \lambda_2 e^{i(\theta_1 + \theta_2)}, \lambda_1 \lambda_3 e^{i(\theta_1 + \theta_3)}, \lambda_1 \lambda_4 e^{i(\theta_1 + \theta_4)}, \lambda_2 \lambda_3 e^{i(\theta_2 + \theta_3)},$$
$$\lambda_2 \lambda_4 e^{i(\theta_2 + \theta_4)}, \lambda_3 \lambda_4 e^{i(\theta_3 + \theta_4)}]$$

So we see that the vector length has been increased from 4 to 6.

After switching to higher-order product terms, the above error relationship remains valid provided that no two terms have been constructed from the same set of raw input values. At the same time, the stimulus vector length can increase considerably, since the number of unique statistics for an initial length n and order of statistic s is

$$\binom{n}{s} = \frac{n!}{s!(n-s)!}$$

In the present implementation, the standard expansion method allows expanding the stimulus vector to any desirable length. Also, any order of statistic can be used. If the chosen length is not equal to the number of unique statistics, then each of the unique terms is chosen with equal probability. It means that very long expanded vectors will consist of nonunique terms, and each of the unique terms will be represented (i.e., repeated) in approximately equal amount. However, the learning capacity for such overblown vectors is still estimated by the number of unique terms used, not by the actual expanded vector length.

Finally, it must be noted that switching to higher-order product terms produces an important side effect. As one increases the order of statistic, the neuron's ability to generalize the learned stimulus-response associations becomes smaller and smaller. In some situations this can be a useful feature, since it allows some control over the generalization characteristics. But sometimes the loss of generalization is unwanted or even not tolerable.

According to our experience, the standard stimulus expansion method behaves very well for a moderately short stimulus vector (e.g., between 20 and 100). But for an extremely short vector, switching to higher-order statistics does not help too much. There are simply not enough unique terms to produce any substantial expansion. Or one is forced to use a very high order of statistic, which can cause an unwanted reduction of the neuron's generalization characteristics. For instance, if the vector length is $n = 4$, then the maximum number of unique statistics is obtained with the order $s = 2$, and it amounts only to 6. If the length is $n = 12$, then we could expand the vector to the length ≈ 1000, but only with a considerably high order of statistic $s = 6$.

Due to the reasons above we propose another method for stimulus expansion, which is suitable for expanding an extremely short vector to a moderate length. Our method adds additional (dummy) elements to the original vector according to the following rules.

1. New elements are uniquely determined by the original elements.
2. Any new element depends on exactly one of the original elements.
3. The dependence is nonlinear.
4. The dependence is continuous.

Rule 1 is necessary in order to produce always the same expanded stimulus for a given original stimulus. Rule 2 tries to neutralize the influence of expansion on the neuron's generalization ability. Rule 3 is needed to avoid replication of the same error patterns in multiple parts of the neuron's memory. Rule 4 assures that similar original stimuli will produce similar expanded stimuli, and this is necessary to enable generalization.

There are many possible variants of the proposed method, since the continuous nonlinear dependence can be chosen in many ways. We will describe in detail a variant based on sines and cosines. Let the original stimulus vector length be n, and suppose that we want to expand the stimulus vector to the length N ($N > n$). Let the original vector elements be $\lambda_j e^{i\theta_j}$ ($j = 1, 2, \ldots, n$). Then the dummy vector elements $\lambda_j e^{i\theta_j}$ ($j = n + 1, n + 2, \ldots, N$) are computed through the following procedure:

```
for j := n + 1 to N do begin
    k := ⌊ (j + n - 1) / 2n ⌋ ;
    r := j + n + 2nk;
    if r ≤ n then begin
        λⱼ := λᵣ;
        θⱼ := π(sin(kθᵣ) + 1)
    end
    else begin
        λⱼ := λᵣ₋ₙ;
        θⱼ := π(cos(kθᵣ₋ₙ) + 1)
    end
end.
```

Note that the purpose of our sine/cosine method is only to expand an extremely short stimulus vector to a moderate length. Then the standard higher-order statistics can further be applied to reach the desired final vector length.

4.4 LIBRARY OF ROUTINES

The preprocessing methods proposed in Sections 4.2 and 4.3 have also been implemented as a set of C functions. In this way, a small library of routines has been created, which acts as a supplement to the original HNeT library. The prototypes of our functions are the following:

```
void distr (int n, COMPLEX *sample, float *func);
void cdistr (float *func, float *cumm);
void symm (float *cumm, COMPLEX dorig, COMPLEX *dsymm,
  float contr);
void Symm
    (int n, float *cumm, COMPLEX *dorig, COMPLEX
    *dsymm, float contr);
void SYMM
    (int n, float **cumm, COMPLEX *dorig, COMPLEX
    *dsymm, float contr);
void expand (int norig, COMPLEX *dorig, int nexp,
  COMPLEX *dexp);
```

In the foregoing prototypes the data type `COMPLEX` is a special type used by the HNeT system to internally represent complex numbers as 16-bit values. The other data types are standard. The first five functions make together the optimal stimulus symmetrization method, while the last one serves for stimulus expansion by sines and cosines. In the following paragraphs we will describe each of the functions in more detail.

`distr` uses a list of n sample values from a given domain to estimate the corresponding distribution for phase elements. The sample list is supplied in the array `sample`. The discretized form of the distribution function is stored into the array `func`. To obtain discretization, the adequate equidistant division of the phase range $[0, 2\pi)$ is used.

`cdistr` computes the cumulative distribution for a distribution already computed by `distr`. The given distribution function is supplied in the `array func`. The resulting cumulative distribution function is stored into the `array cumm`. The same kind of discretization is used as for `func`.

`symm` transforms a given value, whose phase element distribution is known, according to the optimal symmetrization method. `dorig` is the original (given) value and `dsymm` points to the resulting symmetrized value. `cumm` is the array that contains the given cumulative distribution function for phase elements.

To be quite precise, our version of `symm` is slightly more general than required by our optimal symmetrization method. Namely, in addition to a uniform distribution on the full interval $[0, 2\pi)$, the function can also produce a uniform distribution on a "contracted" interval $[0, \text{contr} \cdot 2\pi)$, where $0 < \text{contr} \le 1$. So contraction is regulated by the additional parameter `contr`. To perform symmetrization exactly as described in Section 4.2, we must use `contr` = 1.

The functions `Symm` and `SYMM` are similar to `simm` and in fact redundant. Still, they are supplied for convenience. Both functions perform optimal symmetrization, but instead of transforming only one value they transform a list of n given values at once. The original (given) values are supplied in the array `dorig`, and the resulting symmetrized values are stored into the array `dsymm`. The parameter `contr` has the same purpose as in `symm`. `Symm` assumes that all n given values have the same phase element distribution, which is specified by the array `cumm`. `SYMM`, on the other hand, uses a different distribution for each value; consequently `cumm` becomes an array of pointers to cumulative distributions.

Finally, `expand` performs expansion of a given list of values, by using our sine/cosine method. `norig` is the length of the original (given) list, while `nexp` is the length of the expanded list. The original list is supplied in the array `dorig`, and the expanded list is stored into the array `dexp`.

In addition to these functions, which serve for stimulus preprocessing, our library also contains some auxiliary routines. For instance, there is a set of functions for converting values from the external `float` to the internal `COMPLEX` representation, and vice versa.

4.5 EXPERIMENTAL RESULTS

In order to test our two proposed preprocessing methods, we made a series of numerical experiments. The problem we used through all experiments was the iris flowers classification problem, described in Chapter 5. Our neural network was configured according to the general idea from Chapter 5. We experimented with several variants of stimulus symmetrization and expansion. The network emulation was mostly achieved through the HNeT system, but some preprocessing phases (e.g., sine/cosine expansion, optimal symmetrization) were performed by the routines from our library.

The sample set, consisting of 150 correctly classified flowers, was split into two equal parts called the training and the testing set respectively. The training set served for both training and testing the network, while the testing set served only for testing.

The first group of experiments was designed to test our sine/cosine expansion method. The results are presented in Table 4.1. Each row of Table 4.1 corresponds to one variant of stimulus expansion. Any variant consists of two phases, as shown by the first two columns of the table. In the first phase our sine/cosine method is used to expand the original stimulus vector to a length manageable by the neuron. The second phase further expands the stimulus to the final length by applying higher-order statistics. Between the two phases the HNeT system performs sigmoid symmetrization by default, but the effect of this operation becomes negligible after the final expansion. For all variants the final vector length is chosen the same, 400. It means that the neuron always

TABLE 4.1   Iris Flowers Classification: Various Stimulus Expansion Variants

Initial expansion (sin / cos)	Final expansion (higher-order statistics)	Correct responses (%)	
		Training set	Testing set
Omitted	Second order 400 terms (6 unique)	60	56
From length 4 to length 8	Second order 400 terms (28 unique)	95	76
From length 4 to length 12	Second order 400 terms (66 unique)	97	87
From length 4 to length 16	Second order 400 terms (120 unique)	100	88
From length 4 to length 20	Second order 400 terms (190 unique)	100	95
From length 4 to length 24	Second order 400 terms (276 unique)	100	91
From length 4 to length 28	Second order 400 terms (378 unique)	100	89

uses the same amount of physical memory, and this assures a fair comparison among variants.

Columns 3 and 4 of Table 4.1 describe the network performance, in dependence on the chosen expansion variant. After accomplished training the examples from the training and testing sets, respectively, were presented to the neuron for classification. The percent of correctly classified examples has been recorded in the table. Thus column 3 shows how well the neuron reproduces the learned associations, while column 4 illustrates the quality of generalization.

For the iris flowers problem stimulus expansion is crucial, since the original stimulus vector is extremely short. If no expansion were used, the neuron would have a very limited learning capacity, so that its performance would be completely unreliable. More detailed testing has revealed that without any expansion the neuron is able to memorize only nine training examples. As we see from row 1 of Table 4.1, exclusive use of higher-order statistics does not help too much, since the number of unique higher-order terms is low.

Rows 2 to 4 show how our sine/cosine expansion method increases the learning capacity, so that the neuron eventually becomes able to correctly reproduce all the training examples. The initial expansion to length 20 (row 5) seems to produce the optimal quality of generalization. However, further increase of the initial expansion length (rows 6 and 7) reduces the generalization ability. We explain this phenomenon by the fact that steeper and steeper sine and cosine functions are used.

All experiments presented in Table 4.1 use the second-order statistics for the final expansion. Choosing an order of statistics higher than 2 would not do any better, since it would also restrict the neuron's generalization capabilities.

The aim of the second group of our experiments was to test the optimal symmetrization method. For those experiments, the whole sample set was initially expanded by sines and cosines in order to increase the stimulus vector length to 20. The produced 20 stimulus elements were treated as original and independent data, with possibly different phase distributions. Then the available symmetrization methods were applied. The results are shown in Table 4.2.

TABLE 4.2 Iris Flowers Classification: Various Stimulus Symmetrization Variants

	Correct responses (%)	
Symmetrization	Training set	Testing set
Sigmoid	83	81
Optimal (without contraction)	99	91
Optimal (contraction factor 0.9)	99	93
Optimal (contraction factor 0.7)	99	96
Optimal (contraction factor 0.5)	99	93

Each row corresponds to one variant of stimulus symmetrization. Again, for all variants the vector length was the same (i.e., it remained 20) so that our comparison is fair.

Columns 2 and 3 of Table 4.2 have similar meanings as columns 3 and 4 of Table 4.1 respectively; that is, they describe the network performance in dependence on the chosen symmetrization variant. We see that the optimal symmetrization method outperforms the standard sigmoid method. But even better results are obtained by the use of contraction combined with optimal symmetrization. Our explanation for this fact is the following. If the full phase range $[0, 2\pi)$ is used, then very small (≈ 0) and very big ($\approx 2\pi$) angles become close. So the neuron can easily regard some quite different stimulus data as being "similar" and produce a wrong generalization. When a contracted phase range is used, big and small angles are more clearly separated and distinguished. However, one must not exaggerate with contraction, as shown by row 5 of Table 4.2. Namely, choosing a shorter range results in smaller resolution for internally represented phase data.

4.6 CONCLUSIONS

We believe that holographic neural technology will play a prominent role in the future of neurocomputing. However, the process of designing holographic networks is quite unconventional. Namely, the designer is more concerned with picking an adequate data preprocessing procedure, rather than with choosing a right network topology. Therefore it is important that a diversity of preprocessing methods be available.

The present HNeT software package already includes some preprocessing methods quite suitable for problems where the stimulus consists of many values displaying Gaussian distribution. In this text, we have proposed two additional methods for increasing response accuracy and learning capacity. Our proposals improve the applicability of holographic networks to problems where the stimulus consists of only few values displaying different distributions. Such problems are encountered in financial analysis and in other areas.

We have made an implementation of our methods in the form of C functions. Since the HNeT package is in fact a library of C functions, our code acts as an extension to the original software. At present, our part of preprocessing is performed by the application program. A better solution would be to implement the methods through dedicated operator cells. Then, preprocessing would be done by the network itself.

The ideas presented in this text allow further investigation and experimenting. First, our optimal symmetrization procedure could be simplified for some special cases, such as uniformly distributed discrete domains. Next, our expansion method could be realized with other functions instead of sines and cosines; it would be interesting to find out which choice is optimal.

REFERENCES

[1] R. Hecht-Nielsen, *Neurocomputing*, Addison-Wesley, Reading, Mass., 1990.

[2] B. Souček and M. Souček, *Neural and Massively Parallel Computers*, Wiley, New York, 1988.

[3] J. G. Sutherland, Holographic model of memory, learning and expression, *Internat. J. Neural Syst.*, 1(3) 256–257 (1990).

[4] J. G. Sutherland, "The holographic neural method," in B. Souček, ed., *Fuzzy, Holographic and Parallel Intelligence*, Wiley, New York, 1992.

[5] J. G. Sutherland, *HNeT Development System, Version 1.0*, AND Corp., Hamilton, Ontario, 1990.

[6] D. B. Graddy and A. H. Spencer, *Managing Commercial Banks*, Prentice Hall, Englewood Cliffs, N.J., 1990.

CHAPTER 5 ⎯⎯⎯⎯⎯⎯⎯⎯⎯⎯⎯⎯⎯

Classification with Holographic Neural Networks

ROBERT MANGER
VITO LEONARDO PLANTAMURA
BRANKO SOUČEK

5.1 INTRODUCTION

Various decision-making problems fall into a general category of classification. Our interest in classification is mainly motivated by financial and banking applications [1]. We have in mind certain tasks where companies or loan applicants are rated according to various financial parameters. Of course, similarly structured problems also occur in many other disciplines. For instance, diagnostic decision making can be viewed as a process of classifying patients, and software evaluation can be interpreted as classifying software products. Therefore we expect that this chapter should be of interest to a broad audience, not only to financial community.

Classification problems have traditionally been solved by various methods, which originate from different problem-solving paradigms. The three most important paradigms are statistical analysis, artificial intelligence, and neural networks [2]. Statistical methods usually try to find an explicit numerical formula, which determines completely how classification is performed. Artificial intelligence methods try to deduce exact If-Then-Else rules that can be used in the classification process. The neural networks paradigm leads to a more implicit solution. No formulas or rules are produced. Instead, a neural network is constructed that is "trained" to reproduce and generalize a given set of correct classification examples.

It is very hard to say in general which of the methods guarantees the best performance. It depends heavily on the application involved. However, we

Frontier Decision Support Concepts, Edited by V. L. Plantamura, B. Souček, and G. Visaggio. ISBN 0-471-59256-0   © 1994 John Wiley & Sons, Inc.

believe that for financial classification problems neural networks are most appropriate. Namely, the "knowledge" in the financial area is vague and prone to irregularities. An explicit formula or rule (as produced by statistics or artificial intelligence) would not sound convincing in all circumstances. A model adequate for one type of economy may not be justified in another situation. On the other hand, the implicit solution obtained by neural networks is more flexible. It can adjust to any data reflecting a given economy with all its peculiarities.

The idea of using neural networks for classification and financial modeling is not new. The majority of the related papers employ the most popular "backpropagation layered" type of networks [2, 3]. However, many other variants of the neural paradigm have been proposed. One of them is the "holographic" neural technology, due to Sutherland [4]. Holographic networks seem to be superior to ordinary networks in many aspects. Still, at this moment there are not many reports on their application. It would be interesting to see how successfully can they be employed for classification.

The aim of this chapter is to advocate to use of holographic neural networks for classification. The chapter provides an overview of various classification methods, and compares the novel holographic approach with more traditional strategies. Through this comparison, the reader is convinced that holographic networks lead to a more elegant and straightforward solution of classification problems. The chapter is organized as follows. In Section 5.2 the term *classification problems* is defined, and some concrete examples are given. Section 5.3 reviews the three traditional classification paradigms namely statistics, artificial intelligence, and backpropagation neural networks. Section 5.4 lists the main properties of holographic neural networks, and shows how these networks can be employed for classification. Finally, Section 5.5 gives some concluding remarks.

5.2 CLASSIFICATION PROBLEMS

The term *classification problem* refers to any problem conforming to the following general outline. A set of *entities* of the same type is considered. Each entity is described by a list of *attributes*. The entity set is a partitioned into subsets called *classes*. For given attribute values, one is required to determine the class to which the corresponding entity belongs.

As an example of a classification problem, we will mention the well-known iris flowers problem, which is supplied as a benchmark in many software packages (e.g., SAS, IMSL, NeuralWorks II). In this example, the entities are iris flowers, which are grouped into three species (called Setosa, Versicolor, and Virginica respectively) according to four attributes (sepal length and width, petal length and width).

Another example is bankruptcy prediction. There, the entities are firms, and the attributes are various financial ratios [1] that measure the performance of a

TABLE 5.1   Part of the Iris Sample Set

Flower #	Sepal length	Sepal width	Petal length	Petal width	Class
1	0.224	0.624	0.067	0.043	Setosa
2	0.749	0.502	0.627	0.541	Versicolor
3	0.557	0.541	0.847	1.000	Virginica
4	0.110	0.502	0.051	0.043	Setosa
5	0.722	0.459	0.663	0.584	Versicolor
6	0.776	0.416	0.831	0.831	Virginica

firm (e.g., current ratio, debt/assets ratio, etc.). Firms are classified as "bankrupt" or "nonbankrupt."

We are interested in such problems where the classification criteria are not very well understood. In other words, there is no known formula or algorithm to compute the class identifier from given attribute values. Instead, a sample set of already classified entities is given, which is believed to describe implicitly how classification is being done. Any system performing classification should "learn" these examples and generalize them in order to classify new entities.

For the iris flowers problem, the available sample set consists of 150 flowers which have been correctly classified by an expert. The petal/sepal lengths and widths for these flowers have been recorded. Each class is represented by 50 examples. A small part of the set is reproduced in Table 5.1.

For the bankruptcy prediction problem, data for some past period should be available on a group of firms that includes both companies that went bankrupt and companies that did not. Table 5.2 shows such data. For simplicity, only two ratios are shown, although any serious analysis would require more attributes.

5.3 TRADITIONAL CLASSIFICATION METHODS

As mentioned, there are three traditional classification paradigms: statistical analysis, artificial intelligence, and neural networks. In this section we will say more about these methodologies and their advantages and drawbacks. We have no intention of providing an exhaustive list of all available classification algorithms. Instead, through an informal exposition we will only try to give a flavor of the methods resulting from each of the three paradigms.

5.3.1 Statistical Analysis

The oldest classification methods are based on statistics. The sample set of already classified entities is described by a matrix, whose rows correspond to the entities, and columns to the attributes (including also the class identifier). Learning is accomplished through appropriate numerical operations which are

TABLE 5.2 Sample Data for Bankruptcy Prediction

Firm number	Current ratio	Debt/assets ratio (%)	Did firm go bankrupt?
1	3.6	60	No
2	3.0	20	No
3	3.0	60	No
4	3.0	76	Yes
5	2.8	44	No
6	2.6	56	Yes
7	2.6	68	Yes
8	2.4	40	Yes
9	2.4	60	No
10	2.2	28	No
11	2.0	40	No
12	2.0	48	No
13	1.8	60	Yes
14	1.6	20	No
15	1.6	44	Yes
16	1.2	44	Yes
17	1.0	24	No
18	1.0	32	Yes
19	1.0	60	Yes

applied to that matrix. The result of learning is a formula (or an algorithm) that can be used to compute the class identifier for given attribute values.

Several statistical methods have been employed for classification. Probably the best-known method is the *linear discriminant*. The objectives of the linear discriminant can more easily be explained if we restrict to a particular example of a classification problem. Let us choose bankruptcy prediction. Then we could visualize our sample firms as points in a multidimensional space. The space dimension is chosen equal to the number of ratios. Any firm is represented by the point whose Cartesian coordinates are equal to the corresponding ratios. The linear discriminant tries to find a hyperplane that optimally divides the space into two halves, so that the nonbankrupt sample firms are located in one half and the bankrupt firms in the other half. Analyzing a new firm reduces to putting the corresponding point into the space. If the point falls to the non-bankrupt side of the hyperplane, the firm is not likely to become insolvent; otherwise it is likely to go bankrupt.

In our concrete example of bankruptcy prediction (Table 5.2) there are only two ratios, so the space is two-dimensional (i.e., the ordinary plane). The hyperplane is in fact a straight line. Figure 5.1 shows our sample data. The ×'s represent firms that went bankrupt, while the dots represent firms that remained solvent. The boundary line obtained by the linear discriminant is also shown. Companies that lie to the left of the line are not likely to go bankrupt while those to the right are likely to fail. It may be seen from the figure that one ×, indicating a failing company, lies to the left of the line, while two dots, indicating nonbankrupt companies, lie to the right of the line. Thus, the linear discriminant failed to classify properly three companies.

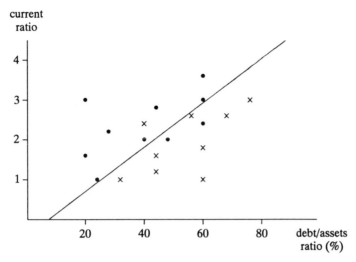

Figure 5.1 *Discriminant boundary between bankrupt and solvent firms.*

The division of the space into halves can of course be described analytically, by an affine function, called the *discriminant function*. Our hyperplane is the set of points for which the discriminant function is zero, and the half-spaces are the sets where the function takes positive and negative values respectively. For our concrete example, the discriminant function is

$$Z = -0.3877 - 1.0736 \times \text{(current ratio)} + 0.0579 \times \text{(debt/assets ratio)}$$

A negative Z value indicates that the corresponding company is nonbankrupt, while a positive Z score suggests bankruptcy.

Our example illustrates a potential drawback of the linear discriminant. Although the method tried its best to construct the optimal boundary line between dots and ×'s, some points remained on the wrong side. There is simply no straight line that divides our dots and ×'s completely. Separation could have been better if the method used some type of curved line instead of a straight line. But then, such a curve would prove inadequate for some other sample data sets. The problem is not caused by the type of the curve, but by the very fact that the method imposes an explicit mathematical model. Even worse, this model is postulated in advance, prior to any data processing. It would be better if the model were not so explicit and fixed, so that it could adapt to the actual data. Similar objections can be imputed not only to the linear discriminant but also to the other statistical methods.

5.3.2 Artificial Intelligence

Artificial intelligence methods for classification are also called *machine learning* methods. Their objective is to construct explicit If-Then-Else rules, which describe and generalize the given correct classification examples. Those rules can then be used for classifying any new entity.

Most of the present machine-learning methods represent the set of rules in a more compact form (i.e., as a *decision tree*). Such a tree is produced by an appropriate algorithm, which takes the sample set as input. Each internal node in the tree contains a criterion expressed in terms of attribute values, while a leaf contains a class identifier. To classify a new entity, one follows a path from the root to a leaf. In each internal node, the given criterion (applied to the actual attribute values) is used to determine the right subtree that must be entered. The path will eventually end up in a leaf, and the corresponding identifier will determine the class to which the entity belongs.

It is obvious that any decision tree is equivalent to a set of separate If-Then-Else rules. If desired, each rule can be constructed by combining the criteria along a path in the tree. But this is usually not necessary.

Various machine learning algorithms differ in their ways of constructing the tree and choosing the criteria. To be more concrete, we shall describe one version of the well-known Quinlan ID3 algorithm [5]. The version is suitable for our bankruptcy prediction problem. The procedure goes as follows:

1. If all entities in the sample set belong to the same class, then there is nothing left to do. The tree consists of only one node (i.e., a leaf) that contains the identifier of that class.

2. Else choose an attribute *atr* and a value *v*. Split the sample set into two subsets. The first subset consists of all sample entities whose value for *atr* is ≤ *v*, and the second subset contains the remaining entities. The subsets define two subproblems—that is, smaller classification problems of the same kind. The tree is formed as a binary tree, whose root contains the condition *atr* ≤ *v*, and the two subtrees correspond to the two subproblems.

These steps are recursively applied to solve the two subproblems, their subproblems, and so on. The binary decision tree is gradually constructed.

From the description above, it is not clear how the attribute *atr* and the value *v* are chosen. Obviously, we must find the "best" combination of *atr* and *v*—the combination that will somehow "maximize" the information obtained by checking the condition *atr* ≤ *v*. In this way, the original sample set will be split into two more homogeneous subsets, namely the subsets with smaller variation of classes involved. That will lead to as small decision tree as possible. But how is information measured?

According to classical information theory, the *entropy* of the original sample set S is defined as

$$E(S) = -\sum_c p(c) \log_2 p(c)$$

where $p(c)$ is the probability that an entity of S belongs to the class c. After choosing the attribute *atr* and the value *v*, and after splitting the set S into two subsets, the resulting entropy will be

$$E(S, atr, v) = -p(atr \le v) \sum_c p(c|atr \le v) \log_2 p(c|atr \le v)$$

$$- p(atr > v) \sum_c p(c|atr > v) \log_2 p(c|atr > v)$$

Here $p(atr \le v)$ denotes the probability that an entity of S satisfies the condition $atr \le v$. Similarly, $p(c|atr \le v)$ is the conditional probability that an entity of S, already satisfying the condition $atr \le v$, also belongs to the class c. The remaining symbols are defined analogously. The *gained information* is measured by $E(S) - E(S, atr, v)$, so the optimal choice of atr and v is the one that minimizes $E(S, atr, v)$.

Numerical realizations of the described algorithm usually work as follows. For a given set S, many (or all) possible combinations of atr and v are generated. For each combination, the corresponding entropy $E(S, atr, v)$ is computed, so that the needed probabilities are approximated by statistics on S. Finally, the combination of atr and v yielding the smallest $E(S, atr, v)$ is chosen.

Let us apply the described algorithm to our concrete example of bankruptcy prediction (Table 5.2). Then, after some computation, the following decision tree (set of rules) is obtained:

if (debt/assets ratio $\le$ 30%) **then**
    firm is nonbankrupt
else
    if (current ratio $\le$ 1.9) **then**
        firm is bankrupt
    else
        if (debt/assets ratio $\le$ 60%) **then**
            firm is (probably) nonbankrupt
        else
            firm is bankrupt

The solution is visually presented by Figure 5.2. Our sample firms are again shown as points in the plane, with the ×'s corresponding to bankrupt firms and the dots corresponding to solvent ones. Similarly as the linear discriminant, our machine-learning algorithm tries to separate the ×'s from the dots by dividing the plane into regions. But now only vertical and horizontal lines are allowed as region boundaries. However, a number of nested divisions may be used. The resulting plane region corresponding to bankrupt and solvent firms, respectively, is no longer a half-plane but a union of "rectangles," as shown by shading.

Note that in Figure 5.2 two bankrupt sample firms are wrongly classified as nonbankrupt. This is only because our recursive splitting procedure was intentionally stopped on the third level. Since most of the firms in the remaining

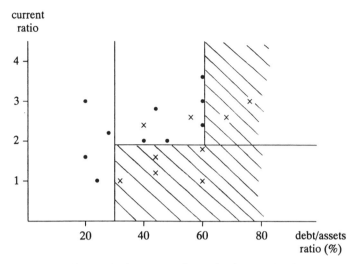

Figure 5.2   *"Rectangles" corresponding to bankrupt and solvent firms.*

set had been solvent, the conclusion was reached that a firm belonging to that set is "probably" solvent. Of course, by additional splitting, all sample firms could be correctly classified, but that would produce a more complex decision tree.

As we have seen from our exposition, artificial intelligence methods try to find a causal interpretation of the given sample data. In fact, they try to put more sense into data, and to derive an explanation for the captured classification process. According to our opinion, this can be dangerous for financial problems. Namely, those problems are quite intractable and noncausalistic. Sample sets always contain irregularities if not contradictions. Such irregularities will cause machine-learning methods to produce a number of complex rules, whose only purpose is to handle rare exceptional cases. An uninformed user can take those rules for granted and generalize them inappropriately.

5.3.3   Backpropagation-Layered Networks

Artificial neural networks are an interesting data processing paradigm that can be used for various purposes including classification. The basic processing element, the *neuron*, has one or more input channels (dendrites) and exactly one output channel (the axon). For any combination of input data arriving from its dendrites, the neuron produces an output and sends it through the axon. More neurons can form a network, so that an axon coming from one neuron is linked to a dendrite leading into another neuron. Still, some dendrites remain unconnected, and they provide input to the whole network. Similarly, some axons provide output from the network. A composite input to the network is called a *stimulus*, and the corresponding composite output is called the *response*.

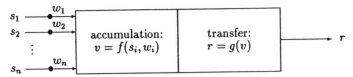

$s_1 \xrightarrow{w_1}$
$s_2 \xrightarrow{w_2}$
$\vdots$
$s_n \xrightarrow{w_n}$

accumulation:
$v = f(s_i, w_i)$

transfer:
$r = g(v)$

$\longrightarrow r$

Figure 5.3 *A conventional neuron.*

The network is expected to have the ability to "learn" a given set of stimulus-response associations. Learning is accomplished by some form of training, where the stimulus-response pairs are exposed to the network. After training, the network must be able to approximately reproduce the learned associations. Also, the network should produce a generalization of the learned associations; that is, it should respond plausibly to new stimuli.

Several authors have proposed various types of neural networks, which differ in neuron properties, network configuration, and training algorithms [6, 7]. A neuron is usually a very simple element built as shown in Figure 5.3. There, the real input values $s_1, s_2, \ldots, s_n$ are transformed into an intermediate value v, by using internally stored weights $w_1, w_2, \ldots, w_n$ and a given accumulation function f. The real output r is computed from v using a given transfer function g. The accumulation function f is usually the weighted sum; $v = \Sigma_{i=1}^{n} w_i s_i$. The transfer function g can be linear: $r = \text{const} \cdot v$, or it can be some kind of modulating function, such as sigmoid, hyperbolic tangent, and others.

If such simple neurons are used, then they must be organized into relatively complex networks in order to be able to solve problems. Thus a network normally consists of a large number of neurons, which can be grouped into layers. There always exists an input layer and an output layer of neurons. Additional "hidden" layers can be inserted between the input and the output layer, as shown in Figure 5.4.

Training is usually realized through an iterative procedure, where the stored weights are simultaneously modified in all neurons. The desired goal is to minimize (in the least square sense) the total error of responses to the sample

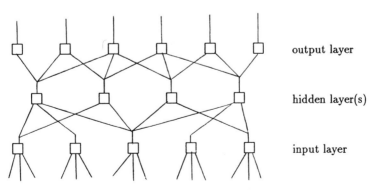

output layer

hidden layer(s)

input layer

Figure 5.4 *A layered network.*

stimuli. During one iteration, the weights are first updated in the last (output) layer, then the changes are successively propagated back from one layer to the previous layer. There are many variants of formulas for updating the weights—we speak about various training rules. After completed training, the network has "learned" the given stimulus-response associations, by optimally adjusting all its weights.

Networks built and trained in such a fashion are presently the most popular kind, and they are called *backpropagation-layered networks* [6, 7]. Problem solving consists of constructing a suitable network and of training that network. Thus, neither explicit mathematical formulas nor explicit rules are involved. Avoidance of exact models is desirable in "soft" knowledge disciplines, such as financial analysis.

Backpropagation-layered networks can directly be applied to classification problems. For this purpose, the list of all attributes has to be interpreted as the stimulus, and the corresponding class identifier must take the role of the response. The network is trained on the sample set of already classified entities. After training, the network will generalize each example; that is, for similar values of the attributes it will respond with the same class identifier.

To be more concrete, let us concentrate again to bankruptcy prediction. Then the corresponding network must use the package of all ratios as the stimulus, and the "bankrupt/solvent" indicator as the response. The network has to be trained on the sample set of firms. One expects that a well-designed and sufficiently large network will be able to memorize all the training examples and reproduce them correctly. Moreover, the network should generalize each example; that is, for similar values of the ratios it should produce the same "bankrupt/solvent" response. In our concrete two-dimensional case, the situation is illustrated by Figure 5.5.

The plane region corresponding to bankrupt and solvent firms, respectively, is neither a half-plane (as with the linear discriminant) nor a union of rectangles (as with the decision tree) but an area consisting of many irregular and disconnected "islands." So the network ideally adjusts itself to the training data; that is, all sample firms are classified correctly. Remember that this has not always been possible with the linear discriminant and has not been very practical with the decision tree. However, there is still a possibility that generalization of the sample data is not reliable enough, so that new firms are not always correctly classified. In our Figure 5.5 it corresponds to plane regions which are far from all islands. Network response for such points (firms) is more or less random. But similar difficulties occur also in statistical and machine-learning methods.

It has been observed that training of backpropagation-layered networks can be a time-consuming task, which can require, say, several thousands of iterations. Moreover, it can happen that the procedure does not converge at all, or that the final least squares error is unacceptably large. In all those cases we try to modify our network. We can change accumulation or transfer functions, the number of neurons, network configuration, or the training rule.

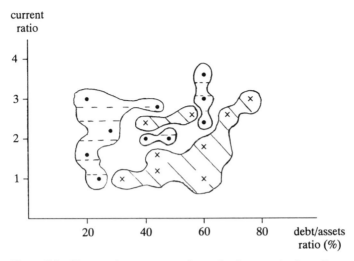

Figure 5.5 *Plane regions corresponding to bankrupt and solvent firms.*

5.4 HOLOGRAPHIC APPROACH TO CLASSIFICATION

Holographic networks are a new kind of artificial neural network that has recently been proposed by Sutherland [4, 8]. Although conforming to the general paradigm, this type of network significantly differs from the conventional backpropagation-layered type. The main difference is that a holographic neuron is much more powerful than a conventional one, so that it is functionally equivalent to a whole conventional network. Therefore there is no need to build massive networks of holographic neurons; for most applications one or few neurons are sufficient. Another important characteristic is that information is represented by complex numbers operating within two degrees of freedom (phase and magnitude).

In this section we first review some basic properties of holographic networks. Then we present a general idea how these networks could be employed for classification. The importance of stimulus preprocessing will be stressed.

5.4.1 Properties of Holographic Networks

A holographic neuron is sketched in Figure 5.6. There exist only one input channel and one output channel, but they carry whole vectors of complex numbers. An input vector S is called a stimulus, and it has the form

$$S = [\lambda_1 e^{i\theta_1}, \lambda_2 e^{i\theta_2}, \ldots, \lambda_n e^{i\theta_n}]$$

An output vector R is called a response, and its form is

$$R = [\gamma_1 e^{i\phi_1}, \gamma_2 e^{i\phi_2}, \ldots, \gamma_m e^{i\phi_m}]$$

Figure 5.6   *A holographic neuron.*

All complex numbers are written in polar notation, so that magnitudes are interpreted as confidence levels of data, and phase components serve as actual values of data. Confidence levels for these complex numbers typically extend over a probabilistic scale (0.0 to 1.0).

The neuron internally holds a complex $n \times m$ matrix X, which enables memorizing stimulus-response associations. Learning one association between a stimulus S and a desired response R reduces to the (noniterative) matrix operation:

$$X+ = S^T R$$

Note that all associations are enfolded onto the same matrix X. Since training is essentially a noniterative procedure, any convergence problem (mentioned in the previous section) is automatically avoided. The response $R*$ to a stimulus

$$S* = [\lambda_1^* e^{i\theta_1^*}, \lambda_2^* e^{i\theta_2^*}, \ldots, \lambda_n^* e^{i\theta_n^*}]$$

is computed through the matrix operation

$$R* = \frac{1}{c^*} S*X$$

Here c^* denotes a normalization coefficient given by

$$c* = \sum_{k=1}^{n} \lambda_k^*$$

The response $R*$ to a stimulus $S*$ can be interpreted as a point in the Riemann plane (i.e., a complex number) composed of many components, as shown in Figure 5.7. Each component corresponds to one of the learned responses. If $S*$ is equal to one of the learned stimuli S, then the corresponding response R participates in $R*$ as a component with a great confidence level (≈ 1). The remaining components have small confidence levels ($\ll 1$), and they produce a "noise" (error).

As we have seen, holographic neurons internally work with complex numbers. Since external data domains are usually real, a suitable data conversion is required. For this purpose the following simple transformation is used: real values from a known range $[a, b]$ are linearly scaled to the range $[0, 2\pi]$ and interpreted as phase orientations of complex values with a unity magnitude. In

error -

Figure 5.7 *Response to one of the learned stimuli.*

the rest of this text we will assume that all data have already been converted to complex.

Holographic networks are available on PCs through an emulator called HNeT [9]. In fact, HNeT is a run-time library of C functions. The user's application must be a program written in Microsoft C or Turbo C. By calling appropriate HNeT library functions, the application program can control the configuration of the emulated network. Similarly, the program can transfer data between the network and its own variables. Execution of working cycles in the network (learning steps, response steps) is also initiated through appropriate calls. Together with neurons, the HNeT system also emulates a number of auxiliary cell types. These are input cells that serve as buffers for data coming from an application program and operator cells that perform various data transformations.

5.4.2 A General Holographic Classifier

Holographic networks can be applied to classification problems in a similar way as ordinary networks. In principle, one holographic neuron is sufficient to accomplish the task. The list of all attributes is interpreted as the stimulus, and the corresponding class identifier as the response. However, since holographic neurons produce analog values, some kind of rounding should be applied when interpreting results. The simplest way is to divide the phase range $[0, 2\pi)$ for the response into an adequate number of equal regions. Each region will correspond to one class, as shown in Figure 5.8.

The required network in the HNeT system will consist of only few cells, as shown in Figure 5.9. The "neuron" cell in Figure 5.9 serves for memorizing stimulus-response associations. The two "buffer" cells serve for storing data coming from the application program. The first buffer cell holds a stimulus A, and the second cell holds the desired response B in the training phase. The computed response is designated with C. The network learning and generalization characteristics can be controlled only through some kind of stimulus preprocessing. This is symbolically shown in Figure 5.9 by introducing an additional "preproc" cell, which transforms the original stimulus A into a transformed vector $\overline{A}$.

To be more concrete, let us see how our general solution can be adapted for bankruptcy prediction. Since the firms are put into only two classes (i.e.,

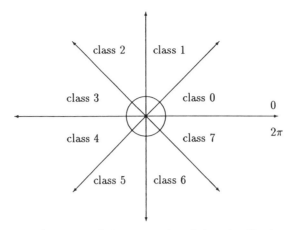

Figure 5.8 *Separation of phase range into distinct classification regions.*

"bankrupt" and "solvent"), the phase range $[0, 2\pi)$ for the response should be divided into two regions, for instance $[0, \pi)$ and $[\pi, 2\pi)$ respectively. The stimulus A has to be a vector consisting of all financial ratios (converted to complex). The desired response B will consist of only one complex number which serves as a code for "bankrupt" and "solvent" respectively. For instance, "bankrupt" can be designated with $e^{i(\pi/2)}$ and "solvent" with $e^{i(3\pi/2)}$. The computed response C is again one complex number, and its value is expected to be approximately equal to either $e^{i(\pi/2)}$ or $e^{i(3\pi/2)}$. However, other responses are also possible. Any value for C whose phase angle falls into the region $[0, \pi)$ will be interpreted as "bankrupt," while the remaining values will be treated as "solvent." The magnitude of C can be interpreted as the confidence level of the response; a magnitude close to 1 suggests a "resolute" response, while a small magnitude ($\ll 1$) indicates that the neuron is "not sure" about classifying the given firm.

The holographic bankruptcy predictor is expected to generalize the learned examples in a similar fashion as the backpropagation-layered network would do. So Figure 5.5, showing the "regions" that correspond to bankrupt and solvent firms, is still appropriate.

Finally, we will say something more about the reasons for stimulus preprocessing. It is obvious that a network designer must have some means to control the performance of his network. The two most important performance char-

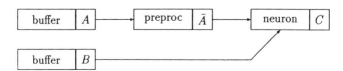

Figure 5.9 *General HNeT configuration for classification problems.*

acteristics are: The quality of reproduction and the quality of generalization. The first characteristic measures how well the network reproduces the learned associations, while the second is concerned with the response to new stimuli. We are interested in achieving a good quality of both reproduction and generalization.

Traditional backpropagation networks are normally controlled by choosing a right network configuration (i.e., the number of layers, neurons and connections). Also, there is a possibility to use various neuron types (i.e., various accumulation and transfer functions) or alternative training rules. For holographic networks, the situation is completely different. Network configurations are simple and do not allow much freedom of choice. Also, the way the neuron works is predefined and fixed. The only variable part of a solution is preprocessing of stimulus data, as shown in Figure 5.9. So, designing a good holographic network in fact means choosing an appropriate preprocessing method.

There are essentially two types of stimulus preprocessing, which are called symmetrization and expansion. Stimulus symmetrization redistributes complex elements within a stimulus vector to achieve more uniform phase distribution. Stimulus expansion increases the length of the stimulus vector (i.e., the number of vector elements). Generally speaking, symmetrization assures accuracy of encoded stimulus-response associations, while expansion increases encoding capacity. Both types of preprocessing can influence both the quality of reproduction and the quality of generalization.

For most classification problems, stimulus preprocessing is necessary to ensure a decent performance of the corresponding holographic classifier. More details about preprocessing can be found in Chapter 4, where concrete symmetrization and expansion methods are described. Those methods can readily be incorporated into our HNeT configuration (Figure 5.9). However, choosing a right preprocessing procedure is not always an easy task. For instance, a method that ensures an excellent quality of reproduction can degrade the network generalization capabilities. So it is desirable to have a list of alternative methods at disposal. Also, some experimenting is necessary in order to reach a compromise solution that satisfies multiple conflicting requirements.

5.5 CONCLUSIONS

Holographic networks are a very promising new type of artificial neural networks. Some of their advantages are:

- Simple network configuration
- Virtually noniterative training algorithm
- Possibility of incremental training
- Explicit control of generalization properties

Holographic networks possess all the virtues normally ascribed to traditional backpropagation networks. Hence, they avoid any strict mathematical modeling or explicit rules, and still lead to an accurate and flexible solution of classification problems. In addition, the solution obtained by holographic networks is simpler and more straightforward than the one obtained by ordinary networks.

Due to the foregoing reasons, we could recommend the use of holographic neural technology for classification. However, in the process of network design, the emphasis should be shifted from the choice of configuration to the choice of adequate data preprocessing. Namely, some sort of stimulus preprocessing may be needed in order to ensure a reliable performance of our holographic classifier. More information on preprocessing methods can be found in Chapter 4. The applications of holographic classifiers in quality control in manufacturing and in software evaluation are presented in Chapters 6 to 10.

REFERENCES

[1] D. B. Graddy and A. H. Spencer, *Managing Commercial Banks*, Prentice Hall, Englewood Cliffs, N.J., 1990.

[2] S. M. Weiss and I. Kapouleas, An empirical comparison of pattern recognition, neural nets, and machine learning classification methods, *Proc. 11th Internat. Joint Conf. Artif. Intellig.*, IJCAI-89, Vol. 1, Detroit, Michigan, Aug. 20–25, 1989, pp. 781–787.

[3] K. G. Coleman et al., Neural networks for bankruptcy prediction, *AI Rev.*, 48–50, (Summer 1991).

[4] J. G. Sutherland, Holographic model of memory, learning and expression, *Internat. J. Neural Syst.*, 1(3), 256–267 (1990).

[5] J. R. Quinlan, Induction of decision trees, *Machine Learning*, 1(1), 81–106 (1986).

[6] R. Hecht-Nielsen, *Neurocomputing*, Addison-Wesley, Reading, Mass., 1990.

[7] B. Souček and M. Souček, *Neural and Massively Parallel Computers*, Wiley, New York, 1988.

[8] B. Souček, *Fuzzy, Holographic and Parallel Intelligence*, Wiley, New York, 1992.

[9] J. G. Sutherland, *HNeT Development System, Version 1.0*, AND Corp., Hamilton, Ontario, 1990.

CHAPTER 6 _____

Quality Control in Manufacturing Based on Fuzzy Classification

GITTE JENSEN

6.1 INTRODUCTION

For many years, vision and neural networks have been discussed and investigated by scientists and researchers. But in the latest years there has been a growing interest in using these tools for industrial quality control applications. This chapter describes a variety of these quality control applications, which are based on neural networks, vision, or both. The applications will be divided into these three main areas in order to make an easy overview of the applications. These are concrete industrial applications and are based on techniques described in Chapters 3, 4, and 5.

6.2 VISION AND NEURAL NETWORK APPLICATIONS

6.2.1 Classification of Seed

Description. This application concerns quality control of seed and is performed by use of a spot test. This spot test determines the percentage of impurity of the seed. The manufacturers of the seed are then obliged to pay a fine according to the amount of impurities.

The impurities are defined as follows: The sample may contain four types of seed—barley, wheat, rye, and oats (Fig. 6.1). One of them is the correct seed, and grains from the others are defined as impurities. Today samples are

Frontier Decision Support Concepts, Edited by V. L. Plantamura, B. Souček, and G. Visaggio. ISBN 0-471-59256-0   © 1994 John Wiley & Sons, Inc.

Figure 6.1   *The four types of seed: (a) barley, (b) wheat, (c) rye, and (d) oats.*

drawn from the seed and a visual control is performed either manually or automatically by means of statistics. This control results in simple statistics consisting of the percentage of the four seed types.

Quality control is performed by a visual inspection of the shape of the seed grain. One of the main problems in seed classification is the variability of the seed grains. Using wheat as an example, the size and shape will vary due to the type of soil, amount of sun and/or rain, and type of wheat. Regarding the latter there is another problem. The shape of one specific type of wheat looks more like rye than any other type of wheat. The same variability can be transferred to the other sorts of seed.

The existing automatic system, based on statistics, has to be calibrated to each type of seed. This calibration can take up to one entire working day, due to the variability of the seed grains and the use of statistics. The direct result of the automatic system is the classification of the seed grains into two classes, good and bad. The good class contains the correct seed grains, and the bad class contains everything not falling within the good class—impurities and correct seed that differs from the standard. The bad class is then manually classified into all four types.

The demands on a new automatic system are

* Easy and fast calibration
* Classification rate of at least 30 seed grains per second with a maximum of 8 seed grains passing the camera at the same time
* Less than 15% of good seed thrown out as bad
* Less than 1% bad seed classified as good

Solution.   This description implies an easily trainable system, based on neural networks to obtain an easy calibration, and thereby reducing the amount of time needed for calibration. This also adds the facility to either start new training or to continue learning on an ''old'' neural network—incremental learning—in the system. This means that you can train the system, then turn it into classification mode. If the system makes a ''misclassification'' due to a nonrepresentative training set, you can train with the grain and then switch it to classification mode.

The seed classification system consists of a vision system containing a line-scan camera, from which the shape information is drawn. This is performed by use of different preprocessing algorithms. This implies that some mechanics have separated the seed grains before the line-scan camera. The neural network will classify the seed grain through the experience obtained by a presentation of classified seed shape data.

The system contains a user interface allowing the user to decide which seed grains to use in the training set. The shape data and the shape of the seed grain are shown on the screen in order to help this decision.

After controlling a spot test the statistics are shown on the screen, and the good and bad seed are physically separated, the bad ones on a tray so they are easy to check manually.

6.2.2 Optical Character Recognition on Labels

Description. The purpose of this system is to check the content, legibility, and print quality of impact-printed date/batch codes on labels. This means in addition to checking that the label carries the correct message, the system should also comment on the print quality and give warning of print degradation, allowing the line operator to take remedial action before products have to be rejected. The system must be capable of checking seven labels per second, where each label carries up to 24 characters in multiple lines of text.

Solution. The system solution is based on a combination of both neural network and rule-based techniques to perform the aforementioned demands of checking the content, legibility, and print quality. The input for the system is coming from a B/W camera with a precision closeup lens in order to obtain an adequate resolution.

The neural network makes the system capable of learning the appropriate codes and fonts. The entire character set is learned in one training session and stored on hard disk. The system then generalizes the learning to cope with reasonable variations in printing. For each batch of production, the required text is transmitted to the system by means of a standard RS-232 port (e.g., from a PC or programmable logic controller (PLC)) or via the keyboard. A trigger signal makes the system check all the following labels.

The system tolerates wide variations in the location of the text characters within its field of view, and tolerates also character-to-character spacing variations and a reasonable degree of rotation.

The system can also be used where the contents of the text is unknown. This just makes the system slower, as all possible characters in the set learned should be compared with those to be checked.

6.2.3 Sorting Bottles

Description. This classification application is especially developed for bottle recycling centers, where bottles are sorted by color, e.g., brown and green.

Until today many traditional color-sensing systems based on spot color measurement have been tried but rejected due to bad performance. Rejections of the systems are due to

Dirty bottles, having been collected from roadside bottletanks

Highly specular nature of glass, which reflects light in unpredictable ways

Large variation in color of bottles in the same class

The latter is due to the recycling, where broken glass in different colors is melted for new bottles. This may cause a highly variable content of green in brown bottles, and vice versa.

The bottles travel on a conveyor belt at a rate of up to 25 bottles per second. The bottles should be classified into two color classes. The classes should be able to represent more than one color, and the user should be able to change the colors of the classes.

Solution. The system for sorting bottles by color should be based on a color camera and a neural network. Hereby the possibility of learning new or other colors is obtained, and can be done by the user through a simple menu. The color camera makes the sorting better, as more than one spot of the picture is used.

The neural network makes the system capable of learning which bottle color belongs to which class, and to tolerate wide variations in the colors. To train the system, the class 1 button is pressed, and some class 1 bottles are sent down the conveyor. The same procedure is followed for class 2 bottles. Then the production button is pressed and the system is fully operational, classifying by the experience, it has gained about the difference between the two classes.

If at a later stage it is decided that, say, blue bottles also should be in class 2 (along with the green ones), simply press class 2, present the blue bottle, and then press production.

Other Bottle Applications. For bottle recycling centers other bottle applications have been developed, which, however, do not include neural networks. One of them is sorting wine bottles. Bottles with ''Bordeaux'' printed in the glass are more expensive, and should be reused and sent back to the producers of Bordeaux wine. The ''Bordeaux'' bottles should be separated from bottles without printing. This is performed by a rather simple check in an area surrounding the ''Bordeaux'' printing.

Another bottle application is sorting bottles by shape. The system is trainable and can easily learn new shapes. Each bottle is matched against all the different shapes the system has learned and the system will choose the shape that is closest.

6.3 NEURAL NETWORK APPLICATIONS

6.3.1 Welding Monitor

Description. This application concerns quality control of spot welding of cans for the food industry. Here it is very important that the weld be of a very high standard and 100% airtight in order to preserve the food; otherwise it might cause food poisoning. This demands 100% quality control; in other words, each can passing through the welding machine should be checked. The speed demand on the system is a maximum of 12 cans per second, but normally 6–8 cans per second.

To perform quality control of the welds three different signals should be used. For controlling the seam weld two signals should be used, namely the seam surface curve and the seam welding current curve. An accelerometer should be used to measure the surface (i.e., the vibration and roughness) of the seam weld on each can. Output from the accelerometer is a curve, of which examples are shown in Fig. 6.2. For the tongue weld 1 signal should be used, i.e. the tongue welding current curve. Control of these three signals should be performed independently of each other, and if one of them is defective the can should be thrown out. A bad weld is due to a number of different errors in the production line, each causing a slight change in the accelerometer curve or in the welding currents. In order to correct the process in-line, the defective cans should be classified into the different faults that occur. This is a desirable state, which should be approached.

Today, different traditional systems exist, which, to a certain point, are capable of detecting some of the bad cans, mainly from the welding current curves, as these should be within certain limits during the welding. The accelerometer curve cannot thoroughly be classified by a rule-based system, due

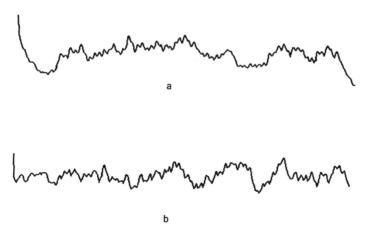

Figure 6.2 *Examples of weld curves: (a) defective can, (b) good can.*

to the high variance of the curves representing good cans. The high variance is due to different factors, such as a slight change in the alloy of the metal or the thickness of the metal.

Solution. The system has to be easily trainable—in other words, training must be performed in-line in real time, due to the variability of the accelerometer curve. This is solved by using neural networks and transputers in combination, neural networks to handle the variations and transputers for the in-line training. The system, however, is a combined traditional and neural-network-based system, as some of the faults, mainly from the welding current curves, are so obvious and easy to find that the neural network is not necessary here.

The cans are today separated into two classes, pass and fail, some by the neural network and some by the traditional system. To perform the fault classification another neural network will be trained to work in cooperation with the rest of the system, so only the curves of defective cans are presented to the "fault-classifying" neural network.

The three signals are all AD converted at a rate of 15.6 kHz, giving 156 samples for the tongue current and 4500 samples for both seam signals, before being presented to the quality control system.

6.3.2   Analysis of NIR Data

Description. Analysis of NIR (near-infrared reflection) data is a prediction application. A sample is exposed by infrared light and the reflection of the infrared light is measured as a percentage of the light exposed. The amount of data measured depends on the sample to be analyzed, but normally 19 NIR data equally distributed in the wavelength range of infrared light are used (see Fig. 6.3). These data are used to predict the proportion of protein, water, and

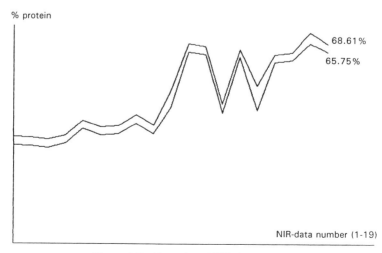

Figure 6.3   *Examples of NIR data curves.*

so forth, in the sample. This method is faster and cheaper but not as accurate as a chemical test performed in a laboratory.

Today systems based on look-up tables exist. The system's look-up tables are based on a combination of the accurate chemical tests and the NIR data of the same tests. Approximately 100–200 test samples are necessary to have a representative table. These systems, however, are not capable of following the change of proportions, from month to month and year to year. The problem for, say, protein is that a change in the content of water influences the entire NIR spectrum. The most protein-informative NIR data are data number 8, 9, 10, and 19 in the NIR spectrum, but these data are influenced by a proportion change of, say, water. This implies the variability of the NIR data.

Furthermore, the system should be able to tell when the NIR data sample presented falls outside the range represented by the table. When this happens, a chemical test has to be performed, and the test sample will be implemented in the look-up table.

The demands on the system are mainly concerned with accuracy, as the system only is for use in laboratories. The prediction has to be made with a maximum deviation of 0.05.

Solution. The NIR data analysis system has to be easily trainable, using the NIR data and the result of the chemical test, because the neural network has to be trained for each new product sample, such as oil and corn. This can be obtained by using a neural network. The neural network is, after training, capable of predicting the proportion of, for example, protein in a sample.

For the neural network to be able to follow a change in range of result, it should tell the certainty of the prediction. When this certainty is below a certain limit, a chemical test will be performed.

6.4 VISION APPLICATIONS

6.4.1 Sorting of Waste Bags by Color

Description. In Vejle, Denmark, a pioneering new scheme for waste management is running. As a part of this scheme, each household sorts its waste into two bags—green bags for organic material, black for plastics, etc.. For environmental purposes, the bags are made from *thin* biodegradable plastic, and so the apparent color of the bag changes depending on the contents. To save money, only one wastebin is provided for each household in which all bags are put. The bags are then collected and brought to a central sorting depot (see Fig. 6.4), where the green bags are separated for composting and the black bags are sent for incineration. The bags are placed on two conveyor belts traveling at 1.5 m/s. Complications arise if a black and a green bag are stuck together. In such cases the green bags must be sorted into the black bags due to the limitations of the mechanical "arms" that push the green bags off the

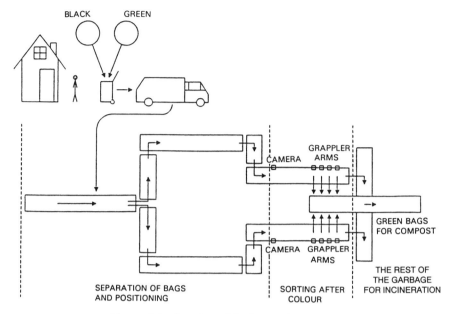

Figure 6.4 *Overview of the bag-sorting system.*

belt to another conveyor belt. A maximum of 6% green bags must be found between the black bags, and a maximum of 1% black bags must be found between the green bags.

Solution. The computer vision system consists of two color cameras, one for each conveyor belt. In order to meet the foregoing description the system checks over 16 pictures per second of each conveyor belt for green bags. When a green bag is detected, a signal is sent to the mechanical arms, which move the bag onto a separate conveyor belt.

The system has the logic built in to make sure that virtually no black bags get sent for composting, and that only a minor proportion of green bags are sent for incineration.

6.4.2 Colorimetry

Description. The colorimetry system is used and designed for checking the colors in a print process. This system checks the decoration on sheets of tinned steel of up to 1×1 m. The user should be able to define in which areas the system should measure. This master tinplate should then be learned by the system, and the data stored on disk. The user should be able to type in the product number and restore earlier settings. The system should check the new plate with the original metal plate and inform the user what colors are wrong and in which square.

Solution. The system will use a camera specially developed for this application to check up to 87,000 pixels. Each pixel's color is measured and classified as one out of over 16 million possible colors. It is possible to check up to 174,000 pixels with the camera, if desired.

The user will use a mouse to draw rectangles on the screen representing the areas the system should check.

Other Color Check Applications. Color check is a widely used quality control measure. It can be used in all areas, where the color is used for separation (e.g., medicine of different colors indicating different degrees of strength for use, say, morning, noon, and evening), sorting objects, boxes that should contain the same objects, and so forth. One of them is inspection of the cap colors of five metal-cap ampoules in a tray. The inspection technique is based on colorimetry plus specularity measurement. The system is able to check 100 trays per minute.

6.4.3 Check Sealing of Plastic Bags

Description. This application system is designed to perform quality control inspection on the plastic seals produced by roll bag machines. The system should measure the distance from the cut to the seal. This distance should keep a predefined value within a certain tolerance. If the distance is too small, the bag will easily break in the bottom. If the distance is too large, the handles of the following bag will break.

The system should be able to communicate with other industrial equipment. The external equipment should through the user be able to program the system to output a variety of different measurements and change the tolerance and predefined distance. The system should, as a minimum, be capable of checking five bags per second.

Solution. The system locates the edge of the stamped-out cut in the bags, and the centerline of the seal. From these parameters the distance between the two is measured. The system compares the measured distance with the programmed expected distance and performs a wide variety of statistical functions on the result.

The system uses optoisolated 24-V signaling to communicate with the other industrial equipment. By this communication the user is able to program the system to change the output of different measurements, and the tolerance and expected distance.

The system is capable of checking around 8–10 bags per second.

6.4.4 Grass Seed Inspection

Description. This system is designed to test the grass-cleaning process to see if the final grass seed product meets customers' specifications concerning amount

Figure 6.5   *Examples of seeds: (a) type 1, (b) type 2.*   a   b

of dirt and foreign seeds, size of the seed, and similar concerns. Different kinds of seeds are shown in Fig. 6.5.

The system should be able to discriminate fully between good and bad grass seed on the basis of size or percentage area of the kernel. Foreign objects larger and smaller than the previously defined parameters should be recognized. Furthermore, the system should perform some statistics on the sample results. The settings of these parameters should be stored on disk so that the system can be switched between all sorts of grass seed, quality, and so on.

The grass seed inspection system should check the specimen grass seed both interactively and automatically. In order to meet this specification the system should use a camera suitable for moving, free-fall, or still camera shots.

Solution.   The system is designed to discriminate fully between good and bad grass seed on the basis of the mentioned parameters. The statistics include the calculation of the ratio of good to bad seed and the running mean of sample results.

The system uses the variations in transparency of the seed to identify husk and kernel, and calculates their relative proportions. Any seed that crosses the boundary of the field of view is totally disregarded due to the size parameters.

In operation, the system has previously defined parameters to work from, which have been saved on disk according to type of seed, particular quality required, and so on. Therefore the user can simply load and start sampling automatically or interactively.

6.4.5   Check for Foreign Objects in Tobacco

Description.   The system is designed to detect foreign objects such as plastic, paper, or wires in a stream of cut tobacco. The detection should be based on color. This implies that all foreign bodies of the same color as tobacco cannot be detected.

The color of tobacco varies from very light brown to almost black, depending on the type. In order to meet this, the system should be easily trainable to check the different types. If the amount of pixels, which are outside the color range learned, exceeds a user-defined threshold for detecting a foreign object, the system should output an error signal.

Solution. The system is designed to detect foreign objects in a stream of tobacco using a specially developed color-map technique. The algorithm is implemented in software, but is designed so that it can be implemented in custom hardware as an upgrade to the system. The software implementation scans the field of view of a single camera at typically three frames per second. The camera used is special selected for optimal accuracy of color rendition.

In operation, the system is first trained to the desired range of colors by running a sample of tobacco past the camera with the system in *teaching* mode. Then the system is placed in *check* mode, where it measures the fraction of the material in view that lies outside the range of colors it has learned to accept, and flags an error if this fraction exceeds the user-selected level, indicating a foreign object in view. A variety of diagnostic and demonstration features are included as well.

The system could also be used for other materials.

6.4.6 Check Compressor Casting

Description. This system is specially developed to classify compressor castings into one of nine possible classes. The classes are based on the number (1–3) of markings (dot or line) embossed in two predefined areas on the casting. The result of the classification should be sent to other production-line equipment and be displayed. The system should be able to classify as a minimum one casting every 4 s.

Solution. Two cameras are used in the system, one for each area of interest on the casting. The system can differentiate *lines* and *dots* as markings and ignore spurious *dots* on *line*-marked castings by use of special lighting. All other demands are met.

6.4.7 Sorting Hot-Water Tanks by Height and Color

Description. The purpose of this system is to classify the type of the hot-water tank passing on a conveyer belt. Besides classification, the system should handle the statistics over the passing hot-water tanks for a predefined period (e.g., this shift, this day, or the entire month).

The hot-water tanks are made of metal, with top and bottom made of polystyrene. The former can be placed askew. The height of the hot-water tanks will be measured along with a color code. These will in combination be used for the type classification.

The height is 1000 to 2500 mm with a minimum 20-mm difference between the types. Seven colors can occur in the color code. The speed is 150 hot-water tanks per hour.

Solution. The system consists of two cameras, a monochrome for the height measurement and a color camera for the color code check. It is programmed with the connection between the color codes and the height so the type can be determined. Furthermore, the system will compensate for the askew mounting of the top, as this otherwise will cause some misclassifications.

It will be possible at any time to print the statistics or to send the data to another computer.

6.5 CONCLUDING REMARKS

In this chapter a variety of applications already implemented in the industry has been described. They show some of the possibilities and the many different areas where neural networks, vision, or both in combination can be used. This is only the beginning of a new era in quality control. Many new projects and applications will arise, even in areas not even thought of yet.

We hope this chapter has given some new ideas of where to use vision and neural networks for quality control.

ACKNOWLEDGMENTS

All applications mentioned are developed by KIA A/S or by KIA A/S in co-operation with QRO Systems.

CHAPTER 7

Quality Evaluation in Software Reengineering Based on Fuzzy Classification

FILIPPO LANUBILE
GIUSEPPE VISAGGIO

7.1 INTRODUCTION

Software quality is a concept that cannot be pinned down to a clear and universally accepted definition. A traditional view of the problem, inherited from hardware engineering, is to consider software quality synonymous with reliability, so that the activity of software quality assurance is reduced to inspecting and testing products to ensure lack of error. This point of view is highly restrictive as it does not take other characteristics into account, such as ease of use or modification, portability, performance, and so on, although these determine our preference for a given product.

The *IEEE Standard Glossary of Software Engineering Terminology* [1] provides the following definitions of *software quality*:

1. The totality of features and characteristics of a software product that bear on its ability to satisfy given needs; for example, conform to specification
2. The degree to which software possesses a desired combination of attributes
3. The degree to which a customer or user perceives that software meets his or her composite expectations

Frontier Decision Support Concepts, Edited by V. L. Plantamura, B. Souček, and G. Visaggio.
ISBN 0-471-59256-0   © 1994 John Wiley & Sons, Inc.

4. The composite characteristics of software that determine the degree to which the software in use will meet the expectations of the customer

The definitions speak of "given needs," "desired combination of attributes," "customer or user expectations." But is software quality then an objective or a subjective concept? Is it independent of the observer or can it be reduced to a mere question of personal taste?

If quality possesses an objective existence in a software product, whoever observes it, then it must be possible to recognize and measure it. If, on the other hand, it is subjective, then it is nothing other than the name we give the things we prefer. To escape from this dilemma, we must concede that quality is simultaneously objective and subjective [2]. In fact, although on the one hand we are all able to recognize opposite extremes (for example, when we agree that a graphical user interface of Windows type is better than a textual interface designed by an inexperienced programmer), in many cases the desired characteristics are in mutual contrast (for example, I might prefer an efficient program with lower possibilities of modification, or give priority to the capacity for modification, accepting a lower level of performance).

A change in observer changes the objective and it is therefore necessary to consider a number of models for quality measurement. A software component is seen as a point in a geometrical space, whose dimensions are determined by the quality model adopted and by the quality objective of interest.

Various techniques to classify software components are described: outlier analysis, threshold analysis, classification trees, score computation, and holographic learning. The use of appropriate techniques to design a decision support system for software reengineering is discussed. A new method for evaluating the quality of software components is based on holographic fuzzy learning. The holographic method is supported by the software package EVA. Fuzzy learning is described in Chapters 3, 4, and 5. The details on software metrics are described in Chapter 8.

7.2 SOFTWARE QUALITY MODELS

To make operational the theoretical concept of software quality it is best to break it down into lower-level characteristics, hierarchically organized, until finally primitive software characteristics are obtained, which correspond to the observable data.

Software quality models can be classified as static or dynamic. Static models offer predefined clusters of software characteristics, starting from primitive constructs that are operationally defined by sets of metrics. Dynamic models, on the other hand, enable the concept of quality to be adapted to the particular characteristics of the organization and the project. The most popular quality models in software engineering are described here.

7.2.1 McCall's Model

McCall et al. [3] subdivided software quality in three parts, according to the desired use of the product: *product operation, product revision*, and *product transition*. Starting from this first level, 11 quality factors can be identified:

- *Correctness:* How far a software system satisfies its specifications and attains the objectives set by the user.
- *Reliability:* How well a software system can perform the required functions with the desired precision.
- *Efficiency:* How many calculation and code resources are required by a software system to carry out a function.
- *Integrity:* How well nonauthorized access to the software or data is prevented.
- *Usability:* How much effort is required to learn, operate, and prepare the input data and interpret the output data in a software system.
- *Maintainability:* How much effort is required to localize and correct an error in a working software system.
- *Testability:* How much effort is required to test a software system and verify that it performs the expected function.
- *Flexibility:* How much effort is required to modify a working software system.
- *Portability:* How difficult it is to transfer a software system from a virtual machine (hardware configuration and/or software environment) to another.
- *Reusability:* How easy it is to use a software system in other applications.
- *Interoperability:* How easy it is to integrate a software system with another.

Behind this second level, a further 23 lower-level factors, called criteria, have been identified. These factors are connected to 41 composed metrics which in their turn use 175 elementary metrics. McCall's quality model is shown in graphic form in Figure 7.1.

McCall et al. also analyze the interrelationships between the quality factors, classifying them as *positive relationships* or *inverse relationships*. In particular, they show how efficiency has an inverse relationship with integrity, usability, maintainability, testability, flexibility, portability, reusability, and interoperability; usability has an inverse relationship with flexibility, portability, and interoperability; and reliability has an inverse relationship with reusability.

7.2.2 Boehm's Model

Boehm et al. [4] have a similar approach to McCall's but differ as regards some of the constructs and metrics proposed. They break software quality down

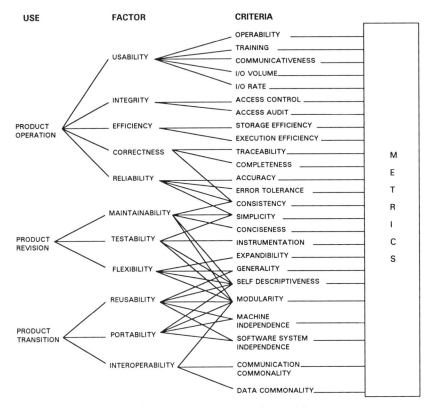

Figure 7.1 *McCall's quality model.*

into three other parts, primary uses, that are interconnected: *general utility*, *as-is utility*, and *maintainability*. From these, they obtain seven intermediate constructs: *portability, reliability, efficiency, human engineering, testability, understandability, modifiability*. Underlying this level there are 12 primitive constructs: device independence, completeness, accuracy, consistency, device efficiency, accessibility, communicativeness, structuredness, self-descriptiveness, conciseness, legibility, and augmentability. The primitive constructs are operationally defined by sets of metrics that act as guides to the collection of observable data. Figure 7.2 illustrates Boehm's quality model in graphic form.

7.2.3 GQM paradigm

The best-known and most fully experimented dynamic model is the goal/question/metric (GQM) paradigm [5]. The GQM paradigm is a mechanism for defining and assessing the goals of interest by using top-down measurement. A three-step approach is proposed for selecting and interpreting measures of

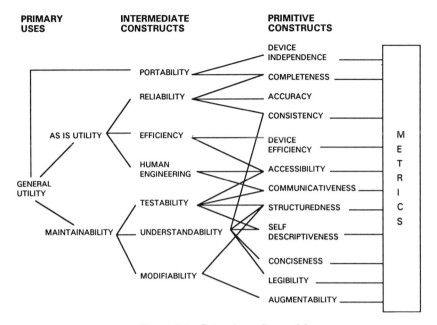

Figure 7.2 *Bohem's quality model.*

any kind, not only quality measures:

- Identify the organizational *goals*.
- Formulate the relevant *questions* for these goals.
- Select those *metrics* that respond to the questions asked.

The GQM paradigm also includes a set of templates for defining the goals and a set of guidelines for deriving the questions and metrics. The template parameters include the *purpose*, which describes the object of and reason for the measurement; *perspective*, which describes the focal point and who is interested; and finally, the *environmental characteristics*.

- *Purpose:* To analyze some objects (processes, products, methodologies, metrics, etc.) for some reason (characterization, assessment, forecasting, supplying reasons, improving, etc.).
- *Perspective:* To analyze a focal point of interest (costs, efficiency, defect elimination, changes, etc.) from the observer's point of view (i.e., user, customer, manager, designer, company, etc.).
- *Environment:* To analyze a given context (problem factors, human factors, resource factors, process factors, etc.).

For example, "analyze the integration test process in order to assess the efficiency from the designer's point of view."

The models generated by the GQM paradigm differ from one project to another and from one organization to another. Static models can be seen as specific examples of a GQM with preset models and metrics. The aim is to analyze a software product for assessment, but the perspective and environment remain generic.

7.3 DATA COLLECTION

The collection of the data required for measuring software quality thus needs a model that clearly indicates what to collect. The ''measure everything you come across'' approach indicates scientific immaturity, demonstrating the lack of a theoretical reference model.

Data collection methods differ according to the typology of the measurement. Product measures can be obtained automatically with analyzers that extract the data directly from the source code. The presence of CASE (computer-aided software engineering) tools, which enables models to be created and information saved on project data bases, also makes it possible the automatic extraction of metrics referring not to the final product but to the models created during the analysis and design phases.

While the collection of product measures can also occur in an asynchronous fashion with respect to the development process, the collection of process measures requires timely intervention, since most of the information is of a volatile nature, as it depends on the time factor. For example, to know the number of modifications a module has had to undergo, it is necessary to record the information before a new change is made, as the product will only show the effects and have no trace of its history. Process measures are generally obtained by means of questionnaires or forms to be filled in manually, like the weekly report, for example, which programmers must fill in, describing in detail what activities they have carried out, on what objects and for how long. In the future, the realization of technological support to all the software development processes, tracing all the events in the project's history, will make it possible to automize the collection of process measures, too.

7.4 DATA INTERPRETATION TECHNIQUES

As software quality is modeled by a number of characteristics, some of which are in mutual contrast [6], it is necessary to consider a *metric vector* $X = (x_i)$, composed of the metrics that quantify the primitive characteristics of the quality model adopted. A software component, be it a simple module or a composed module, can be seen as a point in a geometrical space, whose dimensions are determined by the quality model adopted and by the quality objective of interest. In fact, the *quality objective* (QO) has its corresponding metric vector $X_{QO} \subseteq X$, whose metrics are included in the transitive closure of the subgraph having QO as initial node. Thus the same software component may be subject to different quality evaluations, according to the goal being pursued.

Once a multidimensional quality measurement system is available, the problem arises of how to relate two elements to a quality objective whose metric vector X_{QO} has more than one dimension. It is possible, for example, to define the following partial order relation on X_{QO}: Given two components A and B, to which the metric vectors (a_i) and (b_i) are respectively associated, we can say that

$$A > B \Leftrightarrow \forall i : a_i > b_i$$

This relation is not very useful, as it is not possible to compare elements that are not covered by the partial order. For example, if A has a value of (3, 48) and B of (13, 28), which must be considered better with respect to the quality objective incorporating these measures? The limits set by the partiality of the relation become more restrictive as the number of dimensions of the metric vector increases.

This kind of problem arose in the past when some researchers proposed the use of composite metrics to measure software complexity [7–9]. For example, in [7], the couple (cyclomatic complexity, Halstead's effort) is proposed as complexity metric.

Nowadays, various techniques for interpreting data exist that use vectors of measures. Some can classify the components according to how critical they are, while others also enable intercomparison of the elements.

7.4.1 Outlier Analysis

Outlier analysis consists of localizing those software components having higher values for some metrics of the vector X_{QO}. In [10], the outliers are identified by ordering the components for each dimension of the metric vector and selecting the first positions for each ordered list.

The outlier analysis technique is only effective if there is a limited number of critical components, since only the relatively higher values are selected, without verifying whether there may be other values that make the components unacceptable. There is therefore a risk of underestimating dangerously complex systems.

7.4.2 Threshold Analysis

The technique of threshold analysis involves the division of the metric values composing the metric vector into intervals delimited by threshold values. Each time a measure goes beyond the threshold value, an anomalous situation has occurred, which must be justified. If the number of thresholds is identical for each metric vector dimension, then it is possible to associate meanings to the intervals, connected with the quality of the software component. For example,

TABLE 7.1 Threshold Analysis per $X_{maintainability}$

	Safe Zone	Flag	Alarm
LOC	< 50	[50, 100]	> 100
Effort	< 50000	[50,000, 100,000]	> 100000
$v(G)$	< 10	[10, 20]	> 20

in [11], for the metric vector $X_{maintainability}$ = (LOC, Effort, $v(G)$), three intervals are defined: safe zone, flag, and alarm. The values associated with the metric vector are shown in Table 7.1.

However, the threshold analysis technique does not specify how to compose signals coming from different dimensions with respect to the metric vector. If inspection of the components flagged as critical is activated when at least one metric exceeds the safe zone, there is a risk of flag overload with respect to components whose improvement is not proportional to the effort required. On the other hand, if inspection of the critical components is set in motion when all the measures of the metric vector have exceeded the alarm threshold, there is a risk of ignoring many problems that may arise later in the life cycle of the software.

7.4.3 Classification Tree

A classification tree uses the quality measures of the metric vector to study the difference between the software components. Classification trees were used by Porter and Selby [12] to identify components subject to error and by Esteva and Reynolds [13] to recognize reusable components.

A classification tree is automatically constructed by means of inductive learning by example. The training set is composed of historical data or heuristics, which contain both positive and negative data with respect to a target class represented by the quality objective. A decisional procedure is created to discriminate the components of different classes, using the values of the measures in the metric vector. The decisional procedure is modeled like a tree whose leaf nodes contain the final values of the target class. For example, if the quality objective is reliability then the final values of the target class can be reliable (+) or unreliable (−). Each nonterminal node of the classification tree corresponds to a metric. The edges of the classification tree correspond to an interval of metric values belonging to the father node. It is not necessary for all the metrics to appear in the classification tree, and in the same way it is possible to have several intermediate nodes with respect to the same metric. An example of a classification tree relative to the metric vector $X_{maintainability}$ = (LOC, Effort, $v(G)$) is shown in Figure 7.3.

The most common algorithm for generating the classification tree is based on Quinlan's ID3 system [14]. The algorithm uses information theory principles, applying them top-down. The measures of the metric vector must have

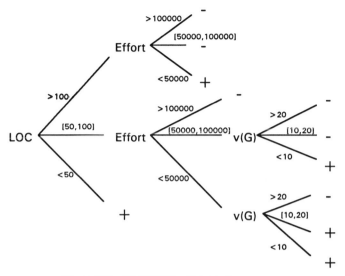

Figure 7.3 *Classification tree per $X_{maintainability}$.*

discrete and mutually exclusive values. If the values of a metric are continuous, then they must be transformed into value intervals having the same properties. These restrictions make it possible to define an equivalence relation between the software components, which partitions them in mutually exclusive and exhaustive target classes.

Let O be the set of objects to be classified. The classification tree is constructed as follows:

- If O is empty or all the objects in O belong to the same target class, then the current node is a leaf node and terminal.
- Otherwise select a metric x_i with the greatest discriminative power on O, partition O into the subsets O_j, create the children nodes corresponding to the partitions, and, for each subset O_j, invoke the algorithm recursively with the set of remaining metrics.

The selection of the metrics is obtained by an assessment function that judges the metric's ability to partition the objects in homogeneous subsets. The metric to be chosen must be the one that minimizes entropy, as the aim of the classification tree is precisely that of identifying objects belonging to different classes.

Once the classification tree has been constructed for a development environment, it is used to recognize the critical components whose paths in the tree lead to a negative target class.

The granularity of the classes in a classification tree determine its precision. In fact, in a classification tree, the elements that can be compared belong to different target classes. To increase the number of comparable elements it is necessary to increase the number of classes considered, restricting the intervals of continuous values of the metric vector measures. However, the use of many different classes also increases the amount of data needed to construct the tree.

7.4.4   Score Computation

To define a total order relation on software components, Conte et al. [15] declared that the ideal would be to be able to combine all the measures of a metric vector so as to produce a single magnitude that would be comparable with those of all the other components.

Let QO_i $(1 \leq i \leq n)$, be a quality objective which interests us, for example maintainability. To each quality objective m_i primitive metrics are associated. Let x_{ij} be the value of the jth metric associated with the ith quality objective. To be able to manipulate values of different metrics, having different orders of magnitude between themselves, it is necessary to apply a normalization function, $S: \{x_{ij}\} \rightarrow [0, 1]$, which aligns all the metrics on a common scale, constituted by the set of real numbers between 0 and 1. The *score* SC_i relative to the ith quality objective QO_i is calculated as follows:

$$SC_i = \sum_{j=1}^{m_i} S(x_{ij})$$

The *total score*, including all the quality objectives, is thus calculated as

$$SC = \sum_{i=1}^{n} \sum_{j=1}^{m_i} S(x_{ij})$$

The formula can be made more flexible by introducing a set of weights, $\{w_{ij}\}$, that takes into account the relative importance of the primitive characteristics with respect to the quality objective, and the importance attributed to the quality objective by our quality model.

$$WSC = \sum_{i=1}^{n} \sum_{j=1}^{m_i} w_{ij} \times S(X_{ij})$$

where $w_{ij} \in [0, 1]$ and $\Sigma w_{ij} = 1$.

Quality Level. *Quality level* is a normalized score, proposed in [16], based on the dichotomy between essential and language-oriented design.

Essential design is a normalized specification of a software structure. It considers the physical environment as perfect from the technological point of view, as its aim is to construct a software structure to satisfy the required objectives while respecting the principles of software engineering. Language-oriented design, on the other hand, is derived as a specialization of essential design that takes into account the limits of the specific programming environment and in particular the programming language. Thus, language-oriented design expresses the resulting software system just as it has been realized. More detailed information on essential and language-oriented design, together with the diagrams for data base design, is found in [17].

The software quality measured in the essential design is the limit toward which the quality measures in language-oriented designs should be aimed. In fact, as it does not depend on any particular programming environment, essential design is constructed taking into account only the quality objective regarded as most suitable. When the quality level is calculated, a language-oriented design represents a viable solution, whose quality should be as near as possible to that of essential design, which constitutes the best possible solution.

Let e_i be the ith metric of a metric vector of n dimensions associated with an essential design component, and let lo_i be the same metric applied to the corresponding component in a language-oriented design. The fundamental axiom for calculating the quality level is

$$\forall i \in [1, n] : e_i \leq lo_i$$

This axiom is supported by the empirical results in [18] that show how the values of the measures grow after each design decision during the software life cycle.

To normalize the metrics associated with the quality objective, let us introduce a scaling function vector S, such that

$$S_i(lo_i) = \begin{cases} 1 & \text{if } lo_i = e_i = 0 \\ 1 - \dfrac{lo_i - e_i}{lo_i + e_i} & \text{otherwise} \end{cases}$$

A *scaling function* measures the distance of a quality metric relative to a language-oriented solution from the equivalent quality metric in essential design. The value calculated by the scaling function is a real number varying from 1 to 0. The scaling function is more sensitive to the differences as e_i nears zero value. This correlates with the observation that, given a quality metric, the difference noticed between the values 1 and 10 is more significant than that between 1000 and 1010.

A vector of normalized weights W specifies the politics that defines the relative contribution of the metrics of X_{QO} to the quality objective QO. This politics may depend on both collected historical data and subjective judgment. If there are not enough elements for a decision to be possible, it is assumed that the measures composing the metric vector have the same importance.

Given a quality objective QO, an essential design E, a language-oriented solution LO, a scaling function vector S, and a weight vector W, the quality level is calculated as

$$QL(E, LO, W) = \sum_i w_i \times S_i(lo_i)$$

It is possible to define a total order relation on the set of solutions for a software component, whereby

$$LO_X \text{ improves } LO_Y \text{ with respect to QO and } E \Leftrightarrow$$

$$QL(E, LO_X, W) > QL(E, LO_Y, W)$$

The calculation of the quality level does not necessarily require a great quantity of historical data to define threshold values or target classes. A lack of historical data on which to base the software quality evaluation is very common in those development environments that most need the control of risks connected with degraded software. The calculation of the quality level supplies this lack by using weights that can be assigned according to the preceding experience, or else by leaving the weights equal when there is not enough information.

Using the Quality Level during Software Evolution. The evolution of a software system is subject to laws, which Lehman calls the *laws of program evolution* [19]. The first, *law of continuing change*, decrees that a software system used in a real environment is permanently subjected to pressures for its modification until it finally becomes more economical to replace it. The second, *law of increasing complexity*, decrees that these modifications degrade the original structure of the software system, thus increasing its complexity, unless a contrary push is made to control the increasing entropy.

The quality level can be used to control the degradation of quality in a system or software component and give warning when it is no longer acceptable. The organization defines what quality level value must be considered the tolerance limit. Figure 7.4 shows a graph of the quality-level values relative to a subsystem as it varies with the modifications made.

The quality level can also be used as coefficient of the technical quality in assessing the portfolio of applications in an organization [20]. Figure 7.5 shows a grid with four quadrants in which the programs are positioned according to their strategic importance and the quality level. The project manager must define which subject areas and functions are relevant to the organization and establish threshold values for the quality levels that make it possible to distinguish between the programs as regards a quality objective.

- Quadrant I contains programs with a low valuation as regards utility and quality. These programs must be discarded or substituted. The advisability of purchasing an applicative package from third parties must be examined, bearing in mind that their poor importance does not justify costly investments.

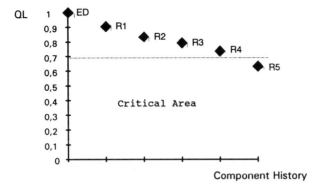

Figure 7.4 *Entropy control by means of quality level.*

- Quadrant II contains programs not considered to be very useful but of good quality. These must be frozen: in other words, no maintenance should be carried out.
- Quadrant III contains programs regarded as important by the user and of good quality. These programs do not need preventive measures to be taken but must be modified only when the requests for changes are made directly by the user.
- Quadrant IV contains programs with a high strategic importance but of poor quality. These programs are the first candidates for reengineering.

In general, system maintenance workers must endeavor to control the entropy of the application so that, once built, the programs stay in the third quadrant and do not require radical intervention.

The quality level can also be useful at a lower level of abstraction, which takes into account both simple and compound modular components. The applications are in a state of continual change, and this obliges us to define

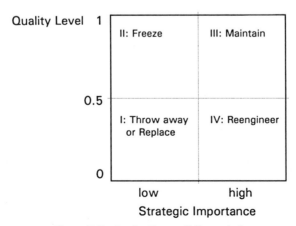

Figure 7.5 *Application portfolio analysis.*

TABLE 7.2 Priorities for the Required Changes

Components	QL (rel)	Rank (corr)	QL (port)	Rank (adapt)	QL (flex)	Rank (perf)
module1	0.7113	6	0.1538	12	0.6222	5
module2	0.8312	3	0.3387	9	0.8088	3
module3	0.5426	7	0.3543	8	0.5063	8
module4	0.7160	5	0.0013	14	0.2245	11
module5	0.7621	4	0.9462	1	0.9103	1
module6	0.8950	2	0.9264	2	0.4716	9
module7	0.4932	8	0.2767	10	0.0450	14
module8	0.3014	11	0.4918	6	0.1791	12
module9	0.0675	14	0.8563	3	0.8424	2
module10	0.4192	9	0.8407	4	0.4426	10
module11	0.4095	10	0.2052	11	0.1097	13
module12	0.2637	12	0.6032	5	0.5552	7
module13	0.0969	13	0.4796	7	0.5978	6
module14	0.9948	1	0.0894	13	0.6738	4

priorities as regards modifications, according to the urgency of the real needs. Table 7.2 shows the quality levels calculated for three different quality objectives. By choosing reliability as the quality objective, the ranks obtained ordering the quality levels of the components give priority to the corrective modifications. When portability is the quality objective, priority is assigned to the adaptive modifications. Finally, choosing flexibility as quality objective defines which components are most suited to perfective-type modifications.

7.4.5 Holographic Learning

A new method for evaluating the quality of software components is based on *holographic fuzzy learning*. Problem solving using a new holographic paradigm [21–23] consists of constructing a suitable network and training that network. Thus, no explicit mathematical modeling is involved, no algorithm design and no programming are needed, provided that a network simulator is available. Avoidance of exact models is desirable in ''soft'' knowledge disciplines, such as software evaluation.

In order to apply holographic networks to software evaluation the metric vector, which comprises all the acquired metrics, has to be interpreted as a stimulus, and the ''good/poor'' attribute must take the role of a response. The network is trained on a sample set of software components. A sufficiently large network will be able to memorize all the training associations and reproduce them correctly. Such a network will also generalize each association; that is, for similar metrics values it will produce the same response. The network comprises a holographic association map. Holographic learning derives its operational efficiency from its ability to superimpose multiple fuzzy metrics–category associations within exactly the same correlation set, composed of complex numbers or vectors. The analog information content is assigned to the phase orientation of the vector. The associated vector magnitude indicates the confidence bounded within a probabilistic range (0 to 1). The user can establish a threshold level for a given confidence value to define the module categories.

The holographic method is supported by a software package *EVA* composed of three main modules: analysis classification, simulation/testing, and user-friendly interface. The package was used for the evaluation of software modules produced by a controlled group of students, obtained from a software house, and derived from a large data base.

The evaluation of software packages by means of holographic fuzzy learning is a new method. Its characteristic features include accuracy, flexibility, defined confidence level, and high speed. The method avoids classification rules and focuses on data and facts. In this respect the holographic method presents a fundamental divergence from rule-based expert systems such as classification trees. Moreover it differs greatly from connectionist neural computing, as a holographic neuron is much more powerful than a conventional one and therefore there is no need to build a huge network. For more details on holographic learning and classification, see Chapters 3, 4, and 5.

REFERENCES

[1] *IEEE Standard Glossary of Software Engineering Terminology*, ANSI/IEEE Std. 729-1983.

[2] R. M. Pirsig, *Zen and the Art of Motorcycle Maintenance*, 1974.

[3] J. A. McCall, P. K. Richards, and G. F. Walters, "Factors in Software Quality," Tech. Rep. 77CISO2, General Electric, Command and Information Systems, Sunnyvale, Calif., 1977.

[4] B. W. Boehm, J. R. Brown, H. Kaspar, M. Kipow, G. J. MacLeod, and M. J. Merrit, *Characteristics of Software Quality*, North Holland, Amsterdam, 1978.

[5] V. R. Basili and H. D. Rombach, The TAME project: Towards improvement-oriented software environments, *IEEE Trans. Software Eng.*, 14(6), 758–773, (June 1988).

[6] N. Abbattista, G. Piscitelli, and G. Visaggio, The software complexity vector, *Proc. 10th European Computer Measurement Assoc.*, Munich, Germany, 1982.

[7] A. L. Baker and S. H. Zweben, A comparison of measures of control flow complexity, *IEEE Trans. Software Eng.*, SE-6(6), 506–512 (November 1980).

[8] W. J. Hansen, Measurement of program complexity by the pair (cyclomatic number, operator count), *ACM SIGPLAN Notices*, 13(3), 29–33 (March 1978).

[9] G. J. Myers, An extension to the cyclomatic measure of program complexity, *SIGPLAN Notices*, 12(10), 61–64 (October 1977).

[10] D. Kafura and G. R. Reddy, The use of software complexity metrics in software maintenance, *IEEE Trans. Software Eng.*, SE-13(3), 335–343 (March 1987).

[11] J. A. Lewis and S. M. Henry, On the benefits and difficulties of a maintainability via metrics methodology, *Software Maintenance: Res. Practice*, 2, 113–131 (1990).

[12] A. A. Porter and R. W. Selby, Empirically guided software development using metric-based classification trees, *IEEE Software*, 46–54, (March 1990).

[13] J. C. Esteva and R. G. Reynolds, Learning to recognize reusable software by induction, *Internat. J. Software Eng. Knowledge Eng.*, 1(3), 271–292 (1991).

[14] J. R. Quinlan, Induction of decision trees, *Machine Learning*, 1(1), 81–106 (1986).

[15] S. D. Conte, H. E. Dunsmore, and V. Y. Shen, *Software Engineering Metrics and Models*, Benjamin/Cummings, Menlo Park, Calif., 1986.

[16] F. Lanubile and G. Visaggio, Software maintenance by using quality levels, *Proc. Workshop on Software Quality: Measurement and Practice*, Napoli, 43–51 1992.

[17] F. Lanubile and G. Visaggio, Maintainability via structure models and software metrics, in *Proc. Fourth Internat. Conf. Eng. Knowledge Eng.*, IEEE Computer Society Press, Los Alamitos, Calif., 1992.

[18] R. G. Reynolds, Metrics to measure the complexity of partial programs, *J. Syst. Software*, 4, 75–91 (1984).

[19] M. M. Lehman, Programs life cycles, and laws of software evolution, *Proc. IEEE*, 68(9), 1060–1076, (September 1980).

[20] G. G. Verdugo, Portfolio analysis—managing software as an asset, *Proc. Sixth Internat. Conf. Software Maintenance Management*, 1988.

[21] B. Souček and IRIS Group, *Fuzzy, Holographic, and Parallel Intelligence*, Wiley, New York, 1992.

[22] J. Sutherland, A holographic model of memory, learning and expression, *Internat. J. Neural Syst.*, 1(3), 259–267 (1990).

[23] J. Sutherland, "A Holographic Neural Method," in B. Souček and IRIS Group, *Fuzzy, Holographic, and Parallel Intelligence*, Wiley, New York, 1992.

CHAPTER 8

Software Quality Metrics as an Input to Fuzzy Classifiers

FILIPPO LANUBILE
GIUSEPPE VISAGGIO

8.1 INTRODUCTION

The main goal of software quality metrics researchers is to transform the software field into an engineering activity inspiring the same trust in software products as is felt today in products of other more consolidated engineering fields like civil, mechanical, or electronic engineering. To avoid reducing software engineering to the level of a list of good intentions, it is necessary to proceed according to the methods of modern science. In fact, one of the weaknesses of computer science in its present state is its poor adaptability to measurement, which holds it back nearer to scholastic science than to modern science, in which knowledge is based on measurement.

In order to develop a scientific theory, the theoretical constructs must be connected to observable data. From this point of view, the theories in physical science are well developed, as the relations take the form of formal equations, while the theories in behavioral science are less well developed, since it is logically presumed that such relations exist and the arguments are only supported by correlation studies of the statistical type. A nonscientific theory, on the other hand, is characterized by nonoperational theoretical constructs whose arguments are expressed verbally and whose acceptance is based on their supported reasonableness.

The theories of computer science are distributed along this scale of scientific viability. For example, theories like the one on reliability [1] or on the com-

Frontier Decision Support Concepts, Edited by V. L. Plantamura, B. Souček, and G. Visaggio.
ISBN 0-471-59256-0   © 1994 John Wiley & Sons, Inc.

putational complexity of algorithms [2] are based on a set of axioms, on formally defined relations with a mathematical base, and on the validation of the equations with real data. In the theories studying the psychological aspects of software,* on the other hand, the scientific level diminishes. The theory that structured programming induces a lower number of errors in the programs, for example, is not based on formal equations, although there are many experimental studies, discussed in [4], that analyze the correlation between theory and real data. Many development methods presented as final solutions to the problems of software, are lacking not only in formal relations but also in any reference that could be verified by observations belonging to the real world.

For the above reasons, the development of scientific theories on which to base any engineering (in this case software engineering) requires a measurement system to be defined.

The first section of this study sets out the basic foundations of the theory of measurement, analyzing the measurement of software quality in depth, while the second describes the most common product metrics in the software engineering field. These metrics are given as input to the classification system EVA, based on the holographic networks. The system supports the decision making in two areas: product and process quality evaluation. The third part of this study analyzes the use of measures in the software life cycle.

The details of software quality evaluation based on holographic networks are described in Chapter 7.

8.2 MEASUREMENT AND ANALYSIS

A metric μ is a function of A in B, there A is a model made up by empirical objects and empirical relationships between these, while B is a formal model made up by formal objects (like numbers, for example) and operations on these. A measurement system may therefore be seen as a homomorphism between the world of theoretical constructs and the world of numbers. In this study we shall use the term *metric* when referring to the function and the term *measure* when considering the result of the application of the function, which often assumes the form of a simple number.

8.2.1 What Is a Software Quality Metric?

A *software metric* is a metric whose input is obtained from observations made on the products or processes of a software project and whose output is a number or a vector of numbers. Some examples of software metrics are the number of instructions in a module, the number of variables in a program, the development

---

*The psychological aspects of software are considered to be the characteristics that influence human performance, since software development and maintenance activities are largely human activities [3].

cost of an application, the number of errors occurring during testing or the percentage of time spent on debugging.

A *software quality metric* constitutes a further refinement in the concept of metrics. A software quality metric is a function in which the input is composed of observables or software measures and the output is a numerical value M, scaled or vectorial, that can be interpreted as the degree to which the software object (product or process) possesses a given attribute affecting its quality. Indeed, the general concept of quality can be considered as the abstraction of a set of attributes that we shall call *quality factors*, for which reason the standard definition of software quality [5] refers to the degree to which the software possesses a desired combination of attributes.

One or more metrics can be associated with a quality factor, called *direct metrics*, as they provide a numerical indicator of a quality aspect as it is perceived by the user. The attribution of a direct measure to a quality factor is made intuitively and is not subject to statistical validation. For example, error count or error density are considered direct metrics of the quality factor reliability.

An *indirect metric*, on the other hand, is a metric presumed to be related to the quality factor of interest and could therefore be used instead of a direct metric if this were not available. Since the relationship between the quality factor and the indirect metric lacks immediacy, it is necessary to construct a theoretical model explaining the relationship between the indirect metric and the quality factor, and to demonstrate the existence of this relationship by statistical validation of the indirect measures with the direct ones, with respect to the same software object. For example, the number of global variables in a program can be considered an indirect measure of its modifiability. To support this claim, a relationship must be modeled between implicit intermodular communication and the inconsistency of the modifications, and then the correlation between the number of global variables and the number of residual errors after a modification must be analyzed.

8.2.2 Measurement Scales

For a correct use of statistical techniques that verify the relationship between the direct and indirect measures of a quality software characteristic, it is necessary to know the measurement scale. The measurement theory subdivides the measures into four basic types, as shown in Table 8.1.

1. *Nominal Scale.* The term *nominal scale* refers to data that subdivide the objects of interest into categories. For example, an application can be classified as function oriented or data oriented, or a program can be classified as defective or nondefective. The only possible operation between two measures in nominal scale is verification as to whether they belong to the same group.

2. *Ordinal Scale.* An *ordinal scale* involves a total order relation defined on the set of components. As a result, each component has its own *rank*, which

TABLE 8.1 Measurement Scales

Scale	Operations*	Description	Examples
Nominal	=, ≠	Categories	Presence of defects, function orient. vs. data orient.
Ordinal	<, >	Rankings	Level of programming experience Index of program comprehension
Interval	+, −	Significant differences	Programming time Debugging time
Ratio	÷	Significant ratios	Error number Instruction number

*Operations are also inherited from lower scales.

can be compared with that of other components to establish whether it is greater or less. For example, the level of programming experience or program comprehension can be expressed on an ordinal scale.

3. *Interval Scale.* An *interval scale* refers to measures with significant differences. In addition to its properties of equality and ordering, addition and subtraction operators can be applied and simple statistics like means can be calculated. For example, time measures, like the number of days it took to develop a program or the number of hours to carry out a modification, are of the interval type, as the difference between 10 and 20 is perceived as the same as the difference between 20 and 30.

4. *Ratio Scale.* A *ratio scale* refers to measures whose ratios, apart from having the properties of equality, ordering, and significant differentiation, possess significance. The existence of an absolute zero makes it possible to measure the distance of a measure from its absolute absence, and therefore to use the multiplication and division operations so as to be able to affirm that a measure is n times another measure. For example, the number of errors in a program is in ratio scale, as also the number of instructions.

8.2.3 Metric Validation

Metric validation consists of proving that an indirect measure is associated with a direct measure of a quality factor, so that it may be possible to use the indirect measure instead of the direct one, since the former is available earlier in the software life cycle. Metric validation requires a cause-effect model and a correct application of statistics.

It is well to stress at this point that the great availability of statistical packages must not lead to the error of undervaluing the theoretical thinking that is at the basis of any scientific experiment. Thus, it is necessary to set up a reasoning model that explains the indirect metric–direct metric relationship as a cause-effect one.

A full review of the experimentation in software engineering can be found in [6]. In general terms, we can say that there is a conflict between small- and large-scale experimentation. Small-scale experiments, common in research laboratories, possess internal validity, thanks to the rigorous control of external factors, but they are lacking in external validity, as their results tend not to be of generalized use. In [7], an experiment was carried out to validate seven metrics, whose experimental samples were algorithms taken from scientific literature. Large-scale experiments, on the other hand, that are performed directly on software programs have good external but poor internal validity, as it is very difficult to reproduce events in a real project, in order to eliminate the influence of variables that are extraneous to the aim of the experiment. In [8], a real software system with several existing versions is used to assess three product metrics.

The statistical techniques used to analyze data fall into two fundamental classes: parametric and nonparametric. *Parametric statistics* require interval- or ratio-type measures that follow a normal distribution. The results are not considered reliable unless these prerequisites are fulfilled. The use of parametric statistics in experimenting software measures is described in [9]. *Nonparametric statistics*, on the other hand, do not impose conditions on the distribution of data and can also be used for ordinal-type measures and in some cases for data in nominal scale. The greater applicability of these statistics is counterbalanced by their low precision and confidence level, since nonparametric statistics use ranks instead of real data. The use of nonparametric statistics for validating measures of software quality is described in [10].

8.3 PRODUCT METRICS

Software metrics can be classified as product metrics or process metrics. *Product metrics* are numerical functions that can be applied to the products of a software project and are usually obtained with an automatic tool for analyzing the software itself, both in final and intermediate form. *Process metrics*, on the other hand, quantify the attributes of the development and maintenance processes. They are used for making estimates and for improving the software life cycle. Process metrics include resource metrics, cost metrics, and productivity metrics. In some cases it is difficult to ascertain whether the software metric is oriented toward the product or the process. For example, the defect count obtained at the end of the testing phase can be interpreted both as a product metric, as it quantifies the reliability of the program, and as a process metric, as it measures the extension of the testing process.

Since the term software quality is generally considered to refer to the product, the measures of software quality fall into the class of product metrics [3], for which reason process metrics are not described in detail in this chapter.

Hundreds of different product metrics have been proposed in the literature but due to limited space we shall only consider metrics that have been the object of numerous experiments or that appear to be more useful due to their predictive capacities. Product metrics have been subdivided according to the phases in the software life cycle in which they can be calculated: analysis, design, and implementation.

8.3.1 Specification Metrics

Specification metrics are extracted from the requirements specifications produced during the analysis phase and are normally used to predict the effort required for the software development or to assess the project productivity.

Specifications metrics are characterized by their aim to measure the requirements the application must fulfill, independently of the solutions adopted. Since they therefore depend heavily on the nature and the complexity of the problem to be solved, they make it possible to establish whether the complexity of a program is inherent to the application or is the result of a degradation in quality.

Function Point. The concept of *function points* is based on the work of Albrecht and Gaffney [11], who set out to measure the functions left to the user. The general approach is to elicit a weighted sum adapted by the inputs, outputs, inquiries, files, and interfaces of an application, obtaining these primitive data from the functional specifications. The procedure for measuring the function points is as follows:

- Count the number of external inputs (e.g., input screens), external outputs (e.g., output screens, reports), logical internal files, external interface files, external inquiries (e.g., requests from user).
- Assign the weights to the counters reflecting the complexity as it is perceived by the user and calculate the weighted sum. Albrecht proposes a worksheet for assigning the weights, as shown in Table 8.2.
- Calculate the complexity adjustment factor, a number varying from 0.65 to 1.35, taking into account the influence of 14 environmental factors: data communications, distributed processing, performance objectives, operational configuration load, transaction rate, on-line data entry, end-user efficiency, on-line update, complex processing logic, reusability, installation ease, operational ease, multiple sites, desire to facilitate change.
- Calculate the function points left by an application as follows:

$$\text{Function points} = \text{unadjusted function points}$$
$$\times \text{ complexity adjustment factor}$$

Albrecht applied these function points to 22 IBM projects, for five years, in order to study productivity factors. Although they have been much used for the purposes of analysis and project estimation, function points have been found applicable mainly to commercial programs, where the function units are easily recognizable.

TABLE 8.2   Worksheet for Calculating Total Unadjusted Function Points

Function Type	Complexity			Total
	Simple	Average	Complex	
External input	__× 3 = __	__× 4 = __	__× 6 = __	_____
External output	__× 4 = __	__× 5 = __	__× 7 = __	_____
Logical internal file	__× 7 = __	__× 10 = __	__× 15 = __	_____
External interface file	__× 5 = __	__× 7 = __	__× 10 = __	_____
External inquiry	__× 3 = __	__× 4 = __	__× 6 = __	_____
			Total unadjusted function points	_____

Bang. Like function points, the *Bang*, proposed by DeMarco [12], is another measure of the functionalities as they are perceived by the user. The Bang, however, uses as information source the models produced by an analysis method, modern structured analysis [13], which has already become very common in industry and is supported by many CASE tools.

A structured specification is composed of a *function model*, represented by a data flow diagram (DFD) and a *retained data model*, represented by an entity relationship diagram (ERD). Once the structured specification has been created, the system is classified using a ratio involving the number of functional primitives (FP) in the DFD and the number of relationships (RE) in the ERD, as shown in Table 8.3.

For function-strong and hybrid systems the *Function-Bang* is calculated in the following way:

- For each functional primitive in the DFD, calculate the token count (TC_i) as the sum of the tokens associated with the data flows in entry and exit. A *token* is a data item that it is not necessary to subdivide within the primitive.

TABLE 8.3   System Classification

System Type	RE/FP
Function-strong	<0.7
Data-strong	>1.5
Hybrid	$[0.7, 1.5]$

TABLE 8.4   Association between Function Class and Complexity Weight

Function Class	Compl. Weight	Function Class	Compl. Weight
Separation	0.6	Synchronization	1.5
Amalgamation	0.6	Output generation	1.0
Data direction	0.3	Display	1.8
Simple update	0.5	Tabular analysis	1.0
Storage management	1.0	Arithmetic	0.7
Edit	0.8	Initiation	1.0
Verification	1.0	Computation	2.0
Text manipulation	1.0	Device management	2.5

- For each functional primitive, calculate the corrected functional primitive increment ($CFPI_i$) as

$$CFPI_i = TC_i \times \log_2 (TC_i)$$

- For each functional primitive, derive the complexity weight (CW_i) according to the class the function belongs to, as shown in Table 8.4.
- Function-Bang $= \Sigma \, CW_i \times CFPI_i$.

For data-strong and hybrid systems the *Data-Bang* is calculated as follows:

- For each object in the ERD, count the number of relationships (RE_i) involving it.
- For each object, calculate the corrected object increment ($COBI_i$) as

$$COBI_i = (RE_i + 1) \times \log_2 (RE_i + 1)$$

- Data-Bang $= \Sigma \, COBI_i$.

Although it has a greater applicability than the function points, the Bang has undergone less experimentation. In addition, it is not very clear how the measurements for Bang should be synthesized in hybrid systems.

8.3.2   Design Metrics

Design metrics are derived from the software architecture produced by the design phase. This architecture, which can be partly reconstructed starting from the source code (reverse engineering), is often represented by means of a structure chart. A *structure chart* is a hierarchical network of modules whose edges represent module invocations. The input/output data for the modules are shown along the invocation lines. One example of a structure chart for a word-scanning problem is shown in Figure 8.1.

Design metrics measure a system in terms of the basic principles of structured design [14]: *cohesion* and *coupling*. A good software architecture consists of modules that carry out clearly defined tasks (high cohesion) and can be read, tested, and modified without involving many other modules (low coupling).

Information Flow. In 1981, Henry and Kafura [15] proposed measuring the complexity of a design in terms of the number of information flows that passed through the design modules.

Information flows are of three kinds: local direct, local indirect, and global. A *local direct flow* exists when a module invokes a second module or when the invoked module returns a result to the caller. A *local indirect flow* exists if an invoked module returns the result to the caller, which then passes it on to a second invoked module. A *global flow* exists if there is a data flow between two modules through a global data structure.

The measurement of the complexity of a module is calculated as follows:

- Calculate the *fan-in* of the module as the number of local flows that end on the module plus the number of global data structures from which the module obtains information.
- Calculate the *fan-out* of the module as the number of local flows that leave from the module plus the number of global data structures that are updated by the module.
- Module complexity = $(\text{fan-in} \times \text{fan-out})^2$.
- System complexity = Σ Module complexity.

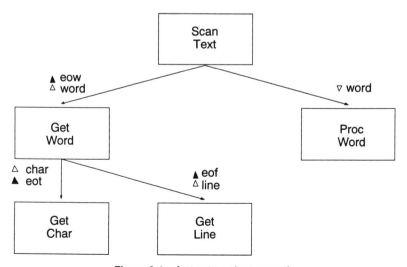

Figure 8.1 *A structure chart example.*

TABLE 8.5   Information Flow Results Applied to Modules

Modules	Fan-in	Fan-out	Module Compl.
Scan Text	1+0	2+0	4
Get Word	3+0	4+0	144
Get Char	1+0	1+0	1
Get Line	1+1	1+0	4
Proc Word	2+0	0+0	0

Table 8.5 reports the intermediate and final measures for the modules in Figure 8.1.

Note that the fan-out of the module Get Word is due to three direct flows and one indirect flow toward the Proc Word module, whereas the fan-in of the module Get Line is due to a direct flow plus a global flow, owing to the file text from which the line is read. The system's relative value is therefore.

$$\text{System complexity} = 4 + 144 + 1 + 4 + 0 = 153$$

The resulting value can also be weighted using a code metric, thus obtaining a hybrid metric that combines both a measure of the module's external connections (macroview) and a measure of the internal complexity of the module (microview).

Information flows are at present the most popular and experimented design metric. The authors too [15] have validated them by correlating the values of the metric with the modification data, relative to the UNIX operative system.

System Design Complexity. System design complexity, too, proposed by Card [16], aims to measure the complexity of a system as it appears after functional decomposition. Analogously to the hybrid version of the information flow, system design complexity takes both *structural complexity* and *intra-module complexity* into account, although the latter is derived without using code metrics.

The procedure for calculating system design complexity is as follows.

• Calculate the structural (intermodule) complexity, St, as

$$St = \frac{\sum f^2(i)}{N}$$

where $f(i)$ is the fan-out (number of modules invoked) of the ith module and N is the number of modules in the system.

- Calculate the data complexity of the ith module, $D(i)$, as

$$D(i) = \frac{v(i)}{f(i) + 1}$$

  where $v(i)$ is the number of input/output variables in the module.
- Calculate the data (intramodule) complexity, Dt, as

$$Dt = \frac{\Sigma D(i)}{N}$$

- Calculate the system design complexity, Ct, as

$$Ct = St + Dt$$

The values of the modules and the program for the word scanning problem are shown, respectively, in Tables 8.6 and 8.7.

System design complexity has been validated by the author using eight software projects belonging to the NASA Goddard Space Flight Center.

Cluster Metric. The cluster metric, proposed by Belady and Evangelisti in 1981 [17], is based on the cluster concept. A *cluster* is a logical aggregation of functional components (modules) and is used as the intermediate level of decomposition of a module system.

TABLE 8.6 System Design Complexity Results Applied to Modules

Modules	Fan-out f	I/O Var v	Data Comp. D
Scan Text	2	2	0.66
Get Word	2	6	2
Get Char	0	2	2
Get Line	0	2	2
Proc Word	0	1	1

TABLE 8.7 System Design Complexity Applied to Program

Structural Compl. St	Data Compl. Dt	System Design Compl. Ct
1.6	1.53	3.13

In the procedure for calculating the cluster metric, the nodes are the system modules and the edges are the communication lines between modules.

- The complexity of a cluster, C_i, is

$$C_i = N_i E_i$$

where N_i is the number of nodes in the cluster and E_i is the number of edges between the cluster nodes.
- The complexity of the entire system, C, is

$$C = NE_0 + \Sigma\, C_i$$

where N is the number of nodes in the system and E_0 is the number of edges between the clusters.

8.3.3 Code Metrics

Code metrics concentrate on the internal mechanisms of the modules in a system, analyzing the source code of the program. Most of the metrics proposed in literature fall into this class because for a long time the only file-based product in the software life cycle available for automatic calculation was the source code of the program. Recently, however, the diffusion of formal and semiformal design methods and the availability of CASE tools, of both forward and reverse type, have enabled analysis and design models to be represented in computer-readable format.

The greatest drawback of code metrics is their limited predictive capacity, as they can only be extracted after the implementation phase or at most after the detailed design phase. Among the many code metrics in the literature, we have selected only a few of the most quoted and used.

Lines of Code. The number of lines of code (LOC) is certainly the most popular metric among programmers, because it is easy to derive. From the intuitive point of view, the lines of code in a program are associated with its dimensions, and the lines of code of a module also measure its quality, as it is considered [18] that modules larger than 50 LOC have low internal cohesion.

Despite the simplicity of this metric, there is no general agreement as to how to count the lines of code. Should the comments, blank lines, program headers, and declarations be counted? Many organizations that measure their programs describe the result of their measurements as LOC but apply a different algorithm from that used by other organizations also using the same name. One solution is to refer to a standard definition. The most authoritative is contained in [9]:

A line of code is any line of program text that is not a comment or blank line, regardless of the number of statements or fragments of statements on the line.

```
{This procedure sorts an array using the quicksort algorithm}
procedure sort(l,r: integer);
var
  i,j,x,y: integer;
begin
  i:=l; j:=r; x:=a[(l+r) DIV 2];
  repeat
    while a[i]<x do i:=i+1;
    while x<a[j] do j:=j-1;
    if i<=j then
    begin
      y:=a[i]; a[i]:=a[j]; a[j]:=y;
      i:=i+1; j:=j-1;
    end;
  until i>j;
  if l<j then sort(l,j);
  if i<r then sort(i,r);
end;
```

Figure 8.2 *A quicksort routine written in PASCAL.*

This specifically includes all lines containing program headers, declarations, and executable and nonexecutable statements.

For example, using the preceding definition, the PASCAL routine in Figure 8.2 has 17 LOC.

Cyclomatic Complexity. Cyclomatic complexity, proposed by McCabe in 1976 [19], is a metric that measures the complexity of the control flow of a program using concepts based on the graph theory.

A program is represented as a direct graph $G = (V, E)$, where the V nodes are sequential code blocks and the E edges correspond to the control flow between the nodes. The graph must have a single entry and exit point. The graph becomes strongly connected if an imaginary edge is added joining the exit point to the entry point. McCabe defines cyclomatic complexity as the cyclomatic number, $v(G)$, of the strongly connected graph. Considering the original graph, without the imaginary edge, the cyclomatic complexity of a module is

$$v(G) = e - n + 1$$

where e is the number of effective edges in the graph and n is the number of nodes.

As $v(G)$ is the number of linearly independent paths in a graph, McCabe proposed this metric as the minimal number of paths to be tested. Later, the purpose of the metric was extended, interpreting it as a measure of the psychological complexity. McCabe himself proposed a threshold, $v(G) = 10$, as an acceptable measure of the complexity of a module.

As nodes with several exit points represent conditional instructions, it can be observed that their presence increases e by one unit with each decision. It is easy to demonstrate that the cyclomatic complexity can also be measured as

$$v(G) = \pi + 1$$

where π is the number of decisions for the module. Instructions of the type *if-then-else*, *repeat-until*, *while-do*, *for-each* correspond to $\pi = 1$, while instructions of type *case* correspond to π = number of *else-if*. The sort routine in Figure 8.2 has one *repeat-until*, two *while-do*, and three *if-then*, equivalent to six decisions and therefore

$$v(G) = 6 + 1 = 7$$

McCabe also proposes a measure of the unstructuredness for a program: the *essential complexity*. Let us remember that structured programming requires the exclusive use of control structures of the one-in/one-out type, like constructs of sequence, alternative, and repetition. If m is the number of proper subgraphs in the graph G, having $v(G)$ cyclomatic complexity, the $ev(G)$ essential complexity is calculated as

$$ev(G) = v(G) - m$$

The essential complexity of a structured module is valued as 1, while $ev(G) = v(G)$ gives the maximum degree of unstructuredness.

Software Science Metrics. The family of metrics proposed by Halstead [20] has undoubtedly been the most subject to experimentation, in order to verify its predictive powers with respect to quality attributes such as reliability, readability, and productivity. Halstead claimed that software obeys natural laws just like physical phenomena do and in this context proposed the existence of a software science.

A program is considered to be composed of tokens that can be classified as *operands* (variables and constants) or *operators* (keywords, delimiters, arithmetical and boolean operators). The primitive metrics are thus defined as

- n_1 = number of unique operators
- n_2 = number of unique operands
- N_1 = total number of operators
- N_2 = total number of operands

Table 8.8 describes an analysis of the operators and operands of the routine in Figure 8.2. The counting strategy adopted is the one in [9].

From these primitives, the following metrics are constructed:

- *Vocabulary.* $n = n_1 + n_2$, which represents the number of single tokens used to construct the program.

TABLE 8.8 Halstead's Primitives for Routine Sort

Operators	Freq	Operands	Freq
Procedure	1	sort	3
( )	4	1	5
,	6	r	5
:	2	i	13
integer	2	j	13
;	16	x	4
var	1	y	2
begin end	2	a	7
:=	10	2	1
+	3	1	4
DIV	1		
[ ]	7		
repeat until	1		
while do	2		
<	4		
−	2		
if then	3		
<=	1		
>	1		
$n_1 = 19$	$N_1 = 69$	$n_2 = 10$	$N_2 = 57$

- *Length.* $N = N_1 + N_2$, which represents the total number of tokens used to construct the program.

- *Estimated Length.* $N' = n_1 \times \log_2 n_1 + n_2 \times \log_2 n_2$, which represents the estimated length of a well-structured program.

- *Volume.* $V = N \times \log_2 n$, which represents the minimum quantity of space, measured in bits, required to memorize a program. The volume can also be interpreted as the number of mental comparisons necessary to write a program of N length, using a binary search method to select the elements of the vocabulary of n dimensions.

- *Program Level.* $L = V^*/V \equiv (2/n_1) \times (n_2/N_2)$, which represents the abstraction level in which an algorithm is realized. The *potential volume* V^* represents the minimal dimension of implementation. As the value of V^* is difficult to calculate, Halstead provides an equation for estimating the program level.

- *Difficulty.* $D = 1/L$, which represents the inverse program level. Intuitively, the idea is that the difficulty of a program increases as the abstraction level diminishes, in other words as the operators are added ($n_1/2$ increases) and the operands are used redundantly (N_2/n_2 increases).
- *Language Level.* $\lambda = L^2 \times V$, which expresses the power of a language, from the point of view of the abstraction capacity, and is independent of the algorithm implemented.
- *Effort.* $E = V/L$, which represents the effort necessary for implementing the program in terms of the number of elementary mental discriminations.
- *Programming Time.* $T = E/\beta$, which represents the time, in seconds, necessary for realizing a program. β is the *Stroud number* (between 5 and 20) and represents the maximum number of elementary discriminations the human mind can make per second, according to psychologist John Stroud [21].

Many experiments have been performed, reported in [22], to verify the correlation between Halstead's metrics and the number of errors, the effective time for programming or the time for comprehension. In later years, however, software science was reopened to discussion both from the theoretical point of view, pointing out the ambiguity of some constructs [23] and the erroneous application of studies on cognitive psychology [24], and from the empirical point of view, as only small programs had been positively experimented. Nevertheless, software science remains the most complete theory ever to be proposed as regards the measurement of the software development process.

8.4 USES FOR SOFTWARE QUALITY METRICS

Software quality measures can provide useful information during the entire software life cycle, including both its development and its successive evolution. In [10], Schneidewind listed three fundamental quality functions: assessment, control, and prediction.

8.4.1 Quality Assessment

Quality assessment refers to the assessment of the quality of a software component in relation to other components. It is not the absolute value of the measurement that counts but its ordinal position with respect to the other objects considered.

If the objects are the product of decomposition then the aim of quality assessment is to assign priority to the efforts to improve the quality and to allocate the resources on the basis of the latter. For example, program modules with a higher number of decisions will be given greater attention during program testing. A real case of quality assessment is described in [25], aiming to assign priority to maintenance work.

If, on the other hand, the objects are potential design or implementation alternatives, then the aim of quality assessment is to help the software engineer make decisions. For example, if the design alternatives of a structure differ as regards the number of references to external variables, the designer will choose the lowest data-binding one. Cardenas-Garcia and Zelkowitz described a system for supporting the implementation decisions in [26], using measures relative to the possible alternatives.

8.4.2 Quality Control

Quality control assess software components with respect to a preestablished threshold of metric values, used as quality standard. These components whose measures exceeds the given threshold are identified as critical. The aim of quality control is to identify components whose quality must be considered unacceptable. For example, many organizations set a maximum length, from 50 to 100 instructions, for program modules: Modules with a greater length must be further decomposed. Otherwise, if the predefined number is exceeded during the system test, the system is rejected and returned to the development team. In [16], some of the most common acceptance criteria for software are described.

The quality control function also acts with the passing of time, keeping trace of the quality of a component during its life cycle. If its quality falls below the minimum level after a modification has been made, then it is necessary to take contrary action against its degradation. The progressive increase in the dimensions of systems and the number of modified objects over a period of time or with the introduction of new releases is described in [27].

8.4.3 Quality Prediction

Quality prediction makes early prediction of the value of a direct quality measure possible by using the value of an indirect measure in its place. For example, the measurement of the complexity of a modular structure, which can be derived at the end of the design phase, can be used as a predictor of the number of errors, which can only be derived at the end of the testing phase. In [12], De Marco uses measures that can be derived in the analysis phase to estimate the design, design measures to estimate its implementation, and code measures to estimate the results of testing and operation.

REFERENCES

[1] J. D. Musa, The measurement and management of software reliability, *Proc. IEEE*, 68(69) 1131–1143, (September 1980).

[2] A. V. Aho, J. E. Hopcroft, and J. D. Ullman, *The Design and Analysis of Computer Algorithms*, Addison-Wesley, 1974.

[3] B. Curtis, Measurement and experimentation in software engineering, *Proc. IEEE*, 68(69), 1144–1157 (September 1980).

[4] B. A. Sheil, The psychological study of programming, *ACM Comput. Surv.*, 13(1), 101–120 (1981).

[5] *IEEE Standard Glossary of Software Engineering Terminology*, ANSI/IEEE Std. 729, 1982.

[6] V. R. Basili, R. W. Selby, and D. H. Hutchens, Experimentation in software engineering, *IEEE Trans. Software Eng.*, SE-12(7), 733–743 (July 1992).

[7] G. Como, F. Lanubile, and G. Visaggio, Evaluation of characteristics of design quality metrics, *Proc. 2nd Internat. Conf. Software Eng. Knowledge Eng.*, Skokie, Ill., 1990, pp. 195–201.

[8] R. J. Leach, "Software Metrics and Software Maintenance," *Software Maintenance: Research and Practice*, vol. 2, 1990, pp. 133–142.

[9] S. D. Conte, H. E. Dunsmore, and V. Y. Shen, *Software Engineering Metrics and Models*, Benjamin/Cummings, Menlo Park, Calif., 1986.

[10] N. F. Schneidewind, Methodology for validating software metrics, *IEEE Trans. Software Eng.*, 18(5), 410–422 (May 1992).

[11] A. J. Albrecht and J. E. Gaffney, Jr., Software function, source lines of code, and development effort prediction: A software science validation, *IEEE Trans. Software Eng.*, SE-9(6), 639–648 (November 1983).

[12] T. DeMarco, *Controlling Software Projects*, Prentice-Hall, Englewood Cliffs, N.J., 1982.

[13] E. Yourdon, *Modern Structured Analysis*, Yourdon Press, Prentice Hall, 1989.

[14] E. Yourdon and L. Constantine, *Structured Design*, Prentice-Hall, Englewood Cliffs, N.J., 1979.

[15] S. Henry and D. Kafura, Software structure metrics based on information flow, *IEEE Trans. Software Eng.*, SE-7(5), 510–518, (September 1981).

[16] D. N. Card and R. L. Glass, *Measuring Software Design Quality*, Prentice-Hall, Englewood Cliffs, N.J., 1990.

[17] L. A. Belady and C. J. Evangelisti, System partitioning and its measure, *J. Syst. Software*, 2, 23–39 (1981).

[18] G. J. Myers, *Software Reliability, Principles and Practices*, Wiley, New York, 1976.

[19] T. J. McCabe, A complexity measure, *IEEE Trans. Software Eng.*, SE-2(4), 308–320 (December 1976).

[20] M. H. Halstead, *Elements of Software Science*, Elsevier North-Holland, New York, 1977.

[21] J. M. Stroud, The fine structure of psychological time, *Ann. N.Y. Acad. Sci.*, 138, 623–631 (1967).

[22] A. Fitzsimmons and T. Love, A review and evaluation of software science, *Comput. Surv.*, 10(1), 3–18 (March 1978).

[23] V. Y. Shen, S. D. Conte, and H. E. Dunsmore, Software science revisited: A critical analysis of the theory and its empirical support, *IEEE Trans. Software Eng.*, SE-9(2), 155–165 (March 1983).

[24] N. S. Coulter, Software science and cognitive psychology, *IEEE Trans. Software Eng.*, SE-9(2), 166–171 (March 1983).

[25] N. F. Schneidewind, Setting maintenance quality objectives and prioritizing maintenance work by using quality metrics, *Proc. Conf. Software Maintenance*, IEEE Computer Society Press, 1991, pp. 240–249.

[26] S. Cardenas-Garcia and M. V. Zelkowitz, A management tool for evaluation of software designs, *IEEE Trans. Software Eng.*, 17(9), 961–971 (September 1991).

[27] M. M. Lehman, Programs, life cycles, and laws of software evolution, *Proc. IEEE*, 68(9), 1060–1076 (September 1980).

CHAPTER 9 —————————————————————

Neurological Fuzzy Diagnoses: Holographic versus Statistical versus Neural Method

RAYMOND HO
JOHN G. SUTHERLAND
IVAN BRUHA

9.1 INTRODUCTION

A holographic neural network for classification of brain stem auditory evoked potentials (BSAEPs) is presented in this chapter. BSAEPs have come to occupy an important role in clinical neurology for assessment of the brain stem function. The BSAEPs are generated in response to brief auditory stimuli invoking characteristic spike potentials within 10 ms following the stimulus in normal subjects. This chapter presents a performance comparison between a statistical classifier–Bayes classifier, a conventional neural network classifier–multilayered perceptron, and a BSAEP classifier based on holographic neural technology (HNeT). HNeT was used in the processing of the evoked potential (EP) waveform for discrimination of correlating signals from electroencephalogram data. Subsequent neurophysiological classification has shown that the holographic technique requires relatively little effort in the initial determination of the correlating factors and a coincident reduction in training time. A substantive improvement in classification accuracy is observed in these experimental results.

BSAEPs have come to occupy an important role in clinical neurology for the assessment of brain stem function. The BSAEPs are generated in response to a brief auditory stimuli with seven peaks appearing within 10 ms following the stimulus in normal subjects [1]. The latencies of the initial five peaks of BSAEPs are highly stable in healthy normal subjects under a wide variety of

Frontier Decision Support Concepts, Edited by V. L. Plantamura, B. Souček, and G. Visaggio.
ISBN 0-471-59256-0   © 1994 John Wiley & Sons, Inc.

physiological conditions such as sleep, wakefulness, and anesthesia [1, 2]. However, pathological states resulting from head injury, acoustic tumors, and multiple sclerosis give rise to delays in the transmission of electrical signals and consequently the peaks are abnormally located [3]. Our research group has attempted to develop pattern recognition techniques for automatically classifying BSAEPs as one component of a decision-support system for neurological diagnoses. Techniques such as Bayes classifiers, multilayered perceptron (MLP), and holographic neural technology were applied to this application. This chapter presents these three classifiers and the performance comparison between them.

This chapter is organized in three sections starting with the background information describing the classification experiments. The classification section presents detailed information about the classification experiments and result obtained from using a holographic neural cell, Bayes classifier, and multilayered perceptron. Performance comparison between these classifier is presented in the conclusion. Details of holographic neural networks are presented in Chapters 3 to 5.

The BSAEP data used in this study were recorded at the neurology clinic run at the McMaster University Medical Centre. Figures 9.1*a*, *b* show typical normal and pathological BSAEPs respectively. The BSAEPs were obtained from the vertex-left mastoid, vertex-right mastoid electrode locations on the scalp by employing a Nicolet Pathfinder II system in the evoked potentials laboratory. The contralateral mastoid was used as the reference. The stimulus was a 0.1-ms pulse delivered 9.8/s at 60 dB above the hearing threshold. The frequency range of recording was 150–3000 Hz. Details of data acquisition of BSAEPs can be found in [4–6].

We have collected 133 BSAEP patterns from patients, 53 of which are used for training and the rest were used for testing. Table 9.1 shows the number of normal and abnormal BSAEP patterns in the training and testing sets.

Feature Selection. A critical issue in any classifier design is the selection of features. Based on several years of investigation of BSAEPs in animal studies and in the clinic, it is now believed that the latencies provide necessary and sufficient information to discriminate between normal and patient's BSAEPs [2]. Further experiments in [4] have shown that the second, third, and fourth peak latencies are the optimal features for classification. Hence we used the second, third, and fourth peak latencies of the initial five peaks as the features for classifying the BSAEPs.

BSAEP Preprocessing. Preprocessing procedures were used to obtain the second, third, and fourth peak latencies: (1) filter preprocessing, (2) extracting a string of symbols as a formal description of the input waveform, and (3) syntactic analysis. These preprocessing procedures are well beyond the scope of the chapter; however, details about these procedures can be found in [6–8].

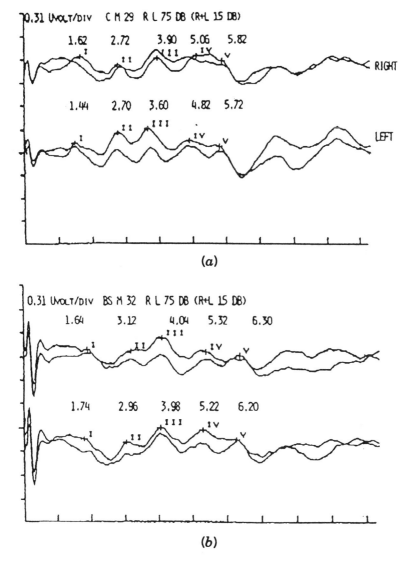

Figure 9.1 *(a) BAEPs of a normal subject. (b) BAEPs of a patient with multiple sclerosis.*

TABLE 9.1 **Number of Normal and Abnormal BSAEP Patterns in Training and Testing Sets**

	Normal	Abnormal (Multiple Sclerosis)	Total
Training set	30	23	53
Testing set	46	34	80

9.2 PATTERN CLASSIFICATION TECHNIQUES

We have studied Bayes classifier, MLP, and HNeT for the classification of BSAEPs. Bayes classifier and MLP have been widely used as classifiers in many different areas [9, 10]. However, both of them have drawbacks. For example, in the case of Bayes classifier, a very large number of training information is needed in order to obtain acceptable classification accuracy. In the case of MLP, there are no formal theories on obtaining the set of optimal network parameters [10] and in many cases it is time consuming to train the network, even if a set of near-optimal network parameters are obtained. HNeT presents a fundamentally different neural system theory. The operational basis stems from holographic principles in the superposition or enfolding of information through complex vectors [11]. Other applications [12] have shown that HNeT can classify complicated patterns with high accuracy in a relatively short training time. This study of BSAEP classification provides a performance comparison between these three classifiers.

In the following sections, brief descriptions of the three classifiers we have used in the study of BSAEP classification are presented along with the classification results.

9.2.1 Bayes Classifier

Bayes decision theory is a fundamental statistical approach to the problem of pattern classification. This approach is based on the assumption that the decision problem is posed in probabilistic terms and that all of the relevant probability values are known [13].

The Bayes classifier treats each pattern as a multidimensional random variable and assigns the pattern to a class with maximum a posteriori probability [13]. For a BSAEP pattern X with features $\{x(0), x(1), x(2)\}$, it can be stated that pattern X belongs to class A (abnormal) or class N (normal), depending on

$$P(A|X) \underset{N}{\overset{A}{\gtrless}} P(N|X) \qquad \text{given } X \in A \text{ or } N \qquad (9.1)$$

In Eq. (9.1) $P(A|X)$ and $P(N|X)$ are the posteriori probabilities of class A and class N, given that the BSAEP pattern X is being observed. Equation (9.1) decides in favor of class A if the left-hand side is greater, otherwise the BSAEP pattern X belongs to class N. By Bayes' theorem, the equations can be written as

$$p(X|A)P(A) \underset{N}{\overset{A}{\gtrless}} p(X|N)P(N) \qquad (9.2)$$

where $p(X|A)$ and $p(X|N)$ are the conditional probability density function of the BSAEP pattern X and $P(A)$ and $P(N)$ are the a priori probabilities that class A or N occurs, respectively.

Assuming that the BSAEP patterns satisfy the multivariate normal density function and there are n features, the multivariate normal density is

$$p(X) = \frac{e^{-[(X-M)^T S^{-1}(X-M)]/2}}{(2\pi)^{n/2}|S|^{1/2}} = N(M, S) \tag{9.3}$$

where X is the feature vector (the BSAEP pattern), M is the mean vector, S is the variance-covariance matrix, and $|S|$ is the determinant.

The n-dimensional multivariate normal density function for class A and class N are

$$p(X|A) = N(M_A, S_A) \qquad p(X|N) = N(M_N, S_N)$$

From the preceding equations, following [13], we get

$$(X - M_N)^T S_N^{-1}(X - M_N) - (X - M_A)^T S_A^{-1}(X - M_A)$$

$$\underset{N}{\overset{A}{\gtrless}} 2 \ln\left[\frac{P(N)}{P(A)}\right] + \ln\left[\frac{|S_A|}{|S_N|}\right] \tag{9.4}$$

The vectors M_A, M_N and matrices S_N and S_A are not known a priori and are estimated from a set of labeled BSAEP patterns. The set of labeled BSAEP patterns is the same training set mentioned earlier and used as the training set for the MLP and HNeT neural network classifiers described in subsequent sections. The values of $P(A)$ and $P(N)$ used in this study were clinical values obtained at McMaster University Medical Centre in 1984.

9.2.2 Classification Result Using Bayes Classifier

Classification results using the Bayes classifier were obtained by using Eq. (9.4). Feature vectors, which contain the second, third, and fourth peak latencies of the BSAEP patterns, were fed into the classifier and the result was compared with the threshold value (right-hand side of Eq. (9.4)). If the result was greater than the threshold value, the pattern was classified as abnormal, otherwise the BSAEP pattern was considered to be normal.

The classification results and performance using Bayes classifier are presented in Table 9.2.

9.2.3 Multilayered Perceptron

It has been found in earlier studies [6, 8] that a three-layer perceptron was not quite stable for classification of BSAEPs. Thus, the MLP architecture used in this study was a two-layer perceptron. Figure 9.2 shows the architecture of a two-layer perceptron used in this study. The BSAEP patterns were inputted to the three input nodes of the neural network. One of the two output nodes would

TABLE 9.2   Classification Results Using Bayes Classifier

	Reference Diagnosis	
	Abnormal	Normal
Classification result: class A	33	12
Classification result: class N	1	34
Overall performance: 83.75%		Learning time $\approx$ 1.5 s

be fired by the neural network classifier indicating either a normal or abnormal pattern.

The learning algorithm used in the experiments was the *backpropagation algorithm*. The backpropagation algorithm is a generalization of the least mean square (LMS) algorithm [9]. It uses a gradient search technique to minimize a cost function equal to the mean square difference between the desired output and the actual output. The network is trained by initially selecting small random weights and internal thresholds and then presenting all training data repeatedly. Weights are adjusted after every trial using supervising information specifying the correct class until weights converge, and the cost function reduced to an acceptable value. The following presents the backpropagation algorithm used in the two-layer perceptron BSAEP classifier:

Step 1. Normalization. Normalize the training BSAEP patterns to the values between 0 and 1 for faster convergence.

Step 2. Initialize Weights and Thresholds. Set all the weights and threshold in the network to small random values in a specific range *iw* (the initial weights range), excluding zero, of the maximum value in the training set.

Step 3. Present Input BSAEP Pattern and Desire Output Class. Present input pattern $X = \{x(0), x(1), x(2)\}$ and desired output $D = \{d(0), d(1)\}$ until weights are stabilized.

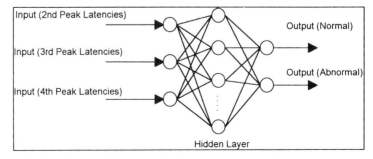

Figure 9.2   *Architecture of a two-layer perceptron.*

Step 4. Calculate Actual Output and Test for Adapting Weights. Use the sigmoid logistic nonlinearity

$$f(\alpha) = \frac{1}{1 + e^{-(\alpha - \theta)}}$$

where $\alpha = \Sigma_i w_{ij} x_i$, θ = threshold, to calculate output $Y = \{ y(0), y(1) \}$.

If weights are stabilized, do not adapt. The weights are stabilized when the error signal ϵ, defined by

$$\epsilon = \tfrac{1}{2} \sum_j (d(j) - y(j))^2$$

is reduced below a preestablished limit where j is all the nodes in output layer.

Step 5. Adapt Weights. Use a recursive algorithm starting at the output nodes and work back to the first hidden layer. Adjust weights by

$$w_{ij}(t + 1) = w_{ij}(t) + \eta \delta_j x'(i)$$

where $w_{ij}(t)$ are the weights from hidden node i or from an input to node j at time t, $x'(i)$ is the output of node i or an input, η is a gain term (learning rate), and δ_j is an error term for node j.

If node j is an output node, then

$$\delta_j = y(j)(1 - y(j))(d(j) - y(j))$$

where $d(j)$ is the desired output class for node j and $y(j)$ is the actual output class. If node j is an internal hidden node, then

$$\delta_j = x'(j)(1 - x'(j)) \sum_k \delta_k w_{jk}$$

where the summation is performed over all nodes in the layer following node j.

Repeat by going to Step 3.

9.2.4 Adjustment of Neural Parameters for MLP

Parameters needed to be specified for the classification of BSAEP using MLP with the backpropagation training algorithm. These parameters were the gain term η (learning rate), the initial weights range iw, and the number of hidden nodes in the hidden layer. Unfortunately, there is no formal method for ob-

TABLE 9.3   Near-Optimal Parameters of MLP

Parameter(s)	Value(s)
Gain term η	2.0
Initial weights range iw	200%
Number of hidden nodes	30

taining the values of these parameters [10], therefore, experiments and analysis were done to obtain the optimal set.

A set of heuristics for determining near-optimal neural parameters for the classification of BSAEP using MLP [6] was followed in these experiments. A large set of classification experiments, however, still had to be conducted in order to obtain the near-optimal neural parameters. Following the heuristics [6], eight, six, and five sets of experiments were conducted to obtain the near-optimal number of hidden nodes, the gain term, and initial weights range, respectively. We needed to execute the MLP classifier 10 times for each set of experiments (i.e., $8 * 10 + 6 * 10 + 5 * 10 = 190$ times) to obtain a more accurate evaluation of the classifier, as the initial weights of the MLP neurons are randomly assigned and the performance in terms of both learning time and classification accuracy of each execution of the MLP classifier varied. The near-optimal parameters (optimal only for the classification accuracy) of MLP for the classification of BSAEPs using the second, third, and fourth peak latencies are listed in Table 9.3.

9.2.5   Classification Result Using MLP

There was a random factor involved in the experiments, since random numbers within a range determined by the initial weights range iw were used in Step 2 of the learning algorithm. Therefore, classification result using the MLP was obtained by averaging 10 separate executions of training and classifying testing patterns.

The classification result and performance based on 10 executions using MLP are presented in Table 9.4.

TABLE 9.4   Classification Results Using MLP

	Reference diagnosis	
	Abnormal	Normal
Classification result: class A	30.3	5.8
Classification result: class N	3.7	40.2
Overall performance: 88.13%	Number of epochs: 23.8	Learning time $\approx$ 19 s

9.2.6 Holographic Neural Technology

Holographic neural technology is a relatively new artificial neural system paradigm that is fundamentally different from conventional neural network theory. The paradigm resembles a class of mathematics found within electromagnetic field theory. A brief description of HNeT for classification of BSAEPs is presented in the following section. A detailed presentation on holographic neural theory can be found in [11, 12, 14].

9.2.7 Information Representation

An element of information within the holographic neural paradigm is represented by a complex number having both phase and magnitude. The input BSAEP patterns $X = \{x(0), x(1), x(2)\}$ (the second, third, and fourth peak latencies) and output class $Y = \{y\}$. ($y = -ve$ (normal) and $y = +ve$ (abnormal)) were converted from real values to the complex representations in the neural system using a sigmoidal preprocessing operation:

$$x(k) \rightarrow \lambda_k e^{i\theta_k} \qquad \theta_k \rightarrow 2\pi(1 + e^{(\mu - x(k)])/\sigma})^{-1}$$

where μ is the mean of distribution over X, $k = 0, 1, 2$, σ is the variance of distribution, and λ_k is the assigned confidence level.

The above transformation maps the input BSAEP patterns to corresponding sets of complex values, illustrated as

$$X \rightarrow X' = \{\lambda_0 e^{i\theta_0}, \lambda_1 e^{i\theta_1}, \lambda_2 e^{i\theta_2}\}$$

9.2.8 Learning (Encoding)

The learning process realizes a holographic effect in its ability to enfold multiple input/output associations onto the identically same correlation set C comprising complex numbers. The learning process is executed, at its most fundamental level, by a complex-valued matrix inner product over the BSAEP pattern and the class to which it belongs. Elements of the correlation set C are evaluated by

$$c_k + = \bar{s}(k) \cdot d \tag{9.5}$$

The preceding maps an association of the BSAEP peaks $s(k)$ to the desired class d (if $d = 0.5$ then abnormal, if $d = -0.5$ then normal). In complex notation, the BSAEP peaks and the desired class are represented by

$$d = \gamma e^{i\phi} \qquad s(k) = \lambda_k e^{i\theta_k}$$

Equation (9.5) can be rewritten as

$$c_k + = \lambda_k \gamma e^{i(\phi - \theta_k)}$$

The learning process for multiple BSAEP patterns—that is, the process to obtain the correlation set C for all the BSAEP training patterns in the training set—may be represented by

$$[C]+ = [\overline{X}']^T \cdot [D'] \tag{9.6}$$

where

$$[X'] = \begin{vmatrix} \lambda_{0,t1}e^{i\theta_{0,f1}} & \lambda_{1,t1}e^{i\theta_{1,f1}} & \lambda_{2,t1}e^{i\theta_{2,f1}} \\ \lambda_{0,t2}e^{i\theta_{0,f2}} & \lambda_{1,t2}e^{i\theta_{1,f2}} & \lambda_{2,t2}e^{i\theta_{2,f2}} \\ \vdots & \vdots & \vdots \end{vmatrix}$$

$$[D'] = \begin{vmatrix} \gamma_{t1}e^{i\phi_{t1}} \\ \gamma_{t2}e^{i\phi_{t2}} \\ \vdots \end{vmatrix}$$

and

$$[C] = \begin{array}{c} \sum\limits_{t}^{P} \lambda_{0,t}\gamma_{t}e^{i(\phi_{t} - \theta_{0,f})} \\ \\ \sum\limits_{t}^{P} \lambda_{1,t}\gamma_{t}e^{i(\phi_{t} - \theta_{1,f})} \\ \\ \vdots \end{array}$$

$t1$, $t2$, . . . are first, second, . . . training patterns, respectively, and P is the number of training patterns. The preceding operations encode the entire set of BSAEP-waveform-and-class associations within a matrix product solution over two complex-valued data sets.

9.2.9 Classifying (Decode)

Classifying or decoding BSAEP patterns may be performed by transforming the patterns through all the BSAEP-waveform-and-class mappings enfolded within the correlation set $[C]$. The response class generated from the BSAEP pattern is in complex form possessing phase and magnitude. In the event that new BSAEP patterns resemble prior learned stimulus patterns, the neural cell will generate the associated class values at a high confidence level (magnitude ≈ 1). The decoding transform used in this is represented by

$$[D'] = \frac{1}{k} [X']^* \cdot [C] \tag{9.7}$$

where $[X']^*$ is the new BSAEP pattern exposed to the holographic cell for issuance of a class. This input BSAEP pattern may be represented by the linear matrix

$$[X']^* = \{\lambda_0^* e^{i\theta_0^*}, \lambda_1^* e^{i\theta_1^*}, \lambda_2^* e^{i\theta_2^*}\}$$

The normalization coefficient k in Eq. (9.7) is a function of the BSAEP pattern. Optimal characteristics are exhibited using the following relation for this coefficient in normalizing the generated class to a probabilistic range (0.0 to 1.0):

$$k = \sum_{n=0}^{2} \lambda_n^*$$

9.2.10 Enhanced Learning (Encoding)

The enhanced encoding method for holographic neural technology was introduced in [11]. These enhancements map out more effectively the input state-space to the set of desired response values. In the basic encoding mechanism multiple BSAEP-class associations are enfolded onto the correlation set, each association encoded at a fixed level of confidence. Learning progresses independently from knowledge previously accumulated, and no control is afforded over attention or the degree to which prior knowledge influences learning within the mapping substrate. In this enhanced process, the recall (decode) error is substantially reduced over that observed in the basic encoding process. Also, the error on recall may be effectively eliminated using relatively few learning trials over the training set. This is achieved by permitting learning to occur as a function of accumulated memory, the effect within the mapping substrate is in inverse proportion to the degree to which similar BSAEP-class associations or mappings have been previously encoded within the holographic cell. The enhanced encoding process used in the classification of the BSAEPs is as follows:

1. Decode a BSAEP pattern through the neuron cell to produce a (complex) class value Y'; that is,

$$Y' = \frac{1}{k} [X'] \cdot [C]$$

2. A vector difference D'_{diff} between the generated class and the desired class D' for this BSAEP-class association is evaluated simply by

$$D'_{\text{diff}} = D' - Y'$$

3. The correlation mapping is generated from the BSAEP pattern X' and the above difference vector. This encoding follows the canonical form

presented in Eq. (6):

$$[C]+ = [\overline{X}']^T \cdot D'_{\text{diff}}$$

The evaluation of a difference term D'_{diff} is somewhat analogous to the back-propagation of error terms used in conventional gradient approaches. This procedure, however, realizes a method whereby the new BSAEP pattern is mapped exactly to the desired class D' following one encoding operation. The enhanced encoding procedure may be performed over multiple reinforcement learning trials in instances where more numerous or difficult generalizations are required.

9.2.11 Higher-Order Systems

Conventional ANS models are reasonably restricted in terms of the numbers of associations that may be accurately encoded into a network. Within the holographic process, limitations on storage density are largely overcome by using a preprocessing operation involving the generation of higher-order product terms or "statistics" from the stimulus basis set. This presents a sigma-pi variation of the basic encoding and decoding schemes. For the learning process the procedure for updating one correlation value (synapse) within the holographic cell is shown in a generalized form:

$$x_j = \sum_{t=1} \gamma_t e^{i\phi_t} \prod_{k=1} \lambda_{f(j,k)} e^{-i\theta_{f(j,k)}}$$

The sigma-pi variation of the decoding or recall process used in classification is similarly structured:

$$r = \frac{1}{c} \sum_{j=1} x_j \prod_{k=1} \lambda_{f(j,k)} e^{i\theta_{f(j,k)}}$$

In this evaluation 50 higher-order terms were generated using default selection parameters from an HNeT evaluation system. By default, the generation of combinatorial product terms (i.e., $f(j, k)$ the set of unique combinatory complex products starting from first order and progressing to higher orders). To illustrate, the distribution of the order of terms using in the BSAEP mapping for this test is given in Table 9.5. Further details regarding the theoretical basis

TABLE 9.5 Distribution of Order of Terms

Order of Term	Distribution Count
1	6
2	12
3	20
4	10

and characteristics of higher-order product encoding/recall can be found in [11, 12].

9.2.12 Classification of BSAEP Waveform Using HNeT

There are parameters to be adjusted in HNeT for optimal performance. The parameters are *number of higher-order product terms, learning rate,* and *memory profile.* Depending upon the nature of different applications, the neural parameters of HNeT may greatly affect the performance of the neural system. In this case with classification of BSAEP waveform, experiments showed that the learning rate and memory profile do not play a significant role in terms of classification accuracy. However, the number of higher-order product terms determines not only the learning time but also the classification accuracy after the training.

The conversion scheme used in the experiments, which convert from real values of the peak latencies of the BSAEP patterns and the desired classes of the patterns to complex representation, is *linear* conversion. The ranges specified were $[-10, 10]$ and $[-1, 1]$ for BSAEP patterns and the output class, respectively. Employing the default setting of 50 product terms in the cell configuration, the results of using HNeT in classification of BSAEPs after the first learning trial are presented in Table 9.6.

9.3 CONCLUSION

The Bayes classification being the most conventional method in this type of determination illustrated rapid solution but tends to require a large number of training prototypes to obtain a reasonable generalization. This method indicated the lowest accuracy in our evaluation. In comparison, the MLP technique requires a reasonably high level of customization to achieve peak performance characteristics. The genetic approach used in optimizing performance for the MLP incurred a time expense of several weeks. The holographic neural technique has a lower dimensionality in terms of the design parameters, this being particularly due to the characteristic that the mapping is more accurate and

TABLE 9.6 Classification Results Using HNeT

	Reference Diagnosis	
	Abnormal	Normal
Classification result: class A	31	0
Classification result: class N	3	46
Overall performance: 96.25%	Number of epochs 1	Training time $\approx$ 1 s

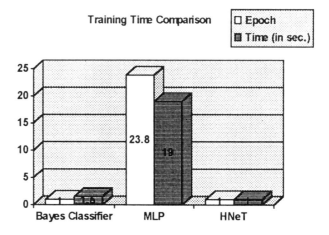

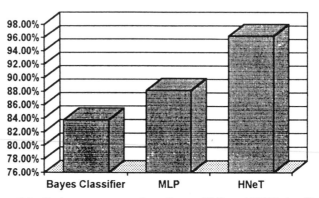

Figure 9.3 *Performance comparison: Bayes, MLP, and HNET classifiers.*

performed with single cells versus the multiple-cell/multiple-layer configurations found in MLP-type systems. The evaluation for the holographic neural
process was performed on an HNeT evaluation system using default parameters. The holographic method was shown to be comparable to the Bayes method
in terms of actual speed of training and classification. Figure 9.3 presents the
performance comparison between the Bayes classifier, MLP classifier, and the
classifier based on HNeT.

REFERENCES

[1] I. G. Kiloh, A. J. McComas, J. W. Osselton, and A. R. M. Upton, *Clinical
Electroencephalography*, Butterworth, London, 1981, pp. 251–255.

[2] M. J. Rowe, III, Normal variability of the brainstem auditory evoked response in young and old adult subjects, *Electroenceph. Clin. Neurophysiol.*, 44, 459–470 (1987).

[3] K. H. Chiappa, K. J. Gladstone, and R. R. Young, Brainstem auditory evoked responses: Studies of waveform variations in 50 normal subjects, *Arch. Neural.* (Chicago), 36, 81–87 (1979).

[4] M. V. Kamath, S. N. Reddy, A. R. M. Upton, D. N. Ghista, and M. E. Jernigan, Statistical pattern classification of clinical brainstem auditory evoked potentials, *Internat. J. Biomed. Comput.*, 21, 9–28 (1988).

[5] J. Fridman, E. R. John, M. Bergelson, J. B. Kaiser, and H. W. Baird, Application of digital filtering and automatic peak detection of brainstem auditory evoked potentials, *Electroenceph. Clin. Neurophysiol.*, 62, 405–416 (1982).

[6] R. Ho, ''A Neural Network System for Recognition of Evoked Potentials,'' M.Sc. Thesis, Dept. Computer Science and Systems, McMaster University, Hamilton, Ontario (1990).

[7] I. Bruha and G. P. Madhavan, Use of attributed grammars for pattern recognition of evoked potentials, *IEEE Trans. Syst. Man Cyber.* 18(6), (1988).

[8] I. Bruha and R. Ho, Evoked potential waveform processing by a 2-layer perceptron: Heuristics for optimal adjustment of its parameters, *Proc. of Neuronet 90*, Prague 1990.

[9] R. P. Lippmann, An introduction to computing with neural net, *IEEE ASSP Mag.*, 4(2), 4–22(April 1987).

[10] D. E. Rumelhart, G. E. Hinton, and R. Williams, *Learning Internal Representation by Error Propagation, PDP: Exploration in the Microstructure of Cognition. Vol. 1: Foundation*, MIT Press, Cambridge, Mass., 1986.

[11] J. G. Sutherland, Holographic model of memory, learning and expression, *Internat. J. Neural Syst.*, 1(3), 256–267 (1990).

[12] J. G. Sutherland, *The Holographic Method, Fuzzy, Holographic, and Parallel Intelligence: The 6th Generation Breakthrough*, B. Souček and IRIS, eds. Wiley, New York, 1992.

[13] R. O. Duda and P. E. Hart, *Pattern Classification and Scene Analysis*, Wiley, New York, 1973.

[14] J. G. Sutherland, A transputer based implementation of holographic neural technology, Transputing '91, *Proc. World Transputer User Group Conf.*, Vol. 2, P. Welch, D. Stiles, T. L. Kunii, and A. Bakkers, eds., IOS press (1991).

CHAPTER 10 ⎯⎯⎯⎯⎯⎯⎯⎯⎯⎯

Holographic Decision Support System: Credit Scoring Based on Quality Metrics

BRANKO SOUČEK
JOHN G. SUTHERLAND
GIUSEPPE VISAGGIO

10.1 INTRODUCTION

Scoring based on quality metrics is a frequent decision-making task. Our interest concentrates on financial problems related to credit scoring. Similarly structured problems occur in many other disciplines. Sections 10.2 to 10.4 deal with the quality evaluation based on the quality metrics. In using measurement to assess quality, we must

Determine the relevant quality attributes. A quality attribute captures an ability of an entity to satisfy a given need. The needs must be clearly identified.

Define quality attributes in terms of quantitative attributes such as power, length, age, volume. This definition is necessary, since otherwise quality cannot be assessed or predicted.

Determine needed measurement quantitative attributes from quality attributes; quantitative attributes can be measured in terms of the entity itself independently from any needs or requirements, whereas quality attributes depend on needs or requirements and are assessed or predicted rather than measured.

Quality assessing can be based on the principles of knowledge domain, inductive or neural learning, pattern recognition, and holographic learning.

Frontier Decision Support Concepts, Edited by V. L. Plantamura, B. Souček, and G. Visaggio.
ISBN 0-471-59256-0   © 1994 John Wiley & Sons, Inc.

Sections 10.5 to 10.8 present the fuzzy holographic classifier for credit scoring. Stimulus-response associations are both learned and expressed in one noniterative mapping using the holographic network (HNeT). An initial network determines the most influential fields of input vectors. The reduced vector is then expanded to higher-order statistics prior to input to the cortex cell. The classifier deals with financial, biomedical, power, and geophysical problems. The loan and credit-scoring application is described. Classification in terms of good versus bad clients has been performed. It leads to the elimination of 88% of financial losses while reducing the good client prospective by only 13%. The training and testing sets contain 1000 client vectors each. The entire training/recall process required approximately 8 min (vs. 10 h for the connectionist package).

10.2 KNOWLEDGE DOMAIN

We discuss how to present and represent the conceptual domain knowledge— the conceptual knowledge about measurement in the quality assurance. One possible idea is to define the domain knowledge explicitly and to structure it independently from particular courses or learning strategies. Based on this domain structure (and additional knowledge), different learning modes can be supported. Thus, for developing the system we first had to develop a structuring for the knowledge such that it could be presented adequately to the users.

Muellerburg, Meyerhoff, and Flacke [1], in their METKIT system, distinguish the following types of conceptual knowledge:

Knowledge about particular terms or objects

Knowledge about groups of terms or objects

Knowledge about the context of a term or object

Knowledge about the context of a group of terms or object

According to Briand, Basili, and Thomas [2], building domain knowledge for quality assessment faces the following difficulties:

There is no theory proven to be effective in any environment that would give a formal relationship among measured metrics in the development process. Therefore the capabilities of classical statistical approaches seem limited.

There is little evidence to support the assumption about the probability density distribution with respect to the dependent and independent variables of interest.

The sample size is usually small relative to the requirements of classical statistical techniques, the quality of data collected, and the number of significant independent variables. This is due to the nature of the studied objects and is difficult to avoid.

Modelers have to deal with missing, interdependent, and nonrelevant independent variables. This is due to a lack of understanding of the processes and interactions.

Data defined on a continuous (i.e., ratio, interval) and a discrete (i.e., nominal, ordinal) range both have to be handled. Collecting data in a real-life environment is a difficult task, and discrete data collection is often performed to facilitate the measurement process. Also, the nature of some of the data may be discrete.

10.3 INDUCTIVE AND NEURAL LEARNING

In general, various methods could be used for machine learning, only some of which have been used for quality assessment.

Candidate learning methods include

Bayes theory, assuming independence of the attributes.

Linear discriminant methods for multivariate normal propulations.

Logistic regression model.

Machine-learning algorithms using decision trees, of which the best known is Quinlan's ID3 [3]. There are also variations of the ID3 dealing with relational data.

Genetic classifier system based on evolution/selection theory and on genetic algorithms [4].

Neural networking learning, where error signals are backpropagated through the network [5].

Several authors have compared these learning methods in different applications. In some applications several learning methods produce similar results. In others a particular learning method outperforms the others.

Michalski [6] defines the inductive learning in the following way: inductive concept learning is a form of learning in which a general concept description is inferred from examples of that concept or in which concepts useful in characterizing a given collection of objects are generated.

Esteva and Reynolds [7] have developed an inductive approach in which the members of a set of object attributes that may possibly describe the concept are outlined. Thus, a decision tree construction tool formulates a decision tree, based on the values of measurable attributes, to accept all positive instances of the concept and to reject negative instances. Thus, the decision tree characterization becomes the basis for forecasting whether an object, previously unseen, is a positive or negative instance of the concept being modeled.

The concept learning system (CLS) developed by Hunt, Martin, and Stone [8] constructs a classification rule using the knowledge contained in a set of objects, called the training set, the classes of which are given. All objects are described here by a fixed collection of attributes, and each object in the set can be said to belong to one of two mutually exclusive classes. A classification rule is expressed as a decision tree in which every interior node consists of a test of an attribute with one subtree for every possible value of that attribute, and each leaf is a class signaling the appropriate outcome of the classification rule. Attributes are selected according to their discriminatory power—that is, to the degree to which an attribute partitions the objects into subsets that are either all positive or all negative. An evaluation function is applied to each subset of objects that have resulted from using the attribute as a partition. The decision tree generation system takes as its input the training set and uses the recursive procedure to generate a classification rule expressed as a decision tree. The module classification system uses the decision tree derived by the decision tree generation system to classify any object in the test set. This is done by searching through the tree, starting at the root node, according to the values assigned to the attributes for that module. The process of searching through the tree stops when the module's class is determined (i.e., when a leaf node is encountered).

Another possibility is to use neural networks [5]. However, it has been observed that training of backpropagation-layered neural networks can be a time-consuming task, which can require, say, several thousand iterations. Moreover, the procedure may not converge at all, or the least squares error for the final network may be unacceptably large. In those cases we try to modify the network. We can change the number of neurons, network topology, accumulation or transfer functions, the training rule, or the paradigm.

10.4   PATTERN RECOGNITION

Quality evaluation based on pattern recognition has been developed by Briand, Basili, and Thomas [2]. The technique has as its goal the recognition of patterns in a data set. These patterns are used as a basis for understanding and assessing the development process, product, and environment. The following definition outlines this technique:

A learning sample consists of N vectors $(DV_i, IV_{1,i} \ldots, IV_{n,i})$, $i \in (1, \ldots, N)$, containing one dependent and n independent variables. These vectors, which we will call pattern vectors, represent measurements taken in the environment. (DV, dependent variable; IV, independent variable).

A measurement vector is defined as the set of independent variables representing a particular object whose dependent variable is to be predicted. That is, it is a pattern vector without the dependent variable.

To be able to make predictions on the dependent variable, its range has to be subdivided or grouped into what we will call DV classes. These classes correspond to natural situations that can be encountered in the measurement environment, with respect to the dependent variable (e.g., productivity). If the dependent variable is "ratio," "interval," or "ordinal," the dependent variable range is subdivided into intervals, if the dependent variable is "nominal," categories may be grouped into a smaller set of classes. They are called *states of nature* in decision theory and *pattern classes* in pattern recognition. We have chosen the name DV classes in order to make the connection with a classical statistical approach for multivariable analysis.

To be able to use the independent variables as a basis for predicting the dependent variable, they, like the dependent variables, must be mapped into IV classes by subdividing or grouping.

A pattern is defined as a nonuniform distribution of probabilities across the DV classes. The further a distribution is from uniformity, the more the pattern is considered as significant (measurable metric developed later).

The results of preliminary experiments have been encouraging, since the predictions obtained were more accurate than those of other modeling techniques.

10.5 THE HOLOGRAPHIC NETWORK

Problem solving by a new holographic paradigm [9–11] consists of constructing a suitable network and training that network. Thus, no explicit mathematical modeling is involved. Also we need no algorithm design and no programming (provided that a network simulator is available). Avoidance of exact models is desirable in "soft" knowledge disciplines such as quality evaluation and analysis.

Holographic networks can be applied directly to quality evaluation. For this purpose, the package of all metrics has to be interpreted as a stimulus, and the "good/poor" attribute must take the role of a response. The network is trained on the sample set of objects. A sufficiently large network will be able to memorize all the training associations and reproduce them correctly. Moreover, the network will generalize each association; that is, for similar values of the metrics it will produce the same "good/poor" response.

The input field is expressed in a form of a vector composed of several elements (10 to 20). The elements belong to four groups, covering continuous (i.e., ratio, interval) and discrete (i.e., nominal ordinal) ranges: (1) binary, (2) grades, (3) Gaussian, and (4) asymmetric.

It is the principle of a azimuthal symmetry that fundamentally enables the superposition of information within the holographic cell. Symmetry is achieved in the following way:

The binary yes/no input elements are converted to representative 0-π phase orientation

In a similar way, the field composed on n grades $(0, 1/n, \ldots, 1)$ is converted into $(0, 2\pi/n, \ldots, 2\pi)$

In a Gaussian distribution, the parameters α, σ are used to find the proper sigmoid conversion curve.

The more complex distribution $f_1(x)$ of input elements displaying asymmetric cases employs the optimal conversion function $g(x) = F_1(x)$, where $F_1(x)$ is the integral distribution of $f_1(x)$, as described in [12].

10.6 INPUT DATA FOR CREDIT SCORING

A point description of the input field for credit scoring is listed here. The external data base supplied 13 of these fields, the internal data the remaining five.

GE	Age client
SEX	Male/female
MAR_STAT	Martial status (single/married)
HHLD_STAT	Household status of client
	H - head of household
	W - wife
	P - aged parent
	C - college-aged child
CHILD	Does client have children (yes/no)
DWEL_TYPE	Type of dwelling client resides in
	S - urban single family
	A - urban apartment
	M - urban multifamily
	R - rural
HOMEOWNER	Does client own property (yes/no)
AGED_PAR	Does aged parent live in household (yes/no)
LENGTH_RES	Period of time that client has been living in current accommodation
INCOME	Personal income of client
	J - $15,000 or less
	K - $15,001 to $25,000
	L - $25,001 to $35,000
	M - $35,001 to $50,000
	N - $50,001 to $75,000
	O - $75,001 to $100,000
	P - $100,001 to $120,000
	Q - $120,001 and up
HHLD_INCOME	Cumulative income of persons living in household
	H - $8,000 or less
	G - $8,001 to $9,999
	F - $10,000 to $14,999
	E - $15,000 to $19,999

D - $20,000 to $24,999
C - $25,000 to $44,999
B - $35,000 to $49,999
A - $50,000 to $74,999
I - $75,000 and up

NUM_ADULTS	Number of adults living in household
ZIP	Zip code of client
ORIG_BAL	Original loan balance
LN_TERM	Term of loan in months
APR	Annual percentage rate
V_AGE	Vehicle age at time of loan inception
RT_NEW	Vehicle rate type, assigned by the bank based on vehicle type

Data were taken in raw numerical form for input to the holographic network. For instance, character codes as used in the case of RT_NEW were converted to their equivalent integer ASCII values. A significant improvement in the mappings generated by the holographic system may be realized by breaking these codes into appropriate divisions within their associated complex phase representations. For instance, one may segregate the phase regions into type (i.e., car/truck) and expense category (economy/luxury). An appropriate representation within the complex field is illustrated in Figure 10.1. A similar type of breakdown could be performed with zip codes (i.e., segregating area code by economic factors) to increase the meaningfulness of the mapping generated within the holographic neural system.

10.7 FORECASTED VARIABLES

The system was trained to learn the most significant indicator within the data base, this being LN_STAT loan status—the loan was either paid out by the client or charged off by the bank. This is probably the most important indicator. Other important factors can also be predicted, namely claim status, money

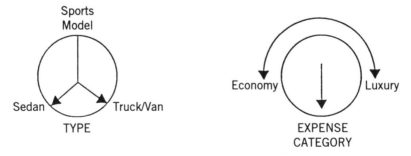

Figure 10.1 *Phase representation for discrete vs continuous ranges.*

amount of insurance claims filed, the total amount of money written off by the bank, and so on.

10.8 DETAILS OF THE HOLOGRAPHIC SCORING

A subset of the input fields were converted to the complex domain using a straightforward linear conversion. For instance, in the case of binary or yes/no decisions, these fields were assigned a representative $0/\pi$ phase orientation. In a similar fashion the HHLD_STAT and DWELL_TYPE fields were linearly scaled to four phase regions (i.e., 0, $\pi/2$, π, $3\pi/2$). The remaining fields employed a sigmoidal conversion in the generation of the internal complex representation. The mean and standard deviations for each input field were evaluated over the 650 vectors within the training set and used as the conversion coefficients to achieve a symmetrical distribution in phase space. The mean and standard deviation values used in this conversion are presented in Table 10.1.

An initial network was constructed to rank the importance of the input field, evaluating only the first-order terms. This process involves encoding a representative set of input vectors to their associated credit assignment and determining the magnitudes of the correlation elements generated in the cell's internal mapping. The 650 vectors within the training set have been used for this evaluation. The magnitude of the correlation element indicates the degree of correlation between input/output for the associated fields. These results are presented in Table 10.2. It was found from this analysis that the most important

TABLE 10.1 Distribution Parameters for Input Fields

Field	Mean of Distribution	Standard Deviation
1	38.4	12.9
9	3.34	3.89
10	3.55	1.1
11	4.9	2.1
12	2.2	1.23
13	1060	813
14	9830	486
15	50	14
16	12.6	2.2
17	1.55	2.6
18	74	10.4

TABLE 10.2 Correlation Magnitudes over Input Fields

Field	Correlation Magnitude	Field	Correlation Magnitude
1	935	10	929
2	593	11	664
3	524	12	451
4	446	13	2303
5	269	14	1397
6	697	15	4554
7	291	16	1309
8	573	17	2809
9	399	18	256

indicators were ranked as follows:

1. Term of loan
2. Age of vehicle
3. Zip code
4. Amount of loan
5. Annual percentage rate charged on loan
6. Age of client
7. Client income

The final evaluation used the 15 most significant fields as determined from Table 10.2. This reduced set was then expanded to 135 first- and second-order statistics via the stat cell prior to input into the cortex cell of the HNeT system. The data files were constructed from alternating high/low risk profiles in order to train the neural system symmetrically. Again, 650 vectors were used in the training set and the same number in prediction. One learning trial was used over the training data set requiring approximately 1 min of processing time. During the recall (prediction) portion of the program, the input vectors used in prediction of the clients credit risk category were then encoded in time series format to allow the network to adapt to the dynamically changing ambient (presumably economic) conditions. It was found that this mode of training/ prediction significantly improved the accuracy of the results over those obtained when not allowing the neural system to adapt to time series trends.

The prediction results obtained over the 650 vectors within the test set displayed a very significant improvement over prior results using only the financial institutions internal database. These results are shown in terms of nonloss versus loss clients whom have been classified as bad credit risks by the neural system. The net benefit in terms of dollar savings for the bank or other con-

TABLE 10.3   Rejection Ratios for Client Groups

Confidence Threshold	Good Rejected (% Total Good Clients)	Bad Rejection (% Total Bad Clients)
−0.5	3	65.0
−0.4	4.3	70.1
−0.3	6.2	75.1
−0.2	8.3	80.9
−0.1	11.4	84.0
−0.0	13.2	87.7
−0.1	17.2	91.7
−0.2	20.3	92.6
−0.3	25.2	94.5
−0.4	30.8	96.0
0.5	38.5	96.9

tingencies is reflected in the difference between these two percentages as shown in Table 10.3. In addition, the holographic neural process assigns a confidence level to the response prediction. One may further establish a threshold level about a given confidence value at which clients may be rejected as bad credit risks, thereby customizing system performance to meet operating constraints. For instance, the bank may find it acceptable to reject 13% of nonloss clients for loan applications at which point the network will reject 87% of the clients who have defaulted (i.e., eliminating 88% of losses while reducing their good client prospective by only 13%). The results expressed in terms of the rejection ratios are again presented in Table 10.3 as a function of the confidence threshold. Further indicators may of course be mapped within the neural system (such as net dollar value of losses) to obtain a more thorough risk assessment for the prospective client.

Further analysis using another set of data shows that a large number of the input parameters may be discarded without adverse effect on the accuracy of the system. In all, the number of input variables used in the most recent analysis is 30 out of the original 52.

The network (one cell with 500 synopses) was trained on 2000 patterns, then tested on 2000 patterns not used within the training set. The entire training/recall process required approximately 5 min (vs. 8 h for the connectionist neural package). The summary in Table 10.4 illustrates the increase in classification accuracy on the test set as one increases the threshold for allowable confidence levels. In this manner one may minimize the number of high risk client classifications, however, at the cost of greater numbers of loss misclassifications. The total accuracy for the system is approximately 75%; however, the ratios

TABLE 10.4   Loss vs Nonloss Ratios as a Function of Confidence

Confidence	Percent Losses Incorrectly Classified	Percent Nonlosses Correctly Classified	Absolute Error (% Total Records)
0.0	25.7	73.3	26.2
0.05	27.7	76.4	25.6
0.1	30.4	78.9	25.7
0.15	31.8	81.2	25.3
0.2	33.7	82.5	25.6
0.25	34.9	84.5	25.2
0.3	37.0	86.3	25.4
0.35	38.7	87.9	25.4
0.4	40.5	88.9	25.8
0.45	41.9	90.1	25.9
0.5	44.7	91.3	26.7

of losses vs nonlosses may be skewed by varying this confidence level. For instance, the network is capable of correctly classifying approximately 85% of nonlosses at the point where one third of all losses will be misclassified. This ratio occurs at a confidence level of 0.25 and may again be modified to suit the institution's specific resources or requirements.

In this analysis the initial set of data was reduced to a core set of 30 fields. A statistical measure of the mean and standard deviation over the training data was evaluated for these input fields and used within a sigmoidal transfer to map the real-valued inputs to the complex representation used within the neural system. The neural configuration allocated within the HNeT system expanded this input field up to 500 first- and second-order statistics.

It was found that accuracy improved somewhat if the input fields with a 0 tag were assigned to a confidence value of zero. This method of varying confidence assignment within the stimulus field was used to filter out extraneous or missing parameters during the encoding/decoding processes. In this manner the holographic neural system can automatically adapt to record lengths of variable size. The additional demographic profiles could increase absolute accuracy levels by a further 10–15%.

REFERENCES

[1] M. Muellerburg, D. Meyerhoff, and S. Flacke, "Supporting Software Measurement: The METKIT CAI System," Information Processing Systems and Software, *ESPRIT*, XIII, 372, 256–261, (1991).

[2] L. C. Briand, V. R. Basili, W. M. Thomas, "A Pattern Recognition Approach for Software Engineering Data Analysis," Technical Report 2672, University of Maryland (1991).

[3] J. R. Quinlan, "Introduction of Decision Trees," *J. Machine Learning*, 1(1), 81–106 (1986).

[4] J. H. Holland, *Adaptation in Natural and Artificial Systems*, University of Michigan Press, An Arbor, 1975.

[5] B. Souček and M. Souček, *Neural and Massively Parallel Computers*, Wiley, New York, 1988, p. 460.

[6] R. S. Michalski, ed., *Machine Learning: An Artificial Intelligence Approach*, Carbonell, Mitchell, Morgan Kaufmann, 1983.

[7] J. C. Esteva and R. G. Reynolds, Identifying reusable software components by induction, *Internat. J. Software Eng. Knowledge Eng.*, 1(3), 271–292 (1991).

[8] E. B. Hunt, Martin, and Stone, *Experiments in Induction*, Academic Press, 1966.

[9] J. Sutherland, A holographic model of memory, learning and expression, *Internat. J. Neural Syst.*, 1(3), 259–267 (1990).

[10] J. Sutherland, The holographic neural method, in B. Souček, ed., *Fuzzy Holographic, and Parallel Intelligence*, Wiley 1992, pp. 7–92.

[11] B. Souček and IRIS Group, *Fuzzy, Holographic, and Parallel Intelligence*, Wiley, New York, 1992, p. 350.

[12] R. Manger, V. L. Plantamura, and B. Souček, Stimulus Preprocessing for Holographic Neural Networks, Chapter 4 of this volume.

CHAPTER 11

Credit Scoring Based on Neural and Machine Learning

JÜRGEN GRAF
GHOLAMREZA NAKHAEIZADEH

11.1 INTRODUCTION

The traditional approach of granting credit is based on a "judgmental" concept that uses the past experiences of credit officers and some credit applicants' characteristics such as income, occupation, residential stability, and so on. This approach suffers, however, from some drawbacks such as high costs of training of credit officers, often wrong decisions made by credit officers, and different decisions of credit officers for the same case. These difficulties have encouraged finding some means of automating credit management decisions. An alternative approach is based on classical statistical classification tools such as discriminance analysis. Recently, some knowledge-based credit-scoring systems were developed with expert system technology. In practice, many of the attributes used to characterize credit applicants are qualitative attributes, and as is well known, discriminance analysis is not an appropriate tool in such circumstances. On the other hand, in development of knowledge-based credit-scoring systems, normally one encounters the knowledge-acquisition bottleneck problem. As an alternative to these approaches, consider the application of neural nets and machine-learning algorithms. In this study we discuss the performance of different approaches that can contribute to automating credit-granting procedures. We concentrate, in particular, on the application of machine-learning and neural network approaches in solving the credit-scoring problem. To evaluate the performance of the different approaches, we use several real-world data sets. The empirical results of the evaluation procedures will be reported and dis-

Frontier Decision Support Concepts, Edited by V. L. Plantamura, B. Souček, and G. Visaggio.
ISBN 0-471-59256-0 © 1994 John Wiley & Sons, Inc.

cussed. The results show that, in particular, machine-learning-based classification approaches can be regarded as a very efficient alternative to credit-scoring systems.

Credit-scoring (CS) is a procedure used to evaluate customers of financial institutions as good or bad credit risk. Credit demand has increased rapidly in recent years. For example, private households in Germany have applied on average for DM 5.7 Mrd new credit in the period 1970–1974. From 1990 to 1991 the applied new credit has been on average 28.4 Mrd (monthly report of the Bundesbank for April 1992). In 1980 only 9% of private households in Austria had a bank credit, but in 1990 it was 15% (see [1]). Especially in the field of consumer credit, a combination growth in the supply and form of credit has contributed very strongly to increasing the demand. Credit cards have made obtaining consumer credit much easier. There is also an increase in the demand for commercial credit. In Germany, decreasing the capital rate of private companies from 30% in 1967 to 18% in 1989 has led to increasing credit demand (see [2]). On the other hand, it is estimated that about DM 15 Mrd of the granted credit to the private companies will never be repaid.

These points show the importance of the CS as a framework for prediction of credit risk, credit decisions, and credit management support. The benefits of CS systems have been realized by many companies, and their applications are well established. Although scoring is the main part of the CS systems, their application is not limited only to scoring. Modern CS systems make not only the judgment of new credit applications possible but they can also be used for

- Periodic evaluation of possible risk, especially, for revolving credit
- Evaluation of the alternative limit strategies
- Determining if the quality of the overall portfolio is changing over time

In this study we discuss recent developments in solving the CS problem. We emphasize the application of new learning techniques such as neural nets and symbolic machine learning. In this connection, we present the results of some empirical works we have done, using different neural and symbolic learning algorithms. Section 11.2 describes the traditional approach in credit scoring. In Section 11.3, we regard credit scoring as a classification task and discuss some statistical and machine-learning classification algorithms used in the empirical part. The different data sets used are presented in Section 11.4, where we discuss empirical evaluation results as well. The last section is devoted to conclusions and final comments.

11.2 TRADITIONAL APPROACH IN CREDIT SCORING

The traditional approach of granting credit is the "judgmental" approach (see [3]). According to his past experience and using a conceptual framework based on income, occupation, and residential stability, a credit officer has to decide, subjectively, whether to grant or reject credit to an applicant. Such judgmental methods suffer from drawbacks such as

- High costs of training and employing of credit officers.
- Often wrong decision made by credit officers.
- For the same case, different credit officers often have different judgments.

These difficulties have led creditors to find means of automating credit management decisions. Early numerical scoring systems can be seen in this connection. According to Capon [3], the first scoring systems were developed in the mail order industry in the 1930s and were later used by large finance companies. The framework of the early systems was based on some predictor qualitative attributes used to discriminate between good and bad credit risks. Such attributes also build the core of modern CS systems and usually consist of factors such as income, occupation, length of employment, personal references, and the like. Each level of these attributes is awarded points. The achieved score of each applicant was determined by summing the points across different attributes. This score was compared with a cutoff value to decide whether to accept or reject the application. Table 11.1 shows a very simple example for an early numerical scoring system.

Suppose a married male applicant applies for credit amount that is about 30% of his disposable income. Setting the cutoff value, for example, as 40, he must be at least an unskilled employee to obtain the credit. In this case, he will achieve 45 points, which is higher than the cutoff value. From this example, it is clear that the creditors can change the amount of granted credit by changing the cutoff value.

TABLE 11.1 Example for Point Awarding in a Numerical Scoring System with Three Attributes

Attribute	Attribute Value	Awarded Points
Occupation	Unemployed	10
	Unskilled employee	20
	Skilled employee	30
	Manager, self-employed, highly qualified employee or officer	40
Installment rate in percentage of disposable income	$\geq 40\%$	5
	$25 \leq \cdots < 40\%$	10
	$20 \leq \cdots < 25\%$	15
	$< 20\%$	20
Personal status and sex	Male: divorced or separated	5
	Female: divorced, separated, or married	10
	Male: single	10
	Male: married or widowed	15
	Female: single	20

Awarding of points to different values of attributes was, mostly, in the early numerical CS systems ad hoc. In the scoring systems developed later, this procedure is based on the distribution of the attribute values in the selected sample of good and bad credit applicants. One of these methods, which is applied often in practice, will be described.

Suppose that we have selected a sample of good and bad credit applicants from the creditor's files and A is an attribute whose values $A_1, A_2, \ldots, A_k$ should be awarded by points. Denoting the relative frequency of the attribute value A_i for good and bad applicants by π_{i1}, π_{i2}, respectively, the awarded points to A_i will be calculated as

$$
v_i = \begin{cases} (\pi_{i1}/\pi_{i2}) - 1 & \pi_{i1} \geq \pi_{i2} \\ 1 - (\pi_{i2}/\pi_{i1}) & \text{else} \end{cases}
$$

One can find in the literature some other methods for awarding points based on the relative frequencies of the attribute values (e.g., see [4]).

It can be seen that the awarding procedures based on relative frequencies use the past experiences of credit officers more objectively because they apply, in contrast to the ad hoc method, all available information about the former credit applicants, explicitly. On the other hand, these procedures can be used only if solved cases are available. It means the creditors should have already granted a certain number of credits and have registered the good and bad credit applicants. In both of these point-awarding procedures, it is possible to change the amount of credit granted by changing the cutoff value. Lowering the cutoff value allows creditors to grant more credit, and vice versa. Of course, a higher cutoff value corresponds to a higher risk rate. It means there is a trade-off between the risk and acceptance rates, which can be described very well by the strategy curve (see Figure 11.1).

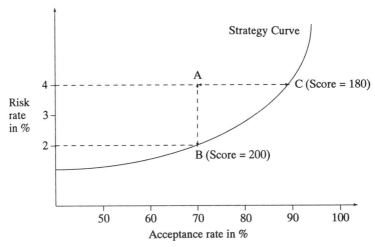

Figure 11.1 *Strategy curve.*

The strategy curve is an instrument for portfolio planning (see [5]). Each point of the strategy curve represents a certain score associated with an acceptance and a risk rate. Using the strategy curve, the portfolio manager can analyze the various effects of changing cutoff values on acceptance and risk rates. For example, decreasing the cutoff value from 200 to 180 changes the acceptance rate from 70% to 90%. At the same time the risk rate will be increased from 2% to 4%.

Up to now we have discussed only the different procedures of awarding points for attribute values. The selecting of relevant attributes is a very important task in developing scoring systems. In early numerical scoring, attribute selection was, as point awarding, an ad hoc procedure. It was not clear if the selected attributes are statistically related to the payment performance of credit applicants. Meanwhile there are several methods for attribute selection. Most of these procedures are based upon statistical approaches such as discriminance and regression analysis, discussed in the next section.

11.3 CREDIT SCORING AS A CLASSIFICATION TASK

11.3.1 General Remarks

Regarding the fact that credit scoring is a classification task, one can use all available tools appropriate for classification. A classification tool or a classifier accepts a pattern of data as input; its output is a decision. For example, in credit scoring the classifier input could be information about the attribute values of the credit applicant, such as level of income, occupation, marital status, and the like. As shown in Figure 11.2, the classifier produces as output the decision of whether the applicant is a good or bad credit risk. Most of the procedures used to develop classifiers are based on a general concept called *learning from examples* or *supervised learning*. In learning from examples, the learning task

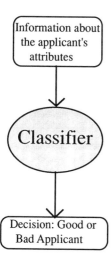

Figure 11.2 *Credit scoring as a classification task.*

TABLE 11.2   Pattern of Data in Learning from Examples

Examples	Attribute Values	Classes
1	a_{11} a_{12} $\cdots$ a_{1n}	c_1
2	a_{21} a_{22} $\cdots$ a_{2n}	c_2
.		.
.	$\cdots$	.
.		.
m	a_{m1} a_{m2} $\cdots$ a_{mn}	c_m

can be formulated as follows: *Given a mutually exclusive set of solved examples (cases), find a concept for classifying an unseen example (case) as a function of its attribute values.*

As this case shows, in learning from examples the learning system needs solved as *learning* or *training data*. Table 11.2 demonstrates the pattern of the examples that can be seen as input for the learning system. The learning system learns from this type of example and develops a classifier that can be used later for classifying cases with unknown class. The traditional learning systems that learn from examples are the classical statistical tools. Recently, some other classifiers are developed that are based on concepts like *neural nets* and *machine learning* (see Figure 11.3). We briefly describe these learning systems.

11.3.2   Statistical Approaches

As mentioned, the classification systems based on statistical approaches learn from examples. The classification problem has been widely studied in statistics. Most of the statistical classification methods have a very strong theoretical foundation, and some of them are implemented in statistical packages like SAS and SPSS. To the standard statistical classification algorithms belong linear discriminant, logistic regression, nearest-neighbor, and Bayesian classifiers. Besides these standard methods, other classifiers are implemented in program packages, such as ALLOC80, SMART, and CASTLE. We describe the main

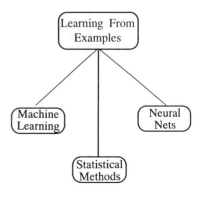

Figure 11.3 *Alternative approaches for learning from examples.*

idea of the linear discriminant that we will use in the empirical part of this study. ALLOC80 is described in [6], information about SMART can be found in [7], and the theoretical background of CASTLE is given in [8].

Similar to other multivariate procedures, LD is a parametric approach and, usually, it is assumed that the statistical populations are normally distributed. Under this assumption, the objective is to find a rule—a discrimination function—that can be used to classify objects with unknown classes. For simplicity, we regard the case in which only two populations are available, which means that the elements of the sample belong with certainty to population 1 or 2. Furthermore, we assume that each object is characterized by p attributes, which means that we represent the objects by a p-dimensional space W. The aim is now to find a boundary that divides W into two subspaces, R and $W - R$, such that as many objects as possible of population 1 lie on one side, and as many objects as possible of population 2 lie on the other side (see, for example, [9]). It is clear that such a boundary cannot divide the space W precisely into two desired subspaces and an error risk is always available. Two kinds of error can be considered: An object may belong to population 1 and yet be assigned by the boundary to population 2, or vice versa. Denoting the frequency distributions of populations 1 and 2 by f_1 and f_2, respectively, and assuming that the probabilities of misallocation are the same for the two kinds of error, we get

$$\int_R f_2 \, dx = \int_{W-R} f_1 \, dx = 1 - \int_R f_1 \, dx \qquad (11.1)$$

Equation (11.1) shows that the total error e is

$$e = 1 + \int_R (f_2 - f_1) \, dx \qquad (11.2)$$

Among all possible boundaries, LD selects the boundary that minimizes the total error e. For the case in which f_1 and f_2 are continuous, e will be minimized if

$$f_1 = f_2 \quad \text{or} \quad \log f_1 = \log f_2 \qquad (11.3)$$

Under the assumption that the populations are normally distributed with equal covariance matrix Σ, Eq. (11.3) leads to

$$(x - \mu_1)^T \Sigma^{-1} (x - \mu_1) = (x - \mu_2)^T \Sigma^{-1} (x - \mu_2) \qquad (11.4)$$

After slight manipulation we get

$$x^T \Sigma^{-1} (\mu_1 - \mu_2) - \tfrac{1}{2}(\mu_1 + \mu_2)^T \Sigma^{-1} (\mu_1 - \mu_2) = 0 \qquad (11.5)$$

Equation (11.5) represents the desired discrimination function. To classify an unknown object, we can use the equation

$$D = x^T \Sigma^{-1}(\mu_1 - \mu_2) - \tfrac{1}{2}(\mu_1 + \mu_2)^T \Sigma^{-1}(\mu_1 - \mu_2) \qquad (11.6)$$

If $D > 0$, the object will be assigned to class 1; otherwise it is assigned to class 2.

11.3.3   Neural Networks

Many contributions in the literature report the application of neural nets in solving classification tasks in different domains. There are also some studies that report applying neural nets for solving the CS problem. In [10], for example, the authors use neural networks to predict bond ratings, which represent the default risk of bonds. For this reason we describe the topology of the networks used in this study.

Adaline Network. One of the earliest contributions to neural computing is the Adaline (*ada*ptive *li*near *ne*uron) from Bernard Widrow, a threshold logic device that used outputs of -1, $+1$. The input to the unit was also bistate (-1, $+1$; see [11], p. NC-35). Like perceptron, the Adaline can only be applied to data sets with discrete-valued classes. The Adaline learning algorithm used in this study is Widrow-Hoff learning.

Madaline Network. The first approach to solving linear separability was the multiple Adaline or Madaline. This paradigm uses several Adalines in parallel with a single output unit that takes a majority vote on the inputs. If half or more of the inputs are $+1$, the output is $+1$. Otherwise, the output is -1. Since the Madaline has a binary output, it can only be used to discriminate between two classes. In Madaline learning an input pattern and a desired output are presented to the network. If the actual output matches the desired output, no learning takes place. However, if they differ, the Adaline with the closest output to zero in the wrong direction is adapted. The process is repeated until the network converges.

Counterpropagation Network. Counterpropagation was invented by R. Hecht-Nielsen, who developed it as a means for synthesizing complex functions (see [11], p. NC-157). Counterpropagation is able to learn the categories and to separate them. There are three requirements (see [11], p. NC-160):

- The classes must be discrete valued.
- The competition layer must have enough processing elements to ensure that they can adapt to form the boundaries.
- The inputs must be selected so that they uniformly cover the class categories. Concentrating them may skew the concentration of elements in the competitive layer, creating faulty class boundaries.

Coding Inputs and Outputs. One of the techniques used in several of the Adaline and Madaline experiments is the use of "linearly independent codes." This is basically a method of decomposing a single input value into a series of "codes" that form an invertible matrix consisting of only 0 and 1 terms. One example of a linearly independent code used in this study for decomposing one attribute with four values is shown in the following:

Value of X		Code		
value 1	1	0	0	0
value 2	0	1	0	0
value 3	0	0	1	0
value 4	0	0	0	1

The disadvantage of this method is the length of the input layer. Complex problems need input layers with hundreds of nodes. The requirement of time, hardware, and software is very high in this case.

We used two forms of coding for outputs:

- In the Adaline we use two output nodes; one represents the good risks, one the bad.
- In the Madaline and Counterpropagation net, we use only one neuron as output node, the interval [0.5, 1.0] represents the good and the interval [0.0, 0.5] the bad risk.

11.3.4 Machine-Learning Approaches

As mentioned, some machine-learning algorithms can be used to solve the classification tasks. Machine learning is a subarea of artificial intelligence (AI) with the objective to imitate the learning ability of a human being. In recent years AI researchers developed some machine-learning algorithms based on the concept *learning from examples*. These algorithms were originally developed to solve the well-known knowledge-acquisition bottleneck problem that arises normally in development of classical expert systems. Using past experiences, available in the form of *examples*, machine-learning algorithms can generate production rules for the knowledge base of expert systems. It was later realized that many machine-learning algorithms can solve the classification tasks as well, and they can be regarded as a very useful alternative to classical statistical approaches.

The machine-learning approach in classification was not totally unknown to statisticians (see, for example [12]). The popularity of this concept is, however, due to the contributions of AI researchers like Michalski (see [13]) and Quinlan (see [14]).

The most important machine-learning algorithms that learn from examples can be divided into two major groups (see Fig. 11.4). The first group, mainly based on the AQ-Family developed by Michalski, learns from examples and

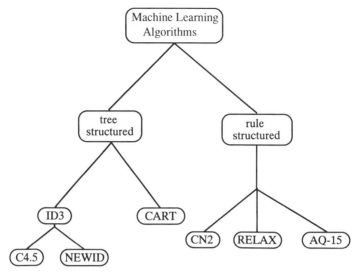

Figure 11.4   *Some machine-learning algorithms.*

generates If-Then rules. To this group belong algorithms like AQ-15, CN2, and RELAX. The other group generates decision trees involving algorithms like ID3, CART, C4.5, and NEWID. We discuss briefly some of the algorithms used in the empirical part of this work.

Tree-Structured Algorithms

ID3 Concept. Most of the tree-structured algorithms are based on the concept of ID3. ID3 generates a decision tree from which one can derive the If-Then rules. As shown in Fig. 11.5, the generated decision tree consists of a root, some middle nodes, and some terminal nodes. To generate the decision tree from a training data set the following procedure is used:

1. From the list of available attributes ID3 selects the most informative attribute, using a selection criteria based on the entropy measure. Suppose that X is a random variable that takes the values $x_1, x_2, \ldots$, with probabilities $p_1, p_2, \ldots, p_n$, respectively. The entropy measure is defined as

$$\text{ent}(X) = -\sum_{i=1}^{n} p_i \log (p_i)$$

In practice, probabilities are replaced by relative frequencies. It can be showed that

$$0 \leq \text{ent}(X) \leq \log n$$

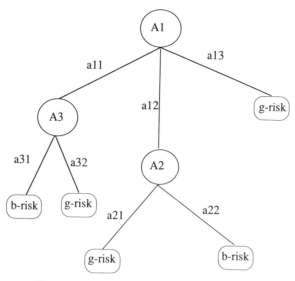

Figure 11.5 *An example for the decision tree.*

The minimum of ent(X) is zero and can be achieved if

$$p_j = 1 \quad \text{and} \quad p_i = 0 \quad \forall i \neq j$$

In this case, the random variable X takes the value x_j with probability 1. The information content of ent(X) is, in this case, maximum. On the other hand, if the probabilities are all $1/n$, then ent(X) $=$ log n. In this case the information content of ent(X) is minimum.

ID3 uses a weighted version of the entropy measure. Suppose that the attribute A has the values $a_1, a_2, \ldots, a_m$. Denoting the relative frequency of a_i with $R(a_i)$, we define the entropy of the attribute A as

$$\text{ent}(A) = - \sum_{i=1}^{m} R(a_i) \sum_{j=1}^{k} r(c_j|a_i) \log r(c_j|a_i)$$

where k denotes the number of classes and for the attribute A, and $r(c_j|a_i)$ denotes the relative frequency of all examples belonging to class c_j and having the value a_i.

2. After selecting the most informative attribute, ID3 divides the examples into different groups according to values of the most informative attribute and assigns each group to a node. If all examples of a node belong to the same class, then this node will be regarded as a terminal node and ID3 stops splitting at this node. In the other case, the algorithm again selects another most informative attribute and continues splitting as long as the examples of each node have the same class value.

The foregoing description of the main idea of ID3 is further developed in different directions by Quinlan and other authors to handle

- Continuous-valued attributes and classes
- Data sets with missing values
- Noisy data

C4.5. The algorithm C4.5 is based on ID3 and was also developed by Ross Quinlan at the University of Sydney, Australia. The theoretical issues of C4.5 are discussed in a series of Quinlan's contributions, among them [15–17]. The output of C4.5 is a decision tree. But it is possible to derive from this tree the production rules, too. Like all ID3-based algorithms, C4.5 uses various criteria that make it possible to reach a decision in the following situations:

- When should a node be regarded as a terminal node, or, in other words, when should splitting be stopped? A criterion, also used by NEWID, could be the membership of the examples of each node in the same class. In practice, and especially in dealing with noisy data, this criterion is not applicable and generates very complex decision trees with poor classification power. C4.5 uses a χ^2-statistic as stopping criterion. It means, however, that after stopping, not all examples of each node belong to the same class. To overcome this problem, one can use the class with highest frequency as the common class for the examples of each node.
- How can the most informative attribute be selected? Like ID3, C4.5 uses the entropy criteria. But some other versions of the entropy criterion are also implemented in C4.5.
- How can continuous-valued attributes be handled? It is obvious that it is not possible to use the attribute values to divide the examples into different groups. C4.5 uses a binary approach. Suppose that the attribute A takes values that can be increasingly ordered as $a_1, a_2, \ldots, a_n$. Now, a threshold s can be defined as

$$s = \frac{a_i + a_{i+1}}{2} \qquad (i = 1, \ldots, n)$$

which can be used to divide the examples into the nodes. Values of A greater than s can be assigned to the left, and the other values to the right nodes. The entropy criterion can be used to find the optimal threshold.
- How can noisy data be handled? As mentioned, noisy data lead to very complex trees with poor classification power. Some pruning methods are implemented in C4.5 to overcome this difficulty, among them cost-complexity pruning, error-reduction pruning, and pessimistic pruning. Furthermore, it is possible to derive production rules from unpruned trees and then generalize these rules (see [16] and [17] for more details).

Besides the preceding possibilities, C4.5 can handle large-scale data sets using the "windowing technique." It is also possible to handle data sets with missing values.

NEWID. The NEWID algorithm was developed by Robin Boswell at Turing Institute, Glasgow, and generates as C4.5 decision trees. It is also possible to derive production rules from generated trees, automatically. Almost all properties of C4.5 can be found in NEWID as well, except for the windowing technique. On the other hand, NEWID can handle continuous-valued classes, which is not possible with C4.5. Only two other algorithms can do so, namely, CART (see [12]) and a procedure recently implemented in the statistical package S-Plus.

To handle continuous-valued classes, one needs another strategy to select the most informative attribute. It is the same for assigning class values to the middle and terminal nodes of the decision trees. Instead of an entropy criterion, which is not applicable in this case, NEWID uses a variance criterion. Assigning the class values to the nodes is discussed in our other contribution to this book.

Rule-Structured Algorithms. As mentioned, the outputs of the rule-structured algorithms are If-Then rules. Among such algorithms, we used CN2 in the empirical part of this study.

CN2. This algorithm was developed by Tim Niblett and Peter Clark at Turing Institute, Glasgow. One can find the theoretical issues of CN2 in [5] and [6]. The initial version of AQ-Algorithm could not handle noisy data. To overcome this shortcoming, different strategies from ID3 and AQ-type algorithms are implemented in CN2.

The algorithm starts with an empty rule set and searches a general complex covering a large number of examples of a single class c and a few examples of the other classes. The complex evaluation approach in CN2 consists of a two-stage heuristic procedure. To test the quality of generated rules, CN2 uses in the first stage an evaluation function based on different criteria, among them

- Accuracy rate, which is the number of correctly classified examples divided by total number covered.
- Entropy criteria (see "Tree-Structured Algorithms").
- The Laplacian error estimate L defined as

$$L = \frac{n - n_c + k - 1}{n + k}$$

where k is the number of the classes, n is the total number of examples and n_c the number of positive examples covered by the rule.

In the second stage, CN2 tries to determine if a complex is significant by using the likelihood ratio test given by

$$2 \sum_{i=1}^{n} f_i \log \left(\frac{f_i}{e_i} \right)$$

where $F = (f_1, f_2, \ldots, f_n)$ is the observed frequency distribution of examples among classes that satisfy a given complex and $E = (e_1, e_2, \ldots, e_n)$ is the expected frequency distribution of the same number of examples under the assumption that the complex selects examples randomly (see [19] for more details).

Like NEWID and C4.5, CN2 can handle attributes with missing values.

11.4 EVALUATION RESULTS

11.4.1 Used Data Sets and Empirical Results

To evaluate different methods described in Section 11.3 we used two real-world data sets. Some information about these data sets is summarized in Table 11.3. The first data set is a sample of 1000 consumer credits and stems from a large bank in south Germany. By traditional and statistical methods, this data set has been analyzed often in the literature. The results reported in [20–22] are examples of such empirical studies. These studies use, however, traditional or statistical approaches of credit scoring. An exception is Hofmann (see [23]), who uses the CART methodology described in [12]. As can be seen from Fig. 11.4, CART is a tree-structured approach that uses a similar procedure as NEWID. The original version of the first data set includes 700 good- and 300 bad-risk bank customers. Regarding only the distribution of good and bad classes, one can get a default accuracy of 70%, assigning an unknown case to good risk class. Thus, to be acceptable other classifiers should have an accuracy better than 70%.

To examine the performance of the evaluated classifiers for the other cases with different good- and bad-risk distributions, we created an additional version of the first data set, selecting randomly only 300 good risks from 700. This led to a new version of the first data set, including 300 good- and 300 bad-risk customers with a default classification accuracy of 50%.

As Table 11.3 shows, in the first data set the credit applicants are charac-

TABLE 11.3   Used Data Sets

Data Set	Number of Examples	Number of Attrib. Categorical	Numerical	Number of Classes
I	1000	13	7	2
II	8900	23	16	2

TABLE 11.4 Description of Attributes in First Used Data Set

Attribute	Type	Description
1	Categorical	Status of existing checking account
2	Numerical	Duration in month
3	Categorical	Credit history
4	Categorical	Purpose
5	Numerical	Credit amount
6	Categorical	Savings account/bonds
7	Categorical	Present employment since
8	Numerical	Installment rate in percentage of disposable income
9	Categorical	Personal status and sex
10	Categorical	Other debtors/guarantors
11	Numerical	Present residence since
12	Categorical	Property
13	Numerical	Age in years
14	Categorical	Other installment plans
15	Categorical	Housing
16	Numerical	Number of existing credits at this bank
17	Categorical	Job
18	Numerical	Number of people liable to provide maintenance for
19	Categorical	Telephone
20	Categorical	Foreign worker

terized by 20 attributes, 13 categorical and 7 numerical. More information about attribute types is given in Table 11.4.

To evaluate the first data set we used a fivefold cross-validation. To perform a V-fold cross-validation the data set $\mathcal{L}$ is partitioned into V disjunct subsets $\mathcal{L}_1, \ldots, \mathcal{L}_V$, leading to V-learning sets characterized by $\mathcal{L}^{(v)} = \mathcal{L} - \mathcal{L}_v$. Using this procedure, learning set $\mathcal{L}^{(v)}$ corresponds to testing set $\mathcal{L}_v$. For $V = 5$ one gets in each repetition of cross-validation 800 examples as learning sets and 200 as testing sets.

The calculated confusion matrices for the two versions of the first data set using machine-learning algorithms are given for the test examples in Tables 11.5 and 11.6, respectively.

The rows of the confusion matrices in Tables 11.5 and 11.6 represent actual values, the columns the predicted values. For example, the first row of Table 11.5 says that the learning algorithms CN2 could classify 643 good credit risks as good and 57 good credit risks as bad. The accuracy rates are calculated as the number of correctly classified examples divided by the total number of examples. Both the elements of the confusion matrices and the accuracy rates are calculated as averaged over fivefold cross-validation.

To compare the foregoing results with those using traditional and statistical approaches in credit scoring, we mention the results reported in [24]. Using the linear discriminant described in Section 11.3, the authors obtained 71.1% accuracy for the testing data set. They applied, however, the leaving-one-out

TABLE 11.5 Empirical Results for First Data Set Version 1 (700 good and 300 bad credit risks)

			Predicted		
			G	B	Overall Accuracy
CN2	Actual	G	643	57	72.0%
		B	223	77	
NEWID	Actual	G	505	195	65.1%
		B	154	146	
C4.5	Actual	G	573	127	72.7%
		B	146	154	

method, which is a special case of cross-validation. Using the traditional approach of Section 11.3, they report 71.8% accuracy.

To examine the performance of different methods in dealing with large-scale data sets, we used a second data set of 8900 examples. The credit applicants are characterized in this data set with 39 attributes, 23 categorical and 16 numerical. As this has been a confidential data set, the meaning of the attributes is unknown. Half of the examples are good risks, and the other half are bad risks. We partitioned this data set into two learning and testing data sets, including 6230 and 2670 examples, respectively. The empirical results for testing data sets are reported in Table 11.7.

We have also used the two versions of the first data set to evaluate the performance of the different neural networks described in Section 11.3. We tried to use the second data set as well. However, on the one hand, the accuracy obtained was too low; on the other hand, the learning time was too high in comparison with the learning time needed for machine-learning algorithms. Hence, we do not report the results for the second data set, but we discuss this shortcoming of neural networks later when we analyze the results. The achieved

TABLE 11.6 Empirical Results for First Data Set Version 2 (300 good and 300 bad credit risks)

			Predicted		
			G	B	Overall Accuracy
CN2	Actual	G	189	111	65.5%
		B	96	204	
NEWID	Actual	G	173	127	56.8%
		B	132	168	
C4.5	Actual	G	199	101	65.7%
		B	105	195	

TABLE 11.7 Empirical Results for Second Data Set (4450 good and 4450 bad credit risks)

			Predicted		
			G	B	Overall Accuracy
CN2	Actual	G	1172	163	87.8%
		B	165	1170	
NEWID	Actual	G	1124	211	87.0%
		B	136	1199	
C4.5	Actual	G	1184	151	91.8%
		B	67	1268	

accuracy for two versions of the first data set using different neural networks is reported in Tables 11.8 and 11.9.

11.4.2 Analysis of Results

To have a better overview about the performance of the different algorithms, we report all achieved accuracy in Table 11.10. As the results show, the accuracy achieved by different algorithms is generally higher than the default accuracies based on the distributions of the classes in the training data sets. Exceptions are the results delivered by NEWID and Counterpropagation for the version 1 of the first data set. Regarding accuracy, Counterpropagation performed very badly for version 2 of the second data set as well.

It can be seen also from Table 11.10 that the performances of Adaline and C4.5 are the best for version 1 of the first data set. For version 2 of the first data set, Adaline provided the best performance as well. As mentioned, we could not use the three neural networks to handle the second data set because it was too complex for the applied networks. Among the other algorithms, the

TABLE 11.8 Empirical Results for First Data Set, Version 1 (700 good and 300 bad credit risks)

			Predicted		
			G	B	Overall Accuracy
Adaline	Actual	G	610	90	72.7%
		B	183	117	
Madaline	Actual	G	559	141	70.9%
		B	150	150	
Counprop.	Actual	G	589	111	68.7%
		B	202	98	

TABLE 11.9 Empirical Results for First Data Set, Version 2 (300 good and 300 bad credit risks)

			Predicted		
			G	B	Overall Accuracy
Adaline	Actual	G	189	111	69.0%
		B	75	225	
Madaline	Actual	G	182	118	60.7%
		B	118	182	
Counprop.	Actual	G	149	151	47.3%
		B	165	135	

performance of C4.5 was the best. In summary, we can say that the Adaline network would be appropriate to handle small-scale samples of credit-scoring data. For large-scale data sets, however, the neural networks are not appropriate, at least under the usual computation facilities.

Accuracy is, however, only one of the criteria that can be used to compare the performance of different algorithms. In many situations and especially concerning the CS problem, the cost of misclassification is a more important criterion. It is obvious that classifying a bad credit risk as good would cost more than classifying a good credit risk as bad. Unfortunately, credit institutes cannot give a precise estimation about the cost of misclassification. On the other hand, most of the algorithms we applied in this study cannot use a cost matrix in performing the classification task. Recently, some effort was devoted to considering the cost of misclassification in learning algorithms such as NEWID and C4.5 (see [25]). Therefore, we could not use the cost of misclassification as an evaluation criterion, generally. But under certain assumption, one can provide a criterion to compare the performance of different algorithms considering the cost of misclassification.

Suppose that $C(b, g)$ is the cost of misclassifying a bad credit risk as good

TABLE 11.10 Accuracy Rates of Different Algorithm/Data Set Pairs in Percent

Algorithm	First Data Set Version 1 Default Accuracy 70%	First Data Set Version 2 Default Accuracy 50%	Second Data Set Default Accuracy 50%
CN2	72.0	65.5	87.8
NEWID	65.1	56.8	87.0
C4.5	72.7	65.7	91.8
AD	72.7	69.0	—
MAD	70.9	60.7	—
Counprop	68.7	47.3	—

as $C(g, b)$ is the cost of misclassifying a good credit risk as bad. Denoting the prior probabilities of good and bad risks by $P(g)$ and $P(b)$, we can calculate the cost of misclassification as

$$K = C(b, g)P(b)F(b) + C(g, b)P(g)F(g) \qquad (11.7)$$

In relation (11.7), $F(b)$ and $F(g)$ are the error rates of the classification of bad and good risks, respectively. As mentioned, in practice, it is very difficult to find out the values of $C(b, g)$ and $C(g, b)$ (see for example [23]). Hence, it is often assumed that

$$\frac{C(b, g)}{C(g, b)} = \frac{P(g)}{P(b)} \qquad (11.8)$$

Concerning assumption (11.8), one can get from (11.7) that

$$K = C(b, g)P(g)[F(b) + F(g)] \qquad (11.9)$$

Regarding the fact that in (11.9) the factor $C(b, g)P(g)$ is the same for all algorithms, one can use

$$\phi = F(b) + F(g) \qquad (11.10)$$

as an additional evaluation criterion to compare different algorithms. Since $C(b, g)$ is usually higher than $C(g, b)$, a default classifier would classify all credit applicants as bad risks. In this case we would have $F(b) = 0$ and $F(g) = 1$, meaning that for default classification $\phi = 1$. The calculated values for ϕ using different algorithm/data set pairs are given in Table 11.11.

It can be seen from Table 11.11 that the values of ϕ are generally less than unity. An exception is the Counterpropagation on the second version of the first data set. It turns out that learning algorithms perform better as the default classification under consideration the costs of misclassification. For the first data set the performances of neural networks Adaline and Madaline are superior

TABLE 11.11 Values of ϕ for Different Algorithm/Data Set Pairs

Algorithm	First Data Set Version 1 Default Accuracy 70%	First Data Set Version 2 Default Accuracy 50%	Second Data Set Default Accuracy 50%
CN2	0.82	0.69	0.24
NEWID	0.79	0.86	0.18
C4.5	0.72	0.69	0.26
AD	0.74	0.62	—
MAD	0.70	0.78	—
Counprop	0.83	1.05	—

to other algorithms. For the second data set, which could not be handled due to its complexity by neural networks, the performance of NEWID is superior to that of other learning algorithms.

One advantage of the traditional approach to credit scoring is that the result is a score that can be simply compared with a cutoff value. As mentioned, using the strategy curve the portfolio manager can analyze the various effects of changing the cutoff values on acceptance and risk rates. The output of the systems based on decision trees and neural networks (Sec. 11.3), however, is a class assigning, which is not comparable with a cutoff value directly. For this reason, some modifications are necessary to make such procedures appropriate for practical applications. For decision-tree-based algorithms one can think, for example, about probability values that should be assigned to the final nodes of the tree. It means the algorithm would decide for a good or bad credit risk but with a certain probability, say 0.8. In this case, one can regard a number in the interval [0, 1] as a cutoff value and accept the decision delivered by the algorithm if 0.8 is greater than the cutoff value (see for this point [26]). This is also possible in the case of some neural networks. Back-propagation and counterpropagation networks, for example, realize a value between 0 and 1 by using one output node. The value 1 represents the class of a good credit risk, and the value 0 represents a bad credit risk. The realized values by the net, of course, are not exactly 0 or 1 but something between 0 and 1. Similar to the last case, one can choose also a number in the interval [0, 1] as a cutoff value (see [27]).

11.5 CONCLUSIONS

In this study we gave an overview of traditional and statistical approaches contributions to solving the CS problem. But our emphasis has been on evaluating different machine-learning and neural network algorithms. Put together, this study shows that such algorithms can be considered as alternatives and can contribute efficiently to development of CS systems.

After evaluating different algorithm/data set pairs by using the accuracy rate as an evaluation criterion, we can say that there is no significant difference between the performance of neural networks and machine-learning algorithms. In practice, the data sets used to develop the CS systems are large-scale data sets. Our study shows that in such circumstances neural networks are not appropriate tools, at least with the usual computation facilities.

We concluded that accuracy is not the best criterion to evaluate algorithms. The cost of misclassification would be a better alternative. There are some problems, however, in this connection. On the one hand, it is very difficult to estimate a precise cost of misclassification. On the other hand, most of the learning algorithms cannot handle misclassification costs at all. This is especially true for many neural networks. We think that application-oriented research can contribute to overcoming these shortcomings and to preparing the machine-learning and neural networks algorithms so that they can be used in the development of practical CS systems.

ACKNOWLEDGMENT

The authors would like to thank Michael Pechowski for research assistance.

REFERENCES

[1] P. Provaznik, Herausforderungen durch dynamisches Wachstum des öster-reichischen Privatkreditmarktes, *Bank und Markt*, 26–29 (1992).

[2] G. Köpf, Zukunftsbezogene verfahren der bonitätsanalyse, *Bankkaufmann*, 2, 35–37 (1992).

[3] N. Capon, Credit scoring systems: A critical analysis, *J. Marketing*, 46, 82–91 (1982).

[4] T. M. Bretzger, "Die Anwendung statistischer Verfahren zur Risikofrüherken-nung bei Dispositionskrediten," dissertation, Universität Hohenheim (1991).

[5] P. Hub, Credit scoring in Deutschland (Aktuelle Situation und Zukunftsperspek-tiven), *Bank Markt*, 7, 16–21 (1992).

[6] J. Hermans, J. D. F. Habbema, T. K. D. Kasanmoentalib, and J. W. Raatgever, *ALLOC80 Discriminant Analysis Program*, Department of Medical Statistics, University of Leiden, Netherlands, 1980.

[7] J. H. Friedman, *SMART: Smooth Multiple Additive Regression Technique*. Stanford University, Calif., 1984.

[8] R. Molina, L. M. de Campos, and J. Mateos, *Using Bayesian Algorithms for Learning Causal Networks in Classification Problems*, University of Granada, 1992.

[9] M. S. Haque, R. J. Henery, and J. M. O. Mitechell, "Classical Statistical Algorithms in Discrimination," Mimeo, University of Strathclyde, Glasgow, 1992.

[10] S. Dutta and S. Shekhar, Bond-rating: A none-conservative application of neural networks, *IEEE Proc. 2nd Annual Internat. Conf. Neural Networks*, II, 433–450 (1988).

[11] Neural Ware Inc. *Neural Computing*, NeuralWorks Professional II/Plus and NeuralWorks Explorer, Pittsburgh, 1990.

[12] L. Breiman, J. H. Friedman, A. Olshen, and C. J. Stone, *Classification and Regression Trees*, Wadsworth, Belmont, Mass., 1984.

[13] R. S. Michalski, Computer implementation of a variable-valued logic system v11 and examples of its application to pattern recognition, *Proc. 1st Internat. Joint Conf. Pattern Recognition*, 3–17 (1973).

[14] J. R. Quinlan, "Discovery Rules from Large Collections of Examples: A Case Study," in D. Michie (Hers.), *Expert Systems in the Micro Electronic Age*, Edinburgh University Press, 1979.

[15] J. R. Quinlan, Induction of decision trees, *Machine Learning*, 1, 81–106 (1986).

[16] J. R. Quinlan, Simplifying decision trees, *Internat. Man-Machine Stud.*, 27, 221–234 (1987a).

[17] J. R. Quinlan, Generating production rules from decision trees, *Internat. Joint Conf. Artif. Intell.*, 304–307 (1987b).

[18] P. Clark and R. Boswell, ''Rule Induction with CN2: Some Recent Improvements,'' in Y. Kodratoff, ed., *Machine Learning-EWSL-91*, Springer-Verlag, 1991, pp. 151–163.

[19] P. Clark and T. Niblett, The CN2 induction algorithm, *Machine Learning*, 4, 261–283 (1988).

[20] W. M. Häußler, Empirische ergebnisse zur diskriminationsverfahren bei kreditscoringsystemen, *Zeits. Oper. Res.*, Ser. B, 23, 191–210 (1979).

[21] W. M. Häußler, *Punktebewertung bei Kreditscoringsystemen*, Knapp, Frankfurt (1981).

[22] W. M. Häußler, Methoden der punktebewertung für kreditscoringsysteme, *Zeits. Oper. Res.*, 25, 79–94 (1981).

[23] H. J. Hofmann, Die Anwendung des CART-Verfahrens zur statistischen Bonitätsanalyse von Konsumentenkrediten, *Zeits. Betriebswirtschaft*, 9, 941–962 (1990).

[24] L. Fahrmeir, W. Häußler, and G. Tutz, ''Diskriminanzanalyse,'' in L. Fahrmeir and A. Hamerle, (eds.), *Multivariate statistische Verfahren*, Verlag de Gruyter, Berlin, 1984.

[25] U. Knoll, *Kostenoptimiertes Prunen in Entscheidungsbäumen*, Daimler-Benz, Forschung und Technik, Ulm, 1993.

[26] C. Carter and J. Catlett, Assessing credit card applications using machine learning, *IEEE Expert*, 71–79 (Fall, 1987).

[27] M. Schumann, T. Lehrbach, and P. Bährs, *Versuche zur Kreditwürdigkeitsprognose mit künstlichen Neuronalen Netzen*, Universität Götingen (1992).

CHAPTER 12 ──────────────────

Symbolic-Numeric Learning and Classification

M. LIQUIÈRE
H. RALAMBONDRAINY

12.1 INTRODUCTION

Along with the development of expert systems and the rapid increase in the amount of data stored in data bases is the need of learning techniques for extracting knowledge and relevant information (concepts, decision rules, etc). Traditionally, numerical methods, such as data analysis techniques, neural networks, or genetic algorithms, are opposed to symbolic learning techniques developed in artificial intelligence. Numerical techniques are efficient and fast when dealing with important and noisy data but provide a low-level description of knowledge. Symbolic techniques are more concerned with rich knowledge domains and represent facts and knowledge using tools such as first-order logic or graph representation. In this chapter, we first propose a hybrid numeric-symbolic method of concepts acquisition that integrates a numerical clustering method [1] for cluster determination and a symbolic technique for deriving concepts from clusters. In the second part, we show how to use numerical techniques to optimize a graph-learning technique from examples.

Learning research is concerned with various areas such as knowledge acquisition, concepts formation, problem solving, organization of knowledge bases, or knowledge discovery in data bases. The last few years have seen the development of many learning systems. They can be classified from different viewpoints, for example, application domains, underlying learning strategies, type of knowledge representation, and so on. Traditionally, numerical methods developed in statistics and data analysis have been opposed to symbolic tech-

Frontier Decision Support Concepts, Edited by V. L. Plantamura, B. Souček, and G. Visaggio. ISBN 0-471-59256-0   © 1994 John Wiley & Sons, Inc.

niques issued from artificial intelligence. For example, Langley [2] compared numerical and symbolic clustering approaches. Statistical clustering methods [3] are older and much used in fields such as biology, where extensive data sets are stored. They can efficiently process large amounts of data, but they have been criticized on the following points. Clustering methods are more concerned with structures discovery and data exploration than finding conceptual descriptions. They produce clusters that are difficult to interpret, and they do not use any background knowledge in the clustering process. Conceptual clustering, such as Cluster 2 [3], has been developed to overcome these limitations. They focus on finding clusters describable by a concept expressed in a high-representation language, such as logical predicates or frames. They are useful for dealing with complex and rich application domains, but the logical inferences used by the learning process are not well suited to large, noisy, numerical data.

In the first section, we propose a characterization method that finds intensional descriptions from clusters obtained by the well-known numerical clustering method k-means. We introduce the notion of "statistical concept." The hybrid clustering method that results combines the efficiency quality of numerical algorithms and the conceptual interpretation orientation of symbolic clustering methods.

In the second section, we propose an algorithm that researches patterns common to a set of examples using graph conceptual representation. Algorithms using this kind of representation are complex. We show how to use a numerical clustering method to reduce the complexity.

12.2 SYMBOLIC EXTENSION OF THE k-MEANS ALGORITHM

Clustering methods are made of two phases: the aggregation phase, where a partition of the observations is determined, and the characterization phase for describing the classes. The popular k-means algorithm is chosen for the first phase because it is a fast algorithm whose complexity is polynomial in the number of observations. We first give the main features of the k-mean algorithm and then show how the results are used in the characterization phase.

12.2.1 The Aggregation Phase

The data must be presented as a set of observations O characterized by a fixed set of numeric attributes $(X_j, \mathbf{R})_{1 < j < p}$. A given observation $o \in O$ is described by a tuple $o = (X_1, a_1) \cdots (X_p, a_p)$ that can be represented by a vector $o = (a_1, \ldots, a_p) \in \mathbf{R}^p$. The method requires the choice of a dissimilarity measure for every pairwise combination of the observations. In practice, if the attributes are homogeneous the Euclidean distance is suitable; otherwise the normalized distance must be used. The Euclidean distance between the given observations $o = (a_j)_{1 < j < p}$ and $o' = (b_j)_{1 < j < p}$ is $d^2(o, o') = \Sigma_{1 < j < p}(a_j - b_j)^2$, and the normalized distance is $d^2_{1/\sigma^2}(o, o') = \Sigma_{1 < j < p}(a_j - b_j)^2/\sigma_j^2$, where σ_j is the standard deviation of the jth attribute. This distance is independent of the attribute's unity of measures and amplitude.

Let $P = \{C_1, \ldots, C_k\}$ be a partition into k classes of the set of observations O, and $g_1, \ldots, g_k$ be the gravity centers of the clusters. The k-means algorithm is an optimization method that researches a partition that minimizes the intra-class inertia $W = \Sigma_{1 < l < k} \Sigma \{ p_l d^2(o_i, g_l) | o_i \in C_l \}$.

The attribute X is called symbolic if the values (or modalities) domain $D = \{d_1, \ldots, d_m\}$ is finite (for example, (sex, $D = \{$man, woman$\}$)). In order to be processed, symbolic attributes must be coded numerically. The usual way to do that is to substitute the binary attributes $(X_l, \{1, 0\})_{1 < l < m}$ for the attribute X. For a given observation o, X_1 takes the value 1 if $X = d_1$, and 0 otherwise. When all the attributes are symbolic, a given observation o is represented by a binary vector $o = (a_i)_{1 < j < q} \in \mathbf{R}^q$, where q is the total number of modalities. The distance between two objects $o = (a_j)_{1 < j < q}$ and $o' = (b_j)_{1 < j < q}$ is

$$d^2(o, o') = \sum_{1 < j < q} (a_j - b_j)^2 \qquad (12.1)$$

which is interpreted as the number of different modalities of o and o'.

12.2.2 The Characterization Phase

The usual numerical clustering programs give extensional descriptions of clusters. The observations and attributes are classified from the most typical to the less typical. The complex problem of determining the meaning of the clusters is left to the user.

In this section we present a learning algorithm from examples and counterexamples to derive automatically conceptual descriptions. The definition of the term *concept* has given rise to numerous works [4]. Traditionally, a concept is a precise definition of a set of objects using necessary and sufficient conditions. Work in philosophy and cognitive psychology [5] has shown that, in real applications, useful concepts of humans are related to fuzzy or uncertain classes of objects. Hanson and Bauer [6] then claim that categories can be best described by a polymorphy rule (m features out of n, $m < n$) than with necessary and sufficient features. We propose here the notion of "statistical concept," which is more consistent with the characteristic of the k-mean algorithm used. Let $(X_j, a_j)_{1 < j < l}$ denote the typical values of the attributes for a given class C to be described. A typical observation of C will have many values that do not differ much from the typical values $(a_j)_{1 < j < l}$ of C. The goal of our algorithm is to make precise this class recognition rule that expresses that the observations of C have statistically many common typical values of attributes.

12.2.3 Graph Conceptual Representation of a Tuple

In this section we use the conceptual graph formalism [7]. A tuple object $o = (A_1, a_1) \cdots (A_p, a_p)$ is easily represented by a conceptual graph Γ_o (Fig.

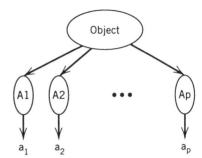

Figure 12.1 *Graph representation.*

12.1). The set of nodes is $\{object, A_1, \ldots, A_p, a_1, \ldots, a_p\}$, and the vertices are $\{object \rightarrow A_j\}_{1 < j < p}$ and $\{A_j \rightarrow a_j\}_{1 < j < p}$. We provide a generalization structure of the set of conceptual graphs Γ_o.

We associate to a symbolic attribute $(X, D = \{d_1, \ldots, d_m\})$ a generalization structure $l = (E, gen, <)$, where

> E is a set of subsets of D that contains the set D and the singletons $\{d_j\}_{1 < j < m}$ denoted also by $\{D\}$. The set E is called the research space associated to X. E is chosen by the user.
>
> $<$ is the partial order is less general than, which we identify with the inclusion relation.
>
> l is a sup-complete lattice, which means that every couple (e, f) in E has one least upper bound in E, denoted by $gen(e, f)$, and called the *generalization* of e and f. $gen(e, f)$ may be different from $e \cup f$, but the inequality $e \cup f < gen(e, f)$ always holds. The largest member of E is D, and the singletons $\{d_j\}_{1 < j < m}$ are the minimal elements.

Two important research spaces must be mentioned:

1. The sup-complete lattice l_0 related to $E_0 = \{D, \{D\}\}$ is the simplest structure possible.
2. The sup-complete lattice l_1 where the research space E_1 is the set of all subsets of D: $E_1 = p(D)$ is the most complete structure.

The research space chosen may be an intermediate structure, such as a tree, between l_0 and l_1 (Fig. 12.2).

Let $(X, \mathbf{R})$ be a numeric attribute. We provide a generalization structure of X by defining a generalization operator gen on the set of real intervals. This operator will taken into account that data are noisy and that the classes are uncertain as the result of the k-means algorithm. An attribute value is typical of a class if it is not very different from the attribute mean in the class. More precisely, for a given class C_1, the typical values of the attribute X_j are in $[m_j^l - \sigma_j, m_j^l + \sigma_j]$, an interval denoted by "$===$." Let "$---$" $= (-\infty, m_j^l - \sigma_j]$ and "$+++$" $= [m_j^l + \sigma_j, +\infty)$.

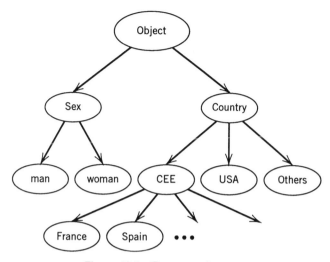

Figure 12.2 *The research space.*

The generalization operator gen is defined as follows:

If min (r, r') **and** max $(s, s') \in$ $===$ **then** gen $([r, s], [r', s']) = $ $===$
If max $(s, s') \in$ $---$ **then** gen $([r, s], [r', s']) = $ $---$
If min $(r, r') \in$ $+++$ **then** gen $([r, s], [r', s']) = $ $+++$
otherwise gen $([r, s], [r', s']) = \mathbf{R}$

The attribute X has then the generalization structure $l = (E, \text{gen}, 1)$, where $E = \{[r, s] \mid r, s \in \mathbf{R}\}$ is the set of real intervals; l is a sup-complete lattice; the largest member of E is $\mathbf{R}$; and the reals $\{[r] \mid r \in \mathbf{R}\}$ are the minimal elements.

12.2.4 Representation of the Observations

We suppose that we have a set of p numerical or symbolic attributes represented by the triplets $(X_j, D_j, l_j = (E_j, \text{gen}, <))_{1 < j < p}$ defined as before. A tuple object $\omega = (A_j, e_j)_{1 < j < p}$, where $e_j \in E_j$, belongs to the space $\Omega = E_1 \times \cdots \times E_p$, which has a sup-complete lattice structure:

$$l_1 \times \cdots \times l_p = (\Omega = E_1 \times \cdots \times E_p, \text{gen}, <)$$

as the set product of the sup-complete lattice structures l_i. As a tuple object, ω can be represented by a conceptual graph Γ_ω. The associated conceptual graph space $\mathbf{l} = (\Gamma_\Omega, \text{gen}, <)$ has, by construction, a sup-complete lattice structure such as

$$\Gamma_\omega < \Gamma_o \Leftrightarrow \omega < o \Leftrightarrow (\omega_j < o_j)_{1 < j < p}$$
$$\text{gen}(o, \omega) = (\text{gen}(\omega_j, o_j))_{1 < j < p}$$
$$\text{gen}(\Gamma_\omega, \Gamma_o) = \Gamma_{\text{gen}(\omega, o)}.$$

We associate to every element Γ_ω of Γ_Ω, the logical assertion A_ω, such as

$$A_\omega: \Gamma_\Omega \to \{\text{true, false}\}$$

$$\Gamma_o \to A_\omega(\Gamma_o) = \text{true} \Leftrightarrow \Gamma_o < \Gamma_\omega$$

Let $\mathbf{A}_\Omega = \{A_\omega | \; \omega \in \Omega\}$ be the set generated by the assertions related to Ω. The implication $\Rightarrow$ defines a partial order an $\mathbf{A}_\Omega$. It is easy to show that there is a lattice isomorphism between $(\Gamma_\Omega, \text{gen}, <)$ and $(\mathbf{A}_\Omega, \text{gen}, \Rightarrow)$. The operator gen in $\mathbf{A}_\Omega$ is such that $\forall \omega, o \in \Omega$, $\text{gen}(A_\omega, A_o) = A_{\text{gen}(\omega, o)}$. An object ω will be now represented by the assertion A_ω.

12.2.5   The Characterization Algorithm

Let be C the class of the partition P to be described. We define a set of examples $EX = \{ex_i\}_{1 < i < nex}$ of C as the typical observations of C. We call counterexamples CX, the observations of the other classes. The cluster C will be represented by the assertion $A_C = \vee \{A_o | \; o \in C\}$, which is a characteristic function of C.

The algorithm we propose is an ascending learning method from examples and counterexamples. It is a heuristic search through a space of symbolic descriptions generated from generalization rules. Let $a_\Omega = \{A_C = \vee_{\omega \in C} A_\omega | \; C \in p(\Omega)\}$ be the set of assertions generated by the assertions of $\mathbf{A}_\Omega$. The problem of cluster characterization of C will be formulated as the research of an assertion $\hat{A}_C \in a_\Omega$, which is an approximation more general and simpler than A_c. Its expression will be $\hat{A}_C = \vee_{1 < j < q} A_j$ with $A_j \in \mathbf{A}_\Omega$.

To be selected, the assertions A_j must verify the following conditions:

1. The assertions A_j must be α-discriminating. It means that the number or percentage of counterexamples recognized must be less than α.
2. The number or percentage of elements of the cluster C recognized by A_j must be greater than β.

The proposed algorithm has the following steps:

1. The research of a set of assertions A_j more general than A_{exi} using the lattice structure l. We start from the set of examples. We compute all the generalizations of the examples $\text{gen}(o, o')$ two by two. Only the resulting associated assertions that verify condition 1 are kept. The process is repeated until it stops because the computed generalizations recognize more and more counterexamples. The assertions A_j verify conditions 1 and 2 will be used to be the input of the next step.
2. Let $S = \{A_1, \ldots, A_m\}$ be the set resulting from the previous step. The assertion $R_S = A_1 \vee \cdots \vee A_m$ is an answer to our problem, but R_S can still be simplified. The assertions $A_1, \ldots, A_m$ are ranked in a decreasing

way according to the number of recognized elements of C. If the set of recognized elements of A_l is included in the one recognized by $A_1 \vee \cdots \vee A_k$, then the assertion A_l can be dropped.

We applied our method to data concerning 169 desk computers described as follows: color monitor: (no, optional, yes); CP/M system: (no, optional, yes); MS/DOS system: (no, optional, yes); other operating system: (no, optional, yes); microprocessor: (8 bits, 16 bits, 32 bits); parallel interface: (no, optional, yes); series interface: (no, optional, yes); IEE488 interface: (no, optional, yes); hard disk: (no, yes). The k-means algorithm provides one partition having five clusters. The conceptual rule for class 1 is the disjunction of the following assertions:

Assertion 1. Well classified 44 (88%), misclassified 0. If color monitor = optional and microprocessor = 16 bits and parallel interface = yes, then class 1.

Assertion 2. Well classified 41 (82%), misclassified 0. If color monitor = optional and MS/DOS system = yes and microprocessor = 16 bits, then class 1.

Assertion 3. Well classified 41 (82%), misclassified 0. If color monitor = optional and MS/DOS system = yes and other system = no, then class 1.

Assertion 4. Well classified 41 (82%), misclassified 0. If color monitor = optional and MS/DOS system = yes and parallel interface = yes, then class 1. This set of rules recognizes 92% of class 1. This class is related to 16-bit computers running under MS/DOS system and with optional color monitor and parallel or series interfaces.

12.3 A STRUCTURAL LEARNING ALGORITHM

In this section we describe an algorithm that researches common patterns to a set of examples. Such patterns, which are seen on a majority of examples, may be used to discriminate a concept characterized by examples and counterexamples. The knowledge representation language is conceptual graphs, which we already used to represent tuples. This language has the power of first predicate formalism; it describes knowledge using bipartite oriented and labeled graphs. A node is labeled as a concept or as a conceptual relation. Figure 12.3 gives the representation of the well-known Winston arches.

This set of conceptual graphs [7] is the internal representation of Winston's conceptual graph of an arch. The essence of the concept arch is deemed to be the structure of a "physical object being supported by two bricks, one of which

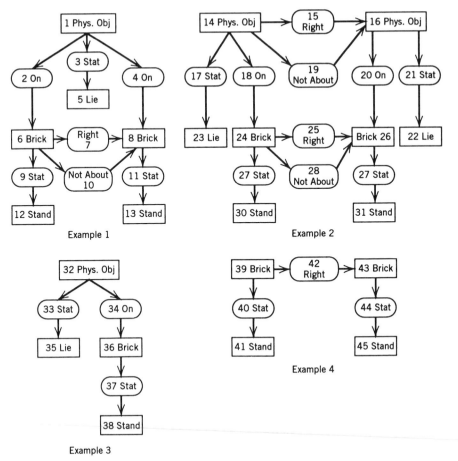

Figure 12.3   *Conceptual graphs.*

is right of the other but not touching.'' We have the following, very noisy, set of examples:

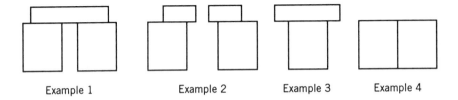

Example 1   Example 2   Example 3   Example 4

12.4   GRAPHS AND LEARNING

A limitation of many statistical methods is the descriptive language. In many cases this language is a vector of measures (attributes). In our work we use a descriptive language based on graphs. A convenient form of a structural description is an attributed graph that is, a graph with symbolic attributes or labels attached to its vertices [7, 8]. Our goal is to find a classification of these graphs. In many works [9, 10] the authors define a similarity measure between the graphs and use this measure in a classical classification process. The problem of this technique is the interpretation of the results.

In other works, the user defines a set of structural attributes. Each example is described by a vector of attributes that can be structurally interpreted. In our work we merge these techniques.

First, each example is described by a graph. In our method, we have chosen to describe objects as conceptual graphs. Each conceptual graph may be mapped into a formula in the first-order predicate calculus [7].

Second, we search for subgraphs in a subset of the graphs describing the examples. This problem is NP-hard, so we use heuristics to deal with this intrinsic complexity. The base of our heuristic is a statistical method. We use this method as a function of our structural learning method. For a specific problem we can change this statistical method, so we have a set of algorithms based on the same structure. The result of the algorithm is a set of clusters. Each cluster is a repeated *subtree* of the set of graphs describing the examples.

Third, we have found a set of structural attributes. Each attribute is associated with a subtree. We can now describe each example by a vector of attributes and use a classical method.

Consider two nodes X, Y in a graph, and consider the nodes $\{X_1, \ldots, X_n\}$ linked with the object X and the node $\{Y_1, \ldots, Y_n\}$ linked with the object Y. Each node is labeled.

A similarity measure between two nodes can be

1. 0 if X and Y do not have the same label.
2. Otherwise the similarity between X and Y is equal to the number of $X_i \in \{X_1, \ldots, X_n\}$ that can be associated to Y_j such that the label of X_i is the same as the label of Y_j.

In our set of examples the similarity between the vertex 1 and the vertex 14 is 2, the vertex 6 and the vertex 24 is 3, ... This method has been used in [11].

Now we have a very trivial similarity measure. In fact this measure can be structurally interpreted. The node X can be interpreted as the root of a tree T_x and the node Y as the root of a tree T_y such that T_x and T_y are isomorphic.

In our example the similarity between vertex 1 and vertex 14 can be interpreted as

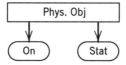

and the similarity between the vertices 6 and 24 as

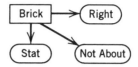

This crude approach has two problems: (1) A procedure, which compares all the objects of one example to all the other objects of another example, has $O(n^2)$ complexity. In real-world experimentation n can be very big. We do not want to find formulas covering all the positive examples and exclude all the negative ones because we have many errors in our examples and in the classification of the examples. In this case the 1-1 procedure we described cannot be used. (2) We only consider the neighbors of a node, so we do not use all the structural description of the example. Therefore, for a given pair of entities, the similarity measure for this pair should take into account the similarities of the other pairs.

12.4.1   Problem 1: A Resolution by Partitioning Nodes

We want to group in a class all similar nodes. This is a partition problem. In propositional domains the partition problem has been well solved if we have a criterion to optimize. The problem is: How can I describe my node? Which is the criterion to optimize?

Node Description for the Partition Process. Consider a set of nodes {6, 8, 24, 36, 39, 43} such that each node has the label "Brick." We represent the local description of a node by the following array:

	Right	Stat	NotAbout
6	1	1	1
8	0	1	0
24	1	1	1
26	0	1	0
36	0	1	0
39	1	1	0
43	0	1	0

Each row is associated with a node. Each column is associated with a label for a row I and a column J, the number of k means that the node I is linked to k nodes with label J.

Now our aim is to regroup nodes that are similar with respect to this local description. This partition problem is solved if we have a criterion to optimize. Here we can use a greedy algorithm [12] or a classic statistical method [13].

In our example we can construct the following partitions: {6, 24, 39} associated with the structural similarity

{8, 26, 36, 43} associated with the structural similarity

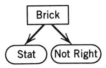

So the problem is now to define a criterion to be optimized.

Criterion. We consider that a learning algorithm learns if the results can be used to compress the description of the example. So we decide to use a compression criterion close to minimal representation criterion. This criterion [9] was introduced to guide inference of concepts in case the maximum likelihood fails. This kind of criterion is obviously equivalent to a minimal description length principle and related to the Kolmogorov complexity [14]. With this criterion we can use statistical methods, but we do not have a statistical validation of the found classes. The validity of a class may be given as a function of different criteria.

A simple but interesting one is used in [15]. This description of this criterion is as follows: A concept is valid if we have many examples that verify this concept and few counterexamples that verify this concept. In many cases this criterion is useful—for example, if we want to find a concept that covers all the positive examples and excludes all the negative ones.

12.4.2 Problem 2: Structural Similarities

We have defined a similarity measure and showed that this similarity can be interpreted as stated before: If two nodes are similar, then they are roots of two isomorphic trees with depth 1. Our goal is to find a rooted tree with depth greater than one. We know that a rooted tree can be described as a root and a set of subtrees. Let us consider now that for each node X_i, we know that this node is a root of a specific tree. The label of the node X indicates this kind of information.

We may now generalize the similarity computation described above:

1. X and Y can be similar if X's label is equal to Y's label. This equality is interpreted in the following way: X is the root of a tree T_1 and Y is the root of a tree T_2 with T_1 isomorphic to T_2.

2. The similarity between X and Y is equal to the number of $X_i = \{X_1, \ldots, X_n\}$ that can be associated to Y_j such that the tree T_i of X_i is isomorphic to the tree T_j of Y_j.

This similarity measure gives the following iterative algorithm:

1 Repeat
   2   For each set E_T of node X root of a tree isomorphic to T
            Creation of a local table
            Partition of the set E_T
       We give to each partition a specific number (label).
       Modification of the label of the nodes with respect to the new partition.
Until no new results

We have based our algorithm on the classic problem of partitioning a graph [16]. Partitioning is the main tool used by most algorithms that test graph isomorphism.

12.4.3 Example

The application of our algorithm, with our set of examples, gives the following results. Consider that a class is valid if the associated tree is present in two examples or more.

Step 1. First we find a trivial partition of the nodes

{1   14   16   32} Class of objects with label PhysObj
{2   4   18   20   34} Class of objects with label On
{6   8   24   26   36   39   43} Class of objects with label Brick
{3   9   11   17   21   27   29   33   40   44} Class of objects with label Stat
{5   22   23   35} Class of objects with label Lie
{12   13   30   31   37   41   45} Class of objects with label Stand
{7   15   25   42} Class of objects with label Right
{10   19   28}} Class of objects with label Not About

Step 2. The table created for the class {1   14   16   32} is

	PhysObj	On	Brick	Stat	Lie	Stand	Right	NotAbout
1	0	2	0	1	0	0	0	0
14	0	1	0	1	0	0	1	1
16	0	1	0	1	0	0	0	0
32	0	1	0	1	0	0	0	0

A class {1, 14, 16, 32} with interpretation

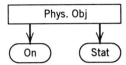

First results are given in Figure 12.4. We make a new description of the examples with this new knowledge and new label set that we obtain. See Figure 12.5. On this new description, with the same method, we obtain the trees shown in Figure 12.6. So after the second step we have built trees of depth 2 (Fig. 12.7). Step by step, we reduce the description of the examples and we increase the depth of the found trees. We obtain the maximal results shown in Figure 12.8.

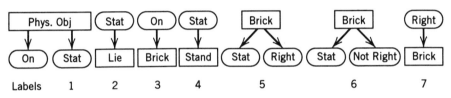

Figure 12.4 *Depth one A1.*

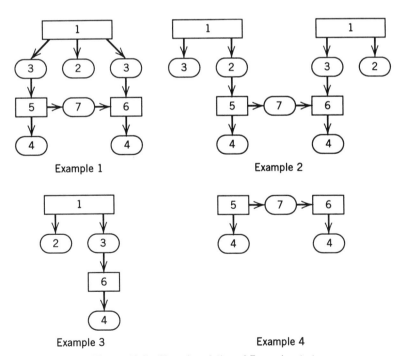

Example 1

Example 2

Example 3

Example 4

Figure 12.5 *New description of Examples 1–4.*

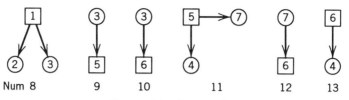

Num 8   9   10   11   12   13

Figure 12.6 *Step two A2.*

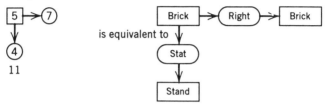

Figure 12.7 *Interpretation of a result.*

12.5 CONCLUSION

The purely numerical methods have two problems:

1. Interpretation of the results
2. Limitation of the description language

In this chapter we have described two symbolic and numeric methods. The first treats the interpretation problem. This method gives statistically valued results that can be symbolically interpreted. The second method treats the language problem. It uses a graph description of the examples and a statistical method as a heuristic inside the learning process. The structural similarity between examples can be directly interpreted by the user.

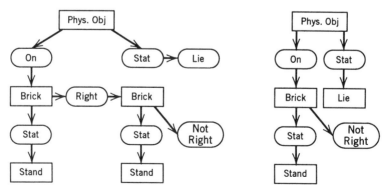

Figure 12.8 *The maximal results.*

REFERENCES

[1] B. Everitt, *Cluster Analysis, Heineman:* Educational Books, London, 1977.

[2] D. Fischer and P. Langley, Approach to conceptual clustering, *Proc. Ninth Internat. Joint Conf. Artificial Intelligence*, 1985.

[3] R. S. Michalski and R. E. Stepp, Learning from Observations: Conceptual Clustering, *Machine Learning*, Vol. 1. Tioga Publishing, Palo Alto, Calif., 1983.

[4] C. Mattheus, "Conceptual Purpose: Implications for Representation and Learning in Machines and Humans," thesis, 1987.

[5] E. Smith and D. Medin, *Categories and Concept*, Harvard University Press, Cambridge, Mass., 1981.

[6] S. Hanson and M. Bauer, *Uncertainty in Artificial Intelligence, Conceptual Clustering, Semantic Organization and Polymorphy*, 1985.

[7] J. F. Sowa, *Conceptual Structures*, Addison Wesley, 1984.

[8] M. Liquière, Inne (Induction in networks): A structural learning algorithm for noisy examples, *EWSL* 89, 111–123.

[9] J. Segen, Graph clustering and model learning by data compression, *Proc. 7th ICML*, 93–100 (1990).

[10] A. Wong and M. You, Entropy and distance of random graphs with application to structural pattern recognition, *IEEE Trans. Pattern Anal. Machine Intell.*, PAMI-7 (1985).

[11] C. Vrain, OGUST: A system which learns using domain properties expressed as theorems, *Machine Learning*, Vol. 3, Morgan Kaufmann, pp. 360–382.

[12] J. Dunstan and D. J. Welsk, A greedy algorithm for solving a certain class of linear programs, *Math. Prog.*, 5 (1973).

[13] G. Celeux, E. Diday, G. Govaert, Y. Lechevallier, and H. Ralambondrainy, *Classification automatique des données; environnement statistique et informatique* Dunod, 1989.

[14] L. Ming and P. Vitanyi, Inductive reasoning and kolmogorov complexity, *J. Comput. Syst. Sci.*, 44, 343–384 (1992).

[15] J. Quinqueton and J. Sallantin, CALM: Contestation for argumentative learning machine, in *Machine Learning, a Guide to Current Research*, T. M. Mitchell, J. G. Carbonell, R. S. Michalski, eds., Kluwer Academic Pubs., 1986, pp. 247–253.

[16] B. Peroche, NP-Completeness of some problems of partitioning and covering in graphs, *Discrete Appl. Math.*, 8, 195–208 (1984).

⸻

CHAPTER 13

Time-Series Prediction by Artificial Neural Networks: Electric Power Consumption

MIRKO NOVÁK
EMIL PELIKÁN
HYNEK BERAN

13.1 INTRODUCTION

In this chapter an examination of the theoretical background of time-series prediction by artificial neural networks is presented first. The neural-oriented prediction methods are compared with those based on the linear and nonlinear algorithmic prediction procedures. Some important problems in training the respective neural predictors, maintaining their stability, and predicting their accuracy are discussed. The applicability of prediction through specially designed and trained neural structures is tested.

Forecasting has always been one of the most important human activities. Among many forecasting methods, both heuristic and scientific, time-series prediction is still one of the main tools. In contemporary commerce, business, industry, medical care and science, time-series prediction is applied quite often with significantly good results. For many years, several numerical and statistical methods have been used to this purpose (among them the linear regression, autoregressive moving-average (ARMA) models, and Box-Jenkins methods are well known).

Since the advent of a renaissance of interest in artificial neural networks, starting in the mid-1980s, more approaches have been presented on how to use one-dimensional layered neural structures for estimating future values of various time series, their previous history being known.

Frontier Decision Support Concepts, Edited by V. L. Plantamura, B. Souček, and G. Visaggio.
ISBN 0-471-59256-0   © 1994 John Wiley & Sons, Inc.

The principle of this prediction technology consists of training the appropriate neural network to know the sequence of input signals, composed of the proper part of the respective time-series history and completed by well-chosen auxiliary intervention series, and respecting the main secondary influences (e.g., the temperature, humidity, atmospheric pressure, etc.). After satisfactory long training, which is often a considerably difficult procedure requiring a lot of fast computer power and time, and deep knowledge of the necessary facts, the properly designed and trained artificial neural network is prepared for activation. In this way one usually obtains the necessary forecast estimations easily and quickly, even when conventional PCs are used.

It has been shown that, in certain cases, results reached in this way are better than those obtained using classical prediction procedures.

In this chapter the following aspects of time-series prediction by artificial neural networks are addressed:

a. General principles of neural time-series prediction
b. Learning procedures and problems
c. The role of intervention series
d. Decorrelation and hybrid approaches
e. Sensitivity to network parameter changes and parameter tolerances

Finally, practical experience in neural time-series prediction as applied to electric energy consumption in large power systems and in water resource quality is described.

13.2 PROBLEMS OF PREDICTION

The present stage of development in a very progressive new information technology—neurocomputing based on the use of artificial neural networks and neurocomputers—on which, during the past few years, a good part of the interest in the area of computer science has been concentrated is already able to address some important practical problems. One of these is the prediction of a time series whose principles have been known for several years.

Artificial neural networks are at their most powerful when applied to problems whose solutions require knowledge that is difficult to specify but for which there is an abundance of examples. As time-series prediction is performed entirely by inference of future behavior from examples of past behavior, it is an ideal application for neural network technology.

For time-series prediction, classic mathematical algorithmic methods have long been developed. At present, several methods based on linear models (e.g., autoregressive models, ARMA models, etc.) or nonlinear models (bilinear models, threshold-controlled autoregressive models, etc.), or some alternative approaches (e.g., expert systems) are known.

The usual approach to time-series prediction is to carry out a "manual" analysis of the time-series data, build a model from first principles, and then iterate the design by measuring the proximity of the model to real data. This can be a long process often involving the derivation, implementation, and refinement of a number of models before one with appropriate characteristics is found. In addition, problems arise when the underlying dynamics of the system are poorly understood. In particular, the most difficult systems to predict are those with nonstationary dynamics, where the underlying behavior varies with time. Problems also arise due to the fact that physical data are subject to noise and experimental error. Some series are also relatively short, providing few data points on which to conduct the analysis.

In all these situations traditional prediction techniques are severely limited and a need to use some alternative techniques is apparent. The application of artificial neural networks therefore seems to be quite natural.

During the last two years, interest in time-series prediction has been considered with artificial neural networks used as universal nonlinear approximators between indicators and the predicted value of a time series (e.g., electric power consumption).

In general, linear approaches are successful in such applications where the overall economic and social conditions are satisfactorily stable. However, there are many cases where this requirement is not met. This is typical for many situations of the contemporary rapidly changing world. Here the use of nonlinear neural-oriented adaptive methods is a key to successful solution of the problem of practically applicable time-series prediction systems.

Some research groups at several universities and institutes have reached a satisfactorily deep level of experience in the application of theoretical knowledge in natural and artificial neural networks to some interesting practical tasks in medicine, industrial process control, ecology, meteorology, and other fields. Among them the time series prediction applications play a very important role. For commercial exploitation of this knowledge the development of special prediction methods and systems and the creation of respective software tools for solving the complicated practical problems appearing in commerce, industry, business, health care, and ecology is now frequently performed using progressive neural information technology.

By means of this knowledge it is possible to create and learn artificial neural networks suitable for simulation on personal computers that can predict the future development of considerably complicated time series (e.g., an electric power network's consumption over several days, weeks or months, daily temperatures, water-level statistics, etc.) with much higher accuracy and efficiency than can be reached by classical methods up to now commonly used in those fields. In such a way one is able to solve cases where other methods are hardly applicable.

One of the main problems of data analysis in many industrial and commercial applications (e.g., in electric power distribution) is the maximum accurate prediction of some needed quantity in the next time period. Such a quantity can be power consumption, level of water in reservoirs, demand for some product, and so on. Because the applications of time-series prediction of electric power consumption are of major importance, this area will be considered in more detail later on.

Electrical energy produced by various power plants is usually bought by power distributors and sold to consumers. The demand for energy varies significantly in time with respect to weather, time of year, day in week, hour and minute in day, and the overall economic and political situation. These changes are of quasi-periodic character. The respective time series have some daily, weekly, and seasonal periodicity, but their actual shape differs quite a lot from one period to another. Power distribution companies are therefore deeply interested in knowing satisfactorily in advance the best estimations of future consumption as are possible.

The range of prediction (prediction interval) can vary from a few hours or days (short-time prediction) to several months or years (long-time prediction). In short-time prediction, special interest can be given to morning or afternoon peaks. Information on such peaks is necessary for economic regulation and control of power consumption and efficient distribution during the day.

The relation between power consumption and the respective determining factors (indicators) is very complicated, and usually its analytical description is practically out of the question because it involves a time-varying combination of various meteorological, economical, social, and political aspects.

Therefore the only way to reach a reasonable prediction of power consumption expected in the next given time interval is to use the previous history of power consumption in combination with some auxiliary intervention time series (such as temperature, wind, humidity, sky cloud cover, etc.), whose proper combination forms the input to the prediction system. Its predictors are not based on physical models of the consumer's activity, but they learn the respective input time series and intervention series given on their inputs.

The problem of time prediction of electric power can therefore be formulated as follows:

a. The goal of the prediction must be specified; that is, one has to determine the physical and mathematical character of the predicted quantities, the length of prediction (prediction interval), and the time in which the prediction has to be realized.

b. The relevant input data must be selected.

c. The requirements on the accuracy of prediction must be specified. (This has to be done very carefully with respect to the overall economy.)

d. How the accuracy of prediction will be tested must be determined.

e. The architecture of the proper set of predictors must be selected and their parameters must be determined using a suitable neural network learning procedure, including the procedure of their testing and subsequent adaptive modification.

f. The requirements on the user friendliness of the program environment of the respective prediction system must be specified.

According to experience, such a neural prediction system can be designed so that the accuracy of the daily morning peak prediction ranges from 97–98%—that the average error in long-time testing (several months or years) is below 2–3% (i.e., almost 80% of predicted values differ from the actual values not more than $\pm 2\%$ or $\pm 3\%$), which is significantly better than may be obtained using traditional numerical algorithmic methods for the considered data sets.

13.3 METHODS OF PREDICTION

Before we describe the methods of forecasting and prediction, let us characterize the basic prediction models. Suppose that we are dealing with the time series y_t, the actual real value of which for $t = t_o$ is y_{to}. The predicted value is $y_{t_o + k}$, where k is a prediction step. For the determination of this, the knowledge of y_t for $t < t_o$ is supposed.

13.3.1 Linear Models

The popular Box-Jenkins methodology (e.g., see [1]) involves linear models.

Assume a stationary stochastic time series for such the autocovariation function is

$$\gamma_k = \text{cov}\ (y_t,\ y_{t+k}) = E(y_t - \mu)(y_{t+k} - \mu)$$

and the autocorrelation function is

$$\rho_k = \frac{\gamma_k}{\gamma_0}$$

for $k = \ldots, -1, 0, 1, \ldots$, where $\mu = E(y_t)$ and $\gamma_0 = \text{var}\ (y_t)$.

If we denote the observed time series as $y_1, \ldots, y_n$, the estimation of its mean value is

$$y^* = \frac{1}{n} \sum_{t=1}^{n} y_t$$

The estimation of its autocovariation function is

$$c_k = \sum_{t=1}^{n-k} \frac{(y_t - y^*)(y_{t+k} - y^*)}{n}$$

and, finally, the estimation of autocorrelation function equals

$$r_k = \frac{c_k}{c_0}$$

for the same values of k.

Usually $n > 50$ and $k < n/4$ should be chosen. The estimation of the autocorrelation function r_k allows one to choose the most suitable model from the Box-Jenkins set.

The basic Box-Jenkins set of models involves the moving-average model $MA(q)$ of order q, having the form

$$y_t = \epsilon_t + \theta_1 \epsilon_{t-1} + \cdots + \theta_q \epsilon_{t-q}$$

where ϵ_t is the white noise with zero mean value and with variance $E(\epsilon_t^2) = 1$ and θ_j are real values. The autocorrelation function ρ_k of this model can be found as

$$\rho_k = (\theta_k + \theta_1 \theta_{k+1} + \cdots + \theta_{q-k}\theta_q)(1 + \theta_1^2 + \cdots + \theta_q^2)^{-1}$$

for $k = 1, \ldots, q$ and $\rho_k = 0$ for $k > q$.

From here one obtains the set of nonlinear equations for θ_j where the values ρ_k are known.

The second model of Box-Jenkins methodology is known as the autoregressive model $AR(p)$ of order p. This can be expressed as

$$y_t = \phi_1 y_{t-1} + \cdots + \phi_p y_{t-p} + \epsilon_t$$

where y_{t-1} are the past values of the time series $y(t)$.

The mean value of the stationary $AR(p)$ is zero, and its autocorrelation function leads to the set of difference equations

$$\rho_k = \phi_1 \rho_{k-1} + \cdots + \phi_p \rho_{k-p} \qquad \text{for } k > 0$$

The combination of the previous two models is known as the autoregressive moving average model $ARMA\ (p, q)$, which can be expressed as

$$y_t = \phi_1 y_{t-1} + \cdots + \phi_p y_{t-p} + \epsilon_t + \theta_1 \epsilon_{t-1} + \cdots + \theta_q \epsilon_{t-q}$$

13.3.2 Nonlinear Models

The aforementioned models, belonging to the well-known Box-Jenkins methodology, may be successfully applied especially when the input data are linear. However, quite often the data coming from the real world do not have such character. This is one reason why in recent years so much interest has been given to nonlinear models.

In this chapter we have no space to present a deep survey of the nonlinear methods for time-series prediction. Our main interest will be given to our experience with those based on the use of artificial neural networks. Nevertheless, we feel the necessity to remind the reader briefly of the principals of some other interesting nonlinear prediction models.

First we take up the *bilinear model*. This can be considered as a straight nonlinear extension of ARMA models. Its basic equation has the form

$$y_t = \sum_{i=1}^{p} \phi_i y_{t-1} + \sum_{j=0}^{q} \theta_j \epsilon_{t-j} + \sum_{n=1}^{P} \sum_{m=1}^{Q} \beta_{mn} y_{t-n} \epsilon_{t-m}$$

where $\{\epsilon_t\}$ is the sequence of independent random values having zero mean value and constant variance σ_e^2. Here also $\theta_o = 1$ usually.

Some modifications of this model, called bilinear models with heterogeneous error, are based on the assumption that m can be zero. Nevertheless, in certain practical applications simplified bilinear models are used. The models with homogeneous output, having the form

$$y_t = \sum_{n=1}^{P} \sum_{m=1}^{Q} \beta_{mn} y_{t-n} \epsilon_{t-m} + \epsilon_t$$

can be mentioned.

Here the most significant is the form of the matrix $[\beta_{mn}]$. According to it, we distinguish the diagonal, superdiagonal, and subdiagonal models reflecting the position of the nonzero values of $[\beta_{mn}]$.

Another group of nonlinear models is the group of *threshold models*.

The forming of such models was stimulated by the theory of nonlinear vibrations in physics. In these models, some parameters are inserted so that if their values rise over a certain predetermined level (critical or threshold level), the basic structure and/or the function of the respective model is changed.

An example of models belonging to this group is the self-exciting threshold autoregressive model (SETAR). For order $(p_1, \cdots p_m)$ this is defined by

$$y_t = \phi_0^{(j)} + \sum_{i=1}^{p_j} \phi_i^{(j)} y_{t-1} + \epsilon_t^{(j)}$$

where the condition is

$$(y_{t-1}, y_{t-2}, \ldots, y_{t-k}) \in S_j, \qquad \text{for } j = 1, \ldots, m.$$

Here again $\{\epsilon_t^{(j)}\}$ for $j = 1, \ldots, m$ is the sequence of m mutually independent strict white noise series, and S_j is some decomposition of k-dimensional space

R^k. The actual form of such nonlinear models depends therefore on past values of the time series $y_{t-1}, \ldots, y_{t-k}$.

Still another group of nonlinear models involves *amplitude-dependent models*. These models are constructed so that they can represent periodic time series whose frequency varies with their values (amplitude). The most important examples from this group are the exponential AR models.

Models of this kind have the form

$$y_t = \{\phi_1 + \pi_1 e^{-\gamma y_{t-1}^2}\} y_{t-1} + \{\phi_2 + \pi_2 e^{-\gamma y_{t-1}^2}\} y_{t-2}$$

$$\vdots$$

$$+ \{\phi_p + \pi_p e^{-\gamma y_{t-1}^2}\} y_{t-p} + \epsilon_t$$

Here again, ϵ_t is the white noise and $\phi_1, \ldots, \phi_p$ and $\pi_1, \ldots, \pi_p$ and γ are the sets of real parameters, whose values depend on the amplitude $|y_{t-1}|$ of the particular member of the time series y_t at time $t - 1$.

Of course, such models can be extended in such a manner that some or all the parameters ϕ_j, π_j, and γ depend also on the amplitudes $|y_{t-2}|$, $|y_{t-3}|$, and so on.

The last group of nonlinear nonneural models we mention are *asymmetrical models*. The origin of models in this group can be seen in the necessity to predict some time series of economical nature, where the prediction of the contemporary development is modified according to the character of time dependence in certain important parts of history. The intensity of these modifications and corrections is modulated according to whether the time series under consideration increases or decreases inside the respective part of its history.

The asymmetrical model of moving average of order q can be defined as

$$y_t = \epsilon_t^+ + \theta_1^+ \epsilon_{t-1}^+ + \cdots + \theta_q^+ \epsilon_{t-q}^+ + \epsilon_t^-$$

$$+ \theta_1^- \epsilon_{t-1}^- + \cdots + \theta_q^- \epsilon_{t-q}^-$$

where ϵ_t is again white noise, $\epsilon_t^+ = \max(0, \epsilon_t)$, and $\epsilon_t^- = \min(0, \epsilon_t)$.

13.3.3 Neural Models

Models based on the application of artificial neural networks form an extraordinarily important class of the nonlinear prediction model family. They differ from both the previously mentioned linear and also the nonlinear models mainly in that their parameters are not determined by straightforward calculation (or by solving the set of corresponding equations), but are adjusted through network learning.

Though network learning or training can also be a very laborious and computer-power-consuming procedure, a great advantage can be found in the absence of the need to know the respective model of the physical problem under consideration. We just train the corresponding artificial neural network like the black box.

Any neural network can, in general, be considered as a dynamically changing oriented graph whose nodes (corresponding to neurons) and branches (corresponding to the synaptic connections acting between some nodes) are characterized by a set of respective sets of numbers. In such a model each node (neuron) is characterized by its input x_i, output y_i, node transfer function f, set of corresponding synaptic weights w_{ij}, and set of thresholds θ_i.

The network structure involves some significant sets of neurons. One of them consists of neurons receiving information from the external world. These are considered as the input set. The respective combination of inputs x_i to all neurons of this set forms the network input X. The second significant group of neurons in the network structure involves those neurons whose outputs y_i influence the external world. These belong to the output set. Suppose that there is no neuron belonging to both these sets. Of course, in the general theory of neural networks, other important sets of neurons are distinguished also. This is true especially when dealing with layered structures. However, we cannot go into more detail in this respect.

The combination of all outputs y_i from the output set forms the overall output Y of the network, while the combination of all inputs x_i in the input set forms the network's overall input X. The ratio Y/X can be considered as the neural network transformation function $\mathfrak{J}$. The existence of some connection and interaction between two nodes in the network structure is determined by the nonzero value of the respective synaptic weight.

When training the particular neural network, one first inserts on its input and output the chosen set of training input and output signals X_T and Y_T. Next, by some interactive learning procedure one determines the network structure and its parameters so that the actual network output Y approximates the required output Y_T in an acceptable manner.

During the past few years a proof (based on the Kolmogorov solution of the thirteenth Hilbert problem) was given that a one-dimensional array with at least three mutually connected layers of neurons having the sigmoid transfer function is able to approximate an arbitrary network transformation function $\mathfrak{J}$. This proof is, however, unfortunately of an existential, not a constructive (synthetic), nature. Therefore we cannot say in advance which network structure will be optimal to represent a given transformation function $\mathfrak{J}$. Nevertheless, from the analogy to the structure of the human brain (and also to all the brains of advanced animals) we usually prefer dealing with layered network structures. Also, all our interest here is focused on such structures.

The learning (training) procedure can be considered in general as an optimization, in the course of which the difference (error) between Y and Y_T is minimized. However, learning usually has many suboptimal solutions differing in the value of the final error. The global optimum is usually not known.

Many learning procedures recommended for different kinds of neural network structures are known. Among them the backpropagation procedure (with various modifications improving its properties) suitable for multilayer feedforward multilayer artificial neural networks is the most popular. Many other learning algorithms and methods are known, such as those based on optimizing principles.

Let us consider a one-dimensional artificial neural network in which the neurons of the first layer are connected with some (or all) neurons of the second layer only. The same is true for the neurons of the second layer with respect to the neurons of the third layer, and so on. The input X comes to the neurons of the first layer, and the output Y is formed by outputs from the last layer.

The application of such an arbitrary multilayer neural network to time-series prediction requires (like other approaches to time-series prediction) careful input data selection above all. One must first choose the training and the testing sets from all the data representing the time series under consideration. For this, no exact theory is yet known, unfortunately. In some cases, the whole set of data representing the time-series history is divided into just two subsequent parts, one (usually the older one) for training and the other for testing. However, there are cases where it is recommended to use the subsequent changing of short training and testing data sets. Another form of learning-testing set arrangement is also very important, where the learning set itself is divided into two parts: proper learning set and validation set.

Usually, approximately 50% of available data is used for training, while the rest is saved for testing. The suitable proportion must, however, be investigated for each case.

The artificial neural network for time-series prediction can be considered as a nonlinear AR model that may be realized in several ways. The common approach is to simulate the functions of such a network on a conventional digital computer. In some special cases, the network can be also realized by suitable special hardware. However, the first approach has, up to now, dominated in most neuron time-series prediction applications.

When dealing with the time-series prediction realized by artificial neural network simulation on a digital computer, one must distinguish between network design and training and its application for the actual prediction. While the first task is usually quite laborious and needs deep knowledge and proper know-how and consumes a good part of computer time running on fast machines, the application of the properly structured and trained neural network for actual prediction can be done without any special knowledge and skill. In most cases, any standard PC is suitable.

For both cases, different software tools are convenient. For the first task, one needs a set of programs that perform the necessary data preprocessing (excluding the eventual outliers, inserting suitable substitutes for missing data and other necessary acts of data refinement) for the creation of a suitable network structure and for its training and testing. Additionally, one needs to use programs for architecture optimizing, for example, network pruning. All these programs need to be satisfactorily universal, fast, and accurate, but need not be too user friendly.

For the second task, the software package must involve programs for inserting respective data into the data store, their actualization, the selection of suitable predictors and their handling, and the requested prediction statistics. As opposed to the previous set, all programs from this one must be as easy for the nonskilled operator to use as possible.

The entire prediction procedure consists at first of inserting in time t the time-series history $x(t - t_1), x(t - t_2), \ldots, x(t - t_p)$ on the input to the p neurons of the first (input) layer of the chosen predictor network.

The determination of t_i is not an easy task. In the course of network learning, the set of p values of the history is inserted into the input neurons many times, shifting its position subsequently with respect to time (the principle of the moving window).

The output layer of the structure under consideration has m neurons. If $m = 1$, one obtains just one member y_t of the predicted time series. Usually, $m = 1$. The case where $m > 1$ can be solved by constructing m networks.

In the case where one deals with such time series, the values of which depend on other parameters or other time series, one can compose the input set X of indicators consisting of some combination of their values. The proper selection of the individual indicators belongs to the most significant part of the prediction know-how. In the next part of this chapter, we mention some of our experience in this respect.

We can conclude that a practically useful procedure of how to design the proper set of neural predictors suitable for certain application is known.

However, when dealing with any realized neural network, one must be very careful of the influence of its parameter changes on overall network properties. Although usually the redundancy of the network structures under consideration is very high, the changes of parameters of some network elements can cause significant unpleasant deviations of the network properties from the preliminary designed nominal values. After finishing the network design procedure, the respective sensitivity analysis is recommended. This is usually quite laborious. As an example, the influence of some variations of synaptic weight coefficients on the network classification ability is presented (see Figure 13.1). From this and other similar results obtained when dealing with not only all the synaptic weights, but also with thresholds and slopes, one can estimate which parameters changes have the most significant influence on network properties. This depends, of course, on network type and complexity of its structure. For example, when dealing with four-layer feedforward structures, simulating cortex column classification properties, the opposite changes in thresholds of neurons in both hidden layers were found to be most critical.

However, artificial, like natural neural, networks are usually very resistant to parameter changes in general. The reason is probably in their high redundancy. Also the quite simple artificial neural networks, dealing with not too many neurons, have some neurons the parameters of which can be changed significantly without influencing the network properties. Quite often some neurons can also be cut from the original structure. This is called network pruning (e.g., see [2, 3]). The procedure for finding the fault-tolerant (resp. maximally

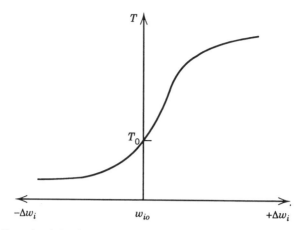

Figure 13.1 *Example of the dependence of neural network classification ability on synaptic weight changes.*

fault-tolerant) network structure requires many numerical computations (see [3]). Recently the method of statistical derivatives was introduced by Šebesta and Novák for technical system tolerances optimization. When applied on neural network optimization and pruning (see [4]), it gives good results. However, when some neuron is suppressed from the original structure, the whole network has to be retrained. This complicates the procedure. One advantage of the approach based on the use of tolerance theory and statistical derivatives is that the respective parameter changes can be determined inherently.

Of course, the degree of network pruning is in contradiction to its resistance to parameter changes, in general. Therefore one needs to find some reasonable compromise. The optimization of the preliminary designed network structure in this respect is very complicated, and the analysis of the network parameter sensitivities and tolerances can represent a useful tool for practical solution of this problem, which is of great practical importance.

13.4 SOME RESULTS OBTAINED

The developed methods of time-series prediction by artificial neural networks were applied to the problem of electric power consumption forecasting in West Bohemia. Some of the results reached in cooperation with H.E.M. Informatics, Prague, are presented. The electrical energy in this area is sold to end users by West Bohemian Power Co., which is the dominant distributor of electrical energy for the entire West Bohemian region, with more than 2 million inhabitants and a lot of industry. They buy daily the necessary amount of energy from the Czech Power Plants Co. and sell it to consumers.

The daily peak here represents about 500 MW. The distributor's profit depends on the difference between the prices of bought and sold energy. These prices depend significantly not only on the amount of purchased energy but also on how accurately the buy and sell agreements are realized.

Therefore, the optimization of the distributor company profit heavily depends on the knowledge of the expected daily consumption. This allows one to influence satisfactorily in advance the company's daily energy policy (e.g., by the use of the HDO system for directly affecting selected groups of small consumers and the distance control of their power consumption, by the use of specialized modifiable contracts with a set of main consumers, and by the eventual starting of the company's own small peak power plants).

The daily course of electric power consumption depends significantly on season, actual weather conditions, day in week, week in month, month in year, on the type of day (working day, weekend, holiday), general economic and political situation, various local events, and such things as expected or unexpected TV transmission of some popular football or hockey match, or other event. The influence of temperature is especially important, because it realizes with some estimable delay significant changes in the daily course of energy consumption in cases of positive and negative temperature variations (this is caused by the inertia of heat accumulation in buildings). Also, wind influence is expected to be significant, while cloud cover appears to be almost negligible. The course of the process of electric power consumption can, however, be significantly influenced by application of control signals for switch-on and switch-off of accumulative electric heaters transmitted in the electric power network in various instants day and night (as a part of the HDO system). These factors all cause the consumption diagram, which is recorded with hour density for several years, to have a very complicated, though quasi-periodical, character. An example of two weeks of recording is presented in Figure 13.2.

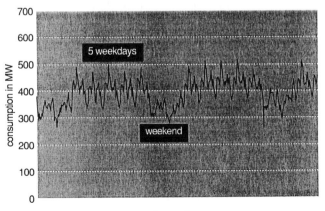

Figure 13.2 *Two-weeks' record of electric power consumption in West Bohemian region.*

Analyses of such a signal, which can be considered as a random process with some known quantitative parameters, made by the use of conventional numerical methods were not very successful. Also attempts to predict daily consumption by linear regression gave unacceptably large errors. Therefore neural-oriented prediction methods were applied.

After many numerical experiments the necessary forecasting methodology was developed and a set of neural predictors was synthesized. At first, a set of special artificial neural networks was designed, and each was trained as a predictor for one season and a different overall situation. Later, on the basis of the decorrelation connectionists approach, mentioned in [5] a whole-year predictor was constructed.

A software prediction system, PREDIP, was designed, which gives the user (distributor company's dispatcher) the ability to operate with various neural predictors in a user-friendly environment of the Windows character.

Even though the training of neural predictors is laborious and time consuming, their application in PREDIP for daily prediction is easy and fast (the prediction is made in a fraction of a second even if a simple PC is used).

Figure 13.3 shows the error histogram for one such predictor, named SUMMER 7, designed for prediction of consumption at eight, nine, and ten o'clock AM when the last information on the previous history was at seven o'clock. The testing was made on unknown actual signal in July and August 1992. In Figure 13.4 the daily statistics of such predictions in these two months are shown. Here three predictions are recorded: the squares show the errors of prediction at eight o'clock, crosses errors of prediction at nine o'clock, and asterisks errors of predictions at ten o'clock. One sees that the channel $\pm 2\%$ involves more than 61% of predicted values, the channel $\pm 3\%$ more than 80%. The maximum error, which is about -7%, appears in only a few events.

By the use of more sophisticated methods of predictor networks synthesis developed in [6], we suppressed the prediction average error to below 2% with maximal error below 5%. The test was performed on data from July and August 1992 where weekends were excluded. The developed predictors were based on combinations of multilayer neural network and linear models with decorrelated residuals. As indicators (inputs to the predictors), the following 10 variables were selected:

$X_{t(1)}$	load today at four o'clock
$X_{t(2)}$	load today at five o'clock
$X_{t(3)}$	load today at six o'clock
$X_{t(4)}$	load today at seven o'clock
$X_{t(5)}$	load yesterday at eight o'clock
$X_{t(6)}$	load yesterday at nine o'clock
$X_{t(7)}$	load yesterday at ten o'clock
$X_{t(8)}$	load a week ago at eight o'clock
$X_{t(9)}$	load a week ago at nine o'clock
$X_{t(10)}$	load a week ago at ten o'clock

Density of Errors

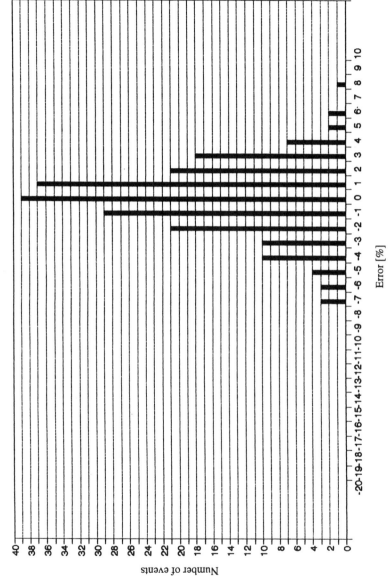

Figure 13.3 *Error histogram for the predictor SUMMER 7.*

235

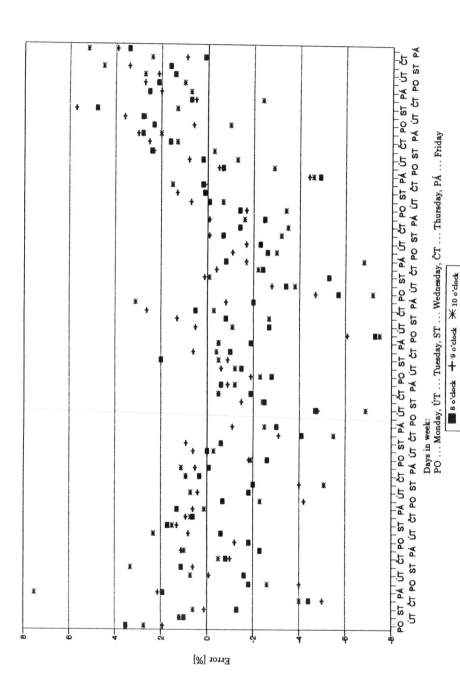

Days in week:
PO ... Monday, ÚT ... Tuesday, ST ... Wednesday, ČT ... Thursday, PÁ ... Friday

■ 8 o'clock + 9 o'clock ✳ 10 o'clock

Figure 13.4 *Daily statistic of predicted value errors.*

Also the influence of some meteorological data (average daily temperatures and cloud-cover variables) were tested, the result of which yielded lower average prediction errors.

Except for applications concerning one-dimensional prediction, several tasks occur in which it is necessary to predict more than one time series. Some of them are usually correlated or mutually dependent. Several strategies are known to obtain such a result [7–10] using different neural network principles and architectures. The input of such a model is a vector $\mathbf{v}$ composed of n components that are varying in time. Taking into account m samples of each component in the past, we obtain a spatiotemporal matrix $V[n * (m + 1)]$, where $m = 0$ means "just now." The vector $\mathbf{v} = (v_{i,j})$ with i fixed and j varying from 0 to m means the particular time series, while the same vector with j fixed and i varying from 1 to n means the input vector sample in time j.

Several approaches exist to use such a matrix as the neural network input. In our example the modified perceptron-like structure was explored.

The multidimensional time-series prediction was carried out in the field of ecology, with the aim of predicting the quality of a river source. Several parameters describing the biological and chemical quality (e.g., oxygen, microorganisms, etc.) have been monitored since 1961 with a period of one month in Vltava River in Bohemia. For our study, seven of them were selected and put into the neural network training set. The values of all of them in last two years were available at the input at every instance with the aim of predicting the value in future months. An example of such a series is presented in Figure 13.5. This represents the relative amount of oxygen in water. The predicted values are on the frontier curve, with the actual values behind them. The relative mean square error of this prediction is less than 5%.

13.5 PERSPECTIVES OF TIME-SERIES PREDICTION BY ARTIFICIAL NEURAL NETWORKS

Prediction of time series by the use of neural predictors, realized as artificial neural networks simulated in a computer under a suitable user-friendly program environment, represents a qualitative new tool for the economic strategy of electric power distribution companies. It allows not only much more precise prediction even in considerably variable situations than is possible by conventional algorithmic numerical methods, but it also allows the possibility of reacting almost immediately to previously unexpected situations in real time and creating in satisfactory time the necessary control signals. The developed predictors are easily adaptable and so can be regularly modified according to the real development of the consumption and with respect to changes in the user's needs.

In the expected development of these predicting tools, interest is going to be given not only to the further diminishing of prediction errors but also to

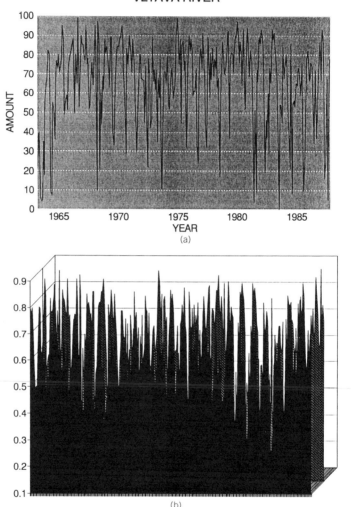

Figure 13.5 *Monitored and predicted values of biological quality of water in Vltava River.*

some other aspects, among them in particular the long-time prediction; that is, the prediction for two to four weeks is to be given attention.

Another interesting aspect is the optimization of the entire economic strategy of the distributor company based on the proper combination of short- and long-time predictions. Also the various prices of energy coming from different sources and various expenses of its transportation will be taken into account.

Besides these applications, the use of neural prediction methods in oncological research was performed. These concerned, for example, the prediction of states of female patients having breast cancer for a few months after application of chemotherapeutic treatments.

REFERENCES

[1] G. E. P. Box and G. M. Jenkins, *Time Series Analysis, Forecasting and Control*, Holden Day, San Francisco, 1970.

[2] J. Sietsma and R. J. F. Dow, Neural net pruning—why and how, *Proc. 1988 IEEE Internat. Conf. Neural Networks*, I, 325–333.

[3] Ch. Neti, M. H. Schneider, and E. D. Young, Maximally fault tolerant neural networks, *IEEE Trans. Neural Networks*, 3(1), 14–23 (January 1992).

[4] M. Novák and V. Šebesta, *Neural Network World*, 2(1), (1992).

[5] E. Pelikán, C. de Groot, and D. Wuertz, Power consumption in West-Bohemia: Improved forecasts with decorrelating connectionist networks, *Neural Network World*, 2(6), 701–711 (1992).

[6] E. Pelikan and V. Šebesta Neural network learning algorithms for electric load forecasting, *Proc. Conf. SPIE94*, Orlando, Florida, (April 1994).

[7] M. Campbell and P. Ormerod, A connectionist vector autoregressive model of the UK economy, *Neural Network World*, 2(6), 571–582 (1992).

[8] I. Grabec, Prediction of a chaotic economic time series by a self-organizing neural network, *Neural Network World*, 2(6), 607–614 (1992).

[7] D. Lowe and A. Webb, Adaptive networks, dynamical systems and the predictive analysis of time series, *Proc. IEE Internat. Conf. Artif. Neural Networks*, 95–99 (1989).

[9] O. V. Pictet, M. M. Dacorogna, R. B. Olsen, and J. R. Ward, Real-time trading models for foreign exchange rates, *Neural Network World*, 2(6), 713–744 (1992).

[10] C. de Groot and D. Wuertz, Analysis of univariate time series with connectionist nets: A case study of two classical examples, *Neurocomputing*, 3, 177–192 (1991).

CHAPTER 14 ⎯⎯⎯⎯⎯⎯⎯⎯⎯⎯⎯

Application of Learning Algorithms to Predicting Stock Prices

JÜRGEN GRAF
GHOLAMREZA NAKHAEIZADEH

14.1. INTRODUCTION

In banking, short- and long-term forecasting of financial time series and, especially, forecasting of the development of stock prices are very important components of management decision models. Besides the application of the traditional methods like technical and fundamental analysis or quantitative classical statistical methods, attention has recently focused on the application of neural networks to prediction of the development of stock prices. On the other hand, some symbolic machine-learning algorithms based on concepts such as regression and decision trees also seem to be appropriate for predicting stock prices. The aim of this work is to contribute to this debate. We describe different methods for predicting stock prices. Section 14.2 discusses the different algorithms used. We also analyze which exogenous variables are useful for predicting the German stock market. In Section 14.3 we describe a model, dealing with daily prediction of DAX (Deutscher Aktienindex) and contributing to short-term prediction of stock prices. In this model, different information like the change of Dow Jones and Nikkei indices, U.S. bonds, German Bund-Future, exchange rate DM/USD, and a technical indicator act as exogenous variables. Section 14.4 deals with another model for long-term prediction of the DAX's development. In this model, fundamental descriptors such as profit expectations, U.S. and German interest rates, and business climate index are

Frontier Decision Support Concepts, Edited by V. L. Plantamura, B. Souček, and G. Visaggio.
ISBN 0-471-59256-0 © 1994 John Wiley & Sons, Inc.

considered as exogenous variables to estimate the "fair value" of DAX and to forecast the development one year ahead. Section 14.5 presents and analyzes the empirical results. Here we use the models to compare the predictivity performance of neural networks, statistical methods, and machine-learning algorithms based on the ID3 procedure. In the last part we summarize our conclusions and present some final remarks.

Most models developed to forecast the movements of stock prices are usually based on traditional methods such as technical, fundamental, and quantitative analysis. Although these three methods are often used, there is no comprehensive study that evaluates their performances. Besides these traditional concepts, one can see recently in the literature some new approaches based on chaos theory, ARCH (autoregressive conditional heteroskedasticity), and GARCH models,* neural networks, and symbolic machine-learning algorithms to predict the development of capital markets.

Technical analysis merely uses past price data to predict the future and is comparable with autoregressive time-series analysis (see also [1]). The first models for predicting stock prices with neural networks were purely autoregressive as well ([2], p. NC-94; [3], p. II-456; [1]). But facing the results obtained by these studies, it can be recognized that the predicted values tend to lag behind the realized values ([4], p. 497). This feature is typical for many statistical methods of univariate time-series analysis relating to exponential smoothing.

Probably the analysis of fundamental information is the most important and most often used method for predicting stock prices. There are many studies examining the relation between stocks and fundamental descriptors like profits and interest rates. In Section 14.2.1 we present the used exogenous variables in fundamental stock-price models in Germany. In Section 14.2.2 and 14.2.3 we describe the algorithms used. We especially consider the neural network back-propagation algorithm and the symbolic machine-learning algorithm NEWID.

A short-term forecasting model is presented in Section 14.3, which is used to predict the German stock market for the following day. This model uses fundamental and technical information to predict DAX.

Quantitative analysis normally uses traditional statistical methods such as regression analysis or univariate time-series analysis. In Section 14.4 we present a dividend discount model using fundamental information to explain the development of stock prices. In this section we also present a neural network, which is able to predict stock prices unconditionally.

The results obtained by simulation are discussed in Section 14.5, while the last section is reserved for concluding remarks.

---

*This model accounts conveniently for the fact that large (small) stock price changes are followed by large (small) stock price changes of unknown sign.

14.2 ALTERNATIVE PROCEDURES IN THE PREDICTING OF STOCK PRICES

14.2.1 Fundamental Analysis of Stock Markets

There are many theoretical studies examining which fundamental exogenous variables will be the best to forecast the stock market. Two important factors determine the development of stock prices: profit expectation and interest rate. Although increases in profit expectation are likely to have a favorable effect, increases in interest rate have an unfavorable effect: the higher the interest rate applied to future earnings, the lower the capital value of the equity. The higher the yield on bonds, the more attractive they become as an alternative to holding common stocks. All other exogenous variables preferred in various models tend to describe these two factors.

In Table 14.1 various exogenous variables are shown, which were used in different German models, generally applied by statistical regression methods.

14.2.2 Neural Networks in Predicting of Stock Prices

Neural networks are computational systems that can be applied to simulate the complex nonlinear* situation on capital markets. Because classical neural nets

---

*It is unlikely that a structure as complex as a Western economy can be captured adequately by a linear system of equations ([9], p. 342).

TABLE 14.1   Exogenous Variables

Author	Frequency[1]	Output[2]	Input[3]
Dresdner[4]	q	FAZ-index[5]	$,[6] UZ,[7] T,[8] GZ[9]
Hielscher[10]	m	stat.B.[11]	E,[12] M,[13] GZ[9]
Rehkugler[14]	q	stat.B.[11]	L,[15] GZ,[9] C[16]

[1]Frequency: m = monthly, q = quarterly.
[2]Output: different stock market indices for representing the German stock market.
[3]Different fundamental exogenous variables.
[4]Dresdner Bank [5].
[5]An acronym for the Frankfurter Allgemeine Zeitung-All Shares Index.
[6]Exchange rate DM/USD.
[7]U.S. interest rate: Treasury bonds.
[8]World trade.
[9]German interest rate: "Umlaufrendite."
[10]Hielscher [6].
[11]Index of the German Statistical Institution.
[12]Expected earnings per share.
[13]Money supply M1.
[14]Rehkugler [7, 8].
[15]Free-liquidity position: money supply M1/nominal GNP.
[16]Business climate index: "ifo Geschäftsklimaindex."

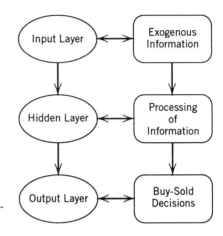

Figure 14.1 *Comparison of alternative prediction processes.*

are well documented in the literature (see also the introductory chapters of this book), we do not describe them here. We will describe the different net topologies we have used to predict the development of stock markets. Figure 14.1 compares the prediction process of stock prices with corresponding neural net layers.

The neural network architecture used in this study consists of three layers: the input layer, one hidden layer, and the output layer. The three layers are completely connected to form a hierarchical network. The *backpropagation* algorithm is used as a learning rule. A problem when using neural networks is that the net tends to overfit the training data and consequently loses its ability to generalize (i.e., perform well on new unknown examples). The overfitting appears when the net starts to fit the noise elements in the data. To solve this problem,* we use a *heuristic algorithm*** described as follows:

1. Create a neural network and fit the training data. Train the network until the mean square error is reduced below a special known bias.†

2. Make a simulation to test the causal connection between inputs and output: for example, change one input variable, keep all others unchanged, and observe the output value.‡ If the output will change in the expected way, the model is well defined. Otherwise the model is not well constructed and you have to go to step 1.

3. Use test data with known output to evaluate the generalization ability of the network to recognize new examples. If the network is not able to

---

*Schumann and Lohrbach (see [1]) have the opinion that there must be a compromise between memorization and generalization.

**This algorithm was developed by the first author by applying the ideas in [10].

†The error of the determined and existing output during the learning period is used as a convergence criteria [2].

‡Ormerod et al. suggests viewing the implied functional relationship critically in economic terms by this method ([9], p. 348).

perform well on these new examples, the network is oversized and you have to prune the hidden neurons. Using one hidden node per pattern type leads to the loss of generalization ability ([4], p. 497).* After reducing the network, begin with step 1.

14.2.3 Machine-Learning Algorithm NEWID

We have described the machine-learning algorithms that are appropriate to solve classification tasks in another chapter of this book. All of these algorithms are not suitable for the case in which the classes are continuous valued. According to our knowledge, only the algorithms CART and NEWID can handle the continuous-valued classes. The statistical package S-Plus can perform this task as well. Since we have used only NEWID in the empirical part of this work, we will describe the parts of NEWID that are related to continuous-valued classes. Information about CART can be found in [11].

As described in Chapter 11 NEWID was developed by Robin Boswell at the Turing Institute in Glasgow and is based on the concept of ID3 due to Quinlan (see [12]). The procedure used by NEWID for continuous-valued classes is almost the same as the procedure used to handle discrete classes. The only difference consists of how class values are assigned to the nodes of the decision tree. Instead of the common discrete class value, NEWID assigns the average class values of the objects to the nodes. We demonstrate this procedure by a very simple example.

Suppose that we want to use two attributes A and B to predict the values of the class C and suppose that C can accept only continuous values. Attributes A and B can accept discrete or continuous values. In this example, we suppose that they are continuous-valued as well. To develop the needed decision tree,** we suppose also that we have five examples listed in Table 14.2. Regarding, for example, A as the most informative attribute and 5 as a threshold value for splitting, we get the first partition of the decision tree as in Figure 14.2.

---

*Given enough hidden nodes, it can be shown that a neural net can approximate each problem to an arbitrary accuracy. But as mentioned, it is not always desirable to minimize the mean square error as much as possible, because of the possibility of overfitting.
**In continuous-valued classes, the decision trees are called regression trees. See, for example, [12].

TABLE 14.2 A Simple Example for Continuous-Valued Classes

Examples	A	B	C
1	6	12	12
2	4	14	6
3	8	18	18
4	10	10	6
5	2	16	24

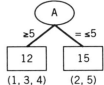

Figure 14.2   *The first partition of the decision tree.*   (1, 3, 4)   (2, 5)

We see that examples 1, 3, and 4 are assigned to the left node and examples 2 and 5 are assigned to the right node of the tree. Now the question is, which class value should be given to the right and left nodes? Algorithms like NEWID and CART use the average of the class values of the examples of each node. It means that the average class value of examples 1, 3, and 4, which is 12, will be assigned to the left node. Similarly, the average class values of examples 2 and 5, which is 15, will be assigned to the left node. From Figure 14.2, we can now derive the following prediction rules:

If A is greater than 5, then the prediction value for C is 12.

If A is less than or equal to 5, then the prediction value for C is 15.

It is obvious that the decision tree in Figure 14.2 can be split further at each node. For example, using the attribute B and the threshold value 15, we can get the decision tree shown in Figure 14.3, which corresponds to the following prediction rules:

If A is greater than 5, then the prediction value for C is 12.

If A is less than or equal to 5 and B is greater than 15, then the prediction value for C is 24.

If A is less than or equal to 5 and B is less than or equal to 15, then the prediction value for C is 6.

Such rules can be used to predict the C values for the examples for which only A and B values are known.

Especially in dealing with noisy data, the decision tree generated as above becomes very complex and its prediction power reduces. In such cases the tree should be pruned (see Chapter 11 or [13]).

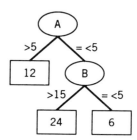

Figure 14.3   *The second partition of the decision tree.*

14.3 SHORT-TERM PREDICTION

There are many possibilities for explaining the daily change rate of the stock market. Professional traders of banks, investment funds managers, and foreign investors have a significant influence upon this development. For example:

The investors react to new information such as revised profit expectations or general economic developments.

The application of technical analysis systems leads to feedback trading: for example, an increase of stock price will be reinforced ([14], p. 1).*

The development of interest and exchange rates at the *same time* could explain the changes of stock prices.

As shown, many factors influence stock prices. A short-term prediction system should satisfy the following requirements:

It must be easily adaptable to new facts.

Linear and nonlinear relations should be reproduced by such a prediction system.**

In Tables 14.3 and 14.4, we show the correlations between various important exogenous variables and DAX. The exogenous variables are

(a)	(b)
Dow Jones Index$_{t-1}$	$(\text{Dow}_{t-1} - \text{Dow}_{t-2})/\text{Dow}_{t-2} * 100$
Nikkei Index$_t$	$(\text{NDJ}_t - \text{NDJ}_{t-1})/\text{NDJ}_{t-1} * 100$
U.S. interest rate$_{t-1}$	$\text{USR}_{t-1} - \text{USR}_{t-2}$
German Bund Future$_{t-1}$	$\text{GBF}_{t-1} - \text{GBF}_{t-2}$
Put/call ratio$_{t-1}$	Put/call ratio$_{t-1}$
DAX$_{t-1}$	$(\text{DAX}_{t-1} - \text{DAX}_{t-2}/\text{DAX}_{t-2} * 100$
Exchange rate DM/USD$_{t-1}$	$\text{DM}/\text{USD}_{t-1} - \text{DM}/\text{USD}_{t-2}$

The correlations between the percentage changes of the exogenous variables and DAX are presented in Table 14.4.

As Tables 14.3 and 14.4 show, there are obviously significant changes in the structure of correlations. In the prediction model we use these seven variables to forecast DAX. The learning period encloses three months, and the test data is the following month. The complete examination period is 01/01/91–

---

*Kirman [15] writes in the context of the foreign exchange market: "Although the foreign exchange traders may claim that the dollar is overvalued they may still buy, perceiving the market trend to be upward in the short term."
**There is some evidence that short-term movements of stock prices behave nonlinearly ([16], p. 82).

TABLE 14.3 Correlations between Exogenous Variables (a) and DAX

	Sign[1]	DAX (1/91)[2]	DAX (2/91)[3]	DAX (1/92)[4]
Dow	+	0.89	0.30	0.76
Nikkei	+	0.51	0.09	−0.75
DAX-1	+	0.98	0.86	0.98
Bund-Future	+	0.80	−0.44	−0.07
DM/USD	+	0.78	0.49	0.21
Put/call ratio	−	−0.48	−0.57	0.05
U.S. int. rate	−	0.31	0.53	0.66

[1]The expected sign of correlation.
[2]01/01/91–30/06/91.
[3]01/07/91–31/12/91.
[4]01/01/92–30/06/92.

30/06/92. The first learning data set is 01/01/91–31/03/92, and the first test data is 01/04/92–30/04/92. The last learning period is 01/03/92–31/05/92, and the test will be realized in 01/06/92–30/06/92. It means that there are altogether 15 different samples.

As mentioned we use the back-propagation algorithm with one hidden layer, seven input nodes, and one output node. Only four nodes are situated in the hidden layer. That should be sufficient to fit the training data and to prevent overtraining the neural network.*

14.4 LONG-TERM PREDICTION

14.4.1 Conditional Forecasting Model

To determine the influences of exogenous variables on price formation of the German stock exchange, we performed statistical investigations with a data base from January 1980 to November 1991. Using the software package RATS,

---

*The number of hidden neurons is optimized by applying our heuristic algorithm described in Section 14.2.2.

TABLE 14.4 Correlations between Exogenous Variables (b) and DAX

	Sign[1]	DAX (1/91)[2]	DAX (2/91)[3]	DAX (1/92)[4]
Dow	+	0.28	0.30	0.27
Nikkei	+	0.22	0.47	0.51
DAX-1	−	−0.07	−0.07	−0.09
Bund-Future	+	0.14	0.14	0.14
DM/USD	+	−0.18	−0.06	0.25
Put/call ratio	−	0.18	0.09	0.00
U.S. int. rate	−	−0.05	−0.09	−0.19

[1]The expected sign of correlation.
[2]01/01/91–30/06/91.
[3]01/07/91–31/12/91.
[4]01/01/92–30/06/92.

we examined the influence of general economic indicators on the movement of DAX by means of stepwise multiple regression.

As the general economic indicators are published only monthly, we used the end-of-the-month single quotation as the dependent variable. The general economic indicators are mainly taken from Monatsberichte der Deutschen Bundesbank. After using many different economic indicators, we took into account the following figures as exogenous variables in a linear regression model:*

1. Index of expected earnings per share, which is calculated by aggregating the earnings per share of all stocks of DAX. No time lag is used.
2. Index of the German business climate, which is provided by the IFO-Institut, Munich. The information lag is two months.
3. Seasonally adjusted order receipts of manufacturing industries. We use a lag of 11 months.
4. U.S. Treasury bond rate as a percentage monthly average. We chose a lag of one month.

Taking absolute value levels, we obtained very high values for multiple regression coefficients R^2, but the Durbin-Watson statistic differed substantially from 2.0, indicating high autocorrelations. The occurrence of such a trend effect is not surprising when we compare the absolute values of time series.** But using the test of cointegration, introduced by Engle and Granger [18], we realized that all exogenous variables are cointegrated with DAX. Especially when examining the index of earnings per share and DAX, the null hypothesis of no cointegration is strongly rejected.

The equation for estimating the "fair fundamental value" of DAX_t can be now represented formally as

$$DAX_t = aE_t + bC_{t-2} + cO_{t-11} + dI_{t-1}$$

with E_t = index of expected earnings per share in t
    C_{t-2} = business climate in $t - 2$
    O_{t-11} = orders in $t - 11$
    I_{t-1} = U.S. interest rate in $t - 1$

and $a, b, c > 0, d < 0$.

One problem arising from this approach is the prediction of DAX development. It is possible to estimate the actual "fair" value of DAX, but for predicting the value for the following month it is necessary to estimate the index of expected earnings, realized next month. So we call this approach conditional forecasting requiring scenarios for the exogenous variables.

For comparison, we trained a neural network with the same input data as

*The time structure is optimized by using the partial correlation coefficients.
**This effect can be eliminated by using growth rates instead of absolute values ([17], p. 136).

mentioned. Furthermore, we trained a neural network using the following inputs without any time lag structure optimized.

1. Index of expected earnings per share; no time lag
2. Index of the German business climate; information time lag two months
3. Seasonally adjusted order receipts of manufacturing industries; information time lag 11 months
4. U.S. Treasury bond rate; no time lag
5. Money supply M1; information time lag two months

14.4.2   Unconditional Forecasting Model

Influenced by the problem of conditional forecasting mentioned in Section 14.4.1, we trained a network using the idea of information structure in Figure 14.1 in Section 14.2.2.

In our model we take as exogenous information

Exchange rate DM/USD

German interest rate, long-term bonds with maturities of 10 years (R10)

German seasonally adjusted order receipts of manufacturing industries

The common feature of these input data is that DAX will react with time lag upon changes in these variables. Figures 14.4, 14.5, and 14.6 represent the significant relationship between these time series and DAX.

The exchange rate DM/USD influences the profits of German enterprises with time lag. If the dollar increases, the profits of German companies that export to the United States will also rise. This should also influence the stock prices positively. Figure 14.4 supports this fact.

As can be seen from Figure 14.5, there is a significant negative correlation between interest rates and stock prices. Normally interest rates fall before stock prices rise.

Order receipts are also a leading indicator, showing the future profits of the enterprises.

The original input data, existing as quarterly data will be transformed by calculating the percentage annual difference: For example, instead of the German orders in 01/75 (first quartal in 1975) we use the percentage difference defined as

$$\text{Input} = \frac{\text{orders } (01/75) - \text{orders } (01/74)}{\text{orders } (01/74)} \times 100$$

In Figures 14.4–14.6 this equation is described as

$$\frac{\text{orders } (t) - \text{orders } (t - 1)}{\text{orders } (t - 1)} \times 100$$

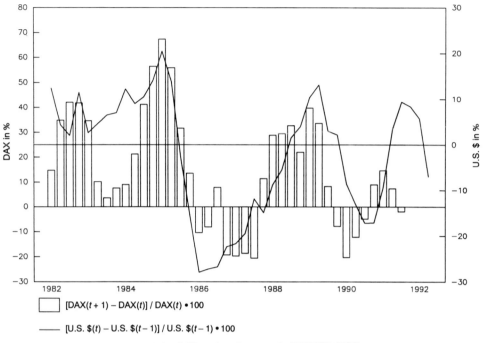

Figure 14.4   *DAX and exchange rate DM/USD (US$).*

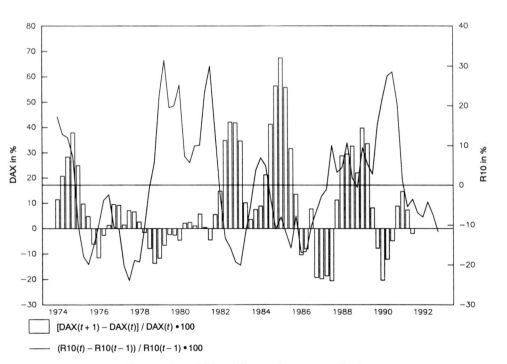

Figure 14.5   *DAX and German interest rate (R10).*

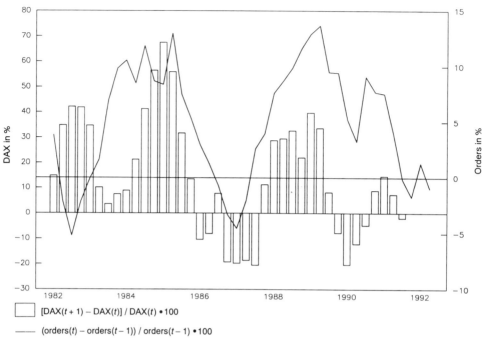

$\square$ [DAX(t + 1) – DAX(t)] / DAX(t) • 100

—— (orders(t) – orders(t – 1)) / orders(t – 1) • 100

Figure 14.6   *DAX and order receipts (order).*

So $t - 1$ represents the annual difference between year t and $t - 1$. The output is the change of DAX in the following year:

$$\text{DAX}_{t+1} > \text{DAX}_t =: 1 \quad \text{and} \quad \text{DAX}_{t+1} < \text{DAX}_t =: 0$$

with t = 01/74, 02/74, .03/74, .04/74, 01/75, ... In the simulation an output higher than 0.8 will show increasing DAX, an output less than 0.2 decreasing DAX. The interval [0.2, 0.8] is neutral.

The simulation period begins 01/74 and ends 04/91. We use 24 learning data examples for training, and after training the neural network forecasts if DAX will increase or decrease in the following year.

In the next section we present the empirical results obtained by using the backpropagation and machine-learning algorithm NEWID.

14.5   EMPIRICAL RESULTS

14.5.1   Short-Term Prediction

The results of the quantitative short-term prediction of the test data using back-propagation* and the NEWID algorithm are presented in Table 14.5. For in-

---

*All examinations with neural nets are done by using the software package NeuralWorks Professional II.

TABLE 14.5 Comparison of Results of Short-Term Prediction

Sample	Neural Network		NEWID	
	RMSE[1]	Accuracy[2] (%)	RMSE	Accuracy (%)
1	1.21	64.2	2.58	85.7
2	0.90	72.7	1.08	54.5
3	1.10	68.7	1.55	68.7
4	1.16	71.4	1.70	50.0
5	1.37	70.6	1.73	41.2
6	0.76	70.0	0.69	40.0
7	0.76	58.8	0.73	47.1
8	0.89	60.0	0.82	60.0
9	0.85	60.0	0.51	80.0
10	0.75	60.0	1.13	33.3
11	0.93	50.0	0.85	64.3
12	0.57	76.9	0.96	46.2
13	0.72	57.1	0.76	57.1
14	1.12	71.4	0.91	46.2
15	0.41	66.7	1.21	50.0
Average	0.90	65.2	1.15	55.0

[1]RMSE = root mean square error
[2]The rate of accuracy will be defined as $t = a/(a + b) \times 100$ with $a =$ correct predictions of tendency, $b =$ false predictions of tendency. The accuracy rates are derived from the quantitative value of prediction.

formation about the samples used see Section 14.3. As Table 14.5 shows, the accuracy rate achieved by neural networks is, on average, higher than the result achieved by NEWID. This better performance of neural networks is also supported by the calculated values for RMSE. A problem of the used machine-learning algorithm consists of overfitting the training data. For a sample of about 60 examples, NEWID has generated 40 different rules. Consequently, there is no generalization ability and prediction performance is rather poor.

14.5.2 Long-Term Prediction

Conditional Forecasting Model. One criterion to compare the different methods is the validity of the sign of correlation that they realized. Another measure is the goodness of fit. As expected, the neural net realized a better fit than the regression model. Nevertheless, as Table 14.6 shows, the validation of its economic performance is rather poor. A negative correlation between orders and DAX seems not to be strange,* but shows the importance of choosing the right time lag structure. Furthermore there is a positive influence of U.S. interest rates on DAX, which is rather doubtful. The machine-learning

---

*"In case of no lag, the correlation was always negative which seems to indicate a lead-lag structure" ([17], p. 137).

TABLE 14.6   Comparison of Results of Conditional Modeling

DAX	Sign Th.[1]	Sign NN[2]	Sign Reg.[3]
Business climate	+	+	+
Expected earnings	+	+	+
Orders	+	−	+
U.S. interest rate	−	+	−
Money supply M1	+	( )	+

[1]Sign of the theoretical expected correlation: + = positive correlation, − = negative correlation.
[2]Sign of realized correlation by the neural network.
[3]Sign of realized correlation by the statistical regression model.

Goodness of fit
Neural network   MAPE = 4.1%
Regression   MAPE = 5.1%

with MAPE = mean absolute percentage error.

algorithm NEWID was not applicable to determine the sign of correlation. The data used for conditional modeling are described in Section 14.4.

Unconditional Forecasting Model. The results realized by using backpropagation and the NEWID algorithm are listed in Table 14.7. For information about the data used see Section 14.4.

Furthermore we calculated the trading profit realized by applying the different methods. Tables 14.7 and 14.8 show that the results achieved by neural nets are better than the performance achieved by the machine-learning algorithm NEWID. An interesting aspect is the fact that NEWID performed better in the difficult prediction period 1980–1982, characterized by a deep recession in Germany.

TABLE 14.7   Simulation Results: Rise/Fall Using the Test Data

Model	NN 3-3-1[1]	NEWID	Naive Prediction[2]
Accuracy[3] (%) 4/80–4/90	68.4	63.4	58.5
Accuracy[3] (%) 1/83–4/90	76.7	56.3	59.4

[1]Neural net with three input nodes, three hidden layer nodes, and one output node.
[2]The naive prediction assumes that the last development realized will also be the next prediction.
[3]The rate of accuracy will be defined as $t = a/(a + b) \times 100$ with a = correct predictions, b = false predictions.

TABLE 14.8   Simulation Results: Trading Profit Using the Test Data

Model	NN 3-3-1	NEWID	Naive Prediction	Buy & Hold[1]
Trad. prof. (%)[2] 4/80–4/90	503.6	421.6	331.4	218.1
Trad. prof. (%) 1/83–4/90	493.8	281.8	287.5	170.7
Add. prof. (%)[3] 4/80–4/90	130.9	93.3	51.5	—
Add. prof. (%) 1/83–4/90	189.2	65.1	68.4	—

[1]The buy-and-hold model represents the development of the German stock market during the simulation period.
[2]Trading profit is calculated by the following strategy: rise = long position, fall = short position. The open position will be completely closed one year later.
[3]Additional profit is calculated as $m = (c - d)/d \times 100$, with c = trading profit, d = buy-and-hold profit.

14.6 CONCLUSION AND FINAL REMARKS

The object of this study has been to evaluate the practicability of neural nets and machine-learning algorithms in predicting short- and long-term development of stock prices. We have discussed possibilities of developing systems that advise the right timing for buying and selling, using German stocks represented by DAX. In simulations, different models are compared. The results are

- Short-term prediction of stock prices is a very difficult task (see also [8]) and seems to be nonlinear. Consequently a neural network seems to be the best approach (perhaps in addition to a GARCH model, which is not tested here). The neural network used in this study was able to outperform linear regression and the machine-learning algorithm NEWID.

- NEWID has often overspecified the data and could not generate rules with high prediction power.

- Long-term prediction can be subdivided into two areas: conditional and unconditional forecasting. Conditional forecasting working with the scenario technique is usually realized by statistical multiple regression techniques. This method uses elaborate resources and seems to perform well on long-term structure modeling. Neural networks are able to get a good fit between input and output, but it is difficult to choose the best input data for neural nets. Using the input data obtained by correlation analysis leads necessarily to similar results.

- In long-term forecasting, the best approach for using neural networks seems to be unconditional predicting. In this approach, the used neural net had a superior performance compared with NEWID.

The results obtained lead to the conclusion that neural networks can be considered as one of the most interesting technologies for analyzing nonlinear relationships in financial markets.

On the other hand, there are some problems in using neural networks. Trained neural nets are complex systems with linked layer nodes and nonlinear functions whose relationship cannot easily be described in qualitative terms. Generally, it is difficult to understand such systems. Furthermore, the user has to select and adjust many parameters—for example, the correct number of hidden layers and the number of nodes at each layer. Adjusting these parameters is often difficult.

Consequently, one major weakness of neural networks is the lack of diagnostics help. If bad results are obtained, it is difficult to detect the responsible node from the mass of interrelated weights and connectivities in the net. In any case the question of how to train the network best is still subject to some uncertainty.

Further research should be carried out in the following areas:

- Theoretical methods to verify neural network systems should be developed, especially for determining the best input data. In our opinion this is the only possibility of preventing loss of generalization ability. It might be possible to combine statistical methods with neural net technology.

- Solving the problem of overfitting: One important idea is to prune hidden neurons that are not necessary for creating the best model. Perhaps it would be possible to implement the pruning methods used in machine-learning algorithms.

- Some previous studies show that machine-learning algorithms like NEWID are very useful tools to solve classification tasks. To get a better idea about the applicability of such algorithms to prediction tasks, further research is necessary.

REFERENCES

[1] M. Schumann and T. Lohrbach, Artificial neural networks and ARIMA—models within the field of stock market prediction—a comparison, *Prelim. Proc. BANKAI Workshop on Adaptive Intelligent Systems*, S.W.I.F.T., Belgium, 1992.

[2] Neural Ware Inc. *Neural Computing*, NeuralWorks Professional II/PLUS and NeuralWorks Explorer, Pittsburgh, Pa., 1990.

[3] H. White, Economic prediction using neural networks: The case of IBM daily stock returns, *IEEE Internat. Conf. Neural Networks*, San Diego, II/451–II/458 (1988).

[4] J. Graf, ''Stock Market Prediction with Neural Networks,'' in R. Gritzmann, R. Hettich, R. Horst, and E. Sachs, eds., *Operations Research '91*, GMÖOR, Tagungsband, Heidelberg, 496–499, 1992.

[5] Dresdner Bank, Lassen sich Aktienkurse erklären?, *Trends* (August 1991), pp. 14–18.

[6] U. Hielscher, *Investmentanalyse*, München, 1990, R. Oldenbourg Verlag München Wien.

[7] H. Rehkugler and T. Poddig, ''Statistische Methoden versus Künstliche Neuronale Netzwerke zur Aktienkursprognose—Eine vergleichende Studie,'' *Bamberger Betriebswirtschaftliche Beiträge, Nr. 73/1990*, Otto-Friedrich-Universität Bamberg, 1990.

[8] H. Rehkugler and T. Poddig, Künstliche Neuronale Netze in der Finanzanalyse: Eine neue Ära der Kursprognosen, *Wirtschaftsinformatik* 5, Oct. 1991, pp. 365–374, 1991.

[9] P. Ormerod, J. C. Taylor, and T. Walker, ''Neural Networks in Economics,'' in M. P. Taylor, ed., *Money and Financial Markets*, Oxford, 1991.

[10] Siemens AG, Projektabschlußbericht für das Innovationsprojekt ''Entwicklung Neuronaler Netzwerke für Prognosezwecke,'' September 1991.

[11] L. Breimann, J. H. Friedman, A. Olshen, and C. J. Stone, *Classification and Regression Trees*, Wadsworth, Belmont, Mass., 1984.

[12] J. R. Quinlan, Discovery Rules from Large Collection of Examples. A Case Study, in D. Michie, ed., *Expert Systems in the Micro Electronic Age*, Edinburgh University Press, 1979.

[13] G. Nakhaeizadeh, ''Inductive Expert Systems and their Application in Statistics,'' in F. Faulbaum, ed., *SoftStat'91. Advances in Statistical Software 3*, Gustav Fischer, Stuttgart, pp. 31–38, 1992.

[14] L. Menkhoff, ''Feedback Trading auf Devisenmärkten,'' in *Jahrbücher für Nationalökonomie und Statistik*, 1992.

[15] A. Kirman, ''Epidemics of Opinion and Speculative Bubbles in Financial Markets,'' in M. P. Taylor, ed., *Money and Financial Markets*, Oxford, 1991.

[16] J. B. Ramsey, ''Economic and Financial Data as Nonlinear Processes,'' in G. P. Dwyer and R. W. Hafer, eds., *The Stock Market: Bubbles, Volatility, and Chaos*, Proc. Thirteenth Annual Economic Policy of the Federal Reserve Bank of St. Louis, pp. 81–134, London, 1990.

[17] T. Landes, O. Loistl, and W. Reiß, ''The Determinants of the Fundamental Value Part of a Share Price,'' in O. Loistl and T. Landes, eds., *The Dynamic Pricing of Financial Assets*, Hamburg u.a., 1989.

[18] R. F. Engle and C. W. J. Granger, Co-integration and error correction: Representation and testing, *Econometrica*, 55, 251–276 (1987).

PART II

Frontier Optical and Parallel Systems

CHAPTER 15 ⎯⎯⎯⎯⎯⎯⎯⎯⎯⎯⎯⎯

Parallel Evolutionary Algorithms and the Concept of Population Structures

MARTINA GORGES-SCHLEUTER

15.1 INTRODUCTION

Many problems in science and engineering, economics and statistics, as well as management can be formulated as optimization problems in which some cost function must be minimized or some profit function must be maximized.

The systems to be handled in practice are usually very complex, so that a mathematical analysis is hardly possible. In those cases where we are able to specify the goal function explicitly (i.e., to derive an analytic expression) and may assume additional specific features of the search space (e.g., the goal function is differentiable, linear, or quadratic), we may be able to apply numerical optimization methods efficiently. These methods compute gradient approximations to calculate search directions leading to an optimum. For nonlinear constrained optimization, sequential linear programming (SLP), sequential quadratic programming (SQP), the modified method of feasible directions (MMFD), and the generalized reduced gradient method (GRG) [1] are the best numerical techniques.

Real-world problems often have high dimensionality and a nonlinear coupling of parameters, a multimodal search space, and a noncontiguous search space. Constraints and further noise and time-dependent behavior may complicate an efficient solution of optimization problems.

Of specific practical interest are combinatorial optimization problems. They arise if the variables can assume only a discrete value out of a finite set of values. In that case the search space is enumerable. Methods commonly used

Frontier Decision Support Concepts, Edited by V. L. Plantamura, B. Souček, and G. Visaggio.
ISBN 0-471-59256-0   © 1994 John Wiley & Sons, Inc.

in operations research and management science to solve combinatorial optimization problems rely chiefly on one variant or another of linear programming. The integer programming formulation of real-world problems may easily involve millions of zero-one variables and thousands of constraints.

During the last decade more and more problems from all scientific disciplines were found to be especially hard and difficult to solve even with the assistance of powerful computers. These problems have the property that numerical efforts to find the exact solution increase exponentially with the problem size in the worst case. These problems are called $\mathfrak{N}$(ondeterministic) $\mathcal{P}$(olynomial time)-complete problems [2]. Unfortunately, numerous problems with immediate practical relevance are known to belong to the $\mathfrak{N}\mathcal{P}$-class [2]. Among them are the, perhaps, most famous problems from combinatorial optimization: the job shop scheduling problem and the traveling salesman problem.

Moreover, even if a deterministic polynomial-time bound algorithm exists to solve a given problem to optimality, the search effort required may easily reach enormous figures with growing sizes of the instances of a problem, unless the order of the deterministic polynomial time bound is not very small.

When optimization tasks arise in practice, they are often large scale, complex, and include numerous constraints. Thus, due to time considerations, one is often forced to relax the optimality requirement and settle for finding ''good'' solutions using only a reasonable amount of search effort. Whenever the acceptance criterion tolerates a neighborhood about the global optimal solution, a semioptimization problem ensues. Most practical problems are of a semioptimization type, requiring some reasonable balance between the quality of solution found and the cost of searching for such a solution. Thus, relaxing optimality is an economic necessity.

The basic problem in handling a semioptimization task is to device algorithms that guarantee bounds on both the search effort and the extent to which the optimization objective is compromised. A more ambitious task would be to equip such an algorithm with a set of adjustable parameters so that the user can meet changes in emphasis between cost and performance by controlling the trade-off between the quality of the solution and the amount of search effort.

In addition to numerical parameter optimization problems and combinatorial optimization problems, we may be interested in a quite different challenging task: the development of strategies. A very popular example comes from game theory. The Prisoner's Dilemma is a two-agent game defined by a payoff matrix, an example of which is given in Figure 15.1. Each of the two agents can either cooperate or defect. For a one-round game, no matter what the other does the selfish choice of defection yields a higher payoff than cooperation, but if both defect then both do worse than if both had cooperated.

The situation is not so obvious if the game is played repeatedly. In an iterated Prisoner's Dilemma, a strategy is a decision rule that specifies the probability of cooperation or defection as a function of the history of the interaction so far. The too-nice strategy of always cooperating with an opponent yields best scores for the entire group. The too-nasty strategy of always defecting yields

	B cooperates	B defects
A cooperates	(3 , 3)	(0 , 5)
A defects	(5 , 0)	(1 , 1)

Figure 15.1 *The Prisoner's Dilemma. The payoff matrix specifies for players A and B the four possible outcomes of one game. The first score is assigned to player A, the second to player B.*

highest individual scores if the other cooperates. The best strategy found is called TIT FOR TAT, submitted by Rapoport to a computer tournament conducted by Axelrod [3, 4]. TIT FOR TAT is a strategy of cooperation based upon reciprocity; if an opponent has defected the last time, defect, and if he has cooperated, then cooperate. TIT FOR TAT needs only a memory of one move in the past. Interesting is the observation that even if more moves are remembered no better strategy has been found, except in very specific environments.

The iterated Prisoner's Dilemma is a very simple nonlinear dynamical system. In a more realistic situation we like to model a small number of competitive sellers. Assuming that each competitor is neither powerless, which would result in pure competition, nor powerful, the case of monopoly, we are interested in strategies maximizing the total profit of each. On one hand, we might be interested to find strategies being robust across a variety of situations; on the other, we might search for a specific successful strategy for a particular environment of competitors. These questions are in contrast to the usual oligopoly problem in which we search for the equilibrium pattern of price and quantity across the sellers, if any.

15.2 WHY DO WE NEED JUST ANOTHER PROBLEM-SOLVING STRATEGY?

Let us first consider an example from function optimization. Assuming a rugged search space, say in the two-dimensional case the topographic map of the Alps, with one global optimum, the Mont Blanc, and several local optima being more-or-less close to the global best, such as those mountains higher than 4000 m, we are still faced with the problem of finding any of them quickly.

This example is especially nice, because it reflects some kind of problems occurring in the real world. Although we can determine for each point in the search space its quality (i.e., the meters above sea level), we cannot give a numerical expression to compute the quality function. Numerical methods are not applicable in those cases. We could use a Monte Carlo method to search for the highest mountains. Starting from a randomly chosen point we climb until we reach the top (a local optima). This procedure is repeated several times. Each iteration is independent of those performed before. But the search space (the topographic map) is not structureless, and thus it might be more appropriate if knowledge gained from previous trials could be reused to learn a search strategy. In this example it might be more promising to search higher mountains in the vicinity of high mountains already found.

The problem becomes even harder, if we assume a nonstationary search space (i.e., one changing over time). A good example is the domain of process control, where certain parameters of a complex industrial process are manipulated in order to achieve a stable optimal operation. In fact, simple adaptive control of time-evolving systems remains a problem not fully solved by traditional means. The amount of a priori information needed about the process is considerable [5]: Even the extension of traditional control theory known as adaptive control theory requires precise knowledge of both the disturbances possible and the process to be regulated, as well as qualitative knowledge about the process. Moreover, this knowledge has to be very precise and complete, and any slight imprecision can degrade dramatically the quality of the control. Adaptive control theory further relies on slow deviation of the process parameters with respect to the adaptive capacity of the controller.

The following two problem classes come from combinatorial optimization. Both have immediate practical relevance and have resisted all attempts to find an optimal solution efficiently.

Machine scheduling problems arise in diverse areas such as flexible manufacturing, production planning, and logistics. One is known as the job shop scheduling problem. Informally, the problem can be described as follows. We are given a set of jobs and a set of machines. Each job consists of an ordered list of operations, each of which needs to be processed during an uninterrupted time period of a given length on a given machine. Each machine can process at most one operation at a time. A schedule is an allocation of the operations to time intervals on the machines. The problem is to find a schedule with minimum makespan. The job shop scheduling problem belongs to the class of $\mathcal{NP}$-hard problems and appears to be one of the more difficult ones. A commonly used assumption is that the number of operations of each job equals the number of machines and each job has exactly one operation on each machine. In that case the number of schedules of each instance is given by $(n!)^m$. An especially notorious 10-job, 10-machine instance published by Fisher and Thompson [6] has defied solution to optimality for more than 20 years, and a solution found in 1984 with cost 930 has only recently been proven to be the global minimum.

Employee scheduling problems arise in a variety of service delivery settings, including scheduling of nurses in hospitals, check encoders in banks, airline and hotel reservation personnel, and others. Analytic methods are only applicable for problems with low-complexity size, where we have limitations such as employee homogeneity. A typical problem is days-off scheduling. The scheduler gives appropriate days off to each of several employees who work standard shifts with differing start times while ensuring that the required number of employees are on duty throughout the day and the week. The shift-scheduling problem is more complex. The scheduler works with part-time as well as full-time employees, and shift types differ in duration, start times, and number and placement of breaks. With medium complexity (i.e., number of shifts up to 500) a combination of linear programming and heuristics may be used. Lately, the general employee scheduling problem has been considered [7]. It differs from the previous simpler models by including important real-world features such as nonhomogeneous employees with limited availabilities, linking constraints between blocks of time periods, numerous shift types, and management rules. This model has wide applicability, especially in the supermarket, reservation office, and fast-food fields.

15.2.1 Optimization by Heuristics

Semioptimal solutions may be generated by heuristics. Besides the amount of search effort, heuristics possess other attributes that are recognized as valid criteria for comparison of heuristic algorithms [8], including

- Quality of solution
- Ease of implementation
- Flexibility
- Simplicity

Flexibility refers to the ability to handle problem variations, and simplicity means a simply stated algorithm.

There exist two basic strategies for heuristics: divide-and-conquer and iterative improvement. The former works by splitting the problem into subproblems, solves these subproblems independently, and then puts the solutions to the subproblems together to form a solution of the original problem. The main disadvantage of this approach is that to perform well the problem needs to be separable into disjoint subproblems so that the error occurring by merging the subsolutions does not offset the gains obtained by solving the small subproblems either to optimality or, if still not possible, by more sophisticated methods.

Iterative improvement methods start with a valid solution, obtained by random or constructive means. That solution is modified until a better one is bound. Then this new solution becomes the starting point of the next improvement step. This process is continued until no further improvement is possible. Iterative improvement is easily trapped in locally optimal, globally inferior solutions, since they can never accept a solution that worsens the cost function in the hope of climbing out of the local optima. Thus, it is customary to start the iterative improvement process several times from different starting points and to save the best solution.

Although there exist sophisticated iterative improvement strategies, they are good in local search, but only weak in global search. The main drawback is that whenever a new iteration loop begins the method starts from scratch. The question is; Why should it not be possible to use information gathered from previous trials to guide the search process?

An analogy may be found in human problem-solving strategies. To solve a problem a human being might work alone and eventually end up with a solution. A team of workers might be more efficient. In solving difficult open questions such as cancer research, it might be even more promising if several workers and/or teams work independently and exchange their results from time to time (e.g., by publishing or joining a conference). The central idea of using both competition and cooperation is to use collective properties of a group of individuals, which are separately performing the search, to generate solutions that are better than those obtained by each individual without interactions within the group, or by only one individual during a number of search attempts equal to the number of members of the group.

15.2.2   Designing a Parallel Algorithm

With single-processor systems we will end up in the near future at a technological barrier, so we cannot hope that the computation time of our algorithms will decrease drastically by using faster machines. Parallel processing offers a speedup beyond technological limitations.

Von Neumann computer systems consist of a control sequence (the instructions) and a collection of data elements. Those machines are called single-instruction, single-data-stream (SISD). Parallelism may be encountered either on the control level or data level.

Data-level parallelism tries to identify independent data elements and then process them on separate processors; that is, in each cycle all processors perform the same instruction. This approach works best on problems with large amounts of independent data. In addition, the "old" software can be used with only minor changes. Machines that use single-instruction, multiple-data-stream (SIMD) parallelism are, for example, vector computers and array processors.

Control-level parallelism tries to identify sequences of instructions that can operate independently and thus may be executed on different processors. The main problem is to identify and synchronize the independent parts of the program. With multiple-instruction, multiple-data-stream (MIMD) parallelism we have reached the stage where any further real advance will entail rethinking of our software.

The MIMD machine is the most general possible. It has become a feasible proposition over the last years due to the cheapness of microprocessor systems. Numerous microprocessors can be linked in a loosely bound network in which they all have their own independent memory, or they can be combined as a tightly bound multiprocessor in which each processor can access any memory; these machines are called shared-memory systems. It turns out that access control to the common memory is a bottleneck that limits the system size to relatively few processors. In the former proposition, information is exchanged between processors via message passing, offering the possibility of building up massive parallel systems with hundreds and even thousands of processors.

The program that runs on a MIMD machine is obeyed by all the processors, but each processor will be at a different place in the program at any one moment. A helpful programming paradigm for massive parallelism is the view of computation as a complex dynamical system—a large collection of possibly disparate entities. These entities have in general a dynamic connectivity; the system evolves by a statistical or deterministic set of rules.

This idea of distributed computation is common to most approaches toward natural computation. The entities might be particles (thermodynamics), cells (artificial neural networks), individuals, or populations (evolutionary algorithms). The interaction between these entities is completely asynchronous.

15.3 OPTIMIZATION METHODS GLEANED FROM NATURE

The large-scale experimental laboratory earth offers us methods to deal with various kinds of "messy" problems. From nature we may get inspired to design methods for solving continuous and discontinuous optimization problems as well as methods for breeding strategies (i.e., the methods).

One such method, optimization by simulated annealing, originated in spin-glass physics. The innovative aspect of simulated annealing is a controlled mechanism for accepting a trial solution x that increases the value of the cost function $f(x)$. A Boltzmann-like distribution is the choice of the accept criterion. Better trial solutions are always accepted; those being worse are accepted with a probability $e^{-\Delta f(x)/T}$, where the temperature T is a control parameter, being initially high and then slowly reduced to zero. This means that the larger the worsening of the goal function and the lower the current temperature, the smaller is the probability that a trial solution worsening the goal function is accepted.

The quality of the final solution found by a simulated annealing process depends heavily on the cooling schedule—the rate at which the temperature parameter is reduced. Only if the system is cooled sufficiently slowly may the process eventually reach the globally optimal solution. The main advantage using simulated annealing is that, in contrast to iterative improvement methods, the final solution does not depend on the starting point. Simulated annealing has been successfully applied, for example, for the placement problem in VLSI chip design, especially gate array and standard cell integrated circuits.

Other methods are inspired by biology. Artificial neural network models are stimulated by neurophysiology. They consist of numerous simple interacting processors. In contrast to the conventional von Neumann system, the storage and processing of information is not separated. Artificial neural networks are distributed learning signal processing structures. They have received wide attention lately. Main fields of application are pattern recognition (e.g., vision and speech) and classification problems.

This chapter focus on methods based on ideas from biological evolution. Evolution implies change with continuity, usually with a directional component. Biological evolution is best defined as change in the diversity and adaptation of populations of organisms. The general theory of life currently accepted by many scientists—the theory of evolution through natural selection, propounded more than 100 years ago by Charles Darwin—has since been modified and explicated and stands today as the organizing principle of biology.

Darwin, in his famous book *On the Origin of Species*, composed a number of postulates. Two of them were consistent with Lamarck's thinking. The first postulate is that the world is not static but evolving; the second is that the process of evolution is gradual and continuous. The other two main postulates, both of which were long resisted by most biologists and philosophers, are common descent and the theory of natural selection, the key to his findings.

Darwin stated that evolution through natural selection is a two-step process. The first step is the production of genetic variability through recombination, mutation, and chance events. The production of variation is random in that it is not caused by, and is unrelated to, the current needs of the organism or the nature of its environment. The second step is selection through survival in the struggle for existence; it is an intrinsic ordering principle. Those individuals with the most appropriate combination of characteristics for coping with the environment would have the greatest chance for surviving, of reproducing, and of leaving survivors, and their characteristics would therefore be available for the next cycle of selection. Thus, selectionist evolution is neither a chance phenomenon nor a deterministic phenomenon, but a two-step tandem process combining the advantages of both.

Living nature did not come up with the most complex optimization method. Instead evolution developed a process of generating new organisms as well as the organisms themselves. Starting from a simple mechanism of self-reproduction with noise,* more and more complex mechanisms** have evolved. At last it became so complex that the mechanism in all its details and consequences is still unknown.

Evolution algorithms such as genetic algorithms [9, 10], evolution strategies [11, 12], and classifier systems [13, 14] use simplified models of population genetics and Darwinian evolution. They try to adopt some of these natural metaphors to guide the search in different kinds of applications, as, for example, parameter optimization, combinatorial optimization, and learning strategies. They are different from most other algorithms in that they process a population of individuals (the structures representing potential solutions).

Of course, evolution algorithms evolved by starting from simpler strategies and extended by simulating nature's mechanism more accurately and by incorporating new mechanisms gleaned from nature.

Early evolutionary models were based on mutation and natural selection only and were not notably successful. In the early 1970s, John Holland's work at the University of Michigan led to genetic algorithms as they are known today. At that time Ingo Rechenberg and collaborators at the University of

---

*Self-reproduction with noise is an exogenous characteristic of the system.
**These are endogenous strategy characteristics.

Berlin independently introduced an algorithm that they called the evolution strategy. Whereas Rechenberg and Schwefel [11, 12] developed the evolution strategy from the viewpoint of an engineer, Holland [9] set up a mathematical framework for the study of the adaptation process found in nature and introduced generalized genetic operators to guide a search process in artificial systems. What makes both genetic algorithms and evolution strategies superior to earlier evolutionary models is the introduction of a crossover operator to mimic the effect of sexual reproduction.

15.3.1 Evolution Strategies

At the time when the evolution strategy (ES) started its own evolution, a simple mutation-selection strategy was used with only one parent creating one child, which competes against its parent for survival. The internal representation of an individual consists of genes x_i ($i = 1, \ldots, n$) coding the position in an n-dimensional Euclidean space R^n called the object parameters, representing a potential solution, and of a single gene coding the strategy parameter σ, the step size. From the only parent an offspring is generated via the mutation operator. If the new position is better than that of the parent, then the offspring becomes the new parent; otherwise the offspring is rejected. This completes one generation.

The mutation operator is realized by normally distributed random numbers with expectation value 0 being added to each object parameter from one generation to the next. The step size specifies the standard deviation of the normally distributed random changes. Thus, according to nature, small changes occur more often than larger ones.

What makes this simple evolution strategy, the (1 + 1)-ES, superior to previous ones is the adaptive change of the step size. The *1/5 success rule* is used to control the step size exogenously:

The ratio of successful mutations to all mutations should be 1/5. If it is greater than 1/5, increase the variance; if it is less, decrease the variance.

This rule was postulated by Rechenberg by theoretical considerations of two model functions.

$$f_1(x) = c_0 + c_1 x_1 \qquad \forall x_i \ (i = 2, \ldots, n) \qquad -b \le x_i \le b$$

$$f_2(x) = \sum_{i=1}^{n} x_i^2$$

where $x = (x_1, \ldots, x_n) \in R^n$. The corridor model f_1 is a linear, monotone function with constraints where improvement of the objective function is only accomplished by moving along the first axis of the search space inside a corridor of width $2b$ in all other directions. The sphere model f_2 is the simplest kind of nonlinear function and has only one optimum.

Rechenberg extended the two-membered $(1 + 1)$-ES to a multimembered $(\mu + 1)$-ES, where two parents out of μ individuals generate an offspring via mutations and recombination. Each of the μ members of the population have equal probability to be chosen as parent. Recombination is realized by randomly sampling genes from either parent. The offspring replaces the worst population member.

Although the step size is adjusted over the optimization process, it is the same for all object parameters. Thus, we may not expect an optimal step size for functions with other characteristics than those of the corridor and sphere model. Thus, Rechenberg proposed to extend the representation of an individual by using for each object parameter x_i $(i = 1, \ldots, n)$ genes coding the strategy parameters s_i $(i = 0, \ldots, n)$. The actual step sizes are calculated as $\sigma_i = s_0 s_i$, where the deviation factor s_0 is in common for all step sizes.

The creation of an offspring starts with a heuristic change of the strategy parameters. The deviation factor s_0 is doubled with probability $1/4$, stays unchanged with probability $1/2$, or is divided by 2 with probability $1/4$. Then each s_i $(i = 1, \ldots, n)$ is multiplied by 1.2 with probability $1/4$, stays unchanged with probability $1/2$, or is divided by 1.2 with probability $1/4$. The mutation operator modifies the object parameters with respect to these actual step sizes. This learning population gave a drastically improved convergence velocity when applied to the model functions f_1 and f_2.

A great evolutionary step of ES took place when Schwefel [12] extended the $(\mu + 1)$-ES to a strategy with a number of parents producing a collection of offspring: the $(\mu + \lambda)$-ES and the (μ, λ)-ES $(\mu < \lambda)$, where μ denotes the size of the parent population and λ the number of generated descendents within one generation. In the former strategy, called the plus strategy, the selection process operates by choosing the μ best individuals of the joint set of parents and offspring to form the parent population of the next generation. In the latter strategy, termed the comma strategy, only the offspring undergo selection; thus the lifetime of every individual is limited to one generation. The limited lifetime allows one to forget inappropriate parameter settings that may result in short phases of stagnation during the search and, by allowing even regression, early termination may be prevented.

The most important aspect of Schwefel's extensions of the evolution strategies is a completely different view of the genetic information an individual contains. Now the object and strategy parameters are viewed as part of the genetic information of an individual $A = x_1 x_2 \cdots x_n \sigma_1 \sigma_2 \cdots \sigma_n$.

The mutation operator works as follows. First, the individual strategy parameters σ_i undergo a mutation: They are multiplied with a Gaussian random number with expectation zero and standard deviation $\Delta \sigma$, an exogenously specified metalevel mutation rate parameter. Second, the variation of the object parameters is now controlled by the mutated strategy parameters.

Thus, the strategy parameters may adapt themselves via the evolutionary process endogenously. Those individuals with better-adjusted strategy parameters are expected to perform better; that is, their offspring have a higher chance to be fit enough to become part of the next generation. Thus, selection will favor indirectly those individuals with better-adjusted strategy parameters and as a result over time a better parameter setting will emerge by means of self-adaptation.

Recombination takes place between two randomly chosen individuals of the population, the parents. Recombination may be either discrete (the offspring's structure is a random sample of the parents' genes) or intermediate (the offspring's genes are computed by interpolation of the corresponding genes of the parents). It is also possible to use different recombination types for the object and strategy parameters. A further extension is to allow recombination between multiple members of the population; that is, for each parameter recombination the second parent is chosen anew. This results in a higher mixing of genetic information.

We are now ready to formulate the multimembered evolution strategy with recombination. Figure 15.2 outlines Schwefel's evolution strategy.

Within the ES the parents are determined with uniform probability; that is, each individual of the parent generation produces the same number of offspring except stochastic deviations. Selection takes place by reducing the population to its original size by deletion of those individuals with the least fitness.

In ES the selection pressure may be controlled via the ratio of μ/λ. Schwefel [12] theoretically investigated the restricted case of a $(1, \lambda)$-ES with a non-controlled step size. From an approximation of the rates of convergence Schwe-

---

1. Initialization :
   Set t=0.
   Generate a start population: either select at random a master individual serving as starting point for the generation of μ individuals by large mutations or choose μ individuals randomly to form $P(0)$.

2. Variation :
   From the population $P(t)$ parents are randomly chosen to produce λ offspring. An offspring is created through the application of the recombination operator, either none, discrete, or intermediate recombination is possible. Then the mutation operator is first applied to the offspring's strategy parameters and these mutated strategy parameters are then used to guide the mutation of the object parameters.

3. Selection :
   Select the μ best individuals out of λ ($\lambda > \mu$) offspring in case of a (μ, λ)-ES or out of $\mu + \lambda$ individuals in case of a $(\mu + \lambda)$-ES to form population $P(t+1)$.

4. Increment t by 1 and goto 2 to begin a new time-step.

Figure 15.2 *Schwefel's evolution strategy.*

fel deduced the optimal value for λ, the number of offspring per generation. For the corridor model f_1, the number of offspring generated should be $\lambda_1 \approx 6.0$ and for the sphere model f_2, $\lambda_2 \approx 4.7$. For a wide range of problems Schwefel's experiments showed that with the assumption $\lambda = c \cdot \mu$ and $c \approx 5$ the selection pressure of a (μ, λ)-ES is relatively well adjusted. For multimodal functions the selection pressure can be made softer by decreasing c, resulting in an increased explorative characteristic at the expense of a reduced convergence velocity. In the limit of $\lambda = \mu$ we end up in a pure random search strategy.

In ESs the mutation operator and the selection procedure together realize a kind of hill-climbing mechanism. Using the one-to-one association of object and strategy parameters, the evolution strategy may only learn search directions that are parallel to the axes of the coordinate system. In general, the optimal search direction (the gradient) is not aligned with the axes. Schwefel [15] extended the mutation operator to handle linear correlated mutations by introducing an additional strategy parameter, the vector θ specifying the correlation coefficients or inclination angles of the main axes of the hyperellipsoid in n-dimensional space. Thus, the ES may adapt the direction of search by self-learning a simple "internal model" of the topology of the environment, the "real world." Figure 15.3 visualizes the difference between simple and correlated mutations in a two-dimensional search space. The quality surface is given as a contour map. The step size σ_i of an individual make up an ellipsoid of equal probability density to place an offspring if these step sizes are applied to the individual's object parameters x_i.

15.3.2 Genetic Algorithms

The most significant difference between evolution strategies and genetic algorithms (GA) is the genetic representation. As a consequence they differ in the interpretation of mutation, recombination, and selection. Nevertheless both algorithms are conceptually identical.

The basic GA use a binary string of length l to encode the individuals. As

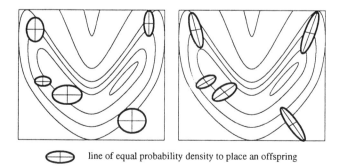

⊕   line of equal probability density to place an offspring

Figure 15.3 *Searching with simple and correlated mutations.*

the GA operates on a subsymbolic level, the binary representation requires for many applications a mapping from bit strings to the object parameters.

Using a binary alphabet in particular dates back to John Holland, who proposed choosing the cardinality of the alphabet Γ over which the structures are defined to be as small as possible. The argument is that the simulated evolutionary system processes the current sample of structures, the population of individuals, and by doing so it finds properties that contribute to a better performance by favoring those individuals that are "better" than others. These properties, called building blocks, are then tested in a new context, the sample generated by continuous modification of the structures of the old sample. The representation must therefore reflect common and useful properties of the structures yielding better-than-average performance. This requirement has been called the principle of meaningful building blocks [9, 10].

The advantage of choosing the cardinality of the alphabet Γ over which the structures are defined to be as small as possible may be easily illustrated by counting the similarities of different structures over two differently sized alphabets.

For illustration assume a binary alphabet Γ_1 and a hexadecimal alphabet Γ_2 and that structures over Γ_1 have length 20 and structures over Γ_2 have length 5. That is, both search spaces have the same cardinality: $S_1 = 2^{20} = 16^5 = S_2$. But, if we consider common attributes, there are many more similarities in the smaller alphabet. Introducing a "don't care" symbol ($\square$) indicating that it does not matter which symbol of the alphabet (an allele in biological terms) occurs at that specific position (a gene in biological terms), we have $17^5 = 1.42 \times 10^6$ versus $3^{20} = 3.48 \times 10^9$ different schemata. The term *schemata* refers to a similarity template.

Using a binary representation allows simple interpretations of the mutation and the crossover operator. Mutations are realized by flipping bits randomly according to an exogenous specified mutation rate. Holland defined a one-point crossover: A position in the range $[1, l - 1]$ is chosen randomly and both parents are cut at that position. By composing the substrings, two offspring are generated. Figure 15.4 gives an illustration of Holland's one-point crossover.

Since Holland, the simple one-point crossover has evolved to a broad family of crossover operators. But it seems no single crossover operator could be identified to be the best independently of the task to be performed.

What remains to be described is how within the context of GAs the process of selection is interpreted. In ES, each member of the parent population has

The parents   The offsprings

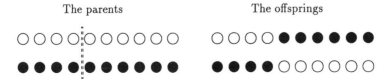

Figure 15.4 *The one-point crossover.*

an equal probability to create an offspring, and selection only occurs through the early death of an offspring (i.e., by discarding them from reproduction). In GAs the selection process operates by assigning those individuals being fitter a higher probability to contribute offspring to the next generation, but all individuals have some chance to contribute.

Let M denote the size of the population and $P(t) = \{A_1(t), A_2(t), \ldots, A_M(t)\}$ the population of structures (individuals) at generation t. The given set of all structures is $\mathcal{Q}$. For example, using a binary representation, this is the set of all strings of length l. The function $f\colon \mathcal{Q} \to \mathbf{R}^+$ assigns to each individual a positive real value $f(A_i)$. The object of the adaptive search is to find a structure that performs well in terms of the quality measure f.

Holland proposed the use of an assignment of offspring based on the absolute values of $f(A_i)$ $(i = 1, \ldots, M)$. The probability of an individual to contribute offspring is

$$p_{A_i} = \frac{f(A_i)}{\displaystyle\sum_{j=1}^{M} f(A_j)}$$

The average number of offspring an individual should receive is a real number computed as $\mathrm{tsr}(A_i) = M \, p_{A_i}$ (termed target sampling rate). During the selection phase this number is converted into an expected value indicating the average number of offspring that individual should receive. As the population size remains constant and is relatively small, a stochastic error occurs, giving some individuals the opportunity to contribute to more offspring than indicated by its target sampling rate, whereas others contribute to fewer offspring.

Figure 15.5 outlines a basic GA in analogy to Holland's reproductive plan of type $\mathcal{R}$.

The genetic search is primarily the search for coadapted sets of alleles, the schemata. The important feature of proportional selection is that reproduction allocates exponentially increasing numbers of trials to above-average schemata and exponentially decreasing numbers of trials to below-average schemata. This has been termed an *extinctive* selection scheme. The selection pressure may be guided by the ratio of μ/λ; decreasing the ratio increases the selection pressure.

In GAs the mutation operator acts as a background procedure to allow the reintroduction of lost variability. Basically, new variants are produced by crossing over. The parent selection probabilities depend on the absolute or relative fitness of the individuals; thus better-than-average individuals have a chance to contribute to more than one offspring. This selection scheme has been termed *preservative*, as every individual has a chance greater than zero to reproduce; the only exception is ranking with max $= 2$, where the least fittest has no chance to reproduce. Using proportional selection with scaling the selection pressure is adjusted adaptively over the course of optimization. Using linear rank selection [16] the selection pressure may be controlled by increasing or decreasing the parameter max.

A thorough comparison of GAs and ESs may be found in [17].

1. Initialization :
   Set $t := 0$ and select at random M individuals from $\mathcal{A}$ to form $P(0)$.

2. Next time-step :
   FOR each $A_i \in P(t)$ DO
       compute and store the measure of utility $f(A_i)$.
   Compute and store average fitness of the population $P(t)$:

$$\bar{f} = \sum_{j=1}^{M} f(A_j)/M$$

3. Selection and Variation:
   FOR $k := 1$ TO M DO
       Select an individual $A_k \in P(t)$ according to fitness, that is
           each $A_k \in P(t)$ has a chance $f(A_k)/\bar{f}$ of being selected.
       Determine the genetic operator to be applied: mutation
           or crossover with probability P_M or P_C, respectively.
       IF crossover operator is chosen
       THEN select a mate according to fitness, that is
           each $A_i \in P(t)$ has a chance $f(A_i)/\bar{f}$ of being selected.
       Apply the genetic operators.
       IF crossover
       THEN choose one of the two offspring randomly.
       Add offspring to population $P(t + 1)$

4. Increment t by 1 and goto 2 to begin a new time-step.

Figure 15.5 *A basic genetic algorithm.*

15.4 SUSTAINING EXPLORATION

Considering the nature of search spaces, we have on one side the extrema of a needle-in-haystack type, all flat with a single spike, and on the other a smooth unimodal search space. The former requires an algorithm with robust exploration (i.e., only exhaustive search will do it); the latter asks for an algorithm with pure exploitation, a good example of which is the hill-climbing technique. In most cases the structure of the search space is somewhere between these two extremes, and often we have no a priori knowledge. Therefore, the required strategy should be able to learn while searching, thus focusing the search to promising regions, and should be capable of sustaining exploration. We mentioned that the balance between exploitation and exploration of the search space is the potential that makes evolution algorithms so attractive.

15.4.1 The Problem of Premature Convergence

One specific problem arises in actual implementations: premature convergence. The difference between theoretical investigations and practical applications is the limited, usually small, number of individuals and, thus, the occurrence of stochastic sampling errors.

Premature convergence is coupled with the loss of genetic diversity, a phenomenon also observed in nature. Due to stochastic effects some genes get fixed and others are lost. Sewall Wright called this random genetic drift [18]. If genes get fixed too early the search becomes limited to some lower-dimensional subspace. A real problem occurs if that subspace does not include high-quality solutions. Then the search will probably stagnate with rather weak results, with little chance to escape this fate through lucky mutations.

With the basic GA a population $P(t + 1)$ is generated from the previous population $P(t)$ by deriving more offspring from better-than-average individuals. On one side, genetic material contained in better-than-average individuals has a chance to be contained several times in the next population, whereas on the other side the genetic material from below-average individuals may get lost.

The effects of random genetic drift may be reduced by increasing the size of the population. Unfortunately, this is computationally infeasible. Another rather greedy method is to increase the rate at which mutations occur. Mutations, as interpreted in GAs, are completely undirected changes. Thus, high mutation rates disturb the learning and adaptation process, and, consequently, the algorithm is no longer able to exploit promising regions of the search space.

15.4.2 Avoiding Premature Convergence

Premature convergence has been addressed by several authors. The basic idea in common is to reduce the stochastic error occurring due to small population sizes by techniques that reduce or eliminate the replacement error. Thus, generating from the previous population of structures the following population should preserve the variability of the contained genetic material.

One of the first responses was Cavicchio's [19, 10] preselection mechanism. Preselection filters the offspring generated, possibly takes the best, and replaces the inferior parent, if the offspring's fitness is better than that of the parent. As offspring are by definition similar to their parents, a good control over genotype variability may be achieved.

A generalization of preselection called crowding, has been proposed by De Jong [20, 10]. The argument is that in nature like individuals compete for survival in the same ecological niche and thus experience a selection pressure in proportion to other members of the population. Dissimilar individuals tend to occupy different ecological niches, so they typically do not compete. Crowding works as follows: Each time a new offspring has been generated, a set of individuals is chosen randomly from the population. The crowding factor specifies the size of the randomly chosen subpopulation. Now the Hamming distance between the offspring and each member of the subpopulation is computed. The offspring replaces the individual with the lowest Hamming distance—that is, the individual most similar in structure. De Jong applied this scheme successfully with crowding factors of 2 (the better) and 3. Even with crowding, a GA is not able to maintain stable subpopulations on all peaks in multimodal search spaces.

A very effective method, called sharing, has been proposed by Goldberg and Richardson [21]. The basic idea is that individuals that are similar either in genotype or phenotype should form a niche. Within niches the selection probability is shared. That is, an individuals fitness and the number of members in its niche determine the selection probability. Sharing forces the GA to explore different areas of the search space simultaneously and this leads implicitly to a higher variability of the search space.

The modern synthetic theory of evolution has identified four major factors of evolution: replication, mutation, selection, and isolation. Whereas replication, mutation, and selection are basic features found in any evolutionary algorithm, the importance of including isolation has been realized only recently. Indeed, the introduction of more-or-less isolation by restricting mating (i.e., introducing a degree of inhomogeneity into the large and only population) is another method to cope with the problem of premature convergence.

This brings us to the study of spatial patterns of populations of organisms.

15.5 IMPROVING THE GLOBAL SEARCH BEHAVIOR: EAS WITH A POPULATION STRUCTURE

So far we have assumed one large panmictic population; that is, we supposed that all members of the population affect one another equally. In living nature this may only occur if we assume mobile organisms contained within a space small enough for any organism to be likely to move freely throughout the whole of it. For large population sizes this is probably unusual. Deviations from panmixia may occur due to relationship or phenotypic similarity. We consider a deviation due to more-or-less spatial isolation of local populations within the species. The subdivision of species introduce a population structure. Introducing a population structure has two practical advantages: (1) reducing premature convergence yields a more robust algorithm; (2) it makes evolutionary algorithms (EAs) explicitly parallel.

Traditional computation involves sequential processing as enforced by the von Neumann machine. An increase of the computing power beyond the limits of the sequential von Neumann machine may only be achieved by alternative computer architectures. The power and cheapness of microprocessors is the reason for the fast-growing interest in massively parallel systems. But with MIMD parallelism we have reached the stage where further real advance will entail rethinking of our software.

Most software relies on an approach where a centralized control mechanism uses global knowledge and global rules to generate the complex behavior of the whole system. This is also true for traditional GAs where the processing of the whole population needs global knowledge and global rules to imitate the process of natural selection. Additionally, global synchronization, at least at the end of each generation, is needed.

The traditional evolution algorithms may be transformed from a sequential one to an explicit parallel evolutionary process by introducing a population structure. Basically, two models of population structure exist; they differ in how the genetic material may propagate through the entire population over time.

15.5.1 Migration Models

The simplest and earliest model of geographical structure described is the subdivision of the entire panmictic population into several subpopulations or *demes*, each forming a breeding unit by itself. Migration refers to the movement of individuals among subpopulations. The amount of migration is measured by a number m that equals the probability that a randomly chosen individual of any subpopulation is a migrant. The pattern of migration and the rate of migration limits the genetic diversity that can occur.

Let k denote the number of subpopulations and n the number of individuals of each subpopulation. If each subpopulation receives migrants from each other at a rate of $m/(k - 1)$, then we obtain a population structure called an *island model* (Fig. 15.6a). In this model we assume that migration takes place at random, in the sense that emigrants from a subpopulation are a random sample of the subpopulation members and are equally distributed to the other subpopulations.

In natural populations, individuals often are distributed more or less discontinuously to form numerous colonies, and individuals may be exchanged only between adjacent or nearby colonies. The geographical situation of the colonies or subpopulations may be linear, circular (Fig. 15.6b), rectangular, toroidal, and so on. Such interdeme migration models are termed *steppingstone models*.

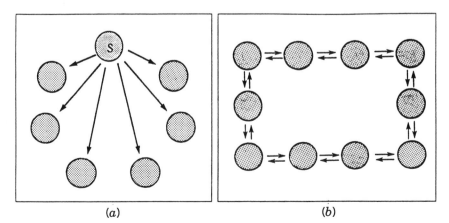

(a) (b)

Figure 15.6 *Migration: (a) island model; (b) stepping-stone model.*

The extension of the traditional EA by using a migration model is straightforward. The entire population is subdivided into subpopulations. Each of the subpopulations runs a traditional EA as described before except for the occurrence of migration. In nature, an emigrant leaving a subpopulation takes its genetic material with him; an immigrant, of course, imports his genetic material. The actual realization of migration in EAs usually sends copies of individuals to other subpopulations, and better individuals are favored to be multiplied.

The first attempt to introduce such a geographic population structure was by Grosso [22]. He studied an island model with five subpopulations. His main result is that semi-isolated subpopulations lead to a performance improvement that will not be fully realized at either of the two extremes of complete subpopulation interdependence (panmixia) or complete subpopulation independence (no migration).

Recent research on parallel GAs focused on a population structure, which looks pretty much like a high-dimensional stepping-stone model of population structure. Tanese [23, 24] and Cohoon et al. [25] placed the subpopulations on the vertices of an n-dimensional hypercube. The reasoning is that a short communication diameter allows efficient travel of migrants from one subpopulation to any other, which in turn should ensure an adequate mixing as time progresses. This corresponds also to the basic assumption of the theoretical investigation of Pettey and Leuze [26]: With adequate mixing the overall behavior of each subpopulation is comparable to that of the entire population of a traditional GA. Their experiments with a three-dimensional hypercube validated that this is a reasonable assumption. All approaches differ in how emigrants are generated and how immigrants are treated.

Another interesting perspective of using several small semi-isolated subpopulations instead of one large population is the observation that small populations develop faster. The amount of sampling errors depends on the size of a population and may be negligibly small for very large populations. Random genetic drift leads to fluctuation about the mean. The fluctuation is larger in smaller populations.

Migration models, as discussed, offer coarse-grained parallelism.

15.5.2 Diffusion Models

An alternative approach is a model of population structure in which a population is distributed uniformly over a large territory, but the parents of any individual are drawn from a small surrounding region, the neighborhood or deme. Figure 15.7 illustrates a linear and a planar continuum with uniform density. Two example overlapping demes are shown; individuals living in the overlapping area may be a mate of either central individual (the individuals marked with hatching).

The model thus passes to a continuum with uniform density in which any local differentiation from sampling depends merely on the limitation of the

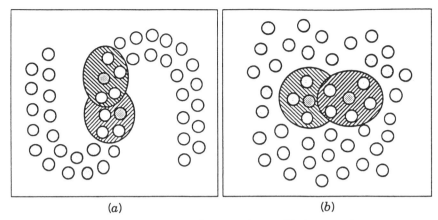

Figure 15.7 *Diffusion: (a) linear continuum; (b) planar continuum.*

range of dispersion. This will produce a sort of isolation, which Wright [27] called "isolation-by-distance." With the continuum model, gene frequencies change smoothly as we move across the manifold, and, thus, we obtain a diffusion process instead of migration.

This model has been inspired by a population concept of species observed in nature. In a widely ranging species, there may be continuity of interbreeding, but forms that are far apart may have differentiated so much that they do not produce fertile offspring on direct crossing. The increasing differentiation along a line may be related to climatic differences (e.g., the situation found in the leopard frog) or merely a function of time since there was common ancestry. A nice example is the herring gull. After the last ice age, by returning from their retreat in a region of the Caspian Sea, the Gulls now habitat the Arctic Coast, a circular region around the North Pole. The immigration of the gulls began in Great Britain. A limited gene flow caused by a long chain of small, poorly linked populations led to sufficient isolation, so different species developed one after the other: *Larus fuscus graelsii* (lives in Great Britain), *L. fuscus fuscus* (Scandinavia), *L. argentus vegae* (Siberia), *L. argentus smithonius* (North America), and *L. argentus argentus* (again in Great Britain). Here the two ends happen to come together to form a circular overlap. There has been so much differentiation, in spite of the line of continuity, that the first species cohabits, without interbreeding, with the last species, although collectively the gulls share a common gene pool. The population model describing the above situation is well known by population geneticists as the isolation-by-distance or neighborhood model [27].

A GA with a continuous population structure and a distributed dynamic was introduced, to my knowledge, by Gorges-Schleuter and Mühlenbein [10, 3]. Results on various applications may be found in [30–33]. A related approach has been published under the name fine-grained parallel GA for function optimization by Manderick and Spiessens [34].

This object-oriented and event-driven approach is (1) capable of reducing the complexity arising from MIMD massive parallelism, and, more important, (2) it simulates the evolution of a population on the basis of distributed and active individuals behaving according to local rules. There is no need of a central control nor of a global time model to synchronize the reproduction. (3) The algorithm scales with the number of processors available from one up to, at most, population-size processors.

15.5.3 The Extended Evolutionary Algorithm

By introducing the neighborhood model, the traditional GA has been completely redesigned. This especially concerns the locally restricted selection of mates, the survival strategy for offspring, the replacement policy of individuals, and the generation model.

The general life cycle of a GA individual as introduced in [35] is as follows:

Each individual i of the population P performs the following actions:

1. Select a mate from the neighborhood with respect to the local fitness distribution.
2. Create offspring by sexual reproduction via crossover and mutations.
2'. Iterative improvement of offspring may be added.
3. If the offspring is viable, which is a function of the fitness of its neighbors and the survival rule, then it replaces individual i and itself becomes parent of the next generation.
4. Repeat 1–3.

Individuals are assumed to be uniformly distributed over a geographical region. The size of a neighborhood and the topological structure determine the degree of geographical differentiation and thus allow keeping genetic variability of the gene pool over a longer period. With a sufficiently large neighborhood the population structure degenerates, ending up at a panmictic population; that is, a mating partner may be selected from the entire population. Two cases of topologies are considered: a linear one, where the individuals are placed on a ring, and a toroidal topology, where the individuals are located at the intersections of a grid with wrapping borders. The generation model describes the time scale on which the population develops. The population as a whole is at all times being depleted by deaths and replenished by births. The traditional GA assumes a *discrete-generation model*, where populations reproduce at discrete time steps. The offspring generation is created on the basis of the parent generation. Thus, at any time we can distinguish a parent population $P(t)$ and an offspring population $P(t + 1)$ (Fig. 15.8).

On the other hand, it is sometimes more appropriate biologically or for implementation reasons to use continuous-time models in which births and

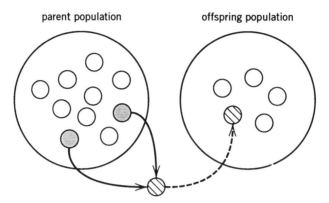

Figure 15.8 *The discrete-generation model.*

deaths can take place at any instance. In the *continuous-generation model* there is just one population at any time. Thus, parents and offspring do coexist in the same population. Reproduction is done on an individual basis rather than on a generational approach. The decision for survival of an offspring, simulating the birth process, and replacement of an individual, simulating the death process, is done immediately after the creation of an offspring rather than after the whole offspring generation has been generated.

We assume a selection model in which each individual included in the population is guaranteed to reproduce and the reproduction is always sexual. The first parent, the mother, is the individual at location i; the second parent, termed mate or father, is selected from the neighborhood according to the fitness distribution within the neighborhood (either proportional or linear rank selection). This parent selection strategy guarantees that the entire pool of genetic material changes only smoothly, and the probability of early loss of genetic material is reduced.

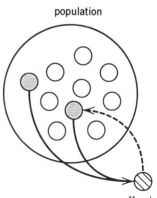

Figure 15.9 *The continuous-generation model.*

The population is assumed to be of constant size. Thus, if at an individual's location a viable offspring has been created, then it needs to replace another individual. We used a simple deterministic replacement strategy: The offspring immediately replaces the individual at that location. Consequently, an offspring always supersedes a parent, to which it is, by definition, similar. The combined effect of parent selection and replacement strategy reduces the sampling error drastically, which in turn results in a more robust algorithm.

The survival strategy specifies which offspring is viable and thus will survive to reproduce. That is, different from selection in traditional GAs, we have an extinctive selection scheme as in the ESs where only the better individuals reproduce. But, different from ES and similar to GA, the assignment of the number of offspring is still based on the individual's absolute or relative fitness, respectively. Thus, the advantages of the different selection schemes in terms of high quality versus search effort are combined, forming a very promising new route to follow.

Five survival strategies differing in the strength of selection pressure have been defined. The term *local* always refers to an individual's reproduction community, the neighborhood or deme.

A   Accept all—each offspring is accepted.

B   1% worse—accept only offspring that are better than the quality of the local weakest +1%. Thus, small degenerations are possible.

C   Local least—accept only offspring that are better than the local weakest.

D   Average—accept only offspring that are better than the local average.

E   Parent—accept only offsprings that are better than the individual itself.

The survival strategy may be modified to be an elitist strategy (ES). In GAs, elitism guarantees that the best solutions found are preserved. We define elitism to be a local property; that is, if an individual is the local best, then it can only be replaced by a better offspring. By definition, survival strategy E is always an elitist strategy. In all our simulation runs we observed that elitism gives faster convergence speed and better final results.

The survival strategy seems to be a very important factor. Although the better-than-parent survival strategy introduces a very strong selection pressure, it offers the possibility that various niches could be established and may be maintained over the simulation run, under the assumption of a small neighborhood size and a linear geographical topology.

15.6   WHY USE AN EVOLUTION ALGORITHM?

Evolution algorithms offer intriguing possibilities for general-purpose adaptive search algorithms, especially, but not necessarily, for situations where it is difficult or impossible to model precisely the external circumstances faced by the program. They do so by searching from a population of points with a cooperation and competition mechanism. In contrast to almost any promising problem-specific heuristic, EAs require no programmer's sophistication. The application domain of EAs is there where conventional methods cannot be used or do not yield satisfying solutions. EAs generate near-optimal solutions. They could operate with almost no problem-specific knowledge, but, if application-dependent knowledge is available it might be used to improve the performance in high-dimensional and very complex search spaces with noisy data and in domains with fixed and varying environmental conditions. In addition, they could take advantage of previously learned information (e.g., by including information in the initial population) to lessen the expense of relearning in approximately recurrent environmental situations.

An interesting perspective occurs if there exist algorithms to solve a problem, but the solutions generated are not "good" enough or the robustness is too low. Then it might be worthwhile to build up an integrated system by combining the existing approach and the evolutionary approach. The advantage is that such a hybrid algorithm is at least as good as the existing algorithm alone, but by adding an EA as a kind of metastrategy there is a good chance of improving convergence velocity, robustness, and, hopefully, the final quality.

Although traditional EAs are inherently parallel, they suffer from the problem that natural selection relies on the fitness distribution of the entire population. The introduction of a population structure makes EAs explicitly parallel, so the algorithms scale with the number of processors available. Nevertheless, EAs by themselves are no real-time method. But, as an example, integrated in an existing process control system they could be used to enhance the performance of a conventional controller.

There is a broad range of applications to which EAs have been applied, as there are, for example, synthesis and optimization of adaptive controllers, design of an adaptive fuzzy controller, task planning and learning, job shop scheduling, time-table problems, load balancing, packing and cutting problems, and function optimization. Good sources for further reading are the proceedings of conferences on genetic algorithms [36–39] and PPSN [40, 41].

REFERENCES

[1] G. Gabriele, *Engineering Design*, Elsevier, Amsterdam, 1985.

[2] M. R. Garey and D. S. Johnson, *Computers and Intractability*, H. W. Freeman, San Francisco, 1979.

[3] R. Axelrod, Effective choice in the prisoner's dilemma, *J. Conflict Resolution*, 24, 247–293 (1980).

[4] R. Axelrod, "The Evolution of Strategies in the Iterated Prisoner's Dilemma," in L. Davis, ed., *Genetic Algorithms and Simulated Annealing*, Pitman, London, 1987.

[5] K. J. Astrom and B. Wittenmark, *Adaptive Control*, Addison-Wesley, Reading, Mass., 1989.

[6] H. Fisher and G. L. Thompson, "Probabilistic Learning Combinations of Local Job Shop Scheduling Rules," in J. F. Muth and G. L. Thompson, eds., *Industrial Scheduling*, Prentice Hall, Englewood Cliffs, N.J., 1963.

[7] F. Glover and C. McMillan, The general employee scheduling problem: an integration of MS and AI, *Comput. Oper. Res.*, 13(5), 563–573 (1986).

[8] M. Ball and M. Magazine, The design and analysis of heuristics, *Networks*, 11, 215–219 (1981).

[9] J. H. Holland, *Adaptation in Natural and Artificial Systems*, University of Michigan Press, Ann Arbor, 1975.

[10] D. E. Goldberg, *Genetic Algorithms in Search, Optimization and Machine Learning*, Addison-Wesley, Reading, Mass., 1989.

[11] I. Rechenberg, *Evolutionsstrategie—Optimierung technischer Systeme nach Prinzipien der biologischen Information*, Frommann Verlag, Stuttgart, 1973 (in German).

[12] H. P. Schwefel, *Numerical Optimization of Computer Models*, Wiley, 1981 (English trans.). Original ed., Birkhäuser, Basel, 1977.

[13] J. H. Holland, "Escaping Brittleness: The Possibilities of General-Purpose Learning Algorithm Applied to Parallel Rule-Based Systems," in R. S. Michalsky, J. G. Carbonell, and T. M. Mitchell, eds., *Machine Learning, Vol. II*, Morgan Kaufman, 1986, pp. 593–623.

[14] L. B. Booker, D. E. Goldberg, and J. H. Holland, Classifier systems and genetic algorithms, *Artif. Intell.*, 235–282 (1985).

[15] H. P. Schwefel, "Collective phenomena in evolutionary systems," *International Conference on Problems of Constancy and Change*, 31st Annual Meeting of the International Society for General Systems Research, Budapest, Hungary, June 1987.

[16] J. E. Baker, Adaptive selection methods for genetic algorithms, in J. J. Grefenstette, ed., *Proc. First Internat. Conf. Genetic Algorithms and Their Applications*, Lawrence Erlbaum, Hillsdale, Calif., pp. 101–111, 1985.

[17] F. Hoffmeister, Th. Bäck, and H.-P. Schwefel, A survey of evolution strategies, in R. K. Belew and L. B. Booker, eds., *Proc. Fourth Internat. Conf. Genetic Algorithms*, Morgan Kaufmann, San Mateo, Calif., pp. 2–9, 1991.

[18] S. Wright, Character change, speciation, and the higher taxa, *Evolution*, 36(3), 427–443, (1982).

[19] D. J. Cavicchio, "Adaptive Search Using Simulated Evolution," unpublished Ph.D. diss., University of Michigan, Ann Arbor, 1970.

[20] K. A. De Jong, "An Analysis of the Behavior of a Class of Genetic Adaptive Systems, Ph.D., University of Michigan, in *Dissertation Abstracts International*, 36(10), 5140B.

[21] D. E. Goldberg, J. Richardson, Genetic algorithms with sharing for multimodal function optimization, in J. J. Grefenstette, ed., *Proc. Second Internat. Conf. Genetic Algorithms and Their Applications*, Lawrence Erlbaum, Hillsdale, Calif., pp. 41–49, 1987.

[22] P. B. Grosso, "Computer Simulation of Genetic Adaptation: Parallel Subcomponent Interaction in a Multilocus Model," Ph.D., University of Michigan, University Microfilms No. 8520908.

[23] R. Tanese, Parallel genetic algorithms for the hypercube, in ref. 37, 177–183.

[24] R. Tanese, Distributed genetic algorithms, in ref. 38, 434–439.

[25] D. P. Cohoon, S. U. Hedge, W. N. Martin, and D. Richards, Punctuated equilibria: A parallel genetic algorithm, in J. J. Grefenstette, ed., *Proc. Second Internat. Conf. Genetic Algorithms and Their Applications*, Lawrence Erlbaum, Hillsdale, Calif., pp. 148–154, 1987.

[26] C. B. Pettey, M. R. Leuze, and J. J. Grefenstette, A theoretical investigation of a parallel genetic algorithm, in J. D. Schaffer, ed., *Proc. Third Internat. Genetic Algorithms*, Morgan Kaufmann, San Mateo, Calif., pp. 398–405, 1989.

[27] S. Wright, *Evolution and the Genetics of Populations*, Vol. 2, *The Theory of Gene Frequencies*, University Chicago Press, Chicago, 1969.

[28] M. Gorges-Schleuter and H. Mühlenbein, The Traveling Salesman Problem—An Evolutionary Approach, in Annual Report of the GMD 1987, GrD, St. Augustin, Germany (in German).

[29] H. Mühlenbein, M. Gorges-Schleuter, and O. Krámer, Evolution algorithm in combinatorial optimization, *Parallel Comput.*, 7, 65–88 (1988).

[30] M. Gorges-Schleuter, "Genetic Algorithms and Population Structures—A Massively Parallel Algorithm," Ph.D. diss., University of Dortmund, 1990.

[31] G. von Laszewski, "Ein paralleler genetischer Algorithms für das Graph Partitionierungs Problem," Masters thesis, University of Bonn, 1990.

[32] H. Mühlenbein, Parallel genetic algorithms, population genetics, and combinatorial optimization, in J. D. Schaffer, ed., *Proc. Third Internat. Conf. Genetic Algorithms*, Morgan Kaufmann, San Mateo, Calif., pp. 416–422, 1989.

[33] H. Mühlenbein, M. Schomisch, and J. Born, The parallel genetic algorithm as function optimizer, in R. K. Belew and L. B. Booker, eds., *Proc. Fourth Internat. Conf. Genetic Algorithms*, San Mateo, Calif., pp. 271–278, 1991.

[34] B. Manderick and P. Spiessens, Fine-grained parallel genetic algorithm, in J. D. Schaffer, ed., *Proc. Third Internat. Conf. Genetic Algorithms*, Morgan Kaufmann, San Mateo, Calif., pp. 428–433, 1989.

[35] M. Gorges-Schleuter, "ASPARAGOS, an asynchronous parallel genetic optimization strategy," in J. F. Schaffer, ed., *Proc. Third Internat. Conf. Genetic Algorithms*, Morgan Kaufmann, San Mateo, Calif., pp. 422–427, 1989.

[36] J. J. Grefenstette, eds., *Proc. First Internat. Conf. Genetic Algorithms and Their Applications*, Lawrence Erlbaum, Hillsdale, Calif., 1985.

[37] J. J. Grefenstette, ed., *Proc. Second Internat. Conf. Genetic Algorithms and their Applications*, Lawrence Erlbaum, Hillsdale, Calif., 1987.

[38] J. D. Schaffer, ed., *Proc. Third Internat. Conf. Genetic Algorithms*, Morgan Kaufmann, San Mateo, Calif., 1989.

[39] R. K. Belew and L. B. Booker, eds., *Proc. Fourth Internat. Conf. Genetic Algorithms*, Morgan Kaufmann, San Mateo, Calif., 1991.

[40] H.-P. Schwefel and R. Männer, eds., Parallel problem solving from nature 1, *Proc. First Internat. Workshop 1990*, LNCS, 496, Springer Verlag, New York, 1991.

[41] R. Männer and B. Manderick, eds., Parallel problem solving from nature 2, *Proc. Second Conf.*, North-Holland, Amsterdam, 1992.

CHAPTER 16 ————————————

Evolutionary TSP Optimization: An Application Case Study

MARTINA GORGES-SCHLEUTER

16.1 INTRODUCTION

The traveling salesman problem (TSP) is seductively easy to state: "Given a set of n cities and a means of obtaining the distance between any pair of cities, find a minimum-length tour that visits each city once and only once and returns to the initial city." On the other hand, the TSP has resisted all efforts to find a "good" optimization algorithm or even an approximation algorithm that is guaranteed to be effective. The simplicity of statement and the difficulty of solution are the elements that made, and still make, the TSP so attractive to mathematicians. But the TSP is also typical of other problems of its genre: combinatorial optimization. And last but not least there are also practical reasons for the importance of the TSP. Many significant real-world problems can be formulated as instances of the TSP. In the last section of this chapter some applications of the TSP, generalizations of the TSP, and related combinatorial problems are described.

Using branch-and-bound techniques together with sophisticated new algorithms for generating cutting planes, two groups have independently reported remarkable success in solving the TSP to optimality. Padberg and Rinaldi have solved real-world instances of size 532, 1002, and even 2392. The 532-city problem seems to be particularly difficult, indicating that the mere size of a problem is not the determining factor for running time. Grötschel and Holland solved a 666-city instance based on the actual location of major cities throughout the world. Working with instances where the distances between cities are

Frontier Decision Support Concepts, Edited by V. L. Plantamura, B. Souček, and G. Visaggio. ISBN 0-471-59256-0   © 1994 John Wiley & Sons, Inc.

random numbers in the interval [0, 1], they claim that these problems seem to be particularly easy on average.

Currently, the best approximation algorithms are derived from a general technique known as local optimization, in which a given solution is iteratively improved by making local changes. The basic step is to discard k edges present in the actual tour and replace them by k new edges, termed a k-move. The most famous local optimization algorithms for the TSP are the 2-Opt (the simplest and fastest method, 3-Opt, and the very sophisticated Lin-Kernighan algorithm. For a review and comparison of TSP algorithms see Johnson [1], where he describes the iterated Lin-Kernighan algorithm, probably the stiffest competitor for any TSP algorithm.

What makes the TSP most attractive as a test bed for our experiments is that the search space is highly multimodal, that numerous near-optimal solutions exist, and that the parameters interact in a nonlinear fashion. This means that very good solutions may not be obtained by simply sampling advantageous genes (the short edges). Instead, an adaptation process is needed to find co-adapted sets of genes. An examination of the configuration space landscape of a specific instance of a combinatorial optimization problem shows that the actual structure of the search space depends on the method used to create the configurations (for the TSP these are the tours). The ''better'' the method the smoother is the surface of the search space; that is, we have a greater chance to reach very good local optima and hopefully the global best.

Another important observation can be made by analyzing the space of local optimal solutions for a specific method. The 100-city problem no. 24 of Krolak et al. [2], shown in Figure 16.1, has been used to generate 400 distinct local optima of the 2-Opt algorithm. We observed that only 378 different edges were present in the sample; 100 edges occurred in more than 40% of the tours, and 200 of the different edges are relatively rare. For each of these edges we computed its frequency in the sample. Figure 16.2 shows a strong correlation between the sum of the frequencies of a tour's edges in the sample and the

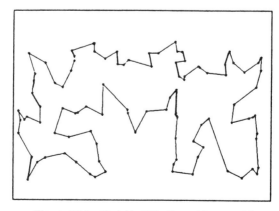

Figure 16.1   *Krolak's 100-city problem no. 24.*

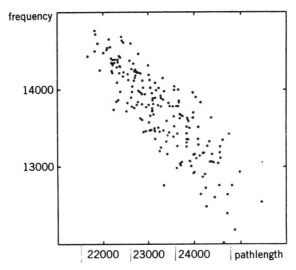

Figure 16.2 *Relative frequencies of edges.*

quality of that solution; that is, the better the solution the more edges are in common with other local optima.

An ideal algorithm should be able to learn from previously performed computations and superimpose on that information a very good solution. Such an algorithm for the TSP may climb the diagonal in Figure 16.2 by favoring those edges belonging to shorter tours.

Therefore we claimed that it might be appropriate to use problem-specific knowledge if it is available. That is, we recommend, first, using a problem-dependent representation and, second, incorporating the method by which the current best algorithm exploits the search space. Thus, the GA acts as a metastrategy on an existing algorithm and adds basically the exploration component, whereas the exploitation might come from an existing algorithm. Experiments with the local optimization algorithm 2-Opt showed that the GA outperformed the multiple-start counterpart by far.

The EA presented for the TSP is relatively easy to implement. We decided to use little problem-specific knowledge, being reflected in the edge-based representation, the realization of mutation and crossover, and in the simple local optimization algorithm added, termed repairing a variant of 2-Opt with reduced search effort. As there is a hill-climbing component for improved exploitation, the GAs operate in the space of local optima as induced by the local optimization algorithm used.

Primarily, the introduced population structure and the local interaction of the individuals are the reasons for the astonishingly good results of the simulated evolutionary search process. Originally the TSP was chosen only as a bench-mark problem. Nevertheless, remarkably good results, when considering the time/tour-length trade-off, have been observed even with the 532-city problem, so that finally the EA described here has been among the best approximation algorithms.

16.1.1 Formal Problem Definition

In the TSP we are given a set of cities $C = \{c_1, c_2, \ldots, c_n\}$ and for each pair c_i, c_j of distinct cities a distance $d(c_i, c_j)$. The problem is to find a permutation of the cities $T = (c_{\pi(1)}, c_{\pi(2)}, \ldots, c_{\pi(n)})$ so that

$$f(T) = \sum_{i=1}^{n} d(c_{\pi(i)}, c_{\pi(i+1)}) + d(c_{\pi(n)}, c_{\pi(1)}) \rightarrow \min$$

T is called a tour and $f(T)$ is the tour length, the quantity to be minimized.

We consider the case of a symmetric TSP; that is, $d(c_i, c_j) = d(c_j, c_i)$. Since the starting point and direction of the symmetric TSP do not matter, there are $(n - 1)!/2$ distinct tours. For $n = 100$ there are 4.661×10^{155} different tours, and for $n = 200$ there are 1.972×10^{372}. Hence, there is a huge search space, growing faster than any finite power of n as the problem size increases.

16.2 THE GENETIC REPRESENTATION FOR THE TSP

For our purpose of combinatorial optimization, we have chosen a representation reflecting the structure of the problem. In addition, the genetic operators have been modified to reflect only valid changes of the individual's genotype.

An intuitive representation is to associate the genes with the cities. Then the genetic representation of a tour is a sequence of cities, and the genetic operators, mutation and crossover, work by exchanging cities and recombining sequences of cities. Although the so-called path representation has been widely used, it seems to not be the best choice. A simple reason is that the configuration space may not be appropriately exploited.

The best current approximation algorithms use edge-based operators. Thus, it seems to be natural to use an edge-based representation. In addition, using an encoding of the current best algorithm also allows us to incorporate the method by which this algorithm solves the problem. The advantage is that "good" substrings (the building blocks) may be easily found by the GA.

The encoding of a tour T is

$$T = (c_{\pi(1)}, c_{\pi(2)}, \ldots, c_{\pi(n-1)}, c_{\pi(n)})$$

This looks pretty much like the usual representation enumerating the cities in the order to be visited. But we always deal with the edges, and thus the encoding is indeed a short form of

$$T = ((c_{\pi(1)}, c_{\pi(2)}), (c_{\pi(2)}, c_{\pi(3)}), \ldots, (c_{\pi(n-1)}, c_{\pi(n)}), (c_{\pi(n)}, c_{\pi(1)}))$$

We refer to the short form as the *string representation*.

16.3 THE GENETIC OPERATORS FOR THE TSP

The problem-oriented approach implies a careful definition of the genetic operators. With the proposed string representation, the application of simple genetic operators as described in Chapter 15 will usually lead to illegal tours—that is, a tour where some cities are visited twice and other cities not at all.

To deal with this situation, typical for combinatorial optimization problems, the offspring tours may be corrected so that the duplicate cities are replaced by the omitted cities. This leads to the destruction of edges found in the parents, resulting in the loss of information gained.

Another route is to guarantee the creation of always feasible solutions (i.e., valid tours). Therefore, we modify the genetic operators themselves.

16.3.1 Mutation

The simplest modification that may be performed on a traveling salesman tour involves two edges:

1. Discard two randomly chosen edges on the tour T, say (c_i, c_{i+1}) and (c_j, c_{j+1}).
2. Replace these edges by (c_i, c_j) and (c_{i+1}, c_{j+1}). This forms a new tour T'.

This modification is equivalent to a 2-move, the basic operator of Lin's 2-Opt heuristic.

We used in our implementation a mutation operator, which usually involves four edges. The mutation operator is defined more specifically as follows:

Choose two cities randomly, say c_i and c_j. Exchange the two cities. This removes the edges (c_{i-1}, c_i), (c_i, c_{i+1}), (c_{j-1}, c_j), (c_j, c_{j+1}) and replaces the edges (c_{j-1}, c_i), (c_i, c_{j+1}), (c_{i-1}, c_j), (c_j, c_{i+1})

Figure 16.3 shows a mutation on a tour.

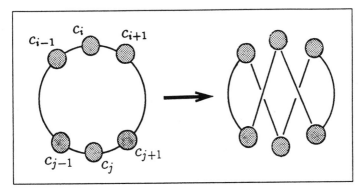

Figure 16.3 *A mutation on the string representation.*

The parameter mutation rate specifies the probability that an edge will be mutated. In principle, the mutation operator needs to decide for each edge whether to change it. To avoid much random number generation, we compute from the mutation rate an expected number of mutations to occur every time an offspring is generated.

We will see that our crossover operator introduces implicit mutations, defined to be those edges of the offspring not found in either parent. More specifically, at the beginning of the genetic search the number of implicit mutations may be higher than expected by the mutation rate, mainly if the specified mutation rate is low. If fewer implicit mutations have occurred than expected by the mutation rate, additional mutations happen to take place.

16.3.2 Crossover

The design of crossover operators for the TSP has received continuous interest. Since the 1985 conference on genetic algorithms, where GAs applied to combinatorial optimization were first described, many crossover operators for the TSP have been invented.

The crossover operator we first introduced in [3] differs from all other crossover operators reported so far in the literature, except the independently proposed genetic edge recombination operator of Whitley et al. [4], in that it is edge based, contains mainly edges of either parent, and preserves subtours already identified. The last argument has not been considered elsewhere.

This ''new'' genetic crossover operator works on the string representation transferring edges from the parents to the offspring as effectively as possible, thus preventing the loss of information by preserving as many edges in the gene pool as possible. Maximal preservative crossover (MPX) is basically an edge-based traditional two-point crossover operator. The MPX operator works very well with the string representation and is invariant to the actual tour representation.

Before we describe the MPX operator we introduce the following notations. The two parents are distinguished and are referred to as the *donator* or the *receiver*, respectively. From the donator a subtour, a continuous chain of edges, is extracted and transferred to the receiver, thus forming an offspring. An edge is called *possible* if in the construction process of an offspring tour the addition of that edge does not generate a cycle.

Figure 16.4 outlines the MPX operator in pseudocode. MPX resembles an offspring from its parents' genes. Sometimes in the process of generating an offspring neither an edge from the receiver nor the donator parent may be added without generating a cycle. In this case an edge is added that preserves the sequence of cities of the receiver parent; that is, a randomly chosen edge is not introduced, but a new edge is formed leading from the current final city of the offspring tour to the first ''possible'' city of the receiver parent.

PROC crossover (receiver, donator, offspring)

    Choose position $0 <= i <$ nodes and
        length $l_{min} <= k <= l_{max}$ randomly.

    Extract the string of cities from position i to
        position $j = (i + k)$ mod *nodes* from the mate (donator). This
        is the crossover string.

    Copy the crossover string to the offspring.

    Add successively further edges until the offspring represents a valid
        tour. This is done in the following way:

        IF an edge from the receiver starting at the end of the last
            edge in the offspring is possible (does not violate a valid
            tour)
        THEN add this edge from the receiver
        ELSE IF an edge from the donator starting at the last city
            in the offspring is possible
            THEN add this edge from the donator
            ELSE add that city from the receiver which comes next
            in the string, this adds a new edge, which we will mark
            as an implicit mutation.

Figure 16.4 *MPX in pseudocode.*

16.3.3. Repairing

Mutation and crossover introduce noise into the genotype. By chance events long edges will be most likely be created.* Although only minor changes occur on the genotype level, drastic effects may occur on the phenotype level (i.e., the length of the tour). Specifically with combinatorial optimization problems the genetic operators transfer the structural information very well, but the disrupted value information used later will then lead to a misjudgment of the offspring's fitness. To prevent those situations in the genetic search process, it seems appropriate to force a genotype to climb to a local optima. In this case the GA will merely work with the peaks in the fitness landscape. We worked out a mechanism that uses the information already gathered in previous generations by the GA. This mechanism considers only the mutated edges, defined to be those edges found in the offspring but not in either parent. The mutated edges are tested for substitution by shorter edges.

We call that mechanism *repairing*. Repairing is an additional operator that makes use of problem-specific knowledge but works without computation of the phenotype.

The design is based on the fundamental theorem of the continuity of the evolution. Repairing starts from the hypothesis that the ancestors are well adapted to their environment. Offsprings should therefore not be too much different from their parents. So changes in the genotype carrying new infor-

---

*Compared to the total number of edges between cities advantageous edges are relatively rare.

PROC two.repair (receiver, donator, offspring)

Let $S = \{(c_i, c_{i+1}) \in T_{\text{offspring}} \mid (c_i, c_{i+1}) \notin T_{\text{receiver}} \cup T_{\text{donator}}\}$
  be those edges of the offspring's tour that don't occur in one
  or the other parent.

WHILE $S \neq \oslash$ DO

   Take an edge $(c_i, c_{i+1}) \in S$ and check if a 2-move is possible:
   FOR $c_j := c_{i+1} + 1$ TO $(c_i - 2 + n)$ MOD n DO
      IF $d(c_i, c_{i+1}) + d(c_j, c_{j+1}) < d(c_{i+1}, c_{j+1}) + d(c_i, c_j)$,
      THEN exchange edges and delete both old edges from
         S and add the new edges to S
         $S = S - \{(c_i, c_{i+1}), (c_j, c_{j+1})\} + \{(c_{i+1}, c_{j+1}), (c_i, c_j)\}$
      ELSE   delete edge (c_i, c_{i+1}) from S:
         $S = S - \{(c_i, c_{i+1})\}$
END WHILE

Figure 16.5   *Repairing in pseudocode.*

mation (the mutated edges), introduced by crossover and mutation, are considered for a 2-move. If it is possible to exchange these edges by better edges this step is performed. These better edges are again marked as new. This is done until all new edges are checked. The local optima reached by repairing is usually not 2-optimal. Figure 16.5 displays the repairing mechanism in pseudocode.

16.4   THE GA WITH POPULATION STRUCTURE FOR THE TSP

So far, we have described all ingredients to formulate how we derive from the previous generation the following generation. What remains to be described is how generation 0 is generated.

The important characteristic of the initial population should be a high variability of the gene pool. So we choose M ($=$ population size) random solutions to be the members of the initial generation. This initial gene pool has almost no structure. That is, the chosen sample of Mn edges out of $(n - 1)(n/2)$ different edges, where n is the problem size, is equally distributed. To set up a gene pool containing some information, we apply a simple iterative improvement algorithm to the random solutions.

We are now ready to formulate the GA with population structure for the TSP. Figure 16.6 outlines the algorithm in pseudocode.

The notation

$$\text{PAR } i = 1 \text{ TO population\_size DO}$$

specifies that the statements enclosed by the PAR . . . ENDPAR braces are replicated independently population size times. We assume that the necessary

```
PAR i = 1 TO population_size DO
    (* Initialization of individual A_i *)
    create start tour A_i randomly
    apply to random tour A_i the startup procedure
    compute the tour length f(A_i)
ENDPAR
PAR i = 1 TO population_size DO
    WHILE NOT terminate
        (* Next generation of individual A_i *)
        mate selection:
            choose a mate according to the local fitness
            distribution from the neighborhood of A_i
        apply crossover operator
        IF fewer implicit mutations have occurred
            than specified by the mutation rate
        THEN apply mutation operator
        apply repairing operator
        compute the tour length of offspring
        apply survival rule
        IF offspring survives
        THEN replace A_i by the offspring
    ENDWHILE
ENDPAR
```

Figure 16.6   *The GA with population structure for the TSP.*

information of other individuals, especially the tour and tour length of neighbors, is provided by a mailbox being updated asynchronously whenever an offspring has been accepted.

When running the algorithm on a sequential machine, the PAR construct degenerates to an ordinary FOR loop

$$\text{FOR } i = 1 \text{ TO population\_size DO}$$

and the mailbox may be realized by an array.

But running the algorithm on an MIMD-type machine gives full benefits. The algorithm is naturally parallel, needs no global knowledge, relies on only local interactions, and behaves completely asynchronously. There is only a single synchronization point needed and this is to ensure that all individuals of the population have been initialized. Thereafter the population consists of independently and asynchronously behaving individuals. The granularity of the algorithm is given by the number of individuals. We refer to this GA as AS-PARAGOS (asynchronous massively parallel genetic optimization strategy).

16.5   SIMULATION RESULTS

The implementation of ASPARAGOS, from which the following results are reported, was done on a parallel system, Parsytec's SuperCluster, built up of 64 T800 transputers, each equipped with 1-MB external memory. An especially nice feature is that the program may run without any software changes on a single processor or on several processors. The programming language used is OCCAM for performance reasons (although the implementation was originally done in parallel C for a network of SUN workstations).

16.5.1 Experimental Setup

The parameters being fixed are the continuous-generation model and the replacement strategy; that is, a surviving offspring replaces the local parent immediately. The neighborhood model with a linear population structure—the ladder population—is the underlying population model, except for those control experiments with a planar population structure where we used a torus. The repairing mechanism is used as local optimization algorithm. This eliminates the negative side effects of mutations—that is, the destruction of problem-specific information learned in previous generations. All remaining parameters may be varied.

We define ASPARAGOS as

$$\mathbf{AS} = (M, D, C, P_M, S, B, O)$$

where M is the population size

D is the subpopulation (deme) size

$C = [c_1, c_2]$ is the size of the crossover interval

P_M is the mutation rate

S is the selection strategy:

(prop, W) proportional selection with window size W

(rank, *max*) linear rank selection with maximal sampling rate

B is the survival strategy (birth or death of offspring)

O specifies the option to be used with the survival strategy:

PS is a pure strategy

ES is an elitist strategy

We experimented with population sizes of 16, 32, and 64 and deme sizes of 8 and 5. Additionally for population size 64 we made simulations with deme sizes of 16 and 64, the latter simulating a panmictic population, thus yielding results comparable to the traditional GA.

The size of the substring to be crossed over could be any fixed length (lower bound = upper bound) or of varying size equally distributed between the lower and upper bounds. The mutation rate was set to $0.02, 0.05$, or 0.1, respectively. This corresponds to an occurrence of at most 2, 5, or 10 mutations, respectively, for the 532-city problem and 2, 4, or 8 mutations, respectively, for the 442-city problem. The clear winner was the strategy with the lowest mutation rate.

The selection strategy may be either linear rank selection or proportional selection with a linear scaling function to keep an appropriate level of competition throughout the simulation run. We define the scaling as

$$q'(A_i) = q_{max} - q(A_i)$$

q_{max} is defined by the scaling window W. $W = 0$ sets the baseline to the quality of the least-fit individual from generation 1. $W = n, n \geq 1$, indicates that the base value is computed from the quality of the least-fit individual from $n - 1$ generations in the past. We tested window sizes of 0, 1, and 10. A window size of 10 offered the best selection pressure; a window size of 0 behaves relatively early like random selection as the population members all have about the same high quality.

With ranking we need to specify the expected value of the local best individual $1 \leq max \leq 2$. In all experiments we set linear rank selection max = 1.7, thus giving the local weakest a chance of 0.3 to be chosen as mate.

In addition to selection, which describes the chance of an individual to be selected as mate, we introduced a survival strategy that specifies how the decision over an offspring's life or death is made. If a new offspring has been created, it competes with its neighborhood for resources. If the offspring is not "fit" enough according to the survival strategy, it immediately dies. The parent then chooses a new mate and reproduces again. We call this the pure strategy (PS). The survival strategy may be modified. The elitist strategy (ES) preserves the local best individual; that is, an offspring whose local parent is the best structure in the deme can only survive if it is fitter than the local parent. The standard parameter setting is

$$AS_S = (64, 8, [N/3, N/2], 0.02, (prop, W = 10), local.least, ES)$$

where N is the problem size and local.least refers to a survival strategy where the offspring survives if its tour length is shorter than the locally longest tour length. But the elitist strategy requires additionally that if the local parent is the best in its deme, the offspring only survives if it is better than the local parent.

In all experiments we refer to this standard parameter setting and will only specify those parameters that differ from that setting.

In each series of simulation runs we modify just one parameter and keep all the others fixed. The experiments thus give an impression on the influence of a single parameter on the behavior of ASPARAGOS. We will see that the most important parameters within the ASPARAGOS simulation environment are those modifying the selection pressure and thus the genetic variability of the population.

The problem of adjusting the control parameters of a GA optimal is again an optimization task with a complex response surface. The control parameters are not independent of each other, and it is not obvious how they interact. The aim of the empirical analysis is not to determine the optimal parameter setting, as this is only possible for a specific problem or, at least, a problem class; for example, an optimal tuning for one problem instance (real-world TSP) may be suboptimal for another problem instance (TSP with randomly distributed cities).

However, the empirical analysis should throw light on questions such as: How sensitive, relative to parameter setting, is the GA with population structure? What is the effect of the population structure? How does it compare to a panmictic population? To answer these more general questions, we examine the progress of the gene pool, the phenotype, and the population. As the test suite for extensive study we decided to use two instances of the TSP with quite different problem structures: the 442 drilling problem from Grötschel [5], which is fairly regular, and the 532 AT&T problem from Padberg and Rinaldi [6].

The optimal tour of the former problem has length 5069, that of the latter has length 27686. The optimal solutions are visualized in Figure 16.7 and Figure 16.8, respectively.

The following notation is used throughout:

Local best, *local* knowledge, and so on, refer to a property relative to a neighborhood.

Global best, *global* knowledge, and so on, refer to a property relative to the entire population.

16.5.2 Performance Measures

In all figures the tour length is plotted versus the average number of generations; that is, the time scale is the average over the generation counter of each individual in the population. In ASPARAGOS all individuals behave completely independently. The computation time needed for one generation is quite different, and thus individuals will usually be in different generations. Just for clarification, each time when an offspring has been created the generation

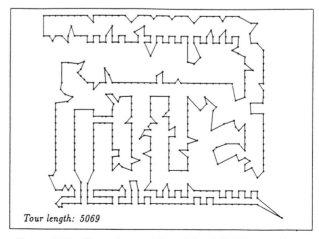

Tour length: 5069

Figure 16.7   *The optimal solution of the 442 drilling problem.*

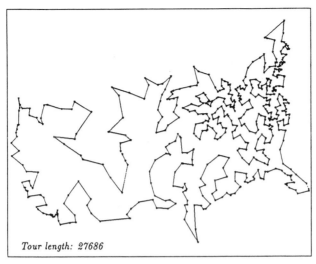

Tour length: 27686

Figure 16.8 *The optimal solution of the 532 AT&T problem.*

counter is increased. Thus the total number of trial solutions generated may be computed as population size × average no. of generations.

The CPU time needed is no invariant measure. Generations take longer with larger problem sizes, at the beginning of a simulation run, and with higher mutation rates, due to our repairing heuristic, which then has more edges to check.

The evolutionary search process adapts very fast at the beginning. Therefore, information is sampled more frequently at the beginning to get enough information in the periods of fast evolution and less frequently later on. As a consequence, in all figures the scale of the x axis showing the number of generations passed is not equidistant, and thus the rate of progress is much faster than it appears from the visualization!

To give an impression about the running time, Table 16.1 gives the CPU time (in seconds) needed for ASPARAGOS (with different mutation rates)

TABLE 16.1   CPU Time (in Seconds) Needed for ASPARAGOS on a Supercluster

	442		532		
	P_M		P_M		
Generation	0.02	0.05	0.02	0.05	0.10
100	110	110	175	175	225
200	190	200	300	310	430
400	340	400	530	580	930
800	580	750	950	1080	1880
1600	1100	1500	1630	2750	4350
2400	1630	2200	3000	4000	6350

running on a system with 64 T800 transputers. The Krolak problem of size 100 needs, on average, only 90 generations to be solved to optimality, taking about 30 s; the optimal solution is always found as long as the population size is larger than 16 with a deme size of 5.

Robustness. Robustness of an algorithm designates, on the one hand, the insensibility of an algorithm relative to the parameter setting and, on the other hand, the certainty of achieving a high-quality solution. We discuss robustness relative to parameter setting by comparing a GA with population structure with a panmictic GA.

Robustness of the algorithm relative to the quality of the solution depends not only on the parameter settings but also on the number of generations computed. Therefore, the termination criterion plays an important role. The algorithm may either stop if time is up (a certain number of generations is computed) and/or if the variation of the gene pool drops below a specified threshold.

Convergence. Another important performance criterion is the number of generations needed until a certain quality of solution is reached. That is, besides the final quality that might be achieved with a certain strategy, another interesting question is the convergence velocity of that strategy.

The main request of a heuristic in practice may, for example, be to get good solutions as quickly as possible even if the chance decreases to reach very high quality solutions. We might think of such a situation in applications where the GA is used to support a decision to be made (e.g., sequencing problems in production planning systems).

Each ASPARAGOS parameter setting was evaluated by using it to perform a number of simulation runs on our TSP test problems. As a measure of comparison we use the final qualities reached and the best-so-far, best, worst, and average qualities of the population over the number of simulation runs and over the course of the simulation. The best-so-far and the best are equal in case of an elitist survival strategy.

The tables give the number of simulation runs performed with each parameter setting, and the best, worst, and average final quality reached after $T = 1600$ generations and for long simulation runs reached after $T = 2300$ generations.

The final quality averaged over all runs is sensitive to extremely good or worse solutions in a set of runs, so we added the median and the standard deviation of the sample to the tables as well. For an easy and fast comparison we added the number of runs of a series of experiments that are below two threshold values, those with a final quality below 1.0% and 0.5% excess of the global optimal solution. For the 532-U.S.-cities problem this means a final result shorter than 27,962 and shorter than 27,824, respectively. With the 442-PCB (Printed Circuit Board) problem from Grötschel a quality better than 1.0% excess is reached if the tour length is shorter than 5120, and a tour shorter than 5094 is less than 0.5% far from the global optimal solution.

16.5.3 Genetic Variation

Mutation is one way to create genetic variation of an individual. The other way is by crossover through sexual recombination of the parents' genes. Repairing is the antagonistic genetic operator.

Within the ASPARAGOS environment it is a poor strategy to attempt to use a high mutation rate to prevent loss of diversity. The price to be paid is that information acquired by the evolution process is destroyed. Chance seems to play a minor role; more important is the recombination of existing information in the gene pool, thus giving information about coadaptation. Very low mutation rates gave best performance; thus, the mutation operator serves as a rare background operator.

The effects of mutation and migration are nearly the same: both introduce variation into the gene pool. The main difference is that mutation is a completely undirected change and therefore often leads to dead ends. With only mutation there is little hope of getting better-adapted individuals. A relatively high mutation rate needed with panmictic populations can be replaced by the only local interaction scheme of ASPARAGOS.

Thus, migration gives an alternative. It introduces variation and at the same time leads the search process. Our empirical analysis with the TSP will demonstrate that instead of a high mutation rate it is much more effective to use a population structure reducing the selection pressure against weak population members and allowing for simultaneous exploitation of different areas of the search space.

Different from most GAs, in ASPARAGOS each individual that survives is guaranteed to reproduce—that is, to become a parent. The individual chooses a mate from the neighborhood, and an offspring is created by combining the parents' genes. Reflecting on convenient lengths of the crossover interval, one will find that it should be no longer than half of the number of genes. With a fixed length of $N/2$ both parents have an equal chance to contribute to the common offspring. Using a shorter string to be transferred from the mate, the offspring contains more information from the local individual. Our experiments showed that the varying interval seems to be the most flexible variant. We prefer to have longer crossover strings at the beginning of a simulation run, to allow a better mixing of information for faster convergence, and shorter strings later, in order to maintain variance by preferring the local individual. A reasonable compromise is the random choice of the length of the crossover string in an interval $[N/3, N/2]$.

16.5.4 Selection

The key to an appropriate parameter setting of a GA is the balance between genetic variability and selection pressure. In that way we can control exploration and exploitation of the search space. One extreme is a very soft selection keeping the variability of the gene pool high, and the other extreme is a strong selection forcing fast fixation of the genes. This section evaluates the influence of selection pressure introduced by the mate selection strategy and the survival strategy on the convergence velocity and final quality of our massively parallel genetic algorithm.

The Survival Strategy. Each individual, together with a mate from its neighborhood, generates a single offspring. Then it is immediately decided if the offspring should be accepted. The offspring's acceptance (that is, the replacement of the local individual) depends on how well adapted the offspring is relative to its neighborhood; that is, the offspring has to compete for survival with other individuals living in its neighborhood. In living nature this may be caused, for example, by limited resources.

We have tested five survival strategies (see Section 15.5.3) differing in the strength of selection pressure: accept all, better than 1% worse, better than local least, better than average, and better than parent (i.e., the local individual).

Figure 16.9 gives the best-so-far performance for all survival strategies, thus showing the progress of the optimization task. The corresponding Figure 16.10 shows the total number of different edges present in the population over the generations performed.

With the accept-all-offspring survival strategy, we see that it is hardly possible to acquire problem-specific knowledge; the gene pool shows at early generations no further fixations of genes, the edges. The learning process stagnates early (Fig. 16.9), resulting in an average final quality exceeding the global optimum by about 3% (Table 16.2). This is still better than the best quality achieved with the Or-opt heuristic in 400 runs, which was 4% off the global optimum.

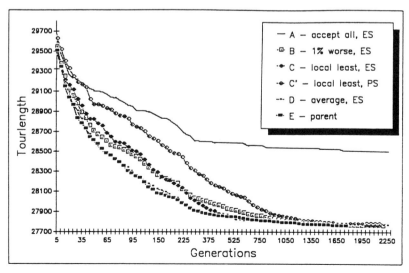

Figure 16.9 *Convergence of the survival strategies.*

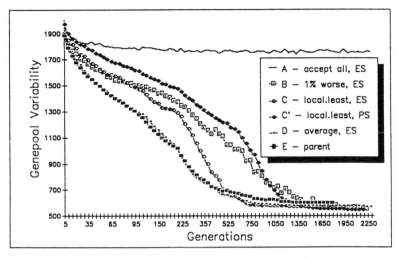

Figure 16.10 *Progress of fixation with various survival strategies.*

Comparing the final quality of the solutions found after generation 2300 (although only slight improvements if any occurred after generation 1600), we find that all survival strategies where the offspring have to compete within the neighborhood, B to E, reach in all runs qualities better than 1% off the global best. Very good solutions, always as close as 0.5%, are found by strategies D and E.

The latter two strategies behave similarly. Both force a fast fixation of the genes (Fig. 16.10). Although the variability of the gene pool decreases rapidly, not all variability is lost. In fact, strategy D (better than average) has a low-level variability that is higher than that of strategies B and C, and this variability is also kept for a very long time. Strategy E (better than parent) once again keeps a higher variability of the gene pool than strategy D.

We observe that the members of the population are not all alike. The behavior of strategies D and E is mainly affected by isolation; that is, local optima once detected are preserved. With strategy E, due to the strong acceptance rule, it is difficult for the information to propagate through the population, and

TABLE 16.2 Quality Depending on Survival Strategy (T = 2300)

Survival Strategy	A	B	C	C', PS	D	E
Number of runs	15	15	15	15	15	15
Best	28465	27752	27733	27776	27733	27726
Worst	28563	27841	27825	27923	27793	27793
Median	28525	27767	27768	27769	27762	27745
Average	28516	27779	27777	27779	27763	27748
Standard deviation	33.09	37.15	36.74	48.99	20.55	15.25
Runs <1.0%	0	15	15	15	15	15
Runs <0.5%	0	12	14	12	15	15

thus niches could establish and exist for quite a long time. Niches may only be left if recombination or chance (mutation) shift to a better optimum.

At first glance one might find it astonishing how good the results of strategies *D* and *E* are, especially if we think of the rapid fixation of genes at the beginning. But looking closer and taking into account that an offspring resembles its parent and the mate, the strong survival policy according to parent best supports the formation and establishment of niches.

Observation 1. The genetic algorithm with a ladder population structure is very robust concerning survival strategies *B*, *C*, *D*, and *E*. With none of these strategies does the average final quality exceed the optimal solution by more than 0.3 %. Isolation due to a strong survival rule forces the survival of different genotypes (solutions). This is the key to the fast convergence and the very high quality solutions of the survival strategy *E* "better than parent" in terms of best final, average final quality, and standard deviation.

Strategy *B* is an appropriate choice if we are interested in keeping the variety of the population as long as possible and gaining a satisfying convergence as well.

Pure versus Elitist Strategy. A pure strategy is a strategy where the local-best solution and thus the global-best solution might be forgotten again. This is very close to nature: every individual has only a limited lifetime. Schwefel [7] argued that "forgetting is as important as learning." He supported this finding by computer simulations.

Grefenstette [8] proposed use of an elitist strategy; that is, the best-so-far structure should always be a member of the population and may only be superseded by a new best-so-far solution. His experiments identified an elitist GA as optimal with respect to on-line performance. On-line performance is an average of all generated individuals during the search. Due to these contrary results the question arises: what is the effect of elitism within the ASPARAGOS environment? Elitism as defined by Grefenstette presumes a panmictic population with global knowledge. Within ASPARAGOS an individual has only local knowledge; that is, each individual knows only the members of its deme. Thus, we need to define elitism within our environment.

> *Elitism* in ASPARAGOS means: If the parent (the center individual of a deme) has the best quality within its deme (i.e., is the local best), then its offspring is accepted only if it is better than the parent.

The elitist strategy ensures a continuous improvement of the local-best individual and consequently also of the global-best individual. Elitism assigns more trials to the region of the search space where we find the local-best solution, because local-best individuals live on the average much longer than other individuals in the deme, leading to a higher chance of being selected as mate.

On the premise of sufficient selection pressure the pure strategy gives as good results as the elitist strategy within the ASPARAGOS environment, the death of the local-best individual and thus the loss of the very best individual of a population neither supports nor disrupts the final quality reached. Of course, the convergence speed of a pure strategy is slower than an elitist strategy.

Proportional versus Linear Rank Selection. We have tested three different selections strategies:

1. Random mating (i.e., ranking with max = min = 1)
2. Ranking with max = 1.7
3. Proportional selection with scaling window $W = 10$

Random mating has been included in the test set because it is an often-made assumption in theory and it isolates the influence of our survival strategy; that is, with random mating, selection takes place only through death events.

We fixed for our test the survival strategy to C. In comparison to survival strategy A, where selection can take place only through mate selection according to fitness, a random mate selection combined with survival strategy C performs much better. The best final quality is 0.5%, and the average final quality is about 1.2% from the optimal solution. But random mate selection compared to the stronger mate selection strategies is the clear loser (Table 16.3). This may be caused by a reduced spread of valuable information. In fact better individuals' genes may only propagate through the population structure by chance events. So it is not surprising that both ranking and proportional selection outperformed random mating.

A small test set with random mating and the other survival strategies showed the following trend: the stronger the survival strategy, the smaller the difference in final quality between random mate selection and proportional or rank selection. But the convergence speed is much slower, and the final quality is still significantly weaker. So, no further investigations were made in random mating.

Proportional selection with window size 10 overestimates at the very begin-

TABLE 16.3 Quality Depending on Selection Strategy ($T = 1600$)

Selection Strategy	C − random	C − rank	C − prop	E − rank	E − prop
Number of runs	15	15	15	15	15
Best	27816	27734	27756	27733	27731
Worst	28006	27913	27867	27835	27793
Median	27868	27753	27779	27772	27756
Average	27890	27782	27786	27770	27758
Standard deviation	56.43	66.15	37.15	28.85	17.73
Runs <1.0%	14	15	15	15	15
Runs <0.5%	1	12	11	14	15

ning of a simulation locally good individuals; they get a relative high chance of being chosen as a mate. Later the expected values compare well with those assigned by ranking with max = 1.7, and in the final stage mating chances are about randomly distributed, because the quality of the individuals in a deme becomes very close.

The convergence speed of ASPARAGOS with proportional selection and appropriate scaling is at the beginning somewhat faster compared to rank selection. This is because proportional selection with $W = 10$ gives the better individuals a higher chance to reproduce, and thus their genes can propagate faster. Using the final quality as a measure of comparison there is no clear winner. Table 16.3 shows us that the best and average final quality reached with proportional selection is better with survival strategy E but weaker with survival strategy C. The softer selection pressure of proportional selection in the later stage of a simulation run (almost random selection) tends to reduce the effects of the strong selection pressure of survival strategy E. The reverse seems to hold for rank selection; its higher selection pressure through mate selection is supplemented better with the softer survival strategy C.

Observation 2. We conclude that mate selection strategy and survival strategy contribute to the high quality and fast convergence of ASPARAGOS. These two aspects together may be used to "tune" genetic search by directly affecting selection pressure and population diversity. With the neighborhood model any combination of mate selection strategy and survival strategy is a good choice, except the two extreme cases of acceptance of all offspring and random mate selection. The simulations show that ranking is very promising, and it is independent of scaling problems.

16.5.5 Selection and Population Structure

The mate selection strategy and the survival strategy affect the selective pressure directly. The following sections discuss those parameters of ASPARAGOS affecting the selection pressure only indirectly. For example, if the population size is increased the selection pressure decreases because more individuals are involved in the search. Assuming a constant pattern of individuals in the continuum, the local differentiation turns out to depend largely on the population number of the neighborhood. The deme size affects the selection pressure by allowing faster or slower propagation of the genes through the total population. In the same way the spatial pattern of individuals in a continuum population works. We compare two spatial patterns: a linear pattern—the ladder population—and a planar pattern—the torus population.

We choose rank selection together with the 1%-worse survival rule for the experiments in this section. The parameter setting is thus

$$\text{AS}_{\text{pop}} = (M, D, [N/3, N/2], 0.02, (\text{rank, max} = 1.7), 1\% \text{ worse, ES})$$

Ranking has been chosen because its selective pressure is constant over the course of the simulation and the 1%-worse survival rule has been used because this results in a more continuous development of the gene pool.

The Population Size. The granularity of the neighborhood model is one individual per processor. So the parameter population size M has a meaningful lower bound of *number of processors* available. If this population size is too small (i.e., the final quality reached is not satisfying), we might hold several individuals on a single processor. Of course the CPU time will then be shared, thus increasing the running time. In the limit of a sequential machine the entire population is processed by the only processor.

We investigated a population size of 16, 32, and 64. A few control runs were made with a population size of 128. The convergence was slightly faster at the beginning of the experiment, and the final qualities were comparable to a population size of 64. It seems as if the TSP problems we considered are not complex enough to justify the use of a large population size of 128, especially if we take into account that with our 64-transputer system two individuals need to share one processor.

The parameters' population size and deme size are not independent of each other. For example, a deme size of 8 with population size 16 means that each individual knows half of the population members; the same deme size with population size of 64 allows more diversification. Therefore we made two sets of experiments: The first set used a deme size of 8, and the second set a deme size of 5. Theoretical investigations in [9] suggest that small deme sizes are most promising even for very large population sizes.

We make two observations concerning gene pool variability with the neighborhood model. First, the gene pool variability does not increase linearly with the population size; that is, with the neighborhood model the increase of the total number of different edges in the gene pool is about the same when the population size increases from 16 to 32 as when it increases from 32 to 64. From the viewpoint of gene pool variability we may conclude that an upper bound for the population size exists where further increase of the population size does not yield a more exhaustive exploration of the search space. Second, with the neighborhood model the loss of variability of the gene pool is much slower with increasing population size. If the population size is doubled, we observe a polynomial increase of the number of offspring created before the gene pool has lost its variability.

A more practical upper bound for the population size may be found by considering average performance and final quality. Figure 16.11 give the performance curves under the assumption that the offspring of a generation are created in parallel. A related figure is Figure 16.18, which gives the performance curve under the assumption that the creation of the offspring is done sequentially. Now we see that the faster evolution of the gene pool of smaller populations leads to a faster convergence in terms of the number of offspring created. Of course, due to the smaller gene pool, the search stagnates earlier.

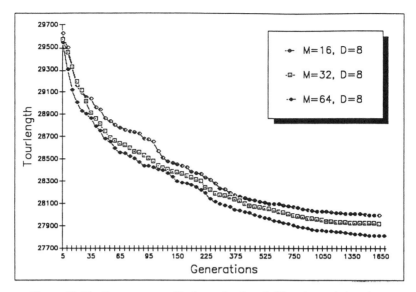

Figure 16.11   *Convergence with deme size 8 and different population sizes.*

Table 16.4 shows the final results for the various population sizes and a deme size of 8 and 5, respectively.

We see that the larger the population size, the better is the final quality and the smaller is the standard deviation; that is, the average quality is also reached with higher certainty. With population sizes 16 and 32 the smaller deme size of 5 gave better results; with population size 64 the deme size of 8 performed better.

All runs with $M = 64$, $D = \{5, 8\}$ and $M = 32$, $D = 5$ reached a quality below the 1% level, and some of these gave a final best solution below the 0.5% level. The small population size of 16 with $D = 5$ ($D = 8$) reached 5 (3) times out of 10 runs a quality below 1% excess, and no run found a solution better than 0.5% far from the optimum. It is remarkable that the results of the

TABLE 16.4   AS with Various Population and Deme Sizes ($T = 1600$)

	Problem Size 532							
	64/64	64/16	64/8	32/8	16/8	64/5	32/5	16/5
Number of runs	10	10	10	10	10	10	10	10
Best	27899	27784	27762	27841	27866	27782	27803	27902
Worst	28018	27870	27835	28050	28199	27852	27875	28067
Mean	27944	27861	27788	27898	28040	27820	27894	27945
Average	27941	27842	27792	27917	28020	27814	27840	27954
Standard deivation	54.54	39.28	22.72	72.39	103.25	29.00	32.18	58.42
Runs <1.0%	5	7	10	8	3	10	10	5
Runs <0.5%	0	2	8	0	0	5	1	0

TABLE 16.5   AS with Various Population and Deme Sizes (T = 1600)

	Problem Size 442					
	64/8	32/8	16/8	64/5	32/5	16/5
Number of runs	10	10	10	10	10	10
Best	5087	5088	5090	5087	5089	5090
Worst	5109	5109	5115	5109	5112	5123
Mean	5090	5093	5098	5089	5091	5109
Average	5093	5097	5099	5090	5095	5109
Standard deviation	6.69	8.66	9.06	5.96	8.64	14.48
Runs <1.0%	10	10	10	10	10	10
Runs <0.5%	8	5	4	8	5	3

panmictic population of size 64, given for comparison in the first column, are only comparable to population size 16 with deme size 5.

A different situation occurs with the more regular and smaller Grötschel problem of size 442. The final best quality is not much affected if the population size is reduced from 64 to 32, and if further reduced to 16 there is still a good chance to yield very good results (Table 16.5). Except for one run with $M = 16$, $D = 5$, all optimization tasks ended up with a quality exceeding the optimal solution less than 1% (5119).

With the Krolak problem of size 100 the neighborhood model always found the global optimum. An early extensive study of this problem [10, 3] showed that an ASPARAGOS strategy is able to find the global optimum as long as the population size is larger than 14 and the deme size is 5.

The Deme Size. A deme size of 5 gave a faster convergence than a deme size of 8 (Fig. 16.12). This superiority of the smaller deme size may be because fewer individuals may immediately choose an individual with high fitness as mate; that is, alleles of relatively good individuals propagate slower through the population structure, thus focusing more on exploration of the search space.

If the deme size is increased, the genetic search process can better exploit a region of the search space since more individuals are forced to occupy this region. But a large neighborhood prevents the massively parallel GA from establishing a search region. The search process is steadily disturbed by the fast propagation of genes through the population.

Thus, we can balance exploitation and exploration of the search space by an appropriate choice of population size and deme size. The smaller the population size the smaller should be the deme size. An extremely small deme size is out of the question because the mate selection process according to fitness cannot work appropriately. For example, with a deme size of 3, AS-PARAGOS can choose a mate only between a best and a worst individual. In contrast a large deme size reduces the error occurring by the assignment of expected values. With error we mean the difference between the expected value assigned in the neighborhood model compared with the expected value assigned in a panmictic population model.

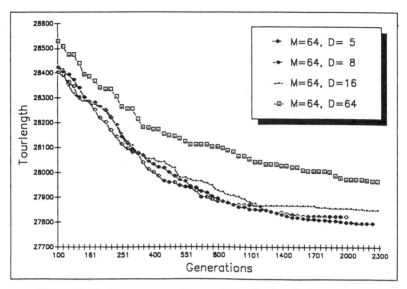

Figure 16.12 *Convergence with population size 64—final generations.*

A deme size of 5 gave the better final quality with the smaller population sizes of 16 and 32. If the population size is large enough, a larger deme size may be the better choice. With population size 64 a deme size of 5 is faster in convergence, but finally the AS strategy with deme size 8 finds better solutions (Fig. 16.12).

Figure 16.12 shows the average performance of AS strategies with a population size of 64. The size of the neighborhood is increased until we finally end up at the panmictic population model if *deme.size = pop.size*. The AS strategy with deme size 16 converged slower than the strategy with deme size 8 and gave weaker final qualities. A deme size of 64, which is a traditional GA where each individual of the population is a potential mate, gave by far the weakest convergence and final quality (Tables 16.4 and 16.5).

Observation 3. The parameters' population size and deme size interact. If the population size is given, then an appropriate deme size can be specified. The optimal deme size is proportional to the population size. A relatively small deme size is always a good choice.

16.5.6 The Spatial Pattern of Individuals

The movement of individuals in the ASPARAGOS environment is defined by the underlying spatial pattern of the individuals. In discussing the effects of the spatial pattern, we are thinking of motile organisms that occupy a fairly small area with definite boundaries specifying the size of an individual's reproduction community. The pattern of individuals is static; that is, the pattern persists throughout the whole simulation.

First, we discuss the formation of species due to the geographical structured population, and second, we compare a linear spatial pattern with a planar spatial pattern. That is, we compare our ladder population, which allows individuals to move only linearly, with another spatial pattern, which allows a movement on the surface of a torus.

16.5.7 The Creation of Species

In the migration models each individual may become a mate of all other individuals in the subpopulation. This is not the case with the neighborhood model. There only the near individuals, as defined by the spatial pattern and the deme size as induced by an individual's mobility, are potential candidates for mating.

The restriction of mating to the deme, the computation of the selection chance relative to the deme, and the replacement of the center individual of a deme by an accepted offspring all lead to the formation of species.

From population genetics we know that in the neighborhood model demes are likely to change their genetic characteristics smoothly across the manifold. In our simulation environment we thus expect that the members of local nearby demes are more similar with respect to the genotype than demes geographically more distant. The following experiment shed light on the process of speciation.

We define the Hamming distance $h(A_k, A_l)$ between the tours (the genotype) of two individuals (A_k and A_l) to be the number of edges found in one, but not in the other, tour.

To compare two demes as a whole, say $\mathcal{D}_i$ and $\mathcal{D}_j$, we use as a measure of comparison the average Hamming distance of all pairs of individuals between the two demes:

$$H_{\mathcal{D}_i, \mathcal{D}_j} = \sum_{k=1}^{D} \sum_{l=1}^{D} \frac{h(A_k, A_l)}{D^2}, \quad \text{with } A_k \in \mathcal{D}_i, \quad A_l \in \mathcal{D}_j$$

Figure 16.13 shows the examined demes. Deme 1 is our reference. Deme 1, deme 2, and deme 3 are very close, whereas deme 4 lies opposite to deme 1 and is thus geographically as far away as possible. Figure 16.14 shows the progress of the Hamming distance between the exemplary demes and as a comparison between deme 1 and the whole population.

During the first generations the species establish; that is, at the very beginning up to about generation 50 the Hamming distance between the demes as well as the Hamming distance between deme 1 and the whole population is about the same. After that the process of species establishment begins. We observe that the Hamming distance between the geographically close demes (i.e., deme 1, deme 2, and deme 3) is comparable and so is the Hamming distance between the most distant demes (deme 4 and deme 1) and the Hamming distance between deme 1 and the whole population. The Hamming distances between close demes are significantly smaller than those between op-

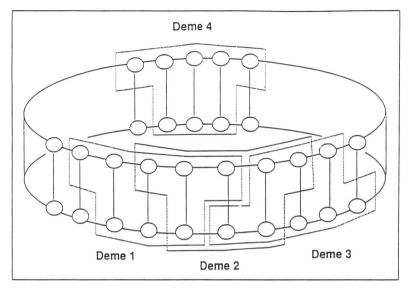

Figure 16.13 *The placement of the examined demes in a ladder population.*

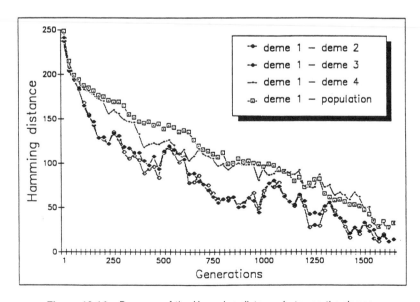

Figure 16.14 *Progress of the Hamming distance between the demes.*

posite demes. Over the course of the simulation the Hamming distance between demes becomes smaller due to the fixation of the genes, but the speciation once established remains over the course of the simulation.

16.5.8 Linear versus Planar Population

In a study of spatial patterns quite different population structures might be thought of. We consider a linear space where the individuals are placed on the rung crossings of a ladder and a planar pattern where the individuals reside on the grid crossings of an 8×8 torus.

The main difference between these two spatial patterns is that the ladder population allows information to flow only along a linear range, whereas the torus population allows a fast flow of information due to the small diameter of order $\sqrt{M}$, where M denotes population size.

Figure 16.15 shows the fixation of genes for the ladder and torus population, respectively. The survival strategy is set to B (1% worse), because the effects on the gene pool variability then become clearly visible. We recognize that the gene pool of the ladder population develops continuously, whereas the torus population has a phase of fast loss of variability. In the torus population the fast propagation of genes allows advantageous genes to quickly dominate the whole population. Thus, the torus population develops faster and the gene pool loses variability very early. The different characteristics of the ladder and the torus population may become more apparent with either a small or a large population size and with highly multimodal problems.

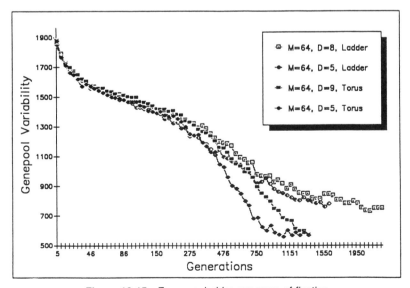

Figure 16.15 *Torus vs. ladder: progress of fixation.*

TABLE 16.6 Final Quality in Percentage Excess: Panmixia versus Ladder- and Torus-Population

Strategy Generations	Torus		Ladder		Panmixia			
	C 2300	C 2300	C 2300	E 1600	C 2300		E 1600	
	64/5	64/9	64/8	64/8	64/64	32/32	64/64	32/32
Number of runs	15	15	15	15	15	15	15	15
Best	0.30	0.20	0.17	0.15	0.29	0.27	0.15	0.18
Worst	0.49	0.53	0.50	0.39	0.99	1.08	0.59	0.82
Median	0.43	0.30	0.29	0.21	0.47	0.57	0.35	0.36
Standard deviation	25.68	26.95	36.74	15.25	53.06	62.12	41.31	63.12
Runs <1.0%	15	15	15	15	15	14	15	15
Runs <1.0%	15	14	14	15	6	5	3	2

Table 16.6 gives the final qualities in percentage excess. The early focus due to fast information flow unbalances exploitation and exploration so that the torus population missed the very best solutions. The important aspect of population structures is the difference in the conditions of selection. The rate of decay of genetic variability in a geographical structured finite population decreases with the diameter of the population structure. A linear spatial pattern may be preferred, with relatively small populations usually being treated. The decreased diameter of the area continuum increases the selection pressure and thus focuses the search. If large populations are processed, the area continuum might be an appropriate choice.

16.5.9 Panmixia versus Population Structure

Panmixia is assumed with traditional GAs. Thus, we are interested in relating the behavior of a panmictic population to one with only local interactions. The experiment uses the somewhat pathological case in the event that the deme size is equal to the population size.

Our experiments show that the panmictic population is very sensitive with respect to the survival rule. Figure 16.17 shows that the gene pool with panmixia and survival strategy E (better parent) loses variability very fast, but with the softer selection pressure of survival strategy C (better local least) fixation is very slow. This corresponds with the findings when looking at the average performance shown in Figure 16.16. The panmictic population of size 64 with survival strategy E is the variant that converges fastest, but is weak in exploration. Improvements after about generation 250 are only due to chance events offered by mutation.

Table 16.6 shows the final qualities reached with a panmictic population and a population with spatial pattern. Comparing the results for panmixia with those obtained with a population structure, we find it astonishing that, using panmixia and a strong selection pressure, the best run out of 15 gave comparable qualities. Nevertheless, the overall behavior is not as good as that reached

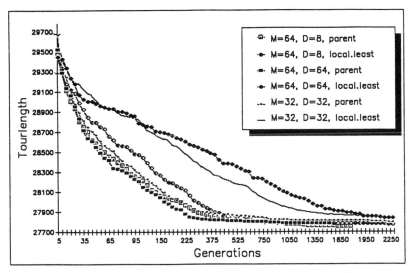

Figure 16.16 *Convergence in percentage excess: panmixia vs. population structure.*

by using a population structure. Using a panmictic population gives a less robust algorithm, as the much higher median and the increased standard deviation indicate.

An interesting phenomenon occurs with the panmictic model if we compare the convergence of population sizes 64 and 32. Except at the very beginning of a simulation the smaller population develops faster. This is due to the oc-

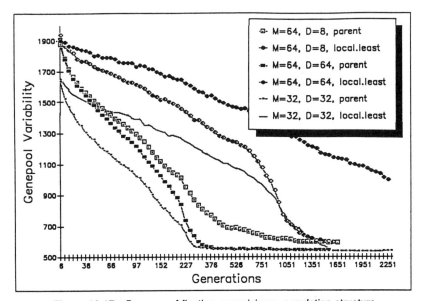

Figure 16.17 *Progress of fixation: panmixia vs. population structure.*

currence of different selection pressures. In a larger panmictic population it takes longer for the genes of the very best individuals to profit, whereas in a smaller population we find faster evolution.

16.6 MULTIPROCESSOR VERSUS SINGLE-PROCESSOR SYSTEMS

Within the ASPARAGOS environment the natural degree of parallelism is one individual per processor. The individuals of a population behave completely asynchronously; that is, after the initialization phase each processor is 100% busy and there are no waiting times due to synchronization. The individuals need only local knowledge, and, thus, if the deme size is sufficiently small no or little, communication overhead is needed for routing activities.

Assuming a shortage in the number of processors available, a processor might be shared by placing several individuals on it. The number of individuals on each processor is determined by *population size/number of processors*. In the case of only one processor, all individuals of the population are generated sequentially. Of course, the arguments improved robustness, better performance, better final quality, and establishment and maintenance of niches speak for the use of a preferably linear population structure instead of a panmictic population.

Assuming a single processor, an interesting question has not been considered yet: "How fast does a population develop first in relation to population size and second with respect to panmixia or population structure?" Figure 16.18 gives an answer. The parameter setting is that of AS_S except for the variation

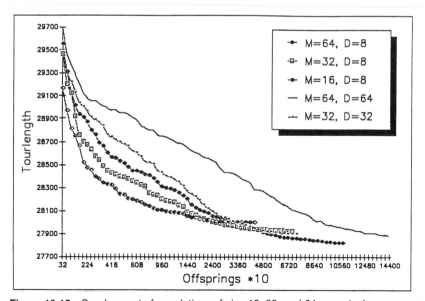

Figure 16.18 *Development of populations of size 16, 32, and 64 on a single processor.*

of the population size and deme size. In contrast to previous figures, where the x axis gave the number of generations, now the x axis shows the number of offspring generated. From this figure it is apparent that in either case (panmixia or population structure) small populations develop faster than larger ones. Of course, the final quality reached with a larger population is always better because it is less prone to premature convergence.

The development of the panmictic population of size 32 is slower compared with the ladder population of size 32 and even slower in comparison with a ladder population of size 64. The final quality reached is comparable to that of an equal-sized population with structure.

The situation changes with larger population sizes. The panmictic population of size 64 develops extremely slowly and even with a large number of generated offspring the final quality reached is only a bit better compared with the panmictic population of size 32 and still weaker than the results of the ladder population of size 64. In terms of generated offspring (i.e., CPU time on a single processor), the convergence of a population of size 64 with ladder structure is faster than that of a panmictic population of size 32. We conclude that the introduction of a neighborhood model is advantageous even on a single processor.

16.7 APPLICATIONS OF THE TRAVELING SALESMAN PROBLEM

The classical TSP as solved earlier has only a few immediate applications, in particular that of a salesman wishing to minimize his or her travel distance or the problem of minimizing the total length of the movements, and hence the time needed by a drilling machine. But several problems could be formulated as instances of the TSP. On the other hand, the proposed approach may be easily expanded to cover other problems.

The vehicle routing problem (VRP) is one such problem related to the TSP that frequently occurs in practice. Given a number of vehicles based at a central depot and a number of customers, the problem to be solved is which customers should be served by which vehicles and in what order. Constraints generally include capacities of the vehicles and time windows for the customers. The VRP is also known as the vehicle scheduling, truck dispatching, or delivery problem. An extension of the VRP is to consider several depots with interdependent depot operations. The time period during which the customer requirements are fulfilled is one of the most important aspects and is a measure of the service level.

Another problem is sequencing a number of jobs on a single machine. Each job requires the machine to be in a certain state; thus to complete a job, the machine must be set up and then the job can be performed. The time to do a specific job is a constant; what we look for is a permutation of the jobs so that the total time to transform the machine is minimized. Therefore, the job sequencing problem is a TSP.

In the design of computers and other technical devices the problem of wiring occurs. Given a number of placed modules with several pins: the problem is to interconnect a given subset of pins due to the constraints that at most two pins may be attached at one pin and the total length of the wires should be minimized. The problem becomes much harder, if the position of the modules is not fixed in advance, but is chosen so as to minimize the total wire length.

Finally, we mention the quadratic assignment problem. It arises, for example, in the placement of VLSI modules, in the design of factories, and in the mapping of processes onto processors in multiprocessor systems. This problem is a generalization of the TSP and a problem of size n has as many as $n!$ different solutions.

REFERENCES

[1] D. Johnson, "How to Beat Lin-Kernighan," TSP Workshop, Rice University (1990).

[2] P. Krolak, W. Felts, and G. Marble, A man-machine approach toward solving the traveling salesman problem, *Communication of the ACM*, 14(5), 327–334 (1971).

[3] H. Mühlenbein, M. Gorges-Schleuter, and O. Krämer, Evolution algorithm in combinatorial optimization, *Parallel Comput.*, 7, 65–88 (1988).

[4] D. Whitley, T. Starkweather, and D'Ann Fuquay, Scheduling problems and traveling salesmen: The genetic edge recombination operator, in J. D. Schaffer, ed., *Proc. Third Internat. Conf. Genetic Algorithms*, Morgan Kaufmann, San Mateo, Calif., (1989), 133–140.

[5] Y. Rossier, M. Troyon, and T. M. Liebling, Probabilistic exchange algorithms and Euclidean traveling salesman problems, *OR Spektrum*, 8, 151–164 (1986).

[6] W. Padberg and G. Rinaldi, Optimization of a 532-city symmetric traveling salesman problem by branch and cut, *Oper. Res. Lett.*, 6, 1–7 (1987).

[7] H. P. Schwefel, "Collective phenomena in evolutionary systems," *International Conf. on Problems of Constancy and Change*, 31st Annual Meeting of the International Society for General Systems Research, Budapest, Hungary (June 1987).

[8] J. J. Grefenstette, Optimization of control parameters for genetic algorithms, *IEEE Trans. Systems, Man, Cybernet.*, 16(1), 122–128 (1986).

[9] M. Gorges-Schleuter, Comparison of local mating strategies in massively parallel systems, in L. Männer and B. Manderick, eds., Parallel problem solving from Nature 2, Proc. Second Conf., North Holland, Amsterdam (1992) 553–562.

[10] H. Mühlenbein, The traveling salesman problem—an evolutionary approach, in Annual Report of the GMD, 1987, GrD, St. Augustin, Germany (in German).

CHAPTER 17 _____

Robot Control Structures for High-Quality Learning in Flexible Manufacturing

MIOMIR VUKOBRATOVIĆ
DUŠKO KATIĆ

17.1 INTRODUCTION

Contemporary research activities in technology and business are focused on the synthesis and application of intelligent control, which as a new paradigm represents one very efficient way for the realization of complex system goals and requirements. A primary concern of intelligent control is cross-disciplinary studies of high-level control in which control strategies are generated using human intelligent functions such as perception, simultaneous utilization of memory, association, reasoning, learning, or multilevel decision making in response to fuzzy or qualitative commands. In this way, using the aforementioned intelligent capabilities, modern manufacturing systems can achieve ultimate machine performance in the presence of many structured and unstructured uncertainties that are inherently incorporated in these systems.

Because of the complex demands that they must accomplish as an integral part of flexible manufacturing systems, manipulation robots represent an ideal object for the application of intelligent control techniques [1–2]. Intelligent robots are the automatic manipulation robots with versatile intelligent capabilities, that can perform various tasks in an unfamiliar or familiar working environment. The first approach to making robots more intelligent was the integration of sophisticated sensor systems such as vision, tactile sensing, and other smart sensors. However, the primary goal of research in this important area is the development and integration of novel intelligent control techniques that can

Frontier Decision Support Concepts, Edited by V. L. Plantamura, B. Souček, and G. Visaggio.
ISBN 0-471-59256-0   © 1994 John Wiley & Sons, Inc.

further improve the overall performance of robotic systems using advanced sensor systems.

In order to ensure high-quality control the new intelligent control techniques must cope with task complexity, heuristic information, and the influence of many system uncertainties. There are many sources of undesirable behavior of robotic systems, when working according to conventional control algorithms, that can be eliminated by new algorithms. For example, it is well known that conventional control algorithms are model-based schemes that in most cases are synthesized using incomplete information and partially known or inaccurately defined parameters. Conventional control algorithms are extremely sensitive to the lack of sensor information and to unplanned events and unfamiliar situations in the robot working environment. The robot is not able to capture and use past experience and available human expertise. All these facts and examples emphasize the necessity that to be used as a tool for solving the drawbacks of conventional control techniques, an efficient robot intelligent control must be based on the following features [3]:

a. Robustness and adaptability to system uncertainties and environment changes
b. Learning and self-organizing capabilities with generalization of acquired knowledge
c. Real-time implementation on robot controllers using fast processing architectures.

The learning properties of intelligent control algorithms in robotics are very important, as they ensure achievement of high-quality robot performance. It is well known that conventional adaptive and nonadaptive robot control algorithms [4] comprise the problem of robot control during execution of particular robot trajectories without considering repetitive motion. Hence, in terms of learning, almost all manipulation robots are memoryless. In this way, previously acquired experience about the dynamic robot model and control algorithms is not applied in robot control synthesis. It is expected that use of a training process with repetition of a control task and recording the results accumulated in the entire process will steadily improve the performance. Also, the state-variables dependency of robot dynamics may be solved by learning and storing solutions, while time dependency of robot parameters requires an on-line learning approach. If the learning control algorithm once learned a movement, it will be able to control quite a different and faster movement using the generalization properties of the learning algorithm.

In this chapter attention will be focused on issues connected to integration of new learning techniques in the intelligent control of robot manufacturing operations with particular emphasis on application of the connectionist (neural network) approach. Recent research reports and extensive simulation studies carried out on models containing neural networks have demonstrated an excellent ability to identify and control sophisticated manipulation robots [5–6]; that is, connectionist robot controllers are capable of producing a large number of efficient control commands in real time. The major concern in this chapter is the application of neural networks in robot control at the executive hierarchical level for on-line learning of inverse dynamic relations used in robot manufacturing operations that are essentially denoted as constrained manipulation or contact tasks. An overview of the basic principles and learning concepts of connectionist control for robot contact tasks is given, with presentation of a new efficient algorithm that uses special neural network structures as an upgrade of conventional schemes for position/force control.

17.2 THE ROLE AND APPLICATION OF LEARNING IN MANUFACTURING ROBOTICS

In contemporary technological systems, robotics and automation technology have an important role in a variety of manufacturing tasks. These manufacturing operations can be categorized in two classes, regarding the nature of interaction between a robot and its environment. The first one is concerned with noncontact—that is, unconstrained motion in a free workspace. In noncontact tasks the robot's own dynamics have a crucial influence upon its performance. A limited number of simple and most frequently performed robotic tasks in practice, such as pick-and-place, paint spraying, gluing, or welding, belong to this group. In contrast, many complex advanced-robotic applications, such as assembly and machining operations (deburring, grinding, polishing, etc.), require the manipulator to be mechanically coupled to the other objects. These tasks are called essential contact tasks because they include phases where the robot's end-effector must come into contact with objects in its environment, produce certain forces upon them, and/or move along their surfaces. Inherently, each manipulation tasks involves contact with the object being manipulated. The terms *constrained* or *compliant motion* usually refer to a contact task.

The objective of using the adaptive and learning capabilities for the aforementioned operations is to simplify the implementation process, to improve the reliability of systems, and, in this way, to achieve a tremendous practical impact. Another important characteristic of learning techniques may be an enhanced capability to design robust hierarchical robotic systems. Namely, there are possibilities of using learning control techniques at all hierarchical control levels. Learning behavior at one hierarchical level will facilitate the technological demands for specific coordination with other levels.

At the strategical and tactical hierarchical control level, there are many opportunities for the application of learning systems to task-planning and task-reasoning problems, particularly those that confront the issue of uncertainty in the task environment. Also, a clear opportunity for the impact of learning systems is the use of sensing and inspection technology for industrial applications. It is important to notice that for this control level, specific methods for machine learning [7] (inductive learning, analytical learning, genetic learning) are dominant learning tools for problems at these levels.

The main concern in this chapter will be integration of learning techniques for control of manufacturing operations at the executive hierarchical level. As is well known, a common and simple way for nonlearning control of manipulation robots at the lowest hierarchical level is the use of local PID regulators for each degree of freedom of the robotic mechanism for position tracking and PID regulators for force regulation. However, this control law is not adequate for advanced industrial robots that must demonstrate capability for high precision and speed in a complex working environment. The influence of couplings between the subsystems and interaction with environment is substantial, so that we should include a "dynamic" control [4, 8] that uses the dynamic model of the robot mechanism and the model of th robot environment in the process of control synthesis.

However a common problem, especially in manufacturing operations, is how to describe correctly the robot environment dynamics and how to synthesize control laws that simultaneously stabilize both the desired position and interactive force. For example, in robot contact operations, such as grinding, deburring, and polishing, it is essential to control the tangential velocity of the tool along the workpiece and the force normal to the work surface. It is very difficult to achieve an acceptable system performance because of a high level of unpredictable interactions between the robot and the environment. Also various system uncertainties need to be taken into account when considering the system behavior. For example, in controller design, we have to cope with structured uncertainties (inaccuracies of the robot mechanism parameters, imprecise position of the workpiece, varying degrees of stiffness of the environment, robot tool, and robot itself, etc.), unstructured uncertainties (unmodeled high-frequency dynamics as structural resonant modes, actuator dynamics, sampling effects), and measurement noise. Besides, the time-varying nature of the robot parameters and variability of the robot tasks can cause a high level of interaction force or loss of contact. In this case, conventional nonadaptive algorithms are not robust enough, because they compensate only a small part of these uncertainties. Hence, a more suitable approach would be one using adaptive control techniques [4]. The adaptive control technique in robotics was applied as a parameter adaptation technique with the possibility of adaptation in feedforward or feedback loops. All such methods usually comprise on-line schemes with recursive least squares optimization criterion and short-term learning in which past experience is completely forgotten. To summarize, conventional adaptive control techniques in robotics can tolerate wider ranges of uncertainties, but in the presence of sensor data overload, heuristic information, limits on real-time applicability, and very wide interval of system uncertainties, the application of adaptive control cannot ensure a high-quality performance.

Therefore, to achieve best performance of the robotic system, a solution to the robot control problem would probably require a combination of conventional approaches with new learning techniques. The application of learning techniques in the field of robot control at the lowest hierarchical level is very important, because these techniques can significantly enhance robotic performance with a priori low level of information about the model of the manipulation robot and the environment. Another important characteristic of learning control in contact tasks is its repetitive nature, which is very important for learning by trial and error.

There are many possibilities in the development of more robust robot controllers by utilizing learning systems to identify more accurately robot kinematics and dynamics, to more efficiently adapt dynamic control parameters to particular tasks, and to more effectively integrate sensory information into the control process. Another possibility for such an application is kinematic calibration of robot arms, utilizing sensing systems to measure positions of the arm end-effector, as the learning system can identify a complex nonlinear model of the robot arm kinematics that could be used to improve the positioning accuracy of the robot arm itself. Also, learning systems may improve the capabilities of execution of fine motion operations, such as force control and grasping. Robotic systems offer a promising domain for experimental exploration of learning systems in manufacturing operations since the practical application of complex robotic systems may require adaptive and learning behavior in order to achieve their desired functionality.

For robot learning control at the executive hierarchical level, we can identify three main paradigms [5]:

1. *Iterative-Analytical Methods.* These methods are based on successive attempts at following the same trajectory. Typically, control input values for each time instant in the trajectory are adjusted iteratively on the basis of the observed trajectory errors at similar times during previous attempts. These iterative learning algorithms may be very precise and rapidly converge. On the other hand, one drawback is that they are applicable only to repetitive operations. Also, these algorithms have no capability of generalization on quite different movements.

2. *Tabular Methods.* This method represents the associative content addressable memories where the robot models learn by storing experience about command signals and current state coordinates in a memory. Each time a particular set of robot positions, velocities, and accelerations is requested, the entire memory has to be searched for the closest experience. In this approach, the problems are long search time due to the large amount of stored experience, ways to measure similarity, and methods of efficient generalization.

3. *Connectionist Method.* It is the neural network approach based on distributed processing.

The connectionist method is the approach that we adopted for learning control of robot manufacturing operations, having in mind excellent capabilities for achieving fast and high-quality control. Hence, special attention will be paid to this approach.

17.3 NEURAL NETWORK APPROACH IN CONTROL OF ROBOTIC SYSTEMS

Basic connectionism theory was founded during the 1960s, but its recent revival is due, in part, to powerful neural network models and learning methods [9]. Besides, interest in this theory is also due to advances in hardware realization of connectionism algorithms.

Connectionism represents the study of massively parallel networks of simple neuronlike computing units. The massive interconnections of the rather simple neurons, which make up the human brain, provided the original motivation for the development of neural network models. The neural networks consist of many interconnected simple nonlinear systems, which are typically modeled by appropriate activation functions. These simple nonlinear elements, called nodes or neurons, are interconnected, and the strengths of the interconnections are denoted by parameters called weights. The activation function of a single unit is commonly a simple nondecreasing function such as threshold, identity, sigmoid, or other complex mathematical function [9]. Neural networks may be distinguished according to the type of interconnection between input and output of network. Basically, there are two types of networks: feedforward and feedback.

In the feedforward network, there are no loops, and the output depends exclusively on the input. With the use of a continuous nonlinear activation function, this network represents a static nonlinear map that can be efficiently used as a parallel computational model of a continuous mapping. For the study and application of feedforward networks it is convenient to use, beside single-layer neural networks, some more structured networks known as multilayer networks or multilayer perceptrons. These networks with appropriate number of hidden levels have received considerable attention because of better representation capabilities and ability to learn highly nonlinear mappings.

If the network possesses some cycle or loop, then it is a feedback or recurrent neural network. In recurrent network, the system has an internal state, and thereby the output will also depend on the internal state of the system. Neural networks can be further characterized by their network topology (i.e., by the number of interconnections), the node characteristics that are classified by the type of nonlinear elements used (activation rule), and the kind of learning rules implemented.

From the point of view of systems theory, we can say that the multilayer neural networks represent static nonlinear mappings, while recurrent networks are nonlinear dynamic systems with feedback loops. But it is important that we can use them in a unified fashion to accommodate both classes of networks in control applications.

The application of neural networks in technical problems consists of two phases:

1. Phase of learning/adaptation/design is the special phase of learning, modifying, and designing of internal structure of network, when the network acquires knowledge about the real system as a result of interaction with the system and the real environment using trial-and-error method, as well as the result of appropriate metarules that are inherent in a global network context.

2. Pattern associator phase or associative memory mode is a special phase when, using the stored associations, the network converges toward the stable attractor or a desired solution.

The computational capabilities of systems with neural networks are amazing and very promising. They include not only "intelligent functions" like logical reasoning, learning, pattern recognition, formation of associations, or abstraction from examples, but also the ability to acquire the most skillful performance in the control of complex dynamic systems. The power of the neural network hinges upon its distinct features of robust processing and adaptive capability in a changing and noisy environment. Neural networks also evaluate a large number of sensors with different modalities, providing noisy and sometimes inconsistent information. The ability to learn is one of the main advantages that make neural networks so attractive. The benefits are most dramatic when a large number of nodes are used and are implemented in hardware. Artificial neural systems can gain a lot of advantage from silicon VLSI technology using commercial architectures and "neural chips" because of the large integration density that can be achieved. The hardware implementation of neural networks is currently a very active research area [10–12], which uses a number of different working principles, implementation technologies (analog and digital neural networks, optical technology, etc.), and interconnection architectures.

Recent research in neural networks has demonstrated an ability for efficient identification and control of a large class of nonlinear dynamic systems. The connectionism approach to control theory comprises the control problem as a special part of the pattern recognition problem. In comparison with human abilities for control functions, neural controllers exhibit the following features: (1) utilization of large amounts of sensor information in planning and control; (2) collective processing capabilities as the basis for fast calculations in real time; (3) adaptation properties using learning by experience.

Within a conventional control system, neural networks can be implemented as a form of feedforward and feedback controllers. In the training phase, using the trial-and-error approach, the learning process gradually tunes the weights of neural networks so that error signal as the deviation between a desired and actual output of the system is minimized. Hence, through training, the model uncertainties are eliminated, and, thus the neural network serves as a compensation tool in control systems.

We can say that robotic systems, as nonlinear dynamic systems, represent a special control plant that is very suitable for the application of advanced concepts from the theory of neural network control. The connectionist computing methods provide an approach to the development of adaptive and learning behavior in robotic systems for manufacturing [13] on the basis of their excellent capabilities for learning and generalization of acquired knowledge about the robotic system. One of the main research goals in modern intelligent robotic systems is to have the robots learn from their experience. As is well known, a robot learns from what is happening rather than from what it expects. Hence, when self-adaptive and autonomous capabilities are required, the application of neural networks in robot control has a great chance. Neural networks are able to recognize the changes in the robot environmental conditions and then react to them, or to make decisions on the basis of changing manufacturing events. Generalization capabilities of neural networks will require more long-term research, but could facilitate the flexibility of systems in their capacity to adapt to new tasks.

The field of possible applications of neural networks in robotics includes various purposes, such as vision systems, appendage controllers for manufacturing, tactile sensing, tactile feedback gripper control, motion control systems, situation analysis, solution to the inverse kinematic problem, sensory-motor coordination, generation of limb trajectories, learning visuomotor coordination of a robot arm in three dimensions, and so on. These applications can be categorized according to the type of hierarchical control level of the robotic system; that is, neural networks can be applied at strategic control level (task planning), at tactic control level (path planning), and executive control level (path control). All these control problems at the different hierarchical levels can be formulated in terms of optimization or pattern association problems [6]. The representative sample of research work being done in neural network approaches to robotics can be found in [5, 14].

As a solution in the context of robot control at the lowest level, the connectionist approaches provide implementation tools for complex input/output relations of the robot's dynamics and kinematics without analytic modeling. The connectionist approach may, in principle, solve the problem of variable-coupling complexity and state dependence of the robot dynamic model, because neural networks, through the process of training, can learn input/output relations. Perhaps the most powerful property of neural networks in robotics is their ability to model the whole controlled system itself. For example, it may be possible to implement by neural networks a complete inverse dynamics model of the robot that includes dynamics of the controlled object, backlash, and gear friction. In this way, the connectionist controller can compensate a wide range of robot uncertainties. The fast computational capability of neural networks enables real-time applicability of robot control algorithms.

The learning process at executive level is inherently connected for the process of training; that is, we use a trial-and-error approach, when in successive epochs the same desired trajectory and force patterns are presented. The process of training by neural networks in kinematic and dynamic cases can be accomplished both off-line and on-line. In the off-line approach, the neural network uses previously stored input patterns and controller outputs with the aim of minimizing the approximation error. On-line learning uses adjustment of the network weights during the real-time control.

Our major concern is the application of neural networks in robot control for constrained manipulation at the executive hierarchical level (motion/force control problem). The connectionist methods for robot noncontact tasks have been extensively studied with excellent results [3, 5, 15].

Hence, we consider two generic control designs for solving the constrained motion problem: supervised control and direct inverse control. Supervised control represents the form of control when a neural network learns the mapping from the desired inputs or sensor inputs to desired actions, by adapting a training set of examples with the desired values of network outputs generated by an external teacher. Supervised learning could significantly improve the efficiency of training and development of robotic systems. *Fuji* has used this method in working robots. On the other hand, direct inverse control is a form of control when the neural network learns the inverse dynamic or inverse kinematic model of the system, so that it can make the system follow a desired trajectory. Let us explain the inverse dynamic problem of robot control in a computational framework. These are casual relations between the robot driving torque and the resulting robot movement coordinates and forces exerted on the robot end-effector. Let $P(t)$ denote the time history of driving torque and $q(t)$ and $F(t)$ denote the time history of the robot internal coordinates and force on the robot end-effector during trajectory tracking. We can denote the casual relation between P and q, or between P and q and F, using the functional f; that is, $f(P(t)) = q(t)$ or $f(P(t)) = (q(t), F(t))$. If we want the robot to track a desired trajectory q_d or we want to track a desired trajectory q_d with desired force F_d, the problem of generation of a desired driving torque P_d that realizes q_d and F_d, is equivalent to finding an inverse of the functional f.

17.4 SYNTHESIS OF LEARNING CONTROL IN ROBOT CONTACT TASKS BY CONNECTIONIST STRUCTURES

A major objective in this section is the application of new connectionist structures for fast and robust on-line learning of internal robot dynamic relations used as part of control strategies in robot contact tasks. Our intention is to extend the whole theory developed for connectionist control in robot noncontact tasks [15], in order to deal with the more general problem of performing the position and force control of robot manipulators. Our synthesis is based on an analysis of the well-known nonlearning control algorithms for constrained manipulation. Here, two general approaches should be distinguished, one of which is hybrid control or admittance control [16] and the other is impedance control [16]. Namely, some essential shortcomings of hybrid control algorithms have been recently observed [8, 17]. The drawbacks of this approach are linked with incorrect usage of the term *orthogonality* [17] and with the impossibility of finding directions for independent stabilization of force and position. Hence, we have not considered synthesis of learning control schemes with basic principles of hybrid position/force control. The second, more important approach (impedance control), was considered as a possible method for including learning principles.

The main feature of the proposed learning control algorithms is the use of multilayer perceptrons with special topology for fast and robust on-line learning of internal robot dynamic relations. The connectionist structure is integrated in two types of nonlearning control laws for contact tasks: (a) stabilizing control laws with a preset quality of the transient processes for position and force [8]; (b) impedance control laws [18]. Also, multilayer perceptrons through input/output mapping include necessary dynamic component in control scheme and, in this way, serve in the training process as an efficient tool for compensation of system uncertainties. Using the proposed connectionist structures, stabilization of the robot motion and interaction force with the environment is achieved.

Another feature of using new learning control laws is the principle of decomposition of robot dynamics in the internal coordinates. The results are simplified dynamic mappings and learning feasibility of robotic dynamic for larger systems with significant reduction of learning time. This method includes a prior knowledge about robot dynamics, which, instead of being particular knowledge corresponding to a certain class of models, incorporates the general knowledge of robot dynamics. In training, we use new fast learning rules [15] that yield benefits in convergence speed and generalization.

The final result of the proposed approach is a trainable robot controller architecture that uses the neural network model as part of stabilizing control laws and the process of training by the feedback-error learning method.

17.4.1 Models of Robot Dynamics and Environment: Task Setting

In contact asks, the dynamics of the robot mechanism and its interaction with working environment have a crucial effect on the system performance. Hence, in control synthesis it is very important to describe more accurately the robotic system model and the working environment.

A general equation describing the nature of robot dynamics model in its interaction with the environment is

$$P = H(q)\ddot{q} + h(q, \dot{q}) + J^T(q)F \tag{17.1}$$

or, in compact form,

$$P = U(q, \dot{q}, \ddot{q}, F) \tag{17.2}$$

where $P \in R^n$ is the vector of driving torques or forces, $H(q): R^n \Rightarrow R^{n \times n}$ is the inertial matrix of the system, $h(q, \dot{q}): R^n \times R^n \Rightarrow R^n$ is the vector that includes centrifugal, Coriolis, and gravitational effects, $J(q): R^n \Rightarrow R^{n \times n}$ is the configuration-dependent Jacobian matrix that relates joint velocities to the linear and angular velocities of the end-effector, $F \in R^n$ is the vector of generalized forces and torques exerted by the end-effector on the environment and measured by a wrist force sensor, $q \in R^n$ is the vector of robot generalized coordinates, U is the vector function, and n is the number of degrees of freedom.

The dynamic model (17.1) can be transformed into an equivalent form in operational space that is very suitable for analysis and synthesis of a robot controller in constrained motion tasks. This form of the model describes the end-effector equation of motion in Cartesian space:

$$\Phi = \Lambda(x)\ddot{x} + \mu(x, \dot{x}) + F \tag{17.3}$$

where the relationships between the corresponding matrices and vectors from Eqs. (17.1) and (17.3) are

$$x = f(q) \tag{17.4}$$

$$\dot{x} = J(q)\dot{q} \tag{17.5}$$

$$\Lambda(x) = J^{-T}(q)H(q)J^{-1}(q) \tag{17.6}$$

$$\mu(x, \dot{x}) = J^{-T}(q)h(q, \dot{q}) - \Lambda(x)\dot{J}(q)\dot{q} \tag{17.7}$$

$$\Phi = J^{-T}(q)P \tag{17.8}$$

The end-effector position and orientation is presented by the vector of external coordinates:

$$x = [x_k \quad y_k \quad z_k \quad \varphi \quad \theta \quad \psi]^T \tag{17.9}$$

where (x_k, y_k, z_k) are the Cartesian coordinates of the reference coordinate frame attached to the manipulator base. To describe the orientation of the end-effector with respect to the base frame, Euler angles (φ, θ, ψ) were adopted.

The model of the working environment represents one of the most complex and least investigated problems in robot contact tasks. In general, the reaction force can be described at the contact point as a complex function of the end-effector motion:

$$F = f_1(q, \dot{q}, \ddot{q}) \tag{17.10}$$

where f_1 is the vector function.

As a particular form of the general model, we assume that this model can be described by a system of nonlinear differential equations [8, 19]:

$$M(q)\ddot{q} + L(q, \dot{q}) = S^T(q)F \tag{17.11}$$

where $M(q) \in R^{n \times n}$ is a positive-definite matrix, $L(q, \dot{q}) \in R^n$ is the vector function, and $S^T(q) \in R^{n \times n}$ is the matrix derived from kinematic variables.

The presented forms of the robot dynamics model and model of the environment that can be used for learning control synthesis have important features that are given in general nonlinear form of generalized coordinates, although commonly used mathematical models for contact tasks are based on linearized models and external coordinates [16]. Hence, it is convenient in practice to adopt a simplified model of the environment, taking into account the dominant effects, such as stiffness,

$$F = K_E(x - x_E) \tag{17.12}$$

or an environment damping during the tool motion,

$$F = B_E \dot{x} \tag{17.13}$$

where $B_E \in R^{n \times n}$, $B_E \in R^{n \times n}$ are the semidefinite matrices describing the environment stiffness and damping respectively, and $x_E \in R^n$ denotes the coordinate vector of the point of impact between the end-effector (tool) and a constraint surface. However, it is more exact to adopt the relationship defined by specification of the target impedance [18]:

$$F = M_E \Delta \ddot{x} + B_E \Delta \dot{x} + K_E \Delta x \tag{17.14}$$

where

$$\Delta x = x - x_E \tag{17.15}$$

and M_E is a positive-definite inertia matrix.

This model represents the basis for an analysis and design of a learning control strategy that is described in this chapter.

A robot control task can be described, in general, as robot motion along a desired trajectory $q_d(t)$ when a desired force $F_d(t)$ acts between the robot and the environment. In this case, it is important to notice that the desired robot motion $q_d(t)$ and desired interaction force $F_d(t)$ are not arbitrary, but they are interconnected by the relation

$$F_d(t) = f(q_d(t), \dot{q}_d(t), \ddot{q}_d(t)) \tag{17.16}$$

The objective of robot learning control in contact tasks can be formulated by the following goal conditions:

$$q^k(t) \rightarrow q_d(t) \tag{17.17}$$

$$F^k(t) \rightarrow F_d(t) \tag{17.18}$$

where k is the number of learning epochs.

17.4.2 Short Survey of Learning Methods in Contact Tasks

In robot control, learning algorithms refer mainly to the control of noncontact robot operations, where the main aim is to achieve that the robot exactly executes a desired motion, even in the presence of uncertainties in the mathematical model of the robot. These algorithms predominantly use iterative learning procedures [20, 21]. However, with recent extensive research in the area of robot position/force control [16, 22], a few learning algorithms for constrained manipulation have been proposed. We can distinguish two essential different approaches: one whose aim is the transfer of human manipulation skills to robot controllers, and an other in which manipulation robot is examined as an independent dynamic system in which learning is achieved through repetition of the working task.

The principle of transferring human manipulation skills to manipulation robots has been developed in the papers of Asada and co-workers [23–27]. The approach is based on acquisition of manipulation skills and strategies from human experts and subsequent transfer of these skills to robot controllers. It is essentially a playback approach, where the robot tries to accomplish the working task in the same way as an experienced worker. Various methods and techniques have been evaluated for acquisition and transfer of human skills to robot controllers. In [23], measured data about position of the tool tip and force exerted on the tool tip in the process of acquisition of human skill are interpreted and translated into a desired strategy through a special program for robot controllers. Precisely, it can be said that the generated strategy represents a desired robot trajectory of the tool tip and a desired force profile on the tool tip during the working task. This approach was limited exclusively to the operation of robot palletizing. In [24] a method is described for identification of impedance parameters in the deburring process on the basis of recording data about worker's holding the tool tip. These identification parameters were used as input data for the robot controller with the aim of making the robot accomplish the same impedance as the human worker. Of course, this method can be efficient only if the conditions of the working task related to the shape of scrapings and stiffness of the working object are similar as in the preceding process of identification. If the working conditions are time varying during the task, the fixed impedance control cannot give satisfactory results. A further development of the basic idea [25] is the use of the pattern recognition techniques for data extraction from the sensor system. These extracted data are the basis for the correlation with the control action. The control law of an experienced worker is defined through a set of If-Then rules, which have for the result a change of the referent trajectory and referent force.

The transfer of human skill to the robot controllers, described in [26], was accomplished through specialized knowledge that was integrated in weighting factors of the neural network (Fig. 17.1). The learning of a neural network is based on an off-line procedure using the standard back-propagation algorithm {9]. The proposed neural controller was analyzed for robot deburring operation, when input of three-layer perceptron represents the characteristics of a process deburring (characteristics of scrapings and tool), while the output of the neural network is a cutting force in normal directions and damping and stiffness system gain. However, no experimental analysis or direct connections with the real-time control action were given. In the last paper on this approach [27], linguistic control rules are used for transfer of human skills in the grinding proces. In real-time control, the working performance was observed, and on the basis of the previously acquired human sills interpreted through linguistic rules, direct adjustment of referent trajectory and tuning of the control gains were accomplished.

This approach is very interesting and important, although there are some critical issues that related to the explicit mathematical description of human manipulation skill because of the presence of subconscious knowledge, inconsistent, contradictory, and insufficient data. These data may cause system instability and wrong behavior of the robotic system. As is known, the dynamics of a human arm and a robot arm are essentially different, and therefore it is not possible to apply in the same way human skill onto robot controllers. The sensor system for data acquisition of human skill can be insufficient for extracting a complete set of information necessary for transfer to robot controllers. Also, this method is inherently an off-line learning method, whereas for robot contact tasks on-line learning is a very important process because of the high level of robot interaction with the environment and because of unpredictable situations that were not captured in the skill acquisition process.

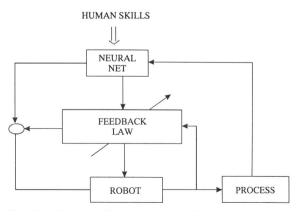

Figure 17.1 *Transfer of human skills on robot controllers by neural network approach.*

The second group of learning methods, based on autonomous on-line learning procedures with repetition of the working task have also been evaluated through several algorithms. The main distinction between these algorithms represents the aim of learning which in the one case is on-line modification of the control signal, while in the other case it is building an internal model of the robotic system.

The algorithms with on-line modification of control signal are basically connected for automated contact operation (precisely, the process of assembling). The control goal in the assembly process is to accomplish the whole set of corrective movements using learning rules in order to achieve valid realization of the working task. Asada [28] considered the problem of nonlinear "compliance" in the process of peg-in-hole insertion. The compliance task is defined as a nonlinear mapping of the measured force and moments on the robot end-effector into corrective velocity movement defined through linear and angular velocity of the robot end-effector. The nonlinear mapping was represented by multilayer perceptron with learning rules defined on the basis of back-propagation method. This is a very interesting approach, but learning analysis was realized off-line using the recorded input/output patterns without experimental verification.

A very interesting approach belonging to this group is the one by Gullapali and co-workers [29]. The authors use reactive admittance control for compensation of the system's uncertainties by on-line control modification and sensor information. Using a similar approach, in [28], the realization of active compliance is based on nonlinear mapping of the admittance from sensors of position and force in commanding velocity movement. The robotic controller learns this mapping through repetitive trial of peg-in-hole insertion. The learning rules are based on the method of associative reinforcement learning [30–31]. This method can be characterized as random search and reinforcement learning. In contrast to the supervised learning paradigm, the role of the teacher in reinforcement learning is more evaluative than instructional. The teacher provides input to the learning system with an evaluation of the system's performance of the robot task according to a certain criterion. Based on both the input to the learning system and action it generated for that input, the environment computes and returns an evaluation "reinforcement." Over time, the learning system has to be able to respond to each action that has the highest expected evaluation. In order to iteratively improve the evaluation obtained for the action associated with each input, the learning system has to determine how modifying the action affects the ensuing evaluation, for example, by estimating the gradient of the evaluation with respect to its actions. The goal of the direct reinforcement learning algorithm is to compensate system uncertainties and sensor noise using learning by position/force feedback. The structure of the neural network is given in Figure 17.2. The neural network has six inputs from the robot sensor system (peg position X, Y, θ from the sensed joint position and force, and moment sensations F_x, F_y, M_z from robot end-effector). Beside two hidden layers with 15 neurons, the output layer contains three stochastic

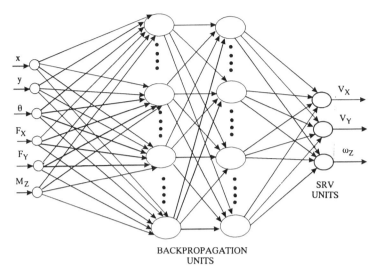

Figure 17.2 *Neural network used for peg-in-hole insertion.*

real-valued (SRV) neural units [31] for generation of linear and angular velocities v_x, v_y, and ω_z. These units generate real-valued output stochastically and use the ensuing evaluation to adjust the output so as to maximize the expected evaluation over time [31]. The units do this by estimating the local gradient of the evaluation with respect to its output and using this estimate to perform gradient ascent. Using the SRV units in the output layer enabled the network to conduct a search in the space of control actions in order to discover appropriate compliant behavior.

The authors have experimentally verified this approach in robot control with a satisfying result even in the presence of a high degree of noise and uncertainties.

Lee and Kim [32] used a special expert system for learning peg-in-hole insertion, starting with an initial rule base. This expert system is implemented as symbolic system with random searching among the expert's rule in order to discover the best control action in the presence of uncertainties and noise. The result of this approach is similar to the previous one.

In learning impedance control, Cohen and Flash [33] evaluated the appropriateness of reinforcement learning for control in a robot surface-wiping task. It is a stochastic scheme of learning without using the model of robot mechanism and environment. The associative searching network put on the controller input parameters of the target impedance. After a new robot action, the impedance robot controller sends from the sensor system to the associative searching network the values of end-effector coordinates and a special signal that represents the measure of compliance between the realized action and desired context. In the learning phase, the network realizes searching that maximizes the value of the special signal for each of the network's input by changing the weighting factors between the input and output of the network. A unique characteristic of this network is generation of the output vectors using a scalar feedback from the robot environment. The reinforcement learning by associative search network might be used for direct adjustment of control signals or parameters, but it is not as efficient as methods for building internal robot models.

For machining operations such as polishing, deburring, and grinding, we can identify two learning techniques: classic iterative methods and connectionist techniques. The well-known iterative learning methods from position control are applied for contact tasks [34–39] that use in repetitive trials various forms of position and force errors from previous control process with the aim of improving robotic performance. For example, we can describe the following control algorithm [39]:

$$u_{k+1} = u_k - \Phi\dot{r}_k + \psi J_\varphi^T(q_k)\Delta f_k \qquad (17.19)$$

where k denotes the number of learning epochs, u_k is the control signal based on some well-known laws for position/force control, $r_k(t) = q_k(t) - q^0(t)$ is the position error from the previous learning epoch k, $f_k = F_k(t) - F^d(t)$ is force error from the previous learning epoch k, $J_\varphi(q_k)$ is the Jacobian matrix of the system, and Φ and ψ are the gain matrices.

The algorithms of iterative learning use the various forms of position and force errors in order to achieve best convergence results, which is some cases are accomplished with restrictive assumptions. Most algorithms have been experimentally verified, but one of the main drawbacks of this approach are the poor generalization properties.

The application of the connectionist method for learning control of contact tasks [40–41] is at its beginning, and a primary aim is the learning of internal robot models with compensation of the system uncertainties.

Fukuda et al. [40] proposed a control scheme that uses the centralized connectionist structure in the frame of explicit hybrid control laws [22]. This approach is very complex because of a large number of input variables and long learning time; hence, it is appropriate only for low-dimensional robotic systems.

17.4.3 Synthesis of Connectionist Learning Laws Stabilizing Robot Motion and Interaction Force

In this chapter we generally adopted the principle of control synthesis on the basis of the preset quality of the transient processes [8]. This principle is important because some requirements defined through transient process are obligatory (the real robot motion should converge to the programmed one), while others are desirable. However, simultaneous stabilization of the perturbed robot motion and perturbed interaction force with independent requirements for a desired quality of their transient process is not possible, because of a strong connection between the desired force and desired robot motion defined by (17.16). Hence, we can divide the synthesis of learning control into two classes: (a) synthesis with stabilization of the robot motion with a preset quality of transient processes; (b) synthesis with stabilization of interaction force with a preset quality of transient processes.

Let us synthesize the control law $u(t)$ in such a way as to ensure a desired quality of robot's motion. For this purpose, we can specify a family of transient processes given by the vector differential equation

$$\ddot{\eta} = N(\eta, \dot{\eta}) \tag{17.20}$$

$$\eta(t) = q(t) - q_d(t) \tag{17.21}$$

where N is an n-dimensional vector function. The function N is chosen such that the system (17.20) is asymptotically stable in the whole:

$$N(\eta, \dot{\eta}) = KP\eta + KD\dot{\eta} \tag{17.22}$$

Using the previous equation, the system (17.20) now has the form

$$\ddot{\eta} = KP\eta + KD\dot{\eta} \tag{17.23}$$

Where $KP \in R^{n \times n}$ is the diagonal matrix of position feedback gains; and $KD \in R^{n \times n}$ is the diagonal matrix of velocity feedback gains. The values for these matrices can be chosen according to algebraic stability conditions.

Taking into account the model of the robot in contact with the environment (17.1), the controlled driving torque has the form [8]

$$P = H(q)[\ddot{q}_d - KP\eta - KD\dot{\eta}] + h(q, \dot{q}) + J^T(q)F \tag{17.24}$$

According to the integral model of the robotic systems (model of robot mechanism with the model of robot actuators), the control variable is defined by the equation

$$u = f_u(P) \tag{17.25}$$

where $u \in R^n$ is the control input, and f_u is the nonlinear function that describes the nature of the robot actuator model.

By substituting (17.24) into the robot dynamics model (17.1), we can obtain the following equation of the closed-form system:

$$H(q)[\ddot{q} - \ddot{q}_d + KP\eta + KD\dot{\eta}] = 0 \tag{17.26}$$

Due to the property of the function N, ensuring an asymptotic stability in the whole of the system (17.20), it follows that the control goals are achieved:

$$\eta(t)_{t \to 0} \to 0 \quad \dot{\eta}(t)_{t \to 0} \to 0 \quad \ddot{\eta}(t)_{t \to 0} \to 0 \tag{17.27}$$

The proposed control law represents a special version of the well-known computed torque method for contact tasks without learning properties, which uses the available on-line information from the position and velocity sensors and from force sensor. Our aim in this chapter is to upgrade this control law into a learning control law by integrating new connectionist structures for efficient mapping of internal dynamic robot relations.

Considering the control law (17.24), we can separate two dynamic terms: (1) $H(q)$ or $F_1(q)$, (2) $h(q, \dot{q})$ or $F_2(q, \dot{q})$. On the basis of this fact, we can integrate two fixed nonrecurrent multilayer perceptrons into control laws (17.24) for approximation of nonlinear mappings F_1 and F_2:

$$P^{NN1} = F_1(w_{jk}^{NN1ab}, q) \tag{17.28}$$

$$P^{NN2} = F_2(w_{jk}^{NN2ab}, q, \dot{q}) \tag{17.29}$$

$$P = P^{NN1}[\ddot{q}_d - KP\eta - KD\dot{\eta}] + P^{NN2} + J^T(q)F \tag{17.30}$$

where F_1 is the nonlinear mapping for the first perceptron NN1, F_2 is the nonlinear mapping for the second perceptron NN2, P^{NN1} and P^{NN2} are the parts of the robot dynamic model generated by NN1 and NN2, w_{jk}^{NN1ab} and w_{jk}^{NN2ab} are the weighting factors for NN1 and NN2, and P is the driving torque at the output of the connectionist structure.

We can see that in the learning control law (17.28)–(17.30), instead of using a centralized connectionist structure, the process of training and learning is accomplished by two integrated neural subnetworks that have simpler input/output relations. In this way, a significant reduction in size of the trajectory input patterns and a great reduction of learning time is achieved.

The topology of the proposed decomposed connectionist structure for learning robot control is defined by a four-layer perceptron with a symmetric sigmoid function as activation functions in both hidden layers. The first network NN1 has an input layer with n neurons and an output layer with n^2 neurons. The second network NN2 has input layer with $2n$ neurons and output layer with n neurons. The activation function for input and output layers is the identity function. The number of neurons in the hidden layers is determined by simulation experiments and on the basis of experience in order to enable the best performance of the learning algorithm.

Training of the proposed connectionist structures can be accomplished exclusively in an on-line regime using various forms of error learning methods. In the *feedback-error learning method* (Fig. 17.3), we can use the position and velocity feedback signals as the output error for the learning algorithm:

$$e = -KP\eta - KD\dot{\eta} \tag{17.31}$$

where $e \in R^n$ is the output error for learning algorithm.

Another solution for output error in learning of the mapping F_1 is the use

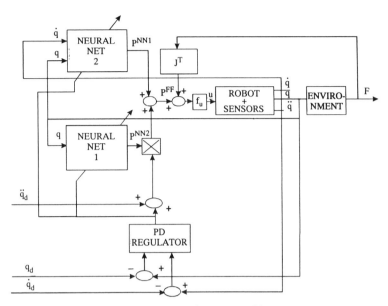

Figure 17.3   *Scheme of learning connectionist control law stabilizing robot motion.*

of the relation [42]

$$e(l) = up(j)(-KP\eta - KD\dot{\eta})$$

$$j = 1, \ldots, n \quad l = n(j - 1) + 1, \ldots, n(j - 1) + n$$

$$up = \ddot{q}_d + KP\eta + KD\dot{\eta} \tag{17.33}$$

As a third solution for output error, we can include driving torque error defined as

$$e = P^r - P \tag{17.34}$$

where P^r is the real driving torque at the robot joint, measured or calculated approximately, and P is the controlled driving torque defined according to (17.30).

Also, it is important to notice that, in order to enhance learning speed, special learning rules based on the RLS gradient algorithm [15] are used.

Let us consider now the second class of stabilizing tasks—stabilization of the interaction force of the robot in contact with the environment. In an analogous way, we can assume that the interaction force in a transient process must have behavior defined by the differential equation

$$\mu(t) = \int_{t0}^{t} Q(\mu(\omega)) \, d\omega \tag{17.35}$$

$$\mu(t) = \int_{t_0}^{t} Q(\mu(\omega)) \, d\omega = \mu(t) e^{-\alpha t} \cos \omega t \qquad (17.36)$$

where $\mu(t) = F(t) - F_d(t)$, Q is a continuous vector function, such that the asymptotic stability in the whole system (17.35) is ensured, and α, ω are parameters of transient process.

On the basis of (17.36), (17.1), (17.11) we can propose the following stabilizing control law (computing the value of controlled torque) [8]:

$$P = H(q)M^{-1}(q)[-L(q, \dot{q}) + S^T(q)(F_d + \mu(t)e^{-\alpha t} \cos \omega t)] + h(q, \dot{q})$$

$$+ J^T(q)[F_d + \mu(t)e^{-\alpha t} \cos \omega t] \qquad (17.37)$$

The control variable u for the whole robotic system is defined in the same way according to Eq. (17.25). By substituting (17.37) into the robot dynamic model (17.1) and using the model of a dynamic environment (17.11), we can obtain the following equation of the closed-form system:

$$(S^T(q) - M(q)H^{-1}(q)J^T(q))[\mu(t) - \mu(t)e^{-\alpha t} \cos \omega t] = 0 \qquad (17.38)$$

In this way, due to the property of the function Q, the control law (17.37) ensures a desired quality of stabilization of the desired interaction force $F_d(t)$. If we want to synthesize a learning control law for stabilization of interaction force, we must identify dynamic terms in Eq. (17.37) that are suitable for nonlinear mapping by decomposed connectionist structures. In this case, we can observe two dynamic terms: (1) $H(q)M^{-1}(q)S^T(q)$ or $F_1(q)$, (2) $H(q)M^{-1}(q)L(q, \dot{q}) + h(q, \dot{q})$ or $F_2(q, \dot{q})$.

In a similar way as stabilization of a desired robot motion, two fixed non-recurrent multilayer perceptrons are integrated into the control law (17.37) for approximation of the nonlinear mappings F_1 and F_2 (Fig. 17.4):

$$P^{NN1} = F_1(w_{jk}^{NN1ab}, q) \qquad (17.39)$$

$$P^{NN2} = F_2(w_{jk}^{NN2ab}, q, \dot{q}) \qquad (17.40)$$

$$P = P^{NN1}[F_d + \mu(t)e^{-\alpha t} \cos \omega t] + P^{NN2}$$

$$+ J^T(q)[F_d + \mu(t)e^{-\alpha t} \cos \omega t] \qquad (17.41)$$

where F_1 is a nonlinear mapping for the first perceptron NN1, F_2 is a nonlinear mapping for the second perceptron NN2; P^{NN1} and P^{NN2} are the parts of the robot dynamic model and model of the environment generated by NN1 and NN2, and w_{jk}^{NN1ab} and w_{jk}^{NN2ab} are weighting factors for NN1 and NN2.

The general principles related to the topology of networks, using fast learning rules and driving torque-error learning method are the same as in the previous case of stabilization of desired robot motion (Fig. 17.4).

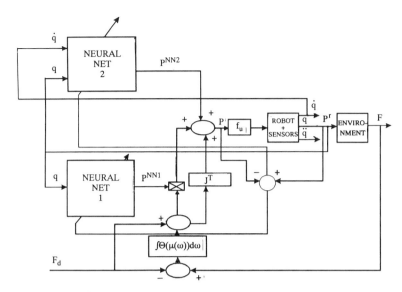

Figure 17.4 *Scheme of learning connectionist law stabilizing interaction force.*

We can conclude that the integration of decomposed connectionist structures ensures the necessary dynamic compensation in learning position and force control laws. Also, it is important to notice that for both classes of stabilization tasks, due to the connection (17.16), the closeness of the real and desired robot motion produces closeness of the real force and desired interaction force, and vice versa.

17.4.4 Synthesis of Connectionist Learning Impedance Laws for Contact Tasks

The primary concern in this subsection is the application of new neural network structures for learning impedance control in the case of robot-constrained manipulation. The fundamental philosophy of *impedance control* [18] is that the manipulator control system should be designed not to track a motion or force trajectory alone but rather to regulate the mechanical impedance of the manipulator. It has theoretically been shown that the approach may also preserve motion stability during contact between the robot end-effector and the environment. However, the implementation of impedance control requires the accurate model of manipulator dynamics as well as perfect measurements of the external force. On the other hand, some parameters of the robot model may be uncertain. In addition, measurements from a wrist force sensor are often found noisy. Model uncertainties and imperfection of the force measurements could severely degrade the performance of a model/sensor-based controller, and, therefore, feasible compensation methods must be developed with the aim of maintaining performance quality as well as motion stability in the presence of parameter uncertainties and measurement noise.

Hence, the main feature of the proposed learning impedance control algorithms is the use of multilayer perceptrons for fast and robust on-line learning of internal robot dynamic relations. The connectionist structures are integrated in control laws as part of three well-known nonlearning impedance control algorithms that enable stabilizing the motion and interaction force of the robot and the environment.

The first impedance control algorithm is *position-based impedance control*. In this method, the inner control loop is conventional positional controller with position sensor, while the outer force loop is closed around positional controller with force sensing. To ensure the successful execution of a constrained motion task, the outer loop includes a feedback compensator whose role is to define the relation between measured contact force and relative displacement, velocity, and acceleration of the end-effector X_d^F, $\dot{X}_d^F$, $\ddot{X}_d^F$; that is, the feedback compensator defines the *target impedance* in an *s*-domain:

$$T_i = (M_E s^2 + B_E s + K_E)^{-1} \tag{17.42}$$

where $M_E \in R^{n \times n}$, $B_E \in R^{n \times n}$, $K_E \in R^{n \times n}$ are the positive-definite matrices that define inertia, damping, and stiffness of the impedance system. The values of these matrices are settled by the control designer in accordance with the task objectives so that the stability of the closed-loop control system is also guaranteed.

The force compensator output X_d^F, $\dot{X}_d^F$, $\ddot{X}_d^F$ is subtracted from the desired external coordinates, velocities, and accelerations X_d^p, $\dot{X}_d^p$, $\ddot{X}_d^p$ resulting in the command input vector for the positional controller:

$$\Delta X_d = X_d^p - X_d^F \tag{17.43}$$

$$\Delta \dot{X}_d = \dot{X}_d^p - \dot{X}_d^F \tag{17.44}$$

$$\Delta \ddot{X}_d = \ddot{X}_d^p - \ddot{X}_d^F \tag{17.45}$$

In this case, for position-based impedance learning control, the left sides of relations (17.44) and (17.45) represent inputs for the position feedforward neural network

$$P_p = g^P(w_{jk}^{ab}, \Delta X_d, \Delta \dot{X}_d, \Delta \ddot{X}_d) \tag{17.46}$$

where g^P is the nonlinear mapping, and w_{jk}^{ab} are the weighing factors of neural networks between the *a*th neuron in the *j*th layer and the *b*th neuron in the *k*th layer.

Using the proposed model of neural network, we can define the position-based impedance learning algorithm (Fig. 17.5):

$$u = f_u(P_p) - K_{pp}\eta - K_{pv}\dot{\eta} \tag{17.47}$$

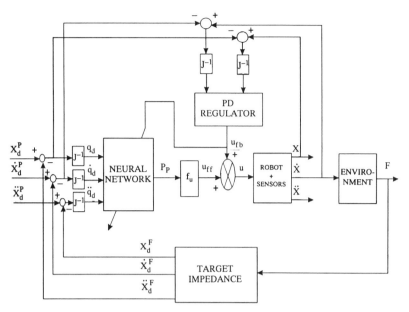

Figure 17.5 *Scheme of learning position-based impedance control.*

where $K_{pp} \in R^{n \times n}$ is the matrix of position feedback gains; $K_{pv} \in R^{n \times n}$ is the matrix of velocity feedback gains.

One of the basic advantages of its approach is its robustness toward disturbances and its reliability. The design of the target impedance is quite clear and straightforward.

In the force-based impedance control approach, an expected reference force is computed to satisfy the desired impedance specification based on the position error and the *inverse target impedance* defined in the s-domain by

$$F_c = (M_E s^2 + B_E s + K_E) \Delta x \tag{17.48}$$

The expected force F_c is compared with the actual force sensed by the force sensor, and the difference of these two forces is the force error ΔF:

$$\Delta F = F - F_c \tag{17.49}$$

This error is further transferred via the transposition of the Jacobian matrix into the control scheme.

In this case, the connectionist model serves as a compensation tool in the feedforward loop, whose inputs are the desired values of the external robot coordinates, velocities, and accelerations:

$$P_p = g^p(w_{jk}^{ab}, X_d, \dot{X}_d, \ddot{X}_d) \tag{17.50}$$

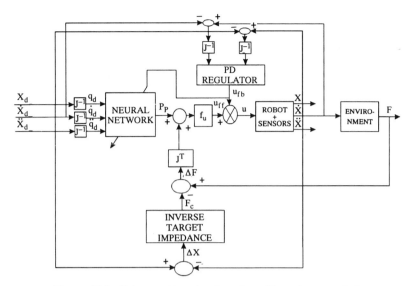

Figure 17.6 *Scheme of learning force-based impedance control.*

Using the proposed model of the neural network and the previously defined force control part, we can define a force-based impedance learning algorithm (Fig. 17.6):

$$u = f_u(P_p + J^T \Delta F) - K_{pp}\eta - K_{pv}\dot{\eta} \qquad (17.51)$$

As in the previous case, the target impedance has to be designed to satisfy specific requirements of the task and guarantee the stability of closed-loop system.

In both learning schemes, we can define the topology of centralized connectionist structure for learning control (input layer $3n$ neurons; first hidden layer $12n$ neurons; second hidden layer $6n$ neurons; output layer n neurons). However, it is more efficient to use some decomposed connectionist structures ("3F-2SF" or "3F-1SF" decomposition) [15], which significantly reduces learning time. In this case we can use the position and velocity feedback signal as the output error for the learning algorithm (17.31).

It is important to notice that for both position-based and force-based learning control algorithms, neural networks are used as a feedforward control part, where the feedback controller serves as a robust controller with the aim of achieving few errors and performing high-quality learning. Hence, in this case, a conventional feedback PD controller provides a moderately skillful function of the system. In this way, the behavior of the positional feedforward network is ever improving, until this network replaces the feedback controller as the main part of the robot dynamic controller for contact tasks.

Also, an important feature of the two previously defined learning algorithms is that impedance control is mainly addressed to the contact tasks whose accomplishment does not require an exact force control. However, under certain circumstances, the synthesis of impedance control may also be applied for the realization and stabilization of desired force. The specification of the impedance control problem can be reformulated in terms of a desired dynamic relationship between the position error and the interaction force error [8, 43]:

$$F - F_d = M_E(\ddot{q} - \ddot{q}_d) + B_E(\dot{q} - \dot{q}_d) + K_E(q - q_d) \qquad (17.52)$$

where the constant matrices M_E, B_E, K_E according to the general impedance model (17.14) are specified by the user in order to ensure an exponential stability of the closed-loop system.

Let us now focus our attention on the fact that the solving of the task of attaining the preset impedance of the closed-loop system defined by (17.52) is a particular case of the control law (17.24), where now a family of transient process is given by the relation

$$\ddot{\eta} = N(\eta, \dot{\eta}) = M_E^{-1}[-B_E(\dot{q} - \dot{q}_d) - K_E(q - q_d) + F - F_d] \quad (17.53)$$

Taking into account the model of robot in contact with the environment (17.1), the controlled law has the form

$$P = H(q)\{\ddot{q}_d + M_E^{-1}[-B_E(\dot{q} - \dot{q}_d) - K_E(q - q_d) + (F - F_d)]\}$$
$$+ h(q, \dot{q}) + J^T(q)F \qquad (17.54)$$

$$u = f_u(P) \qquad (17.55)$$

On the basis of (17.54)–(17.55), we can integrate two fixed nonrecurrent multilayer perceptrons into the control laws (17.54):

$$P^{NN1} = F_1(w_{jk}^{NN1ab}, q) \qquad (17.56)$$

$$P^{NN2} = F_2(w_{jk}^{NN2ab}, q, \dot{q}) \qquad (17.57)$$

$$P = P^{NN1}\{\ddot{q}_d + M_E^{-1}[-B_E\dot{\eta} - K_E\eta + (F - F_d)]\} + P^{NN2} + J^T(q)F$$

$$(17.58)$$

where F_1 is a nonlinear mapping for the first perceptron NN1, F_2 is a nonlinear mapping for NN2, P^{NN1} and P^{NN2} are parts of the robot dynamic model generated by NN1 and NN2, w_{jk}^{NN1ab} and w_{jk}^{NN2ab} are the weighting factors for NN1 and NN2, and P is the driving torque at the output of connectionist structure.

These relations render an ideal solution to the learning control for stabilization of position and force. However, in practice, there are always uncertainties due to limitations in measurement techniques. Hence, in order to enhance capabilities of the learning process, a robust PI controller is added to the basic

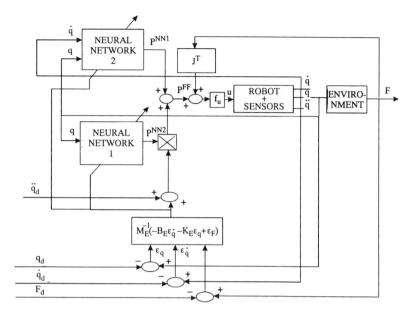

Figure 17.7 *Scheme of learning impedance control with stabilization.*

learning control law according to the idea of Liu and Goldenberg [44] (Fig. 17.7):

$$P = P^{NN1}\{\ddot{q}_d + M_E^{-1}[-B_E\dot{\eta} - K_E\eta + (F - F_d)]\}$$

$$- KPR\gamma - KIR \int \gamma \, dt + P^{NN2} + J^T(q)F \qquad (17.59)$$

$$\gamma = P^{NN1}\{q - \ddot{q}_d - M_E^{-1}[-B_E\dot{\eta} - K_E\eta + (F - F_d)]\} \qquad (17.60)$$

where $KPR \in R^{n \times n}$ is the matrix of position feedback gains for the robust controller and $KIR \in R^{n \times n}$ is the matrix of integral feedback gains.

The previously defined topology of connectionist structures for the mappings F_1 and F_2, and output error for the learning algorithm are the same as in the case of stabilizing algorithms with preset quality of transient processes.

17.4.5 Simulation Examples

In this section, a couple of simulation examples of the robot deburring process are described, whose purpose is to verify the proposed learning connectionist algorithms. We used software package CONMOT [45] and data about industrial robot MANUTEC r3 [46] (Fig. 17.8) with six rotational DOF.

The technological working demands for this operation are defined by the following statements: (a) The robot deburring process takes place in an inclined plane, which represents a constraint to tracking of a desired robot trajectory,

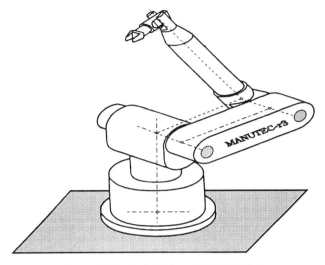

Figure 17.8   *Industrial robot MANUTEC r3.*

which is defined by motion from point *A* with external coordinates (0.; 0.99; 1.505; 0.; 1.; 0.) to point *B* with external coordinates (0.; 0.98; 1.495; 0.; 1.; 0.). During the motion, a triangular velocity profile is used with time duration $t = 1$ s; (b) the robot tool on the end-effector, retains during the process a fixed orientation toward the working surface, while the magnitude of the desired force has a maximal value $F_d = 14.63$ N. PD position feedback controller is adopted in the case of position stabilization with following values for feedback gains $KP = (144.; 144.; 144.; 1024.; 1024.; 1024.)$, $KD = (24.; 24.; 24.; 64.; 64.; 64.)$, while in the case of force stabilization, parameters of the transient process have the next values: $\alpha = 0.01$; $\omega = 0$. In the case of learning impedance control tasks, the following values for parameters of target impedance are adopted: $M = 60$, $B = 1000$, $K = 4000$. In simulation experiments, the model uncertainties are defined by parametric disturbances with approximately 20% variation from nominal values for the link mass and moment of inertia. The roughness of the working surface is simulated using white noise with force variance $\sigma F = 0.5$ N.

Simulation experiments were carried out for the following topologies for multilayer perceptrons in both stabilization tasks: the perceptron NN1 had 6-144-72-36 neurons in the appropriate layers, while NN2 had the 12-72-36-6 topology. In the case of learning position-based and force-based impedance control, a centralized connectionist structure with 18-72-36-6 topology was adopted. The learning of robot dynamics was accomplished through a trial-and-error approach with RLS gradient learning rule [15].

The simulation results for first class of stabilization tasks are presented in Figures 17.9 and 17.10. Figure 17.9 shows internal position error for the first degree of freedom during the learning epochs, while Figure 17.10 presents an

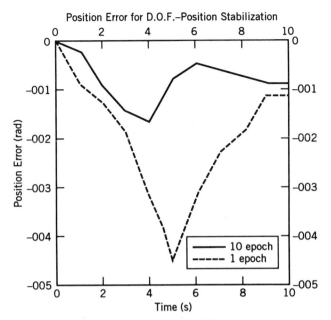

Figure 17.9 *Position error for the first DOF—position stabilization.*

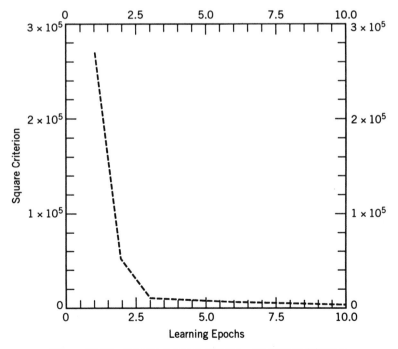

Figure 17.10 *Averaged square criterion—position stabilization.*

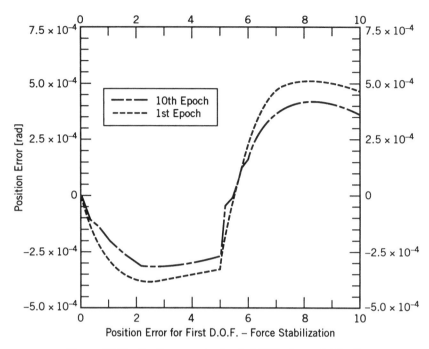

Figure 17.11   *Position error for the first DOF—force stabilization.*

averaged square criterion for both networks during learning epochs. The figures show that with repetitive trials, using RLS method tracking errors are considerably decreased, and thus position robot dynamic learning is accomplished.

For the second class of stabilization tasks, the internal position error for the first DOF and averaged square criterion for both networks during learning epochs are presented in Figures 17.11 and 17.12, whereas the value of force in the first learning epoch and the tenth learning epoch are presented in Figures 17.13 and 17.14. We can see excellent learning properties for position and force, simultaneously.

The simulation results for learning impedance control laws are presented in Figures 17.15–17.18. As can be seen, the tracking errors are considerably decreased during the learning epochs.

17.5   CONCLUSIONS

In this chapter the learning control problem regarding the motion of manipulation robots in manufacturing tasks has been considered. It has been shown that the problem of tracking a specified reference trajectory with a specified force profile can be efficiently solved by means of the application of the so-called decomposed connectionist architectures. The proposed connectionist

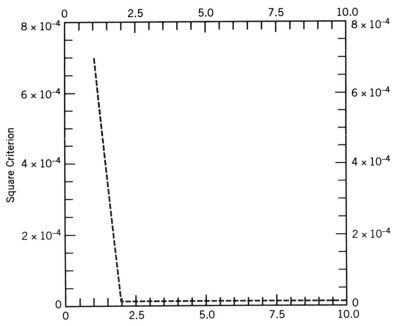

Figure 17.12 *Averaged square criterion—force stabilization.*

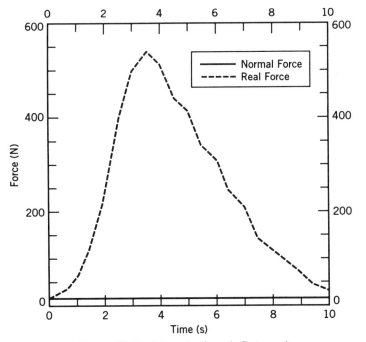

Figure 17.13 *Interaction force in first epoch.*

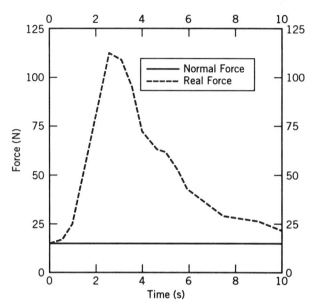

Figure 17.14   *Interaction force in tenth epoch.*

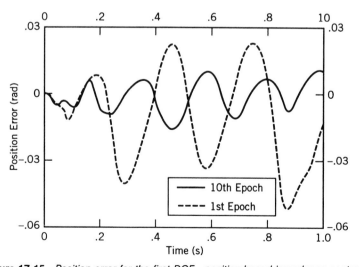

Figure 17.15   *Position error for the first DOF—position-based impedance control.*

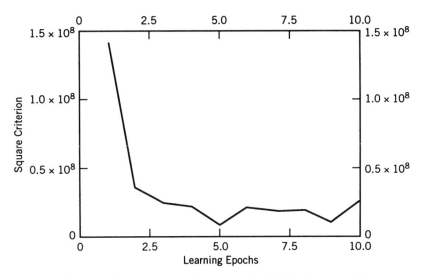

Figure 17.16 *Square criterion–position-based impedance control.*

structures, as integral part of control strategies for robot contact tasks, enable a fast and robust on-line learning of internal robot dynamic relations. The main feature of the proposed learning control algorithms is the use of multilayer perceptrons with special topology that are integrated in nonlearning versions of control algorithms for manufacturing operations: stabilizing control laws with preset quality of the transient processes and impedance control laws.

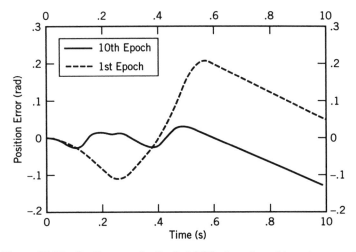

Figure 17.17 *Position error for the first DOF—force-based impedance control.*

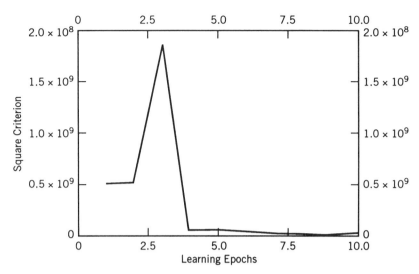

Figure 17.18 *Square criterion–force-based impedance control.*

Multilayer perceptrons through the process of synchronous training use fast learning rules and available sensor information in order to achieve best robotic performance for minimal possible number of learning epochs. Moreover, the results reported have shown that the proposed learning control schemes can guarantee the stabilization of the robot motion and interaction force.

ACKNOWLEDGMENTS

The author gratefully acknowledges the financial support of the National Scientific Foundation of Republic of Serbia through research grant under the project "Robotics," which made this chapter possible. Special appreciation is expressed to Aleksandar D. Rodić for helpful suggestions on preparing the simulation examples.

REFERENCES

[1] G. N. Saridis, "Intelligent robotic control," *IEEE Trans. Automatic Control*, AC-28 (May 1983).

[2] A. Meystel, "Intelligent control in robotics," *J. Robotic Syst.*, 5, 269–308 (1988).

[3] M. Vukobratović and D. Katić, "Connectionist Control Structures for High-efficiency Learning in Robotics," in S. Tzafestas, ed., *Applied Control*, Marcel Dekker, New York, 1993, pp. 705–753.

[4] M. Vukobratović, D. Stokić, and N. Kirćanski, *Non-Adaptive and Adaptive Control of Manipulation Robots*, Springer-Verlag, Berlin, 1985.

[5] D. Katić and M. Vukobratović, Connectionist approaches to control of manipulation robots at the executive hierarchical level: An overview, *J. Intell. Robotic Syst.* (to appear).

[6] S-Y. Kung and J-N. Hwang, Neural network architectures for robotic applications, *IEEE Trans. Robotics Automation*, 5, 641–657 (October 1989).

[7] J. G. Carbonell, Introduction: Paradigms for machine learning, *Artif. Intell.*, 40, 1–9 (1989).

[8] M. Vukobratović and Y. Ekalo, Unified approach to control laws synthesis for robotic manipulators in contact with dynamic environment. in *Tutorial S5: Force and Contact Control in Robotic Systems, IEEE Int. Conf. on Robotics and Automation*, Atlanta, pp. 213–229, May 1993.

[9] D. E. Rumelhart and J. L. McClelland, *Parallel Distributed Processing (PDP): Exploration in the Microstructure of Cognition*, Vol. 1–2, MIT Press, Cambridge, 1986.

[10] S. DeWeerth, L. Nielsen, C. Mead, and K. Astrom, A neuron-based pulse servo for motion control, *Proc. IEEE Internat. Conf. Robotics, Automation*, (Cincinnati), 2, 1698–1703 (May 1990).

[11] C. Mead, *Analog VLSI and Neural Systems*, Addison-Wesley, Reading, Mass., 1989.

[12] A. F. Murray and A. V. W. Smith, Asynchronous VLSI neural networks using pulse-stream arithmetic, *IEEE J. Solid State Circuits*, 23, 688–697 (June 1988).

[13] A. C. Sanderson, "Applications of Neural Networks in Robotics and Automation for Manufacturing," *Neural Networks for Control*, W. T. Miller, R. S. Suton, and P. J. Werbos, eds., MIT Press, Cambridge, 1990, pp. 365–385.

[14] B. Horne, M. Jamshidi, and N. Vadiee, Neural networks in robotics: A survey, *J. Intell. Robotic Syst.*, 3(1), 51–66 (1990).

[15] D. Katić and M. Vukobratović, Decomposed connectionist architecture for fast and robust learning of robot dynamics, *Proc. IEEE Internat. Conf. Robotics Automation* (Nice), 2, 2064–2069 (May 1992).

[16] D. Šurdilovic and J. Timm, "Sensor Based Robotic Control: Review of Contact Control Concepts," Tech. Rep., Fraunhofer Institute for Production Systems and Design Technology, Berlin, April 1991.

[17] J. Duffy, The fallacy of modern hybrid control theory that is based on "orthogonal complements" of twist and wrench spaces, *J. Robotic Syst.*, 7(2), 139–144 (1990).

[18] N. Hogan, Impedance control: An approach to manipulation: Part I—Theory, Part II—Implementation, Part III—Applications, *Trans. ASME—J. Dynamic Syst., Measurement, Control*, 107(3), 1–24 (1985).

[19] A. DeLuca and C. Manes, On the modeling of robots in contact with a dynamic environment, *Proc. Fifth Internat. Conf. Advanced Robotics '91 ICAR* (Pisa), 1, 568–574 (June 1991).

[20] S. Arimoto, S. Kawamura, and F. Miyazaki, Bettering operation of robots by learning, *J. Robotic Syst.*, 1, 123–140 (1984).

[21] P. Bondi, G. Casalino, and L. Gambardella, On the iterative learning control theory for robotic manipulators, *IEEE J. Robotics, Automation*, 4(1), 14–22 (1988).

[22] D. E. Whitney, Historical perspective and state of the art in robot force control, *Internat. J. Robotics Res.*, 6(1), 3–14 (1987).

[23] H. Asada and H. Izumi, Direct teaching and automatic program generation for the hybrid control of robot manipulators, *Proc. IEEE Internat. Conf. Robotics, Automation* (Raleigh), 2, 1401–1406 (April 1987).

[24] H. Asada and Y. Asari, Direct teaching of tool manipulation skills via the impedance identification of human motions, *Proc. IEEE Internat. Conf. Robotics, Automation* (Philadelphia), 2, 1269–1274 (May 1988).

[25] H. Asada and B-H. Yang, Skill acquisition from human experts through pattern processing of teaching data, *Proc. IEEE Internat. Conf. Robotics, Automation* (Scottsdale), 2, 1302–1307 (May 1989).

[26] H. Asada and S. Liu, Transfer of human skills to neural net robot controllers, *Proc. IEEE Internat. Conf. Robotics, Automation* (Sacramento), 3, 2442–2448 (April 1991).

[27] B-H. Yang and H. Asada, Hybrid linguistic/numeric control of deburring robots, *Proc. IEEE Internat. Conf. Robotics, Automation* (Nice), 2, 1467–1474 (May 1992).

[28] H. Asada, Teaching and learning of compliance using neural nets: Representation and generalization of nonlinear compliance, *Proc. IEEE Internat. Conf. Robotics, Automation* (Cincinnati), 2, 1237–1244 (May 1990).

[29] V. Gullapali, R. Grupen, and A. Barto, Learning reactive admittance control, *Proc. IEEE Internat. Conf. Robotics, Automation* (Nice), 2, 1475–1481 (May 1992).

[30] A. G. Barto, R. S. Sutton, and C. W. Anderson, Neuron-like adaptive elements that can solve difficult learning control problem, *IEEE Trans. Systems, Man, Cybernet.*, 13, 834–846 (1983).

[31] V. Gullapali, A stochastic reinforcement learning algorithm for learning real-valued functions, *Neural Networks*, 3, 671–692 (1990).

[32] S. Lee and M. H. Kim, Learning expert systems for robot fine motion control, *Proc. 1988 IEEE Internat. Symp. Intell. Control* (Arlington), 534–544 (1988).

[33] M. Cohen and T. Flash, Learning impedance parameters for robot control using an associative search network, *IEEE Trans. Robotics, Automation*, 7, 382–390 (June 1991).

[34] F. Lange, A learning concept for improving robot force control, in *Proc. IFAC Symp. Robot Control SYROCO '88* (Karlsruhe), 79.1–79.6 (October 1988).

[35] F. Lange and G. Hirzinger, Iterative self-improvement of force feedback control in contour tracking, *Proc. IEEE Internat. Conf. Robotics, Automation* (Nice), 2, 1399–1404 (May 1992).

[36] D. Jeon and M. Tomizuka, Learning hybrid force and position control of robot manipulators, *Proc. IEEE Internat. Conf. Robotics, Automation* (Nice), 2, 1455–1460 (May 1992).

[37] M. Aicardi, G. Cannata, and G. Casalino, A learning procedure for position and force control of constrained manipulators, *Proc. Fifth Internat. Conf. Advanced Robotics* (Pisa), 423–430 (June 1991).

[38] M. Aicardi, G. Cannata, and G. Casalino, Hybrid learning control for constrained manipulators, *Adv. Robotics*, 6(1), 69–94 (1992).

[39] S. Arimoto and T. Naniwa, Learning control for robot tasks under geometric endpoint constraints, *Proc. IEEE Internat. Conf. Robotics, Automation* (Nice), 3, 1914–1919 (May 1992).

[40] T. Fukuda, T. Shibata, M. Tokita, and T. Mitsuoka, Adaptation and learning by neural network for robotic manipulator, *Proc. IMACS Internat. Symp. Math. Intelligent Models System Simulation* (Brussels) (September 1990).

[41] Q. Guo, An adaptive robust compensation control schemes using ANN for a redundant robot manipulator in the task space, *Proc. IEEE Internat. Conf. Robotics Automation* (Nice), 2, 1908–1913 (May 1992).

[42] T. Ozaki, T. Suzuki, T. Furuhashi, S. Okuma, and Y. Uchikawa, Trajectory control of robotic manipulators using neural networks, *IEEE Trans. Indust. Electron.*, 38(3), 195–202 (1991).

[43] R. Kelly, R. Carelli, M. Amestegui, and R. Ortega, On adaptive impedance control of robot manipulators, *Proc. IEEE Internat. Conf. Robotics, Automation* (Scottsdale), 4, 572–577 (May 1989).

[44] G. J. Liu and A. A. Goldenberg, Robust hybrid impedance control of robot manipulators, *Proc. IEEE Internat. Conf. Robotics, Automation* (Sacramento), 1, 287–292 (April 1991).

[45] A. D. Rodić, M. K. Vukobratović, and D. M. Stokić, User-oriented software for modeling, control synthesis and simulation of robots in metal machining processes, *Mechanism Machine Theory* 29, (3), pp. 455–478, (1994).

[46] S. Turk and M. Otter, The DFVLR Models 1 and 2 of the Manutec r3 robot, *Robotersysteme*, 3, 753–768 (1987) (in German).

CHAPTER 18 —————————————

Optical Implementation of a Competitive Network for Pattern Recognition

W. BANZHAF
E. LANGE, M. OITA, J. OHTA
K. KYUMA, T. NAKAYAMA

18.1 INTRODUCTION

This chapter presents first results on the optical implementation of a competitive network for pattern recognition and classification. The actual model we use for implementation is derived from the mode competition model for pattern recognition originally proposed in 1987 by the German physicist H. Haken [1, 2].

We start by summarizing the history of mode competition and its application to information processing problems. After a discussion of related work by other authors we present the actual network model of mode competition including some variations in Section 18.2. In Section 18.3 we point out the technical difficulties in an implementation of this network type. In the same context we will present simulations showing the feasibility of a modified version of the network (with discretized connections). Section 18.4 deals with an optical implementation of the network, including a detailed description of our hardware setup. Section 18.5 describes the recognition task—the recognition and classification of Japanese stamps—and the preprocessing of patterns with a special hardware sensor head extracting color and intensity information. The results of our measurements are given in Section 18.6. Finally Section 18.7 discusses the problems we found in implementing the system as well as future directions of research going on in our laboratory in this field.

The mode competition model was based on Haken's longstanding experience in nonlinear dynamical systems in physics [3] and in the interdisciplinary field

Frontier Decision Support Concepts, Edited by V. L. Plantamura, B. Souček, and G. Visaggio.
ISBN 0-471-59256-0   © 1994 John Wiley & Sons, Inc.

of synergetics [4, 5]. In studying pattern formation processes in different systems, Haken observed deep and striking similarities between seemingly unrelated phenomena. One of his main observations was that systems composed of many subsystems often show global behavior determined by just a few "modes" binding the underlying subsystems. Whether physical subsystems like atoms emitting light were studied, or whether chemical, biological, business, or even sociological subsystems were considered, the notion of a mode of behavior of many subsystems was very useful.

By analyzing the time development of the strength or amplitude of these modes, he was able to formulate general equations governing many different systems. It turned out that, usually, subsystems cooperate to form global modes that compete for the domination of the entire system's behavior. In fact, certain modes can only be observed if system conditions like energetic input, boundary constraints, interaction between subsystems, or fluctuations favor them over others [4]. The whole concept could therefore also be seen as an extension and generalization of Darwin's concepts for adaptation [6] to the inorganic world.

The notion of modes governing the *formation* of patterns was later applied to the "dual" process of pattern *recognition* [1, 2]. The essence of this procedure can be seen if we identify a prototype pattern to be recognized with a mode of a competitive system. The initial state of such a system, that is to say, the amplitudes of different patterns or modes are determined by an input pattern to be recognized. The system's operations are such that a subsequent competition between the modes of the system settles to a state where one mode dominates the system. This can be interpreted as being the pattern or pattern class to which the input pattern was assigned. The most commonly used criteria for an assignment of patterns to classes are similarity measures based on either Euclidean distance or overlap (scalar product) between patterns.

During past years, Haken and collaborators were able to demonstrate the feasibility of this idea [7] (for a recent review see [8] and references therein) very clearly in theory and simulations.

There is another reason for a closer examination of the mode competition network. Besides feedforward networks [9] and feedback networks [10], networks with both sorts of connections have recently become more prominent (see, e.g., [11]). Competitive networks are one subclass of these networks possessing feedforward connections *and* feedback (lateral) connections. After our laboratory was successful in implementing pure feedforward [12] and feedback [13] networks in optical hardware, we felt the time ripe for an optical implementation of a network structure requiring both types of connections. We had, however, to modify the original model somewhat in order to make a hardware implementation more easily. Modifications mainly were introduced in the dynamical laws governing the competition of modes. Since this enterprise is our first trial with the competitive network type, it may not use the strength of the model most effectively. Whereas the network structure requires only $O(n)$ lateral connections, n being the number of grandmother cells, our hardware system could implement $O(n^2)$ feedforward connections. All of these had to be used to realize the lateral network structure required by the algorithm.

Before we discuss the model and its modifications in the next section, a few remarks on related work in competitive networks are in order. In contrast to some differing opinions in the literature, we shall refer to the term competitive network only in connection with the development of state variables, not in connection with learning. The reason is that a competitive learning rule can also be imposed on a network without competing units and therefore does not specify the nature of interactions between units.

Competition is one of the few elementary interactions found in a great variety of natural systems. Particularly many different cell populations in biological systems show competition among their members. One of the first scientists to show a competitive neural system at work was v. d. Mahlsburg [15], who used a distance dependent excitatory/inhibitory interaction between cells to generate orientation sensitivity in cells. Grossberg used lateral inhibition for feature enhancement as early as 1973 [16]. The feature map algorithm devised by Kohonen [17], which was originally proposed in a pure algorithmic fashion, can be implemented using various competitive networks [18–20]. Competition and cooperation were also used by Amari and Arbib (for a review see [21]) for generating various functions in networks (e.g., oscillatory behavior). In 1982, Feldman and Ballard [22] proposed the notion of a winner-take-all network in which competition is so strong as to guarantee one winner in a network.

We hope that from this short and, surely, incomplete list the reader can conclude that their is ample evidence for the usefulness of the competitive network concept and thus enough motivation for implementation trials (see also [23, 24]) in optical hardware.

18.2 THE MODE COMPETITION MODEL

The recognition or classification of static spatial patterns is the function that should be performed by the proposed system. The prototype patterns or classes we want to store in the system are given in advance. These patterns are considered to be unique entities. We assume then that an arbitrary pattern can be decomposed into contributions from these prototypes. Therefore, we assign to every prototype a cell in the network that measures its contribution in a presented input pattern and performs a dynamical competition with other cells measuring their own. Thus we adopt the so-called grandmother cell model, where one cell's activity signals the presence of one pattern or class. In neurophysiology this concept is sometimes called "localized representation of stimuli."

The measurement of contributions can be seen as a continuous mapping A of pattern vectors $\vec{q}$ from the N-dimensional input pattern space $\mathbf{Q}$, $\vec{q} \in \mathbf{Q}$, to the K-dimensional space $\mathbf{D}$ of grandmother cell activity $\vec{d} \in \mathbf{D}$:

$$A: \vec{q} \mapsto \vec{d} \qquad (18.1)$$

After this mapping has taken place, a dynamical recognition process selects the grandmother cell with highest contribution from all cells. Although it may be argued that the same result could be achieved by merely sorting activities and picking the largest one, the fact that a dynamical process is used is important for implementation as well as for learning. For one thing, since Nature is organized mainly in form of dynamical processes, ways of information processing more natural than digital computing will have to rely heavily on dynamical laws. The dynamical processes may therefore be more easily implemented in materials such as those used for optoelectronics. Secondly, processes in general possess distinct phases that may be useful for different purposes, (e.g., learning to distinguish patterns or learning to generalize from examples). Later we shall comment in more detail on these possibilities.

The dynamics we have in mind can be generated by forcing the cells into a competition. This can be achieved via a direct competition of cells for a limited resource. To this end, the offered input pattern should be considered as the resource. Another way to achieve competition is by symmetrical lateral inhibitory connections between cells. This provision will also generate fair competition between grandmother cells. In fact, we used the latter method in our optical implementation.

The original mode competition model [1, 2], as it was conceived from the study of pattern formation processes in natural systems, is depicted in Figure 18.1. For the reader's convenience we summarize its behavior here.

18.2.1 The Formalism

Continuous valued input patterns

$$q_i, \quad i = 1, \ldots, N, \quad q_i \in [-1, +1]$$

are mapped by a connection matrix A_{ik} containing memorized patterns v_{ik} to activities $d_k(0)$, $k = 1, \ldots, K$, of grandmother cells:

$$d_k(0) = \sum_{i=1}^{N} A_{ik} q_i \tag{18.2}$$

We consider $\vec{q}$ as consisting of contributions from each of the known patterns plus noise orthogonal to all of them:

$$\vec{q} = \sum_{k'=1}^{K} \alpha_{k'} \vec{v}_{k'} + \vec{n} \tag{18.3}$$

Then, depending on whether A_{ik} stores the normalized prototype patterns directly

$$A_{ik} = v_{ik} \tag{18.4}$$

Input

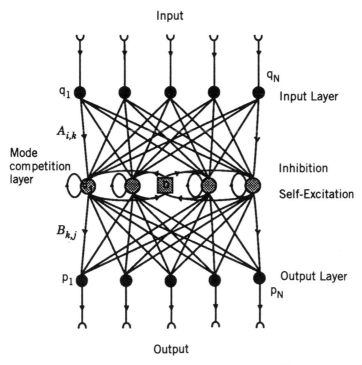

Figure 18.1 *The mode competition network. Three layers with feedforward connections A_{ik}, B_{kj} and feedback connections in the mode competition layer constitute the network. Feeback connections (i) inhibit each neuron according to the overall activity D of all competing cells, (ii) self-excite neurons individually. The number of feedback connections is of O(K).*

or as adjoint patterns

$$A_{ik} = v_{ik}^+ \tag{18.5}$$

indirectly, process (18.1) may be used either measuring correlations between $\vec{q}$ and $\vec{v}_k$,

$$\vec{v}_k \cdot \vec{q} = \sum_{k'=1}^{K} \alpha_{k'} C_{kk'} \tag{18.6}$$

or decomposing $\vec{q}$ into its various contributions

$$\vec{v}_k^+ \cdot \vec{q} = \sum_{k'=1}^{K} \alpha_{k'} \vec{v}_k^+ \cdot \vec{v}_{k'} = \alpha_k \tag{18.7}$$

Here, we have used the definition

$$\sum_i v_{ik}^+ v_{ik'} = \delta_{kk'} \tag{18.8}$$

for adjoint vectors and

$$C_{kk'} = \vec{v}_k \cdot \vec{v}_{k'} \tag{18.9}$$

for the correlation matrix. Due to its definition, noise $\vec{n}$ does not contribute to (18.6) or (18.7).

In any case, a subsequent competition between cells $k = 1, \ldots, K$ governed by the mode competition equation

$$\dot{d}_k(t) = d_k(t)(1 + d_k^2(t) - 2D(t)) \tag{18.10}$$

$$D(t) \equiv \sum_{k'=1}^{K} d_{k'}^2(t) \tag{18.11}$$

decides which activity is most important in terms of its absolute size $\|d_k(0)\|$.

At the same time, an optional third layer performs an association between grandmother cells' activities and other (arbitrary) patterns B_{kj}. The associations are generated as weighted sums p_j, $j = 1, \ldots, L$

$$p_j(t) = \sum_{k=1}^{K} B_{kj} d_k(t) \tag{18.12}$$

Dynamics (18.10) is particular in that it can be derived from a scalar potential $V(\vec{d})$,

$$V(\vec{d}) = -\tfrac{1}{2}D + \tfrac{1}{2}D^2 - \tfrac{1}{4}\sum_k d_k^4 \tag{18.13}$$

In [25] it was shown that we can generalize dynamics (18.10) to

$$\dot{d}_k(t) = d_k^m(t)(1 + d_k^n(t) - 2D^{(n)}(t)) \tag{18.14}$$

with

$$D^{(n)}(t) = \sum_{k'} d_{k'}^n(t) \tag{18.15}$$

provided we restrict $d_k(t)$ to the positive region, $d_k(t) \geq 0$. The overall behavior of the system remains the same, a fact that can be seen better if we rewrite (18.14) as

$$\dot{d}_k(t) = d_k^n(t)\left(1 - \sum_{k' \neq k} d_{k'}^n(t) - \sum_{k'} d_{k'}^n(t)\right) \tag{18.16}$$

The terms in parentheses are responsible for (in the order of their appearance)

(a) Spontaneous growth
(b) Differential amplification
(c) Saturation

According to these functional differences we can discern three different development periods in Eqs. (18.14) and (18.16). As long as $D^{(n)} \ll \frac{1}{2}$ we have exponential growth of all modes. As $D^{(n)}$ approaches $\frac{1}{2}$ we get stronger and stronger differential growth which forces many modes to die out and when $D^{(n)}$ exceeds $\frac{1}{2}$, the saturation term provides for one last growing mode that approaches saturation at $D^{(n)} = 1$.

A particularly interesting dynamics from the point of view of neural networks is the linear dynamics $m = 0$, $n = 1$. In this case, only a linear summation of the inhibitory terms is needed for the system to discern patterns. A variant of the linear dynamics which we use later on in this chapter may be written as

$$\dot{d}_k(t) = d_k(t) - \alpha \sum_{k'} d_{k'}(t) \tag{18.17}$$

In addition to the inhibition felt from other neurons, the activity of each neuron is constrained to lie within the region

$$d_k \in [0, 1]$$

As can be seen readily, these are sufficient conditions for a competition between cells.

18.2.2 A Simulation

Our first simulation is intended to demonstrate the simplest case of competition, namely that between only two cells, under ideal conditions. Figure 18.2a shows the quadratic dynamics. Neuron activities between 0 and 1 for each neuron are used as starting conditions for the competitive dynamics. Shown is the flow field for the derivative for a grid of entry points. Figure 18.2b shows the same setting for the variant of the linear dynamics discussed as Eq. (18.17). In both cases, the boundary between regions is the 45° straight line consistent with the symmetrical inhibition each cell is exerting on the other. We observe that, in general, small values of activity can be discerned faster than large ones, since the absolute value of the derivative components driving away from the separatrix is larger in the former case.

The decision speed can be examined more closely in Figure 18.3. Three networks with different dynamics are compared here with respect to their decision speed, depending on the difference between d_1 and d_2. d_1 was chosen to

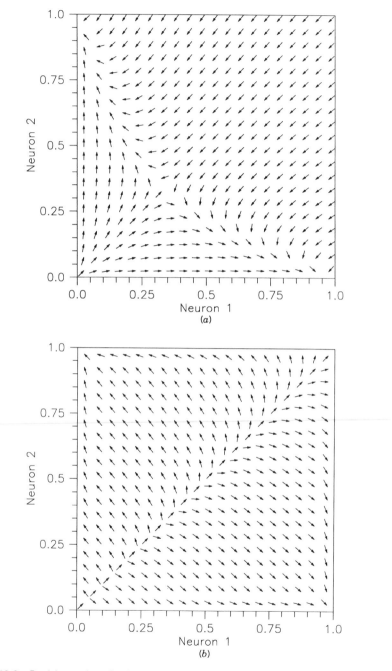

Figure 18.2   Decision regions for the two-neuron case: (a) Quadratic dynamics, m = 1, n = 1, see Eq. (18.16). (b) Linear dynamics, m = 0, n = 1. At each grid point of initial conditions, the directions of the momentary change of activities are shown.

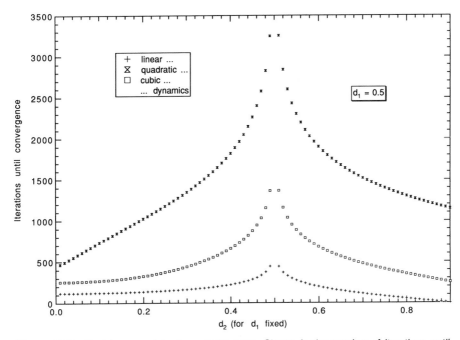

Figure 18.3 *Decision speed for two-neuron case. Shown is the number of iterations until convergence defined as*

$$\begin{cases} 1 - d_1 < \epsilon \text{ for } d_1 > d_2 \\ 1 - d_2 < \epsilon \text{ for } d_2 > d_1 \end{cases} \quad \epsilon = 0.1$$

with a fixed time-discretiation parameter for linear, quadratic and cubic dynamics. $d_2 = 0.5$ was omitted due to (theoretically) infinite convergence time. The dynamical system needs more time to resolve ambiguous initial conditions than unambiguous ones.

be $d_1 = 0.5$. One observes longer decision times to achieve convergence if d_2 is more similar to d_1 initially. Therefore, a clear situation is resolved quickly whereas an ambiguous situation requires a long decision time. Consequently, in addition to the outcome of the competition process, the time until it has settled into the equilibrium is an important signal.

This signal is worth mentioning when learning processes are considered. Equations (18.4) and (18.5) merely specify an algorithmic way of setting connections between the input and the competitive layer without further considerations about a possible process to achieve this. This is the realm of learning which means allowing for time-dependent connections A_{ik}, B_{kj}.

One method to obtain a dynamics for A_{ik} is to force competing cells to specialize on patterns [26, 27]. In this way, starting from randomly initialized A_{ik}, a self-organization process takes place every time a pattern is presented that results in an increase in the specificity with which cells react to patterns. This unsupervised learning process requires the dynamics of the network and, in particular, the different phases of the competition mentioned in the last paragraph, to be successful. We can immediately see that such a dynamics, which can be derived as a gradient dynamics from a scalar network observable (the specialization state of the network), makes very efficient use of the cells present, since it forces cells to win the competition with nearly equal frequency thus covering the pattern space efficiently. The result is a strict classification of input into one out of K classes.

Another method to generate learning behavior is to set up a dynamics which has adjoint patterns $\vec{v}_k^+$ as fixed points. This can be done as described in [28] and again leads to the formation of classes from noisy input patterns.

18.3 TECHNICAL IMPLEMENTATION PROBLEMS

There are some problems in the optical implementation of a competitive network of the sort described in the previous section. Here we shall discuss them briefly. Subsequently, using simulations, a more thorough investigation of one major problem (weight discretization) follows.

In our system, the connections between neurons are made optically using light intensity between light-emitting diodes (LEDs) and variable-sensitivity photodiodes (VSPDs). Light intensity generated by an LED represents the activity of a neuron and the sensitivity of a VSPD represents the weight value. The sensitivity of a VSPD can be controlled externally by the applied voltage and its behavior is basically symmetrical around 0 because positive as well as negative photocurrents may be generated by the photodiode. Since intensity is a unipolar quantity, only positive activity values are allowed.

Practically, the VSPD elements' controlling electronics only allows the implementation of discretized weights. Since it is well known that discretizing connections basically means adding Gaussian noise to ideal continuous weights [29], we expect performance degradation as the number of discrete weight levels decreases. In addition, the device characteristics of LEDs as well as VSPDs are not ideal and show variations from component to component so that each connection may behave in a slightly different way, even under identical conditions. Finally, background noise blurs to a certain degree what may be computed by a connection.

On the level of neurons themselves, the nonuniformity of input/output functions of the VSPDs is the most important source of variation. On the system level, we can single out asynchronicity and temperature dependence of the system's parameters as the most serious problems.

We postpone a discussion of the technical details of our system to the next section and consider now one of the more serious problems in the network, the weight discretization and the restriction to positive neuron activity values. The mapping between input patterns and grandmother cell activities (cf. Eq. (18.1)) is adversely affected by both the weight discretization and the restriction to positive activities, whereas the competition process (cf. Eq. (18.17)) is only affected by the former.

The first simulation studies the aforementioned effects on the mapping process. A certain number of random patterns r_{ik}, $i = 1, \ldots K$, was used to compute a quantity Δ, explained later, which is relevant to the subsequent pattern discrimination process. For the graphs obtained, we varied the number of patterns, K, with the input pattern dimension, N, as a parameter for two cases, the ideal versus a discretized one with only positive activities. Δ is the average distance between diagonal and off-diagonal terms of the matrix c

$$c_{kl} = \vec{r}_k^A \cdot \vec{r}_l^I \tag{18.18}$$

where $\vec{r}_k^A$ is the vector stored in connection matrix A (cf. Eq. (18.4)) corresponding to pattern $\vec{r}_k$ and $\vec{r}_k^I$ is the input vector corresponding to it. The $\vec{r}^A$'s are generated by subtracting the mean, normalizing for the ideal case and additionally discretizing to the number of levels, L, allowed by hardware for the discretized case. The $\vec{r}^I$'s are generated by subtracting the mean, normalizing for the ideal case and additionally setting negative values to zero for the discretized case.

Then Δ reads

$$\Delta = \frac{1}{K} \sum_k \left(c_{kk} - \max_{l \neq k} c_{lk} \right) \tag{18.19}$$

Figure 18.4*a*, *b* show the behavior in a simulation with up to 2048 continuous patterns stored. Δ decreases more or less slowly, depending on the input dimension, to 0. The nearer it is to 0, the more difficult it will be for the subsequent competitive layer to discern patterns. On the other hand, if we consider 32 input dimensions, then even thousands of patterns could be stored while still keeping sufficient distance between off-diagonal and diagonal elements of c_{kl} to be recognized eventually. The situation becomes slightly more unfavorable if we use partially correlated patterns rather than the random patterns used here (cf. Sec. 18.5). As for the discretized case with only positive activities allowed, a negative Δ signals that patterns are now so corrupted that they could not be recognized correctly even if the competition process works perfectly.

Table 18.1 summarizes our results for varying the number L of weight levels allowed by a hypothetical hardware. We can see that the number of input dimensions is far more important than the number of discretization levels. This confirms the view that discretizing weight levels merely amounts to an addition of white noise to continuous weights.

The effect of discretization on the competition process, however, is more serious, in that it restricts the range for the inhibition strength parameter α to

$$\alpha \geq \frac{1}{L - 1} \tag{18.20}$$

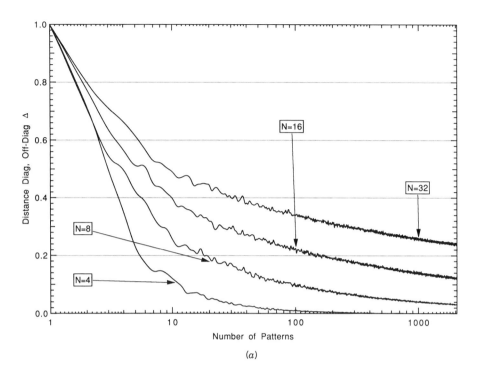

(a)

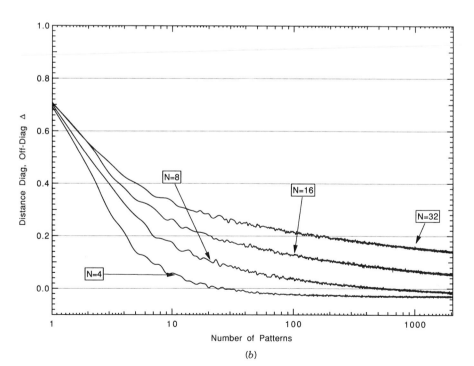

(b)

TABLE 18.1 **Influence of Discretization Levels L for 128 Random Patterns Stored**

Number discrete Levels L	$N = 32$		$N = 16$		$N = 8$		$N = 4$	
	Δ	E	Δ	E	Δ	E	Δ	E
1024	0.247	0	0.175	0	0.076	13	0.005	89
512	0.247	0	0.175	0	0.075	13	0.005	90
256	0.247	0	0.175	0	0.075	13	0.005	88
128	0.247	0	0.175	0	0.075	13	0.005	88
64	0.247	0	0.175	0	0.075	13	0.005	83
32	0.248	0	0.174	0	0.075	12	0.004	86
16	0.245	0	0.171	0	0.073	15	0.002	78
8	0.244	0	0.170	1	0.073	21	-0.002	75
4	0.222	0	0.164	1	0.058	27	-0.002	59
2	0.004	52	0.111	20	0.041	34	-0.002	75

E is the absolute number of erroneously classified patterns, Δ as defined in Eq. (18.19). Influence of input dimension N on recognition performance is stronger than influence of L.

Furthermore, one should keep in mind that only a discretized version of Eq. (18.17) can be used (see Eq. (18.22)). This imposes additional serious requirements on the measurement accuracy of the system.

18.4 THE OPTICAL IMPLEMENTATION

As mentioned briefly in the foregoing section, connections between neurons are realized optically by using light intensities as activity signals (only positive values possible) and externally controlled VSPDs as weights.

Here we discuss in more detail the operating principle to achieve a weight function using metal-semiconductor-metal (MSM) photodiodes. Figure 18.5*a* shows a sketch of one MSM photodiode. The photocurrent generated by incident light is proportional to the transverse electric field across the interdigit

---

Figure 18.4 *Average distance Δ between diagonal and off-diagonal elements of matrix c_{kl} (see Eqs. (18.18), (18.19)). Dimension of random input patterns in $N = 4, 8, 16, 32$ as indicated. With increasing number of patterns stored (log-scale!), Δ decreases toward 0, (a)' or even negative values, (b)' indicating more and more difficulties for a subsequent competitive layer to discern patterns. (a) Ideal case: Continuous patterns stored, positive and negative input activities used. (b) Discretized case: Discretized patterns stored, only positive input activities used.*

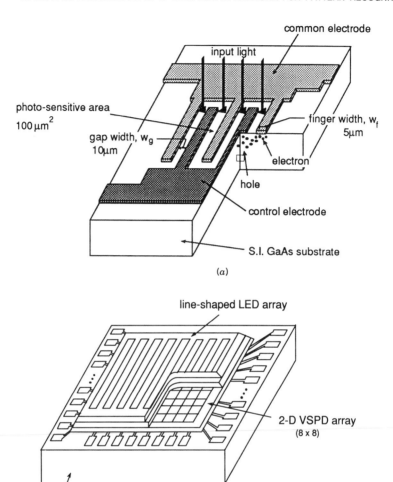

Figure 18.5 *(a) A metal-semiconductor-metal (MSM) photodiode with variable sensitivity (VSPD). Input light causes generation of electron-hole pairs which are separated by the voltage applied to the control electrode. (Reproduced from [30]) (b) 2-dimensional array of 64 VSPDs, together with line shaped LEDs for input and electronic current summation for output constitute the neurochip. (Reproduced from [30]).*

electrodes. The reason for this behavior lies in the charge carrier separation enforced by the applied transverse voltage. It turns out that the relationship between applied voltage and photocurrent generated at the same light intensity is linear over a wide range of voltages.

A set of PDs is arranged in a two-dimensional array as in Figure 18.5*b* with line-shaped LEDs providing the input to each row. An external physical summation of photo currents in each column results in weighted sums of the inputs [30, 31]. The voltage-controlled PDs can assume 256 discrete levels of sensitivity, or weight values. 128 discrete levels are for negative weight values and 128 levels for positive weight values.

In the linear region of operation, an array of LED, VSPD pairs performs

$$I_i^{\text{Out}} = \sum_{j=1}^{N} w_{ij} I_j^{\text{In}} \qquad (18.21)$$

where w_{ij} is controlled separately for each pair. This allows us to implement the mapping of Eq. (18.2) as well as a version of Eq. (18.17), discretized in time

$$d_k(t + 1) = d_k(t)(1 + \epsilon) - \epsilon \alpha D^{(1)}(t) \qquad (18.22)$$

For Eq. (18.22) we used

$$w_{ij} = \begin{cases} 1 + \epsilon(1 - \alpha) & \text{for } i = j \\ -\epsilon \alpha & \text{for } i \neq j \end{cases} \qquad (18.23)$$

with $\frac{1}{5} \leq \alpha \leq \frac{1}{2}$.

Figure 18.6 shows a schematic diagram of the entire system. The hardware is used in a time-multiplexed way, by first computing the activities of grand-

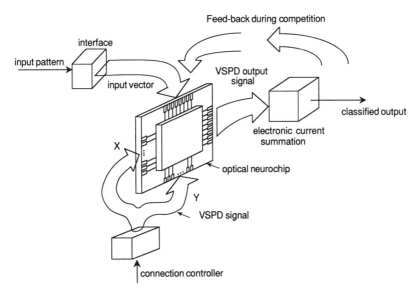

Figure 18.6 *Experimental system arrangement. Externally controlled connections allow a computation of correlations and a competition for the best-matching cell (using the feedback loop).*

mother cells after known patterns are loaded into the connections, and then by performing the dynamical competition process with a fixed and uniform connection matrix according to Eq. (18.22).

Figures 18.7–18.8 show some device characteristics of our optical system. Figure 18.7 plots the photocurrent versus the bias voltage for several PD elements. We can observe a slight variation in each of the PD characteristics. And whereas the relation is nearly linear for higher voltages, a nonlinear behavior is obtained for low voltages. On the other hand, Figure 18.8 shows the photocurrent as a function of the number of active LEDs for one VSPD. A rather linear behavior results after the summation of many inputs.

One of the major advantages of this hardware implementation is the speed of the optical neurochip. In our case, the response time of the VSPD is shorter than 0.1 μs which corresponds to 640 million connections per second for our 64 synapse chip working at 10 MHz. In other words, the speed is high enough as to allow the time multiplexed use of the same hardware [13] without affecting its performance seriously.

The next section deals with the recognition task we have chosen to demonstrate the abilities of the system.

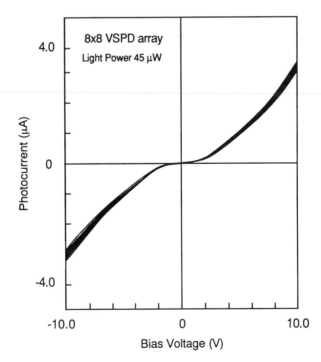

Figure 18.7 *Photocurrent versus bias voltage for 64 VSPD elements. Characteristics vary from element to element. Overall shape: linear in the outer regions, nonlinear in the inner region. (Reproduced from [30]).*

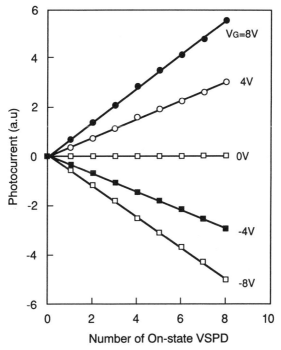

Figure 18.8 *Photocurrent for a number of VSPDs in on-state. Photocurrent, given in arbitrary units, shows linear dependence. (Reproduced from [30]).*

18.5 THE RECOGNITION TASK AND PREPROCESSING OF PATTERNS

Basically it would be possible to test the performance of our optically implemented mode competition system using random input vectors. However, random patterns have usually very low cross-correlation coefficients and are for that reason a rather simple task for a correlation-based system like ours. We selected a more difficult, practical, and attractive task: the recognition and classification of Japanese postage stamps (see Fig. 18.9).*

Figure 18.10 gives an overview of the entire system and the four steps of pattern processing. This section deals with the first processing step, the preprocessing of the patterns. The theoretical background and the optical implementation of the neural information processing in steps 2–4 were already thoroughly discussed in Section 18.2 and 18.4, respectively. For that reason we explain here only the meaning of these steps in the context of stamp recognition. In the second step the preprocessed data from the presented stamp are correlated

---

*The study could equally have been conducted with other postage stamps.

Figure 18.9   *A selection of 32 Japanese stamps was used as recognition task for the optically implemented mode competition network.*

with the stored data from the complete set of stamps, yielding one correlation coefficient per stored stamp. Then the mode competition process (step 3) removes all correlation coefficients except the maximal one. The position of the surviving coefficient indicates the recognized stamp. Finally a mapping network associates the recognized stamp with its price, thereby classifying the stamp in one of the four price classes (step 4).

The preprocessing step has to include a drastic data compression, because only 32 data bytes can be fed into the optical neurochip—one byte per neuron. Due to their two-dimensional nature, the images on the stamps tend to contain a much larger amount of information. For example, scanning a small stamp (2 cm × 3 cm) at a resolution of 600 dots per inch with 24-bit color information per dot results in about 1 Mb of data. For complicated pattern recognition tasks it is often necessary to process such vast amounts of information. Simpler tasks however, like storing and associatively memorizing a limited number of given images, do not require the processing of all the information that an image contains. Rather it is enough to process the image after some smooth data compression. Smoothness means here that small changes in the input image should lead to small changes in the compressed data so that associative image recognition is still possible.

One very simple data compression method for images is downsampling. If the stamp mentioned is scanned with a resolution of 5 dots per inch for instance, only some 70 bytes have to be processed by the subsequent image recognition system. Whether a given pattern recognition task can be solved using only a

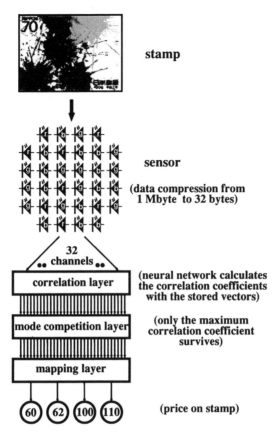

Figure 18.10 *Overview over the entire system. One stamp at a time is presented to the system. A special hardware sensor head that consists of 32 color-sensitive photodiodes performs robust data preprocessing by extracting both color and intensity information from the stamps. The resulting 32 bytes of information are fed into a neural network that recognizes the presented stamp and classifies it into one of four price classes.*

few bytes of information from the images depends on the complexity of the task as well as on the structure of the images itself. When it turns out that the task can be solved however, it is unnecessary to use a more complicated approach.

Concerning the problem of stamp identification, we found that it is sufficient to extract as little as 32 bytes from the images, enabling the use of our neurochip in the subsequent processing steps. For the purpose of data extraction, we developed a special hardware sensor head. The design of this sensor head is described next. In the subsequent part we explain how the problems of shift, rotation, and intensity invariance are addressed. Finally, we present some simulations that illustrate the operation of the sensor head and we show that the extracted information suffices to identify the stamps safely.

18.5.1 The Sensor Head

The underlying motivation for the development of a special sensor head is that the complexities of the pattern identification system and of its front end should be reasonably balanced. A conventional, bulky system consisting of TV camera, frame buffer, and computer would not have matched very well the small and fast optical neurochip used in the pattern identification stage of the system. Therefore we decided to design a special sensor head whose complexity harmonizes with the optical neurochip to a greater degree.

The basic idea behind the sensor head is the fact that the images can be projected on a small array of color-sensitive photodiodes. The photodiodes extract both intensity and color information from the images and at the outputs of the diodes a compressed version of the current input image is available to the neurochip. The number of photodiodes matches the number of neurochip inputs (i.e., 32). Partial preservation of color information is a crucial feature of the sensor head: a look at the colorful stamps in Figure 18.9 makes it obvious that recognition would be much more difficult if the color information is disregarded.

Some of the factors that determine the characteristics of the sensor head are

- The placement of the diodes in the image plane (e.g., regular or random placement)
- The lateral sensitivity profile of the diodes (e.g., small or large, Gaussian or rectangular)
- The spectral sensitivity profile of the diodes (e.g., three types of diodes with maximum sensitivity for red. green, and blue light, or diodes with randomly distributed wavelengths of maximum sensitivity).

Figure 18.11 shows different photodiode configurations. The colors in the drawings match the wavelengths of maximum diode sensitivity and intensity encodes the lateral sensitivity of diodes. In overlapping sensitivity regions the shown color matches none of the wavelengths of the neighboring diodes because of additive mixture of colors.

All these configurations can be implemented in hardware by straightforward methods. For example, a rectangular sensitivity profile can be obtained by using large, rectangular photodiodes and projecting the image on them (see Fig. 18.12*a*). If the photodiodes are placed out of focus of the imaging system (or just above the stamp surface, with no imaging system in between at all), Gaussian-type sensitivity profiles can be obtained (see Fig. 18.12*b*, *c*). This blurred type of projection also facilitates the usage of randomly placed small photodiodes.

The design of the sensor head has some influence on its performance, of course. The smoothness of the data compression process, for example, and with it associativity of the complete recognition system, depends on the size of the total sensitive area of the photodiodes. If the sensitive area is very small, the output of the sensor head depends only on a small area of the input image

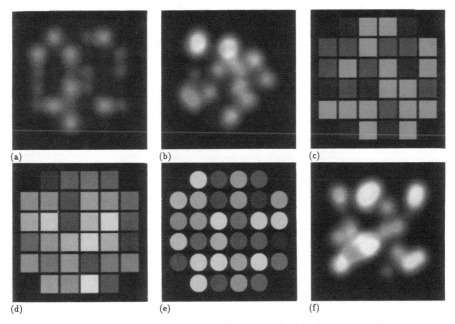

(a)   (b)   (c)

(d)   (e)   (f)

Figure 18.11 *Different sensor head designs. Each photodiode is shown as a bright spot (color and intensity encode wavelength of maximum sensitivity and lateral sensitivity profile, respectively). Placement of diodes: (a, c, d, e) regularly; (b, f) randomly. Sensitivity profile: (a, b, c) Gaussian; (c, f) rectangular; (e) circular. Maximum spectral sensitivity: (a, b, c) for red, green or blue; (d, e, f) for randomly chosen wavelength.*

and becomes therefore very sensitive to distortions and noise in this area. As the sensitive area is made larger, averaging over larger part of the input image takes place, and the generalization ability of the sensor head grows. Ultimately, there is a trade-off between generalization ability and noise sensitivity: if the sensitive area is very large, each photodiode averages over the complete image, making the output of the sensor head unusable for pattern recognition. The

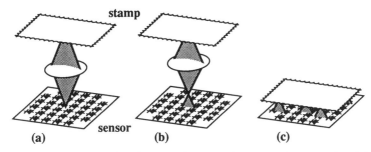

(a)   (b)   (c)

Figure 18.12 *Several possibilities for projecting stamp images on the sensor head: (a) sharp projection; (b) blurred projection—the sensor head is placed out of focus; (c) blurred projection—no imaging system is used.*

exact placement of the diodes and their sensitivity profiles are less crucial parameters for the sensor head performance (see last part of this section).

The complete sensor head consists of 32 photodiodes and amplifiers. The operation speed is only limited by the response times of these diodes and amplifiers. Considering its simplicity and speed, we think that the sensor head is a well-matched front end for our optical neurochip.

18.5.2 How Invariances Are Implemented

The invariance of the recognition process against various transformations of the input images is an important feature of a pattern recognition system. Of course, the intentionally simple design of our hardware sensor head cannot provide complete invariance against shift, rotation, and so forth. However, partial invariances can be achieved, and some invariances are simply not necessary for the purpose of stamp recognition.

Invariance against scaling of size, for example, is not required, because the size of the stamps does not change, and because the sensor head with its imaging system is placed just above the stamp surface.

Full-scale *invariance against shift* is not a built-in feature of our system. Instead, the problem is addressed by requiring the sensor head to be placed roughly above the center of the stamp. Small shifts (i.e., shifts well below the width of the lateral sensitivity profile of the diodes) are tolerated by the system because these shifts lead only to small changes of the sensor head output and therefore do not overstrain the associative properties of the mode competition network.

Invariance against changes of the background the stamp is affixed to is achieved by making the sensor head small enough so that its sensitive area does not jut out beyond the edge of the stamps. Of course, this simple approach cannot be used for general image recognition tasks, because images that differ from each other only in the border area cannot be separated. For the purpose of stamp recognition, however, we found that this method generally works very well.

Invariance against linear transformation of intensity

$$I' = aI + b \tag{18.24}$$

is important in order to ensure stable operation of the recognition system in the presence of illumination fluctuations (expressed by the multiplicative factor a) and stray light from the light source (expressed by the additive constant b). The sensor head itself does not need to be invariant against multiplication by the factor a because in the correlation part of the mode competition network the input vectors are normalized anyway (see Sec. 18.2). The additive constant b is removed by subtracting the average output:

$$x_i' = x_i - \frac{1}{N} \sum_{j=1}^{N} x_j \tag{18.25}$$

Using analog adders, this operation can be implemented in hardware easily. Additionally, this operation enhances the ability of our system to separate input images: usually, output vectors are proportional to the image intensity and lie in the positive corner of state space. Subtraction of the average output spreads output vectors over the complete state-space and therefore increases the angles between output vectors. Consequently, the cross-correlation coefficient of output vectors, nothing more than the cosines of the angles between them, decreases. Output vectors with smaller cross-correlation coefficients can be eventually separated by the mode competition network more easily (see Sec. 18.2).

Basically, *invariance against rotation* is realized to the same degree as invariance against shift. Small rotations cause only small local shifts that are tolerated by the system if they are well below the width of the lateral sensitivity profile of the diodes. In addition, the system can be made invariant against rotation in 90° steps by choosing a sensor head design that is invariant under rotation by 90°. Figure 18.13 shows an example of a sensor head design that meets this invariance requirement. Rotation-invariant design also means that corresponding diodes in the four quadrants of the sensor head have to be connected and operated in parallel. Therefore the shown sensor head has only eight outputs. Generally it is possible to design a sensor head with $m \times n$ photodiodes that is invariant against rotation in $360°/n$ steps (where m and n

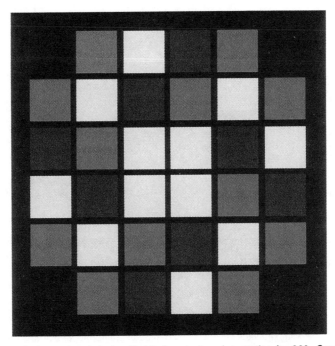

Figure 18.13 *A sensor head design that is invariant under rotation by 90°. Consequently, the output of the sensor head does not change if the projected image is rotated in 90° steps.*

are integers) and has m outputs. For the purpose of stamp recognition, however, an invariance against rotation in 90° steps ($n = 4$) seems to be most useful.

All these invariances and tolerances can be achieved without losing the main advantages of the sensor head (i.e., simplicity and speed). This means, that color sensitive pattern recognition with invariance against background and illumination changes, stray light and rotation in 90° steps and with tolerance to small shifts and rotations can be done very fast (on the order of microseconds).

18.5.3   Performance Simulations

In order to determine whether a certain sensor head can extract enough information from a given set of stamps to enable successful separation and recognition of all the stamps, it is necessary to simulate the behavior of the sensor head before implementing it in hardware. For this purpose, we first scanned a set of 32 different Japanese stamps with a lateral and color resolution of 100 dots per inch and 24 bits, respectively. Then the simulated sensor head was centered above the scans of the stamps. A sample selection of Japanese stamps with placed sensor heads is shown in Figure 18.14. The small, colored rectangles symbolize the photodiodes and their wavelength of maximum sensitivity.

According to the lateral sensitivity profile and the color sensitivity, the expected responses of the photodiodes were calculated. For demonstration, we used the sensor head design from Figure 18.11a: the diodes are placed on a grid with 2.8-mm gaps, are sensitive for either red, green, or blue light and have a Gaussian sensitivity profile with a mean square diameter of 2.535 mm.

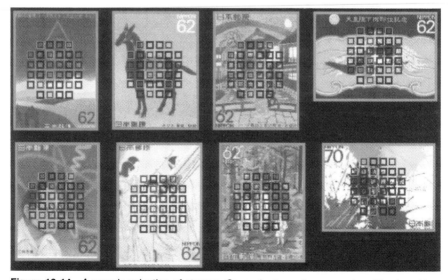

Figure 18.14 *A sample selection of stamps. On each stamp the sensor head is placed in a computer simulation. The photodiodes of the sensor head and their wavelengths of maximum sensitivity are represented as small, colored rectangles.*

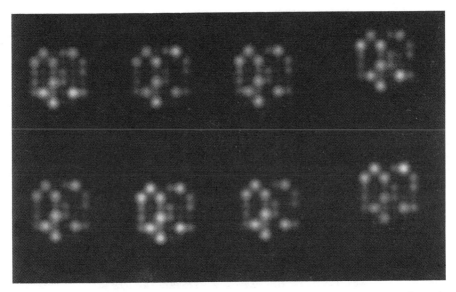

Figure 18.15 *The response of the sensor head from Figure 18.11a on the stamps shown in Figure 18.14. The intensity of each color dot represents the degree of activation of the corresponding photodiode.*

In Figure 18.15 the intensity of the color dots stands for the responses of the sensor head diodes on the stamps in Figure 18.14. For the human eye it is clearly rather difficult to recognize the stamps looking only on the images in Figure 18.15, resulting from data compression by the sensor head. The question is now whether this amount of information suffices for pattern separation and recognition in the optical neurochip. This question can be answered positively, if the output vectors of the sensor head are separated in state-space—that is, if the cross-correlation coefficients (the cosines of the angles between the vectors) are as small as possible. Therefore the distribution of cross-correlation coefficients, and especially the maximum cross-correlation coefficient, are crucial to the overall performance of the system and a valuable measure for the quality of a sensor head design.

Figure 18.16 shows the cross-correlation matrix of the outputs of the sensor head for all 32 stamps. Again, the sensor head design from Figure 18.11a was used. Evidently the diagonal correlation coefficients are equal to one. All off diagonal coefficients are noticeably smaller than one. A look at the distribution of correlation coefficients, shown in Figure 18.17, reveals some more detail. All coefficients, except the diagonal ones, are smaller than 0.78, and 90% are smaller than 0.53. This is an important result: apparently all stamps can be separated using only the output vector of the sensor head. Between the largest cross-correlation coefficient and unity autocorrelation coefficients there is a safety gap of 0.22. This gap allows for some distortions of the input image and for some imprecision during the optical computation of the correlation

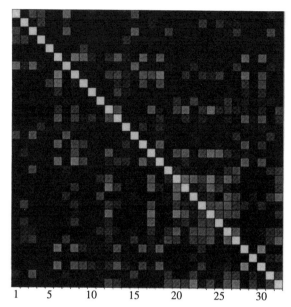

Figure 18.16 *Cross correlation matrix, calculated from the responses of the sensor head on all 32 stamps. Black and white correspond to the correlation coefficients 0.0 and 1.0, respectively. Evidently only the diagonal correlation coefficients are equal to one—all stamps can be separated by the sensor head.*

coefficients, and is therefore important for both the associativity of the system and the feasibility of the optical implementation.

Until now, we have described how we simulated the sensor head from Figure 18.11*a* and how we assessed its performance. With the same methods we now check the image separation quality achieved by sensor heads with different designs. Concerning the stamp recognition task, the sensor heads from Figure

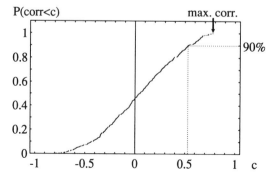

Figure 18.17 *Distribution function of the cross correlation coefficients from Figure 18.16 (P(corr < c) is the probability that a cross-correlation coefficient is larger than c). Each of the 32 × 31 = 992 coefficients is represented by a small dot. The maximum cross correlation coefficient is 0.78, and 90% of the coefficients are smaller than 0.53.*

18.11 show no great differences in performance. This means, that the exact shape of the sensitivity profile of the diodes (rectangular, circular or Gaussian), the distribution of wavelengths of maximum sensitivity (randomly distributed or randomly chosen from the set red, green,, blue) and the exact placement (regular or random) seems to have only limited influence on the sensor head performance.

The size of the sensitive area of the diodes is more crucial, however. If the diameter of the sensitivity profiles in the sensor head from Figure 18.11a is doubled, the overlap of neighboring diodes becomes large, creating dependencies between the sensor head outputs and increasing the cross-correlation coefficients—the image separation quality drops. If, on the other hand, the diameter of each sensitive area is halved, the image separation quality increases slightly, but the generalization capability of the sensor head declines, because each diode averages only over one-fourth of the original area. The size of the sensitive areas shown in Figure 18.11—large, but with small overlaps—represent therefore a reasonable trade-off between generalization and image separation quality. In particular, the output of the sensor head from Figure 18.11a will be used for the experiments in Section 18.6.

Basically it would be possible to optimize the placements and color sensitivities of the diodes in order to ensure optimal separation of a fixed set of stamps. At first, we did not intend to use this approach, since the implicit need to change the sensor head if the set of stamp changes is not desirable for practical applications. However, hardware problems forced a change in our course. Instead of 32 neurons, temporarily only eight neurons were available, limiting subsequently the number of sensor head outputs to eight as well. This posed a serious problem, because simulations showed, that a sensor head with eight diodes is usually not able to extract enough information from the stamps. Actually, the maximum cross-correlation coefficients rose to values around 0.97. We solved the problem by optimizing the sensor head design. As explained, we did not want stamp set changes to affect the hardware implementation. For that reason, we restricted the optimization process on the selection of eight suitable diodes from a given sensor head design (see Fig. 18.11a). If the set of stamps changes, only the optimization procedure has to be repeated, and different diodes have to be connected to the optical neurochip. A random search over 10000 different configurations turned out to be a sufficient optimization method, so that more sophisticated methods, like simulated annealing or genetic algorithms, were not tried. The negative maximum correlation coefficient was used as an energy function. The resulting sensor head performed on a set of 16 stamps as well as the 32-diode sensor head did on the original set (see Figure 18.9).

In a final simulation, we checked the shift tolerance of the sensor head from Figure 18.11a. For this purpose, we simulated the entire system as shown in Figure 18.10.* All stamps from Figure 18.9 are presented to the sensor head,

---

*The final mapping layer was not included.

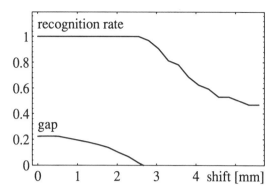

Figure 18.18 *Demonstration of a good shift tolerance of the sensor head. Image shifts below 2.54 mm do not affect the recognition process. The recognition rate (upper curve) begins to decrease when the safety gap (lower curve) between auto and corss-correlation coefficients vanishes.*

and outputs of the sensor head are stored in the correlation layer of the mode competition network. Then horizontally shifted stamps are presented and the recognition rate of the entire system is measured. Figure 18.18 shows that the system tolerates small shifts very well. The stamp (or the sensor head) can be moved up to 2.54 mm without any degradation of the recognition rate. Considering the small sizes of the photodiodes (2.535 mm mean square diameter) and the sensor head (about 17 mm $\times$ 17 mm), this is a very encouraging result: shifts across 30% of the sensor length are tolerated.

All in all the simulations confirmed the feasibility of the sensor head. Although the concept of extracting both color and intensity information from images using a small set of color sensitive photodiodes is very simple, the extracted information still enables associative image recognition in the subsequent simulated neural network. In the next section we show that this is just as true for the optically implemented neural network.

18.6 EXPERIMENTAL RESULTS

As mentioned, due to temporary restrictions in hardware, we were forced to use a dynamical optical neurochip with only eight neurons [30, 31]. Therefore, the input dimension as well as the number of discernible patterns was only eight. As Figure 18.4 has shown, a very low number of input dimensions seriously deprives the system of valuable information. We therefore conclude that in the case of input and competitive layer dimensions of $N, K = 32$ performance can only improve.

Before using prototype patterns derived from Figure 18.9 we performed systematic tests with the competitive dynamics under various parameter settings and initial conditions. Figure 18.19 shows a representative sample of competitive processes.

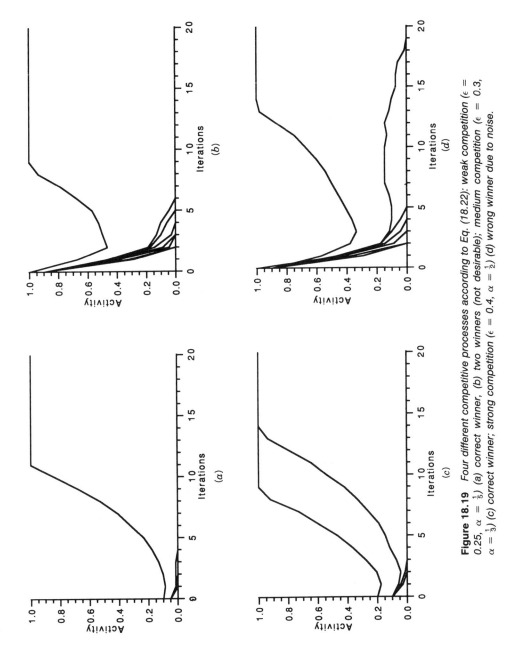

Figure 18.19 Four different competitive processes according to Eq. (18.22): weak competition ($\epsilon =$ 0.25, $\alpha = \frac{1}{5}$) (a) correct winner, (b) two winners (not desirable); medium competition ($\epsilon = 0.3$, $\alpha = \frac{1}{3}$) (c) correct winner; strong competition ($\epsilon = 0.4$, $\alpha = \frac{1}{2}$) (d) wrong winner due to noise.

Three facts can be deduced from these tests:

1. The activity difference required to discern patterns safely is about 0.05.
2. If the competition is too strong, all activities are suppressed and in the end, due to the instability of the system, a cell determined from random noise emerges as the winner.
3. If competition is too weak, more than one cell assumes maximal activity.

If the competition strength is in the right parameter range the system performs correctly for almost all initial conditions.

After parameters have been set to appropriate values, a computation of weighted sums was performed as the first step of the processing. Here, the stamps of Figure 18.14 were used to extract eight-dimensional input vectors through a simulated sensor head of Figure 18.11a. Figure 18.20 shows the computation results in hardware. Only minor differences can be detected as compared to a software simulation. The second step of pattern processing is shown in a typical example in Figure 18.21. It is concerned with the compet-

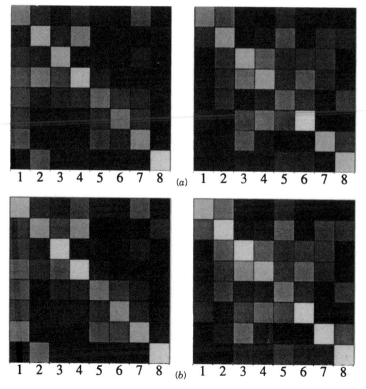

Figure 18.20 Overlaps between stamps as measured by the optical neurochip. Two experiments were conducted (left column and right column). (a) simulation result; (b) measurement. Overlaps in the range [−0.2, 0.4] are encoded as gray levels between black and white.

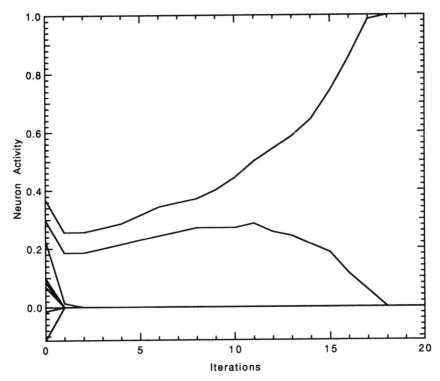

Figure 18.21 *Typical competition process ($\epsilon = 0.4$, $\alpha = \frac{1}{2}$) during a hardware run. After an initial normalization period two activities grow until a decision establishes the winning neuron. Most patterns are suppressed very quickly.*

itive dynamics, realized in hardware. Table 18.2 shows the number of iterations required for the dynamics to converge in our hardware system.

In two experiments we used two arbitrary and mutually exclusive sets of stamps as prototype patterns. In both cases, we were successful and achieved 100% recognition rate for the patterns. Thus, with the input data provided by the sensor head of Section 18.5 we can expect good performance in most cases.

18.7 DISCUSSION

We have seen that a recognition system based on a competitive network can be implemented successfully in optical hardware. Although measurements were somewhat limited owing to the small size of our hardware system, the result of 100% recognition rate is very encouraging.

The main problems for the hardware implementation were

1. The requirements on measurement accuracy in order to resolve contributions from each synapse.

TABLE 18.2 Hardware Performance

Sample 1		Sample 2	
Stamp Number	Iterations	Stamp Number	Iterations
1	8	9	6
2	18	10	11
3	5	11	6
4	7	12	18
5	10	13	11
6	8	14	6
7	8	15	7
8	24	16	6

For each pattern the number of iterations the dynamics has required until convergence is shown.

2. Symmetry requirements for connections to achieve a fair competition between neurons.

Partly, these problems are related to the fact that we have used a (universal) fully connected network in our implementation effort. More specialized hardware with fixed lateral connections could certainly facilitate fulfillment of the above requirements. Also, the other method of competition mentioned earlier (competition for a resource) could be employed [23, 24, 32].

Preprocessing the color patterns with a relatively simple device that worked as a data compression engine turned out to be well adapted to our recognition task. It also has shown potential for a limited invariant recognition of patterns. Thus, the preprocessing device conserved valuable information for discriminating the patterns while removing unimportant information especially under the hard constraint of only 32 or even 8 input components.

Our next steps are (i) to expand the system to 32 neurons for which it was originally designed and (ii) to assemble a 32-photodiode color preprocessing sensor head. By this we hope to achieve a real-time processing ability for color images. We also plan to study more closely appropriate learning algorithms that help in the discrimination of patterns.

Looking further ahead we propose applying more distributed networks, based on neighborhood interactions [19, 20] or a population approach [25] to increase the stability in systems with a considerably increased number of neurons.

ACKNOWLEDGMENT

We thank Dr. S. Tai and K. Hara, T. Ishii, T. Iwamoto, Y. Nitta, and M. Takahashi for numerous valuable discussions. We are grateful to Dr. J. Bell for carefully reading the manuscript.

REFERENCES

[1] H. Haken, "Synergetic Computers for Pattern Recognition and Associative Memory," in H. Haken, ed., *Computational Systems, Natural and Artificial*, Springer, Berlin, 1987.

[2] H. Haken, Nonequilibrium phase transitions in pattern recognition and associative memory, *Z. Physik*, B70, 121–123 (1988).

[3] H. Haken, *Laser Theory*, Springer, Berlin, 1987.

[4] H. Haken, *Synergetics—An Introduction*, 3d ed., Springer, Berlin, 1983.

[5] H. Haken, *Advanced Synergetics*, 2d ed., Springer, Berlin, 1987.

[6] C. Darwin, *On the Origin of Species by Means of Natural Selection*, Murray, London, 1859 (6th ed., 1972).

[7] H. Haken, "Synergetics as a Tool for the Conceptualization and Mathematization of Cognition and Behaviour," in H. Haken and M. Stadler, eds., *Synergetics of Cognition*, Springer, Berlin, 1990.

[8] H. Haken, *Synergetic Computers and Cognition*, Springer, Berlin, 1991.

[9] D. E. Rumelhart and J. L. McClelland, *Parallel Distributed Processing*, MIT Press, Cambridge, Mass., 1986.

[10] J. J. Hopfield, Neural networks and physical systems with emergent collective computational capabilities, *Proc. Natl. Acad. Sci.* (USA), 79, 2554–2558 (1982).

[11] F. J. Pineda, Generalization of back-propagation to recurrent neural networks, *Phys. Rev. Lett.*, 59, 2229–2232 (1989).

[12] J. Ohta, K. Kojima, Y. Nitta, and S. Tai, Optical Neurochip based on a three-layered feed-forward network, *Optics Lett.*, 15, 1362–1364 (1990).

[13] J. Ohta, M. Oita, S. Tai, K. Hara, and K. Kyuma, Opto-electronic implementation of a large-scale neural network using multiplexing techniques, *Trans. IEICE*, E73, 41–45 (1990).

[14] K. Kyuma, foregoing chapter.

[15] C. v. d. Mahlsburg, Self-organization of orientation sensitive cells in the striata cortex, *Kybernetik*, 14, 85–100 (1973).

[16] S. Grossberg, Contour enhancement, short term memory, and constancies in reverberating neural networks, *Stud. Appl. Math.*, 52, 217–257 (1973).

[17] T. Kohonen, Self-organized formation of topologically correct feature maps, *Biol. Cyber.*, 43, 59–69 (1982).

[18] V. Peiris, B. Hochet, S. Abdo, and M. Declerq, Implementation of Kohonen map with learning capabilities, *IEEE Internat. Symp. Circuits, Systems* (Singapore), June 1991, IEEE Press, 1501–1504 (1991).

[19] M. Schmutz and W. Banzhaf, Robust competitive networks, *Phys. Rev.*, A45, 4132–4145 (1992).

[20] W. Banzhaf and M. Schmutz, A dynamical implementation of self-organizing maps. *Proc. Intern. Conf. on Applied Synergetics and Synergetic Engineering (ICASSE)*, Erlangen, 1994, Springer, Berlin (in press).

[21] S. Amari and M. Arbib, "Competition and cooperation in neural nets," in J. Metzler, ed., *Systems Neuroscience*, Academic Press, 1977, pp. 119–165.

[22] J. A. Feldman and D. H. Ballard, Connectionist models and their properties, *Cognitive Sci.*, 6, 205–254 (1982).

[23] J. Lazzaro, S. Ryckebusch, M. A. Mahowald, and C. A. Mead, "Winner-Take-All Networks of $O(N)$ Complexity," in D. Touretzky, ed., *Neural Information Processing Systems 1*, Morgan Kaufmann, San Mateo, 1989, pp. 703–711.

[24] J. Pankove, C. Radehaus, and K. Wagner, Winner-take-all neural net with memory, *Electron. Lett.*, 26, 349 (1990).

[25] W. Banzhaf and M. Schmutz, Some notes on distributed competitive networks, *Internat. J. Neural Syst.* 2, 303–313 (1992).

[26] W. Banzhaf and H. Haken, Learning in a competitive network, *Neural Networks*, 3, 421–435 (1990).

[27] W. Banzhaf and H. Haken, "An Energy Function for Specialization," in S. Forrest, ed., *Emergent Computation*, MIT Press, Cambridge, Mass., 1991, and *Physica*, D43, 257–264 (1990).

[28] H. Haken, R. Haas, and W. Banzhaf, A new learning algorithm for synergetic computers, *Biol. Cyber.*, 62, 107–111 (1990).

[29] D. J. Amit, *Modeling Brain Function*, Cambridge University Press, 1989.

[30] K. Kyuma, Y. Nitta, J. Ohta, S. Tai, and M. Takahashi, "The First Demonstration of an Optical Learning Chip," in *Optical Computing, 1991 Technical Digest Ser. Vol. 6*, Optical Society of America, Washington D.C., 1991, pp. 291–294.

[31] J. Ohta, Y. Nitta, and K. Kyuma, Dynamic optical neurochip using variable-sensitivity photodiodes, *Optics Lett.*, 16, 744–746 (1991).

[32] K. Hara, K. Kojima, K. Mitsunaga, and K. Kyuma, AlGaAs/GaAs pnpn differential optical switch operable with 400 fJ optical input energy, *Appl. Phys. Lett.*, 57, 1075–1077 (1990).

INDEX